OXFORD CLASSICAL MONOGRAPHS

*Published under the supervision of a Committee of the
Faculty of Literae Humaniores in the University of Oxford.*

OXFORD CLASSICAL MONOGRAPHS

The aim of the Oxford Classical Monographs series (which re-places the Oxford Classical and Philosophical Monographs) is to publish outstanding theses on Greek and Latin literature, ancient history, and ancient philosophy examined by the faculty board of Literae Humaniores.

Consoling Heliodorus

A COMMENTARY ON JEROME, *LETTER* 60

J. H. D. Scourfield

CLARENDON PRESS · OXFORD
1993

Oxford University Press, Walton Street, Oxford OX2 6DP
Oxford New York Toronto
Delhi Bombay Calcutta Madras Karachi
Petaling Jaya Singapore Hong Kong Tokyo
Nairobi Dar es Salaam Cape Town
Melbourne Auckland
and associated companies in
Berlin Ibadan

Oxford is a trade mark of Oxford University Press

Published in the United States
by Oxford University Press, New York

British Library Cataloguing in Publication Data
Data available

Library of Congress Cataloging in Publication Data
Consoling Heliodorus : a commentary on Jerome, Letter 60
J.H.D. Scourfield.
Includes text of St. Jerome's Letter 60, in English and Latin.
Includes bibliographical references and index.
1. Jerome, Saint, d. 419 or 420. Letter 60.   2. Consolation–
–History.   I. Jerome, Saint, d. 419 or 420. Letter 60. English &
Latin.   1992.   II. Title.
BR65.J473L5437   1992   270.2'092—dc20   91–30777
ISBN 0-19-814722-8

Set by Latimer Trend & Company Limited, Plymouth
Printed in Great Britain by
Bookcraft (Bath) Ltd., Midsomer Norton

TO MY PARENTS

The financial assistance of the Institute for Research Development of the Human Sciences Research Council of South Africa towards this research is hereby acknowledged. Opinions expressed in this publication and conclusions arrived at are those of the author and do not necessarily represent the views of the Institute for Research Development or the Human Sciences Research Council.

PREFACE

THIS book started life as a thesis submitted to the Board of the Faculty of Literae Humaniores at Oxford for the degree of Doctor of Philosophy in Michaelmas Term 1983. The thesis also included commentaries on two other letters of Jerome, 1 and 107. Since then the commentary on *Letter* 60 has been substantially revised. The introduction has been completely redesigned for a wider readership, while the appendices represent an expansion and elaboration of material treated much more briefly in the thesis. I have included the text of the letter, and added a translation.

The book is intended, first and foremost, as a contribution to the study of an author whose enormous literary output has not received the degree of scholarly attention it deserves. Work on Jerome has tended to focus above all on his biography and on the Vulgate. Certain areas and aspects of his writing have fared better than others, but detailed studies of individual works are few and far between. We have E. Bickel's misleadingly-entitled examination of the sources of the *Adversus Iovinianum* (*Diatribe in Senecae philosophi fragmenta*, 1. *Fragmenta de matrimonio* (1915)), described by H. Hagendahl in 1958 as 'the most comprehensive scholarly research ever made into an individual work of Jerome's', Y.-M. Duval's thorough investigation of the *Commentary on Jonah* (1973, 1985), P. Antin's helpful notes on the same text (1956), P. Lardet's splendidly full discussion of the manuscript tradition of the *Adversus Rufinum* (1982), the studies of the Latin manuscript tradition and the Greek versions of the *Vita Pauli*, *Vita Hilarionis*, and *Vita Malchi*, edited by W. A. Oldfather (1943), and G. J. M. Bartelink's commentary on *Letter* 57 (1980); beyond this, it is no easy matter to name anything significant in this category. Certainly, with the exceptions of Duval (1985) and Bartelink, no commentary on anything like the scale attempted in this book has ever been published. And yet Jerome has a claim to be regarded as one of the most stylish of Latin prose writers, in whose work, perhaps more than in any other's, the classical tradition can be seen to be accepted and adopted by Christianity, rather than shunned, or even rejected as its polar opposite.

In the commentary I have tried to answer all the kinds of questions that might be demanded of a commentator on such a text, while seeking to avoid overloading the book so that it becomes nothing but a collection of amorphous material. I wanted at one and the same time to attempt to serve the interests of different groups of readers and to preserve some sense of the letter as a piece with a specific shape and a unifying theme. On the assumption that the book would have some kind of appeal both to the classicist, who may have only a hazy knowledge of patristic writing and its theological background, and to the patristic scholar or Church historian, who may be relatively unfamiliar with the mainstream classical world, I may on occasion have commented on a matter that some may think could have been passed by in silence; if so, I would beg their indulgence and ask them to remember that I have written also for others of a different cast. What unifies the letter is its consolatory purpose, and this I have attempted, in so far as it is possible in a commentary of this nature, to bring into relief. I hope I have succeeded in showing the continuity of the ancient consolatory tradition from its pagan origins to the mainly Christian world of the late fourth century; while the Christians were able to bring to the task of consolation a completely new perspective and to call on a new range of material, the similarities in approach are striking. This is, in *Letter* 60, the most obvious of the debts Jerome displays to the classical world, but there are many others, and if a reader of this book leaves it with a sense of the grip which that world held on one of the Fathers of the Church, the book will have achieved one of its aims.

A book that has been so long in the making has naturally incurred for its author many debts. The thesis was begun in Oxford and finished in London, where I had the benefit of the excellent resources offered by the Bodleian Library and the British Library respectively. Most of the surgery which

produced the book was carried out in Johannesburg. I
should like to thank the University of the Witwatersrand and
the Human Sciences Research Council of South Africa for
awards which enabled me to spend a fruitful period in
Europe during the first three months of 1987, when I was
able to read a good deal of relevant material which I had
previously neglected, and the Master and Fellows of University College, Oxford, who elected me to temporary membership of their Senior Common Room for the duration of my
stay. Final revisions to the typescript were made during a
further period of leave spent at the Institut für Altertums-
kunde der Universität zu Köln; I am grateful to the Insti-
tutsdirektor, Professor W. D. Lebek, for inviting me to work
in such industrious surroundings, and to other members of
the staff for various kinds of assistance.

More personal debts begin with Dr Michael Winterbottom, who not only supervised the thesis but endured to read
the book, sent to him piecemeal as revisions were completed.
His rigorous scholarship impressed itself upon me from our
earliest meetings, and his comments on successive drafts of
thesis and book have been responsible for countless improvements. No one could have taught me more. My exa-
miners, Mr Leighton Reynolds and Professor Peter Walsh,
whose suggestion it was that I publish the commentary in
the first place, have been constantly supportive and offered
many valuable suggestions. Professor Albrecht Dihle read
the whole of the commentary in its thesis form and supplied
me with many new references, as well as with hospitality in
Cologne. Dr Kathleen Coleman and Dr Marica Frank read
most of the book in a near-final stage, and drew my attention
to omissions and errors that had escaped me. Other friends
and colleagues have helped in numerous, and sometimes
intangible, ways; it would be a long undertaking to name
them all, but special mention should be made of Andrew
Louth for assistance with theological difficulties, Jo and
Robert Parker for allowing me time and again to treat their
home as my own, Peter Riemer for giving unstintingly of his
computer expertise, and Carolinne and Hugh White for
chasing up a number of facts and references and supplying

me with material that I could not easily obtain myself. To all, named and unnamed, I am deeply grateful. I need hardly say that remaining errors and shortcomings are all mine.

J. H. D. SCOURFIELD

Johannesburg/Cologne
December 1990

CONTENTS

References and Abbreviations   xiii

INTRODUCTION   I

  1. Jerome   I
  2. *Letter* 60 and the Consolatory Tradition   15
  3. The Text of *Letter* 60   34

TEXT AND TRANSLATION   41

COMMENTARY   77

APPENDICES

  1. The Date of *Letter* 60   230
  2. Prose-Rhythm as a Feature of Jerome's Style   233

Index of Passages Cited   243

General Index   252

REFERENCES AND
ABBREVIATIONS

Abbreviations for Latin authors follow, for the most part, the practice of *TLL*; the few exceptions should cause no difficulties. I have abbreviated Jerome as 'Jer.' in preference to 'Hier.'. References to Greek authors can normally be elucidated either from LSJ or from G. W. H. Lampe, *A Patristic Greek Lexicon* (Oxford, 1961–8). Periodicals are abbreviated according to the system of *L'Année philologique*.

References to Jerome's letters follow the text of Hilberg (CSEL 54–6); the letter to Praesidius, not included by Hilberg, is cited according to Morin, *Bulletin d'ancienne littérature et d'archéologie chrétiennes*, 3 (1913), 54–8. For Jerome's translation and continuation of Eusebius' *Chronicle* the text of Helm (Die griechischen christlichen Schriftsteller, 47; 1956) is used. Prefaces to books of the Bible follow the edition of the Vulgate by Weber (1969). Other works by Jerome are cited from CCSL 72–9 wherever possible, otherwise from PL 23–6, in the 1845–6 edition. Except in the case of the letters and the prefaces to Biblical books, volume and page numbers in CCSL and/or PL are always given; where references to both series appear and the text is quoted in full, the form of the quotation is always that of CCSL. The Vulgate is cited according to Weber; references to the Vetus Latina are to the Beuron edition (1949–   ) wherever possible, otherwise to that of Sabatier (1743[–9]). For the Septuagint I follow Rahlfs (1935), for the Greek New Testament, Aland–Black–Metzger–Wikgren (1966). In citing other texts I have tried to follow one edition consistently; in selecting these editions I have had regard primarily to their quality, but sometimes (unavoidably) also to convenience.

Many books, journal articles, collections of ancient texts, and works of reference are cited throughout by short title. In general my practice has been to include in this group only items that are cited more than once, but there are a few exceptions. Apart from editions of Jerome, which are cited by the name of the editor (details may be found in section 3 of the Introduction), references may be interpreted according to the following key:

Albers (1921)   P. B. Albers, *S. Ambrosii Mediolanensis episcopi de obitu Satyri fratris laudatio funebris* (Florilegium patristicum, 15; Bonn, 1921).

Alexiou   M. Alexiou, *The Ritual Lament in Greek Tradition* (Cambridge, 1974).

ANRW   *Aufstieg und Niedergang der römischen Welt*, ed. H. Temporini and W. Haase (Berlin and New York, 1972–).

Antin, *Recueil*   P. Antin, *Recueil sur saint Jérôme* (Collection Latomus, 95; Brussels, 1968).

Arns   E. P. Arns, *La Technique du livre d'après saint Jérôme* (Paris, 1953).

Atkinson   J. E. Atkinson, 'Seneca's "Consolatio ad Polybium"', *ANRW* II. 32. 860–84.

Bartelink (1980)   G. J. M. Bartelink, *Hieronymus: Liber de optimo genere interpretandi (Epistula 57): ein Kommentar* (*Mnemosyne*, supp. 61; Leiden, 1980).

Bingham   J. Bingham, *Origines ecclesiasticae, or The Antiquities of the Christian Church* (8 vols., London, 1834).

Booth (1981)   A. D. Booth, 'The Chronology of Jerome's Early Years', *Phoenix*, 35 (1981), 237–59.

Buecheler   *Carmina Latina epigraphica*, ed. F. Buecheler (2 fascicles, Leipzig, 1895–7)= *Anthologia Latina*, ed. F. Buecheler and A. Riese (2 parts, Leipzig, 1894–1906), part 2.

Buresch (1886)   C. Buresch, 'Consolationum a Graecis Romanisque scriptarum historia critica', *Leipziger Studien zur classischen Philologie*, 9 (1886), 1–170.

Cavallera   F. Cavallera, *Saint Jérôme: sa vie et son œuvre* (Spicilegium sacrum Lovaniense, 1–2; 2 vols., Louvain, 1922).

CCSL   Corpus Christianorum series Latina (Turnhout, 1953–).

CIL	*Corpus inscriptionum Latinarum* (Berlin, 1863–).
Courcelle (1948)	P. Courcelle, *Les Lettres grecs en occident de Macrobe à Cassiodore* (Bibliothèque des Écoles Françaises d'Athènes et de Rome, 159; Paris, 1948).
—— (1967)	P. Courcelle, *La Consolation de Philosophie dans la tradition littéraire, antécédents et postérité de Boèce* (Paris, 1967).
CSEL	Corpus scriptorum ecclesiasticorum Latinorum (Vienna, 1866–).
Curtius	E. R. Curtius, *Europäische Literatur und lateinisches Mittelalter* (Berne, 1948).
DCB	*A Dictionary of Christian Biography, Literature, Sects and Doctrines*, ed. W. Smith and H. Wace (4 vols., London, 1877–87).
Dict. spir.	*Dictionnaire de spiritualité, ascétique et mystique, doctrines et histoire*, ed. M. Viller *et al.* (Paris, 1932–).
Duval (1977)	Y.-M. Duval, 'Formes profanes et formes bibliques dans les oraisons funèbres de saint Ambroise', *Christianisme et formes littéraires de l'Antiquité tardive en occident* (Fondation Hardt, Entretiens, 23; Geneva, 1977), 235–91, with discussion, 292–301.
—— (1985)	Y.-M. Duval, *Jérôme: Commentaire sur Jonas* (Sources chrétiennes, 323; Paris, 1985).
Eiswirth	R. Eiswirth, *Hieronymus' Stellung zur Literatur und Kunst* (Klassisch-philologische Studien, 16; Wiesbaden, 1955).
Engström	*Carmina Latina epigraphica*, ed. E. Engström (Göteborg, 1911).
Favez (1928)	C. Favez, *L. Annaei Senecae dialogorum liber VI ad Marciam de consolatione* (Paris, 1928).

xvi   *References and Abbreviations*

Favez (1930*a*)   C. Favez, 'Le Sentiment dans les
                          consolations de Sénèque', *Mélanges
                          Paul Thomas: recueil de mémoires
                          concernant la philologie classique dédié
                          à Paul Thomas* (Bruges, 1930),
                          262–70.
—— (1930*b*)   C. Favez, 'L'Inspiration chrétienne
                          dans les *consolations* de S. Ambroise',
                          REL 8 (1930), 82–91.
—— (1937)   C. Favez, *La Consolation latine
                          chrétienne* (Paris, 1937).
Forcellini   A. Forcellini, *Totius Latinitatis
                          lexicon* (6 vols., Prati, 1858–75).
Gibbon   E. Gibbon, *The History of the Decline
                          and Fall of the Roman Empire*, ed. J.
                          B. Bury (7 vols., London, 1909–14).
Gregg   R. C. Gregg, *Consolation Philosophy:
                          Greek and Christian Paideia in Basil
                          and the Two Gregories* (Patristic
                          Monograph Series, 3; Cambridge,
                          Mass., 1975).
Grützmacher   G. Grützmacher, *Hieronymus: eine
                          biographische Studie* (3 vols., Leipzig
                          and Berlin, 1901–8).
Guthrie   W. K. C. Guthrie, *A History of
                          Greek Philosophy* (6 vols., Cambridge,
                          1962–81).
Guttilla (1977–9)   G. Guttilla, 'S. Girolamo, Seneca e la
                          novitas dell'*Ad Heliodorum
                          Epitaphium Nepotiani*', *ALCP* 14–16
                          (1977–9), 217–44.
—— (1980–1)   G. Guttilla, 'Tematica cristiana e
                          pagana nell'evoluzione finale della
                          consolatio di san Girolamo', *ALCP*
                          17–18 (1980–1), 87–152.
—— (1984–5)   G. Guttilla, 'La fase iniziale della
                          consolatio latina cristiana', *ALCP*
                          21–2 (1984–5), 108–215.
Hagendahl (1958)   H. Hagendahl, *Latin Fathers and the
                          Classics: A Study on the Apologists,
                          Jerome, and Other Christian Writers*
                          (Göteborgs universitets årsskrift, 64;
                          Göteborg, 1958).

—— (1974) H. Hagendahl, 'Jerome and the Latin Classics', *VChr* 28 (1974), 216–27.

Hall–Oberhelman (1985) R. G. Hall and S. M. Oberhelman, 'Rhythmical Clausulae in the *Codex Theodosianus* and the *Leges novellae ad Theodosium pertinentes*', *CQ* 35 (1985), 201–14.

Harnack A. Harnack, *Militia Christi: die christliche Religion und der Soldatenstand in den ersten drei Jahrhunderten* (Tübingen, 1905; translated into English, with a new introduction, by D. M. Gracie, Philadelphia, 1981).

Hatch E. Hatch, *The Organization of the Early Christian Churches* (3rd edn., London, 1888).

ILC *Inscriptiones Latinae Christianae veteres*, ed. E. Diehl (3 vols., Berlin, 1924–31).

Janson (1975) T. Janson, *Prose Rhythm in Medieval Latin from the Ninth to the Thirteenth Century* (Studia Latina Stockholmiensia, 20; Stockholm, 1975).

Jocelyn H. D. Jocelyn, *The Tragedies of Ennius* (Cambridge Classical Texts and Commentaries, 10; Cambridge, 1967).

Johann H.-T. Johann, *Trauer und Trost: eine quellen- und strukturanalytische Untersuchung der philosophischen Trostschriften über den Tod* (Studia et testimonia antiqua, 5; Munich, 1968).

Jones, *LRE* A. H. M. Jones, *The Later Roman Empire, 284–602: A Social, Economic, and Administrative Survey* (2 vols., Oxford, 1986—reprint of the original 1964 3-vol. edn.).

Kaibel *Epigrammata Graeca ex lapidibus conlecta*, ed. G. Kaibel (Berlin, 1878).

Kassel R. Kassel, *Untersuchungen zur griechischen und römischen*

	Konsolationsliteratur (Zetemata, 18; Munich, 1958).
Kelly	J. N. D. Kelly, *Jerome: His Life, Writings, and Controversies* (London, 1975).
Knook	P. C. Knook, *De overgang van metrisch tot rythmisch proza bij Cyprianus en Hieronymus* (Purmerend, 1932).
KS	R. Kühner and C. Stegmann, *Ausführliche Grammatik der lateinischen Sprache, zweiter Teil: Satzlehre* (2nd edn., 2 vols., Hanover, 1912–14).
Kumaniecki	K. Kumaniecki, 'A propos de la "Consolatio" perdue de Cicéron', *AFLA* 46 (1969), 369–402.
Kunst	C. Kunst, *De s. Hieronymi studiis Ciceronianis* (Dissertationes philologae Vindobonenses, 12, part 2; Vienna and Leipzig, 1918).
Lambert	B. Lambert, *Bibliotheca Hieronymiana manuscripta: la tradition manuscrite des œuvres de saint Jérôme* (Instrumenta patristica, 4; 4 vols., Steenbrugge, 1969–72).
Lattimore	R. Lattimore, *Themes in Greek and Latin Epitaphs* (Illinois Studies in Language and Literature, 28. 1–2; Urbana, Ill., 1942).
Lausberg	H. Lausberg, *Handbuch der literarischen Rhetorik* (2 vols., Munich, 1960).
Lewis–Short	C. T. Lewis and C. Short, *A Latin Dictionary* (Oxford, 1879).
LHS	M. Leumann, J. B. Hofmann, and A. Szantyr, *Lateinische Grammatik* (Handbuch der Altertumswissenschaft, 2. 2; 2 vols., Munich, 1965–77).
Lier (1903–4)	B. Lier, 'Topica carminum sepulcralium Latinorum', *Philologus*, 62 (1903), 445–77, 563–603; 63 (1904), 54–65.

Lindholm	G. Lindholm, *Studien zum mittellateinischen Prosarhythmus: seine Entwicklung und sein Abklingen in der Briefliteratur Italiens* (Studia Latina Stockholmiensia, 10; Stockholm, 1963).
Löfstedt (1911)	E. Löfstedt, *Philologischer Kommentar zur Peregrinatio Aetheriae: Untersuchungen zur Geschichte der lateinischen Sprache* (Uppsala and Leipzig, 1911).
—— (1956)	E. Löfstedt, *Syntactica: Studien und Beiträge zur historischen Syntax des Lateins* (Acta Reg. Societatis Humaniorum Litterarum Lundensis, 10; 2nd edn., 2 vols., Lund, 1956—vol. 2 is a reprint of the 1st (1933) edn.).
LSJ	H. G. Liddell and R. Scott, *A Greek–English Lexicon*, 9th edn., revised by H. S. Jones (Oxford, 1940), with a supplement by E. A. Barber (1968).
Luebeck	A. Luebeck, *Hieronymus quos noverit scriptores et ex quibus hauserit* (Leipzig, 1872).
Mitchell	J. F. Mitchell, 'Consolatory Letters in Basil and Gregory Nazianzen', *Hermes*, 96 (1968), 299–318.
Mohrmann, *Études*	C. Mohrmann, *Études sur le latin des chrétiens* (4 vols., Rome, 1958–77).
Murphy, *Monument*	*A Monument to St. Jerome: Essays on Some Aspects of his Life, Works and Influence*, ed. F. X. Murphy (New York, 1952).
Nautin (1972–4)	P. Nautin, 'Études de chronologie hiéronymienne (393–397)', *REAug* 18 (1972), 209–18; 19 (1973), 69–86 and 213–39; 20 (1974), 251–84.
Nisbet–Hubbard (1970)	R. G. M. Nisbet and M. Hubbard, *A Commentary on Horace: Odes, Book 1* (Oxford, 1970).
—— (1978)	R. G. M. Nisbet and M. Hubbard, *A*

	Commentary on Horace: Odes, Book 2 (Oxford, 1978).
Oberhelman (1988*a*)	S. M. Oberhelman, 'The *Cursus* in Late Imperial Latin Prose: A Reconsideration of Methodology', *CP* 83 (1988), 136–49.
—— (1988*b*)	S. M. Oberhelman, 'The History and Development of the *Cursus Mixtus* in Latin Literature', *CQ* 38 (1988), 228–42.
Oberhelman–Hall (1984)	S. M. Oberhelman and R. G. Hall, 'A New Statistical Analysis of Accentual Prose Rhythms in Imperial Latin Authors', *CP* 79 (1984), 114–30.
—— (1985)	S. M. Oberhelman and R. G. Hall, 'Meter in Accentual Clausulae of Late Imperial Latin Prose', *CP* 80 (1985), 214–27.
OCD	*The Oxford Classical Dictionary*, 2nd edn., ed. N. G. L. Hammond and H. H. Scullard (Oxford, 1970).
ODCC	*The Oxford Dictionary of the Christian Church*, 2nd edn., ed. F. L. Cross and E. A. Livingstone (Oxford, 1974).
OLD	*Oxford Latin Dictionary*, ed. P. G. W. Glare (Oxford, 1968–82).
Otto	A. Otto, *Die Sprichwörter und sprichwörtlichen Redensarten der Römer* (Leipzig, 1890).
—— *Nachträge*	*Nachträge zu A. Otto Sprichwörter und sprichwörtliche Redensarten der Römer*, ed. R. Häussler (Darmstadt, 1968).
PG	Patrologia Graeca, ed. J.-P. Migne (Paris, 1857–66).
PL	Patrologia Latina, ed. J.-P. Migne (Paris, 1844–64).
PLRE i	A. H. M. Jones, J. R. Martindale, and J. Morris, *The Prosopography of the Later Roman Empire*, i. *AD 260–395* (Cambridge, 1971).

Powell	J. G. F. Powell, *Cicero: Cato Maior de Senectute* (Cambridge Classical Texts and Commentaries, 28; Cambridge, 1988).
RAC	*Reallexikon für Antike und Christentum*, ed. T. Klauser *et al.* (Stuttgart, 1950–).
RE	*Paulys Real-Encyclopädie der classischen Altertumswissenschaft*, ed. A. F. von Pauly, G. Wissowa, *et al.* (24 vols., 19 vols., and supplement (15 vols.), Stuttgart, 1893–1980).
Sparks	H. F. D. Sparks, 'Jerome as Biblical Scholar', *The Cambridge History of the Bible*, 1. *From the Beginnings to Jerome*, ed. P. R. Ackroyd and C. F. Evans (Cambridge, 1970), 510–41.
Thraede	K. Thraede, *Grundzüge griechisch-römischer Brieftopik* (Zetemata, 48; Munich, 1970).
TLL	*Thesaurus linguae Latinae* (Leipzig, 1900–).
Toynbee	J. M. C. Toynbee, *Death and Burial in the Roman World* (London, 1971).
Trillitzsch	W. Trillitzsch, 'Hieronymus und Seneca', *MLatJb* 2 (1965), 42–54.
VL Beuron	*Vetus Latina: die Reste der altlateinischen Bibel* nach Petrus Sabatier neu gesammelt und herausgegeben von der Erzabtei Beuron (Freiburg, 1949–).
Vollmer	F. Vollmer, 'Laudationum funebrium Romanorum historia et reliquiarum editio', *Jahrbücher für classische Philologie*, supp. 18 (1891–2), 445–528.
Wiesen	D. S. Wiesen, *St. Jerome as a Satirist* (Cornell Studies in Classical Philology, 34; Ithaca, NY, 1964).
Wilkinson	L. P. Wilkinson, *Golden Latin Artistry* (Cambridge, 1963).

INTRODUCTION

I. JEROME

Jerome,[1] scholar, translator, exegete, polemicist, and ascetic, was born into a Christian family[2] at Stridon in the Roman province of Dalmatia[3] around the year 347.[4] His parents were people of property and substance, though we know little else about them, not even his mother's name. To her and his father, Eusebius, two other children were subsequently born, a daughter and a second son, Paulinian. In keeping with the common practice of the time,[5] Eusebius and his wife did not have Jerome baptized as a child, though there is no reason to doubt that they had him instructed in the Christian faith.

Jerome's early life is known to us only in fragments. As a

---

[1] Hieronymus, to give him his Latin name; he once (*chron. a Abr.* p. 1 Helm = PL 27. 33–4) styles himself Eusebius Hieronymus. The most important biographical studies are those of Grützmacher, Cavallera, and Kelly, to whom in particular I am indebted in this part of the introduction. A. Penna, *S. Gerolamo* (Turin, 1949) may also be consulted with profit; but the serious scholar can safely ignore J. Steinmann, *Saint Jérôme* (Paris, 1958), a eulogistic piece of work with the flavour of a novel. C. Favez, *Saint Jérôme peint par lui-même* (Collection Latomus, 33; Brussels, 1958), draws an interesting portrait on the basis of what Jerome reveals about himself in his prefaces. Among other scholars who have contributed to our knowledge of Jerome special mention should be made of P. Antin, thirty-nine of whose papers, on matters linguistic, literary, and historical, are collected in his *Recueil*.

[2] Cf. *pref. in Iob, epist.* 82. 2. 2.

[3] Or possibly Pannonia, a case recently re-argued by I. Fodor, 'Le Lieu d'origine de S. Jérôme: reconsideration d'une vieille controverse', *RHE* 81 (1986), 498–500. For sensible comment on the difficulties of locating Stridon precisely see Kelly, 3–5.

[4] Cf. A. D. Booth, 'The Date of Jerome's Birth', *Phoenix*, 33 (1979), 346–53, whose conclusion is based on careful and commonsensical examination of the evidence. The arguments advanced by P. Hamblenne, 'La Longévité de Jérôme: Prosper avait-il raison?', *Latomus*, 28 (1969), 1081–1119, and Kelly, 337–9, in support of 331, the date recorded by Prosper of Aquitaine, rest on shaky ground; they force us to believe, for one thing, that Jerome was at least thirty-three years older than his brother.

[5] Cf. comm. on 8. 2 *igitur . . . nascatur.*

boy he was sent to Rome to be educated at the school of the famous teacher and grammarian Aelius Donatus, and from there proceeded to the study of rhetoric, the influence of which is evident in later writings.[6] It was almost certainly during this period at Rome that he underwent baptism.[7] After his studies, he spent some time at Trier in north-east Gaul, the city to which the Emperor Valentinian I transferred the seat of government of the western Empire in 367, and at Aquileia in the north Italian province of Venetia-Istria. It is impossible to determine how long he stayed at either place, and his reasons for going to Trier can only be guessed at.[8] There, however, his Christianity took on greater meaning;[9] and Aquileia, a major centre close to his native province of Dalmatia, with a community of Christians in the forefront of the monastic movement, which had recently arrived in the West, provided an enriching and exciting environment for one newly endowed with religious zeal.

The chronology of these years is sketchy in the extreme. But it was probably in 372[10] that this happy phase came to a sudden end. For reasons that are obscure, but appear to involve some misdemeanour on his own part and an assault on his reputation by unknown opponents,[11] Jerome abruptly left Aquileia and travelled east, aspiring to the ascetic life and planning to go to Jerusalem.[12] The journey was long,

[6] *Epist.* 1, the earliest work of Jerome's to survive (AD 375), is an excellent example.

[7] Cf. *epist.* 15. 1. 1, 16. 2. 1, with Kelly, 23.

[8] Probably to enter on a public career, an idea first advanced by Cavallera, 1. 17.

[9] Cf. *epist.* 3. 5. 2 'scis ipse [sc. domine Iesu] . . . cum post Romana studia ad Rheni semibarbaras ripas eodem cibo, pari frueremur hospitio, ut ego primus coeperim velle te colere'.

[10] I follow Kelly, 36. The attempt of Booth (1981) to revise the dating of Jerome's journey to the East and his retreat into the desert begs as many questions as it solves. In particular, I cannot accept his interpretation (255 n. 61) of *epist.* 1. 15. 1, which goes back to Grützmacher, 1. 53–4. Auxentius of Milan was plainly dead when Jerome wrote that letter, and it follows that Jerome did not leave Antioch for the desert until late 375 (cf. my article, 'Jerome, Antioch, and the Desert: A Note on Chronology', *JThS* 37 (1986), 117–21), not 369, as Booth has it. This does not, admittedly, fix Jerome's departure for the East in 372; but, if I am right, this sort of date is much more probable than Booth's 368, which would stretch Jerome's sojourn in Antioch to an unbelievable seven years.

[11] See Kelly, 33–5. Booth (1981), 257 n. 66, plays down the idea that the departure was sudden and forced upon Jerome, but the evidence will not sustain this view.

[12] Cf. *epist.* 22. 30. 1.

hot, and hard, and on reaching Antioch in Syria he put up at the house of his friend Evagrius, whom he had perhaps first met at Aquileia. If his intention was to make a brief stop, it was soon overcome. Jerome stayed with Evagrius for at least two years, before finally renouncing the world, submitting to his ascetic impulses, and withdrawing to the desert in the vicinity of Chalcis, east of Antioch towards the Euphrates, late in 375.[13]

The mortifications of the penitential hermit life which Jerome now undertook were harsh and real enough; yet it should not be imagined that it involved total abandonment of human society. There were many anchoritic monks in Syria, and it is likely that for Saturday and Sunday worship Jerome associated with others who had followed the ascetic path.[14] In any case, Evagrius remained in contact with him, he wrote letters to friends, enjoyed the comforts of his library, and even had copyists available for transcribing books. It was here, too, that he began to learn Hebrew, a decision which was to have far-reaching consequences. In short, it was not because the rigours of the desert life were unbearable that Jerome abandoned it after no more than a year or so.[15]

The fact was that theological controversy had rendered his environment much less congenial. Always an object of suspicion, no doubt, because of his educated, western background and abrasive personality, Jerome found himself under attack from his fellow-hermits for refusing to subscribe to the formulation of the divine Trinity to which they adhered.[16] Eventually the hostility became intolerable, and, leaving the eremitic life for ever, Jerome returned to Antioch.

Further obscurity surrounds the years between the end of

[13] For the date see n. 10 above. P. Nautin, 'Hieronymus', *Theologische Realenzyklopädie*, ed. G. Krause, G. Müller, *et al.* (Berlin, 1976–), 15. 304–15, at 304, questions whether Jerome really withdrew to the desert at all; but this seems to be little more than a hunch.

[14] For this practice see Kelly, 47.

[15] His departure belongs to late 376 or early 377; cf. Cavallera, 2. 16, Kelly, 52.

[16] The problem was terminological. Jerome did not care for the new representation in the eastern Church of the Trinity as one οὐσία, three ὑποστάσεις, which appeared to conflict with the Nicene treatment of οὐσία and ὑπόστασις as synonymous. See *epist.* 15–17, Kelly, 52–5.

Jerome's desert experience and his return to Rome in 382. At Antioch he was ordained priest, but it was with some reluctance, and he rarely exercised this ministry. At some time he journeyed to Constantinople, where he will have observed the events surrounding the great Church council of May–July 381 which condemned Arianism and Apollinarianism and reasserted the Nicene position on the person of Christ. Here he met Gregory of Nazianzus, now in his prime, and Gregory of Nyssa. The Scriptural teaching of the former, and his discussions with Jerome on points of difficulty, made a considerable impression on the younger man, who in later years frequently referred to Gregory as 'praeceptor meus'.[17] Constantinople, too, saw Jerome undertake the translation from the Greek of Eusebius of Caesarea's *Chronicle* of world history, which he extended from 325 to 378, and of a number of homilies by the great third-century exegete and theologian Origen.

Dissension within the Church brought Jerome back to Rome the following year, in the company of Paulinus of Antioch, of whose claim to that troubled see he was a firm supporter, and Epiphanius, Bishop of Salamis in Cyprus. Certain western clerics of importance and standing,[18] unhappy with various decisions reached at the Council of Constantinople, indeed with the general situation of the Church in the East, had persuaded the Emperor Gratian to convene a general council at Rome. In the event their purpose was frustrated, for most of the eastern bishops declined to attend; but Paulinus and Epiphanius followed their summons, taking Jerome with them in the role, perhaps, of interpreter or private counsellor. Thus began one of the most important periods in Jerome's life. He quickly gained the confidence of Damasus, Bishop of Rome, and remained in his service after Paulinus and Epiphanius had departed, employed, it appears, in some secretarial capacity. But it was not this official position that lent his stay at Rome such significance. It was the fact that it was now, at Damasus' request, that he commenced work on a new Latin

---

[17] *Epist.* 52. 8. 2, *vir. ill.* 117 (PL 23. 707), *adv. Iovin.* 1. 13 (PL 23. 230). At *epist.* 50. 1. 3 he refers to Gregory as one of his καθηγηταί in the holy Scriptures.
[18] Chief among them, Ambrose of Milan.

translation of the Bible, which, when completed, was to be his most memorable achievement.[19]

The direction Jerome's life was now to take was also influenced by his meeting at Rome a number of women of high birth who had dedicated themselves to the service of Christ and were living austere and simple existences. Jerome's gift for satire and invective, his vigour in attacking those with whom he disagreed, and the ease with which he seems to have made enemies, have perhaps over-emphasized the cantankerous side of his character; it needs to be remembered that his was also a magnetic and winning personality, capable of the warmest friendships as well as the bitterest hatreds. With the widows Marcella and Paula he now formed relationships that would survive until broken by death. He encouraged their ascetic instincts and elucidated or interpreted Scripture for them. Paula, with her daughter Julia Eustochium, to whom in 384 Jerome wrote the most celebrated of his letters,[20] an exhortation to the life of virginity, was in due course to follow him to the Holy Land; and together the three passed the remainder of their lives in the monastic communities they were to found.[21]

The Roman phase ended suddenly in 385. The death of Damasus in December 384 robbed Jerome of his patron and exposed him to the assaults of many whom he had offended. His unpopularity may be attributed largely to his drive for greater asceticism, his scathing attacks on hypocrisy within the Church, and his association with Paula, which inevitably aroused suspicion.[22] There seems to have been a formal Church enquiry[23] into his behaviour, in consequence of which Jerome quit the city for good. With his brother Paulinian and a small number of monks, he sailed for Palestine.

Jerusalem was his original goal; but it was at Bethlehem that Jerome and Paula, who had caught up with him along the way,[24] decided to settle. Paula's wealth enabled them to

[19] For the Vulgate see below, pp. 8–11.   [20] *Epist.* 22.
[21] For Jerome's association with Marcella, Paula, and Eustochium see esp. Kelly, 91–103 and *passim*.
[22] Cf. Kelly, 108–9, 113.
[23] Cf. *Didym. spir.* pref. (PL 23. 102–3), with Kelly, 113.
[24] At either Salamis or Antioch; cf. Kelly, 116–17.

build a monastery and a convent, which gradually attracted considerable numbers of occupants. Here at last the tempestuous Jerome found some degree of calm, an environment suited both to the ascetic way and to the scholarly activity that now came to play a major part in his life. His literary output in the years from 386 to 420, when he died, was phenomenal. In addition to a continuous flow of letters and his work on the Vulgate, Jerome produced numerous commentaries, sometimes on a vast scale, on various books of the Bible. Original exegesis, however, was not his forte, and for this task he drew heavily on previous commentators such as Apollinarius, Didymus of Alexandria, and above all Origen. There were also miscellaneous works on Scriptural subjects, a few translations, the catalogue of mainly Christian[25] writers called *De viris illustribus*, two hagiographies,[26] and a number of polemical pieces.

Jerome's attitude to Origen calls for some comment, for in the 390s and the opening years of the fifth century the latter was the subject of a heated controversy which raged around Palestine. This bitter and tangled dispute, promoted largely by the activity of the anti-Origenist zealot Epiphanius of Salamis, cost Jerome the friendship he had enjoyed since boyhood[27] with Rufinus of Aquileia, himself the founder of a monastery in Jerusalem, and even had him excommunicated for a time by John, Bishop of Jerusalem, in whose jurisdiction the Bethlehem communities lay. A long-standing admirer of Origen, Jerome crossed to the side of his opponents in 393, in response to a demand that probably came ultimately from Epiphanius.[28] Rufinus and John did not

---

[25] The younger Seneca and the Jews Philo and Josephus are notable exceptions.

[26] The *Vita Malchi* and the *Vita Hilarionis*. Jerome's first essay in the genre, the *Vita Pauli*, was written earlier, probably during his second stay at Antioch (cf. Kelly, 60–1).

[27] The rift may in fact have occurred earlier. Kelly, 169–70, suggests that it may go back to Jerome's decision to translate the OT directly from the Hebrew, an enterprise of which Rufinus disapproved. Reviewing P. Lardet's edition of the *Adversus Rufinum* (CCSL 79), H. Chadwick writes of 'the fiction of a suddenly broken friendship', in reference to the time of the Origenist controversy (*JThS* 37 (1986), 595–6).

[28] Cf. Kelly, 198 n. 12. Whether this dramatic volte-face was motivated largely by a wish to please Epiphanius (so Kelly) is, however, questioned by E. D. Hunt in his review, *JRS* 67 (1977), 166–71, at 167.

subscribe to the theologically dubious doctrines of Origen any more than Jerome, but errors of judgement and conflicts of personality in the months and years that followed caused accusing postures to be adopted on both sides. The clash is reflected in two vigorous pamphlets by Jerome, the *Contra Ioannem Hierosolymitanum* of 397, and the *Adversus Rufinum*, written four or five years later. The firm anti-Origenist stance that Jerome maintained from 393 did not, however, result in his total abandonment of Origen's work. Though he studiously shunned, indeed pointedly criticized, those dogmas that were unacceptable to orthodox belief, he continued to make use of his exegesis, to which his admiration for Origen had always been principally due.

Other issues which exercised Jerome in this period also come alive in polemical works, which again reveal his tendency to go for the jugular in matters of personal and theological difference. He had already shown his mettle at Rome, by disposing brilliantly, though not without insult and distortion, of one Helvidius, who had dared to believe that the married state was as worthy as the celibate, and to suggest that Mary, mother of Jesus, had not remained a virgin for the whole of her life. Jerome's obsession with celibacy, a condition for which his own nature was not especially apt,[29] surfaced again in 393 in the *Adversus Iovinianum*. This vitriolic treatise, carefully composed and deploying Jerome's rhetorical skill to best effect, lambasted the teachings of another moderate, who maintained that extreme asceticism did not make a Christian superior to those who lived a more normal life, so long as they were baptized. The

---

[29] He was not without sexual experience; cf. *epist.* 49. 20. 2, where he admits as much to Pammachius, with regret. All his life it seems to have been a struggle to keep his instincts under control. Writing in 384 of his time in the desert, he tells Eustochium of the fantasies that had beset him there: 'O quotiens in heremo constitutus . . . putavi me Romanis interesse deliciis! . . . scorpionum tantum socius et ferarum, saepe choris intereram puellarum. pallebant ora ieiuniis et mens desideriis aestuabat in frigido corpore et ante hominem suum iam carne praemortua sola libidinum incendia bulliebant' (*epist.* 22. 7. 1–2). In 406, as he approached 60, he could say, in a discussion of old age, 'in malorum comparatione tolerabilius sustinebo morbos, dummodo una et gravissima domina libidine caream. patitur quidem et senectus nonnumquam incentiva vitiorum, nullusque iuxta sanctum martyrem Cyprianum diu tutus est periculo proximus. sed aliud est titillari, aliud obrui voluptatibus' (*in Am. lib.* 2 pref. (CCSL 76. 255 = PL 25. 1023)).

year 406 brought a written assault on the priest Vigilantius, a critic of the cult of martyrs' relics[30] and of the practice of observing vigils at night. Pelagius, the British monk whose radical views on sin and grace later brought about his excommunication, was put in the dock in 415 in a treatise that was, coming from Jerome, surprisingly restrained. Even so, the combative character of this vital and intensely engaged individual is as plain here as elsewhere.

When Jerome died, the world was a changed place. The Roman Empire had been battered by invasions of Goths, Huns, Vandals, and other barbarian peoples; Rome itself had been sacked by Alaric. All this Jerome had observed with feeling;[31] indeed, there was one occasion when the troubles came so close as to threaten to uproot him from his monastery.[32] But the foundations of western Christianity could not so easily be destroyed, and Jerome had played his part in establishing them. His contribution to the monastic movement, which was to prove so rich and important a part of medieval culture, was considerable. His teaching on celibacy informed Catholic dogma for centuries. Above all, there was the Vulgate.

In common usage 'the Vulgate' refers to the Latin version of the Bible followed by the Roman Catholic Church, for which Jerome is generally held to have been responsible.[33] This version, however, is not exclusively Jerome's work. In the Old Testament he did not touch the books of Wisdom, Ecclesiasticus, 1 and 2 Maccabees, and Baruch, all of which he considered uncanonical,[34] and in the Vulgate these sur-

---

[30] For Jerome's attitude to this cult see comm. on 12. 4 *basilicas . . . conciliabula.*

[31] Cf. e.g. *epist.* 60. 16. 2–5 with comm., 118. 2, 123. 15–16, 127. 12.

[32] Cf. *epist.* 114. 1. 1.

[33] In the commentary all Biblical quotations in Latin, except where otherwise stated, are drawn from the Vulgate in the edition of Weber. In citing from the Psalms I give both the Vulgate version (the Gallican Psalter; denoted 'LXX') and Jerome's version from the Hebrew (denoted 'Hebr.'), which never gained full acceptance by the Church and is not reckoned part of the Vulgate (though it is included, conveniently, in Weber's edition). For the details in this and the next two paragraphs I am indebted principally to Sparks, 510–26, and Kelly, 86–9, 158–63, 283–5.

[34] For Jerome's views on the canon of Scripture see Kelly, 160–1, Sparks, 532–5, P. W. Skehan, 'St. Jerome and the Canon of the Holy Scriptures', in Murphy, *Monument*, 259–87. His acceptance of the Hebrew canon of the OT followed easily

vive in an earlier, Old Latin,[35] version. Equally, the whole of
the New Testament apart from the gospels almost certainly
represents the Old Latin text as later revised by persons
unknown. The gospels, and the other books of the Old
Testament, are attributable to Jerome in greater or lesser
degree, some being wholly new translations (though the care
and thoroughness with which they were prepared vary
considerably from book to book), others revisions of the Old
Latin.

Jerome's initial foray into Biblical translation came as the
result of a commission from Damasus to revise the New
Testament, and perhaps the whole of the Bible, in the light
of the Greek. Behind this lay a wish to impose some order on
the chaos of the multiplicity of Latin texts which were then
current. In 384 Jerome completed his revision of the gospels,
the only part of the New Testament we can be sure that he
tackled, and around the same time carried out a revision of
the Psalter on the basis of the Septuagint; this, however,
forms no part of the Vulgate and is probably lost. A second
version of the same book was done during the early years in
the Holy Land (386–*c*.390), where Jerome had available, at
Caesarea, the more critical text of the Septuagint found in
Origen's Hexapla.[36] This later work, known as the Gallican
Psalter, fared infinitely better, becoming the Psalter of the

from his recognition, *c*.390, that the Hebrew text should have priority over the
LXX (see below).

[35] The term 'Old Latin'—'Vetus Latina' (VL)—refers to those versions of
Biblical texts which predate Jerome's Vulgate translations. In the case of the
Hebrew books of the OT they were based not on the original but on the LXX. They
came into being more or less simultaneously in Africa and Europe in the second
century, and by Jerome's day existed in many forms. A new scholarly edition,
offering a text with numerous variants, is in the process of being prepared (referred
to in the commentary as VL Beuron). The parts published so far cover the
following books of the Bible: Gen., Ecclus. (1: 1–3: 31), Wisd., Isa. (1: 1–10: 19),
Eph., Phil., Col., 1 and 2 Thess., 1 and 2 Tim., Titus, Heb. (1: 1–9: 12), Jas., 1 and
2 Pet., 1, 2, and 3 John, and Jude. For the remaining books we are still dependent
on the greatly inferior, though historically important, text of P. Sabatier, *Bibliorum
sacrorum Latinae versiones antiquae seu Vetus Italica* (3 vols., Rheims, 1743[–9]).

[36] This magnificent third-century edition of the OT offered the Hebrew text, a
transliteration of it into Greek, and four Greek versions (Aquila, Symmachus,
Theodotion, LXX). The text of the LXX was equipped with diacritical signs. See
ODCC s.v. 'Hexapla', Kelly, 135.

Vulgate even in preference to Jerome's later translation from the Hebrew original.

Further revisions of a number of Old Testament books on the strength of the Septuagint followed. But around 390 Jerome became convinced that a translation of a translation would not do, particularly when arguing points of Scripture with Jews,[37] and during the next fifteen years or thereabouts he produced a completely new translation of the Hebrew books of the Old Testament, which had never been turned directly into Latin before; except in the case of the Psalter, it is this translation which survives as the Vulgate text. The dates of individual books cannot be given precisely. The books of Samuel and Kings appear to have been translated first;[38] the Psalter and the prophets were complete before 393, Job by 394. By 398 only the Pentateuch, Joshua, Judges, Ruth, and Esther remained to be done. At least some work had been done on the Pentateuch before 401. Esther was begun before the death of Paula in January 404; but Paula was dead before this last group of four was finished. In addition, at the request of his friends Heliodorus and Chromatius,[39] both of whom died in 407, Jerome translated from the Aramaic the books of Tobit and Judith, which he did not recognize as part of the canon;[40] the precise date of composition is unknown.

Jerome's attitude to his own work on the Latin Bible may to some extent be gauged by comparing with the Vulgate text his citations from Scripture in works known to postdate the translation or revision of the book from which the citation is drawn. A study of his *Commentary on Matthew*,[41] which was written after his revision of the gospels, has shown that a substantial majority of the gospel quotations in

[37] Cf. *pref. in Ios.*, *pref. in Is.*, *pref. in psalm.*, *adv. Rufin.* 3. 25 (CCSL 79. 97 = PL 23. 476).

[38] This is the generally accepted view; P. Jay, 'La Datation des premières traductions de l'Ancien Testament sur l'hébreu par saint Jérôme', *REAug* 28 (1982), 208–12, on the other hand, argues that the Psalter and the prophets (in that order) predate Samuel and Kings. Certainty seems to me impossible.

[39] For Heliodorus see below, n. 63; for Chromatius see comm. on 19. 3 *fortitudinem . . . filio*.

[40] Cf. n. 34 above.

[41] A. Souter, 'Notes on Incidental Gospel Quotations in Jerome's Commentary on St. Matthew's Gospel', *JThS* 42 (1941), 12–18.

that commentary do not match the Vulgate text. A similar situation prevails in the case of certain quotations in *Letter* 60 (AD 396), particularly those from the Psalms, which generally resemble the text of the Gallican Psalter more closely than the translation from the Hebrew, though the context never offers more than the hint of a reason why Jerome should have avoided the later, more authentic version, and sometimes not even that.[42]

Such discrepancies are clearly significant; but in assessing them one control must be applied. It is possible, perhaps likely, that in some cases they reflect changes made by scribes in the course of transmission. Jerome's new versions, at least those of Old Testament texts, took centuries to win complete acceptance by the Church;[43] they lived alongside the Old Latin in all its many forms. It is not difficult to imagine a scribe bringing the text of a quotation into line with the version with which he was most familiar. Where this was done at an early stage in the tradition there may be no trace of the original form of the quotation in the extant MSS. It is plain, however, that the discrepancies must be due primarily to the fact that in quoting the Bible *en passant*, where textual points mattered little, Jerome was usually content to rely on his memory. In so doing he would understandably have tended to draw on the forms of the Old Latin which had been embedded in his mind from an early age. The simple fact is that he did not regard even his most authoritative versions of Biblical texts as definitive.[44]

Jerome the Biblical scholar also had more than a nodding acquaintance with the pagan classics.[45] At Donatus' school

---

[42] Cf. comm. on 3. 2 *dixerunt . . . ad unum*, 4. 1 *notus . . . nomen eius*, 6. 1 *ad vesperum . . . laetitia*, 7. 1 *sicut . . . dei nostri*.

[43] Cf. Sparks, 520–1.

[44] At *adv. Rufin.* 2. 24 (CCSL 79. 61 = PL 23. 448) he claims that he was even then, in 402, still using his revisions of OT books on the basis of the LXX as the text for his daily Scripture lectures to his monks. The translations from the Hebrew were important for scholarly theological debate, but not for most practical Christian uses; cf. *pref. in psalm.* 'aliud sit in ecclesiis Christo credentium Psalmos legere, aliud Iudaeis singula verba calumniantibus respondere'.

[45] Jerome's knowledge of the classics has been the subject of a wealth of scholarship. The most important investigations are those of Hagendahl (1958, 1974) and Courcelle (1948), 47–78; much of the pioneering work was done by Luebeck. A useful bibliography, containing work published up to 1970, is furnished by F. Trisoglio, 'San Girolamo e Plinio il Giovane', *RSC* 21 (1973), 343–83,

he will have been introduced to authors such as Terence, Cicero, and Virgil; and the corpus of his works indicates a wide knowledge of classical literature, reflected not merely in quotation and allusion, but even, on occasion, in style, where his rhetorical training will have played a part. But for many years Jerome was troubled by the question whether or not a Christian should read the classics. Writing his letter on virginity to Eustochium in 384, and urging her to shun pagan literature, he recalled[46] a terrifying dream he had experienced years before, which was clearly the product of serious illness and intense guilt at interspersing his Christian practices with pagan reading. In the dream, dragged before a judge, Jerome was accused of being not a Christian, as he claimed, but a 'Ciceronian'. A flogging followed; but the pain of his guilty conscience, he tells his reader, was far more severe. At last the bystanders interceded for him; and Jerome forswore worldly books for ever.

This promise, though made in a dream, Jerome seems to have kept for a long time, reading no classical literature and quoting it, where he did so, only from memory. In the preface to the third book of his *Commentary on Galatians*, which belongs to the late 380s, he declares that he had not looked at any pagan author for over fifteen years.[47] It has been argued[48] that he never again read the classics; but a careful examination of the evidence leads convincingly to the conclusion that this was not so.[49] At some point, perhaps not long after his statement in the Galatians commentary, Jerome returned to reading pagan texts. His revised, more relaxed attitude to the use of the classics by Christian writers is made explicit in *Letter* 70, written in 397 or 398. *Letter* 60, which displays a wealth of classical learning, was almost

---

at 348 n. 39. More recent scholarship includes G. Burzacchini, 'Nota sulla presenze di Persio in Girolamo', *GIF* 27 (1975), 50–72, J. J. Thierry, 'Hieronymus en Ovidius', *Hermeneus*, 50 (1978), 359–61, and W. C. McDermott, 'Saint Jerome and Pagan Greek Literature', *VChr* 36 (1982), 372–82; but McDermott's attempt to show that Jerome was better acquainted with pagan Greek literature than Courcelle would have it, a view based on *c. Ioh.* 12 (PL 23. 365), is speculative, as the author himself admits (379), and not convincing.

[46] *Epist.* 22. 30.   [47] PL 26. 399.
[48] By Eiswirth; see esp. 28–9.   [49] Cf. Hagendahl (1958), 318–28.

certainly written with a text of Cicero's *Consolatio* at his side.[50]

For all the sheer bulk of his writings, our knowledge of Jerome's life would be immeasurably poorer without his surviving correspondence.[51] Though patchy in parts, the collection covers the years from 375, while he was still at Antioch, to 419 or 420. It includes a wide variety of letters, dealing with problems of Scripture and theology, topics such as the ascetic life and Christian education, the consolation of the bereaved, and of course important issues of the moment; but all are united in a common belief and purpose. It should not be supposed, however, that in reading the correspondence we are in all cases eavesdropping upon one side of a private conversation. Some of the letters—and they are not necessarily the most technical or impersonal—suggest explicitly that in writing them Jerome envisaged a readership extending beyond the addressee. There are times, for example, when he refers to a general *lector*.[52] *Letter* 123 is plainly not intended for Geruchia's eyes alone, and this

[50] Cf. 5. 3, with comm. on 5. 1 *Anaxagorae . . . mortalem*, 5. 2 *Platonis . . . percucurrimus*, 5. 2–3 *proponunt . . . explicavit*. The attempt of Eiswirth, 24–6, to dismiss the view that Jerome was drawing directly on the *Consolatio*, is a case of special pleading, and defies belief.

[51] The corpus includes letters which are not by Jerome; where these are cited in the commentary, this is indicated. *Epist.* 148, 149, and 150 are spurious (148 is by Pelagius; 150 is omitted by Hilberg and all three by Labourt). Others are addressed to Jerome by other writers, most notably and frequently Augustine. A further group comprises letters of which Jerome is neither the author nor the addressee; one of these, *epist.* 46, purports to have been written to Marcella by Paula and Eustochium, but bears the stamp of having been composed by Jerome himself (cf. Kelly, 124, 141). Still others are translations by Jerome of Greek originals, mainly by Theophilus of Alexandria. *Epist.* 80 is Rufinus' preface to his translation of Origen's *De principiis*. To the letters printed by Hilberg should be added the letter to Praesidius, rescued from banishment among the unauthentic works of Jerome by G. Morin, 'Pour l'authenticité de la lettre de S. Jérôme à Présidius', *Bulletin d'ancienne littérature et d'archéologie chrétiennes*, 3 (1913), 52–60 (the article contains a revised version of the text), and that to Aurelius of Carthage, found among the Divjak collection of Augustine letters and published in 1981 in CSEL 88. 130–3.

Jerome's characteristics as an epistolographer have not been much studied. Arns, 92–8, makes some useful comments on a few aspects of his practice. Thraede, discussing certain standard epistolary topics, devotes a considerable amount of space to the evidence of Christian letter-writers, Jerome included. On classical epistolography generally the standard work is still J. Sykutris, 'Epistolographie', *RE* supp. 5, 185–220.

[52] *Epist.* 78. 16. 2, 108. 2. 1, 127. 5. 3.

seems to be equally true for Marcella in the case of *Letter* 23.[53] In writing *Letter* 52 Jerome recognizes that he may be opening himself up to attacks from his opponents.[54] It has even been argued that a few of the letters were intended solely for wider distribution; that in these cases the epistolary situation is in fact an imaginary one.[55] There is nothing surprising about any of this; epistolography had, after all, existed as a literary form with a public character since the later Hellenistic period.

In *Letter* 60 there are no internal clues which enable us to say with certainty that it was written with a wider public in mind. Yet, while it is concerned with a deeply personal situation, its tone is so elevated that we may suspect that Jerome had at least half an eye to publication. That he regarded it as an important work is in any case evident from its inclusion with *De viris illustribus*, *Adversus Iovinianum*, and only a handful of other pieces, in the list of works mentioned in the preface to his *Commentary on Jonah*[56] as having been written within the previous three years or so. As the Jonah preface cannot postdate the letter by much[57] it seems likely that an intention to publish accompanied its composition. Even if this was not so, the letter could easily have become more widely available later. We know that Jerome retained copies of some of his correspondence,[58] and from these further copies could be made and distributed; Damasus, for instance, was allowed to read and transcribe Jerome's own copies of letters which he had originally written while in the desert.[59] It is possible that the recipients of his letters also issued copies to others who were interested. Chains of distribution could readily arise. Copies of *Letters* 22, 54, and 79—all ostensibly private correspondence—are known to have circulated, either on Jerome's authority or at

---

[53] Cf. *epist.* 123. 17. 2, 23. 2. 1.   [54] *Epist.* 52. 17.

[55] See D. de Bruyne, 'Lettres fictives de S. Jérôme', *ZNTW* 28 (1929), 229–34, P. Nautin, 'Le Premier Échange épistolaire entre Jérôme et Damase: lettres réelles ou fictives?', *FZPhTh* 30 (1983), 331–44.

[56] CCSL 76. 377 = PL 25. 1117.   [57] See Appendix 1.

[58] See comm. on 9. 1 *Alius . . . nepos.*

[59] Cf. *epist.* 35. 1. 2 (Damasus). The basic point is unaffected even if, as P. Nautin thinks (see n. 55 above), this letter is not by Damasus at all but is a fiction of Jerome himself.

least with his approval.[60] We may be fairly confident that by some means or another so fine a piece as *Letter* 60 will rapidly have become known to others besides its addressee.

2. *LETTER* 60 AND THE CONSOLATORY TRADITION

In 394[61] Jerome wrote a letter[62] to a young priest called Nepotianus, the nephew of his old friend Heliodorus, who was now Bishop of Altinum in the province of Venetia-Istria.[63] The letter offered Nepotianus guidance on how a cleric should conduct his life. But the impact it had was brief. Two years later Nepotianus fell ill and died; and Jerome took it upon himself to send a letter of consolation to Heliodorus, the young man's surrogate father.[64] In this he was doing what many others had done before him, and many would do again. His own extant correspondence contains two consolatory letters written considerably earlier;[65] others were to follow.[66] But, as we shall see, *Letter* 60 occupies a special place not only in Jerome's own consolatory works, but in the whole history of ancient consolation.

To offer consolation to those afflicted by grief is an act naturally human, in which the barriers erected between individuals in consequence of personal enmity or social difference or any other circumstance that tends to separate are readily broken down. So, in the last book of the *Iliad*, the Trojan Priam and the Greek Achilles, both of whom have suffered painful losses in the war, join together in weeping,

---

[60] Cf. *epist.* 52. 17. 1 (22), 123. 17. 3 (22, 54, 79), 130. 19. 3 (22).

[61] I give the generally accepted date; Nautin (1974), 251–3, however, interprets the evidence to mean that the letter was written in 393.

[62] *Epist.* 52. All that we know about Nepotianus is derived from this piece and *epist.* 60.

[63] Jerome's friendship with Heliodorus probably went back to student days (cf. Cavallera, 1. 14 n. 1, Kelly, 19 n. 5). When Jerome left Aquileia for the East in 372, Heliodorus went on his own pilgrimage to Jerusalem and later met Jerome at Antioch. Soon, however, he returned to Italy to look after his sister and nephew, rejecting Jerome's overtures that he should join him as a hermit in the Syrian desert (see comm. on 9. 1 *Alius . . . nepos*). At some time before 381 he became Bishop of Altinum, his native town. He was a great supporter of Jerome's literary projects, and regularly provided him with money for copyists. See *DCB* s.n. Heliodorus 7, Kelly, *passim*.

[64] Cf. *epist.* 60. 9. 1.   [65] *Epist.* 23 and 39 (AD 384).   [66] See below, p. 27.

and Achilles, who has killed Priam's son, comforts the old man.[67] But under rhetorical and philosophical influences a specialized literature began to develop in Greece, leading to the establishment of a tradition which persisted throughout Antiquity and continued into the Middle Ages.[68] This consolatory genre, if such it may be called, embraced a number of literary forms. Philosophers wrote treatises on the subject of grief, considering what remedies should be applied to soothe the sorrowful. Letters of consolation were addressed to individuals, and even to whole communities,[69] upon a bereavement or some other misfortune;[70] these might be highly personal in tone, or they might possess the more detached character of an essay. Poets wrote the occasional consolation in verse. At funerals and other occasions for public mourning orators delivered speeches which had as

---

[67] Hom. *Il.* 24. 507–51.

[68] In the discussion which follows and in general throughout the commentary I do not consider the medieval contribution to the genre. Those who are interested in the continuation of the tradition may consult with profit the massive work of P. von Moos, *Consolatio: Studien zur mittellateinischen Trostliteratur über den Tod und zum Problem der christlichen Trauer* (Münstersche Mittelalter-Schriften, 3; 4 vols., Munich, 1971–2); von Moos conveniently assembles testimonia from classical and patristic as well as medieval *consolationes*. In keeping with the principle of restricting the scope of the study in this way I have ignored almost entirely the most famous of the consolations of the Middle Ages, the *De consolatione philosophiae* of Boethius, which is in any case not a typical representative of the genre (T. F. Curley III, 'The *Consolation of Philosophy* as a Work of Literature', *AJPh* 108 (1987), 343–67, at 352, maintains that Boethius' work borrows from the mainstream consolatory tradition only a single topic). The literary tradition in which this work stands is investigated in detail by Courcelle (1967), with which should be read the review of P. Dronke, *Speculum*, 44 (1969), 123–8.

[69] Such as the letters of Basil to the church of Neocaesarea on the death of Bishop Musonius and the church of Ancyra on that of Bishop Athanasius (*epist.* 28 and 29), or the letter of Ambrose to the clergy and faithful of Thessalonica on the death of Bishop Acholius (*epist.* 15).

[70] For example, Cicero consoles T. Fadius for his conviction in one of Pompey's courts (*ad fam.* 5. 18); Seneca and Plutarch write consolations on the subject of exile (see below, p. 21); the pseudography of Jerome contains a letter of consolation to a sick friend ([Jer.] *epist.* 5 (PL 30. 61–75), on which see H. Savon, 'Une consolation imitée de Sénèque et de saint Cyprien (Pseudo-Jérôme, *epistula 5, ad amicum aegrotum)*', *RecAug* 14 (1979), 153–90); Gregory of Nazianzus comforts a friend who is ill in *epist.* 31–4; among the consolatory letters of Basil are a number to the victims of the Arian persecution (see below, n. 107). Cf. Cic. *Tusc.* 3. 81 'sunt enim certa, quae de paupertate, certa, quae de vita inhonorata et ingloria dici soleant; separatim certae scholae sunt de exilio, de interitu patriae, de servitute, de debilitate, de caecitate, de omni casu, in quo nomen poni solet calamitatis'.

one of their aims the comforting of the mourners.[71] What unites the works in these various categories is that they are all concerned, one way or another, with the treatment of grief, and that they draw to a large extent on a common stock of consolatory topics—which is not to say that they have no individuality, or that the genre was static throughout its history.

Some of the themes and topics of this hard core of consolatory texts also appear, quite naturally, in works that were not designed specifically to console. Early poets— Simonides and Pindar, for example—wrote threnodies, lamenting someone's demise. Later, many turned their hands to *epicedia*, such as Horace's ode on the death of Quintilius, and the elegy of Propertius on the drowned Paetus.[72] The popular philosophy of the 'diatribe'[73] has much in common with the literature of consolation. In the field of epigraphy, close links can be seen with sepulchral epigrams in both Greek and Latin, many of which are really *epicedia*.[74] This additional range of related texts does not, of course, exhaust the areas where consolatory themes and topics may be found: they can crop up almost anywhere.

The origins of consolation as a special branch of ancient literature are to be found partly in the belief of the sophists

[71] Ambrose is explicit about the consolatory function of three of his funeral speeches; cf. *obit. Valent.* 40, *exc. Sat.* 1. 14, 2. 3.

[72] Hor. *carm.* 1. 24, Prop. 3. 7. For other cases see Nisbet–Hubbard (1970), 280.

[73] I use the term in the broad sense, to cover a range of Hellenistic philosophical literature of a generally moralizing character; I fully agree with the view, recently restated by Powell, 12–13, that the word as normally employed by scholars should not be taken to denote a literary *genre*. On the 'diatribe' see in general A. Oltramare, *Les Origines de la diatribe romaine* (Lausanne, 1926), W. Capelle and H.-I. Marrou, 'Diatribe', *RAC* 3. 990–1019.

[74] Themes in these epigrams are usefully organized and discussed by Lier (1903–4), both of whom include a good deal of original source-material; texts are available also in the collections of Kaibel, Buecheler, and Engström. Of less interest from the thematic point of view, but none the less striking in themselves, are the consolatory decrees erected in Greek cities of the Roman world officially honouring a notable citizen who had died, and offering comfort to his or her surviving relatives; for discussion of these inscriptions see K. Buresch, 'Die griechischen Trostbeschlüsse', *RhM* 49 (1894), 424–60, M. Galdi, 'Influssi letterarii sulla composizione degli ψηφίσματα παραμυθητικά?', *Mélanges Paul Thomas: recueil de mémoires concernant la philologie classique dédié à Paul Thomas* (Bruges, 1930), 312–26, O. Gottwald, 'Zu den griechischen Trostbeschlüssen', *Commentationes Vindobonenses*, 3 (1937), 5–18, Kassel, 44–5.

in the power of λόγος.[75] Already in the *Prometheus Bound*
Aeschylus (if he is the author) writes of the healing capabili-
ties of discourse;[76] and the emphasis which in the fifth
century BC came to be given to the skilful handling of words
laid the foundations for the development of the consolatory
art. Upon these built the philosophers. Democritus argued,
along proto-Epicurean lines, that death was not to be feared,
as it brought the end of all sensation.[77] The sophist Antiphon
is said to have invented a τέχνη ἀλυπίας, by which he consoled
those in distress.[78] Plato's *Apology* and *Phaedo* contain
consolatory elements, as do the funeral speech in the *Menexenus*,[79] and the pseudo-Platonic *Axiochus*. Jerome's own list
at *epist.* 60. 5. 2 of philosophers whose consolatory works he
claims to have read includes Diogenes of Sinope, and others
from later periods.[80]

The first figure of major importance in the tradition was
the Academic Crantor of Soli (*c.*325–*c.*275 BC), whose Περὶ
πένθους, a treatise of which only fragments remain, exercised
considerable influence on later writers.[81] Attempts have been

---

[75] Cf. Kassel, 4–12; κράτιστον δὴ πρὸς ἀλυπίαν φάρμακον ὁ λόγος, says pseudo-
Plutarch at *ad Apoll.* 6 (103F). The history of ancient consolatory literature was first
traced in detail by Buresch (1886); this is still worth reading, as are the essays of
A. C. van Heusde, *Diatribe in locum philosophiae moralis qui est de consolatione apud
Graecos* (Utrecht, 1840), A. Gercke, 'De consolationibus', *Tirocinium philologum
sodalium Regii Seminarii Bonnensis* (Berlin, 1883), 28–70, and C. Martha, 'Les
Consolations dans l'Antiquité', in his *Études morales sur l'Antiquité* (4th edn., Paris,
1905), 135–89. A good brief modern history is provided by Gregg, 1–50.

[76] Aes. *PV* 378.

[77] Cf. Democr. fr. 297 Diels–Kranz (= Stob. *flor.* 52. 40 Hense) ἔνιοι θνητῆς
φύσεως διάλυσιν οὐκ εἰδότες ἄνθρωποι, συνειδήσει δὲ τῆς ἐν τῷ βίῳ κακοπραγμοσύνης, τὸν
τῆς βιοτῆς χρόνον ἐν ταραχαῖς καὶ φόβοις ταλαιπωρέουσι, ψεύδεα περὶ τοῦ μετὰ τὴν
τελευτὴν μυθοπλαστέοντες χρόνου.

[78] Cf. Plut. *vit. X orat.* 833C–D.

[79] Though they differ in important respects from the later funeral speeches for
individuals (see below, pp. 21, 24–5), the surviving examples of the collective
Athenian *epitaphioi* of the fifth and fourth centuries BC (those attributed to Lysias
and Demosthenes, that of Hyperides, and of course the speech of Pericles at Thuc.
2. 34–46, as well as that of Socrates/Aspasia in the *Menexenus*) also have a partly
consolatory purpose. N. Loraux, *L'Invention d'Athènes: histoire de l'oraison funèbre
dans la 'cité classique'* (Civilisations et sociétés, 65; Paris, 1981), offers an important
investigation, from a structuralist perspective, of these *epitaphioi*.

[80] While we may doubt the existence of genuine consolatory writings by
Diogenes, Carneades, and Posidonius, there seems no reason to dispute that they
made some contribution to consolatory thought; see comm. on 5. 2 *Platonis . . .
percucurrimus*.

[81] Though the fond notion, which goes back to Buresch (1886), that the treatise

made[82] to reconstruct this work, addressed to one Hippocles upon the death of his children, but in vain; we simply do not possess sufficient material or information about the work to make this a worthwhile task. It was, however, very highly regarded in Antiquity. 'Legimus omnes Crantoris, veteris Academici, de luctu; est enim non magnus, verum aureolus et, ut Tuberoni Panaetius praecipit, ad verbum ediscendus libellus', wrote Cicero;[83] and the judgement of Diogenes Laertius is hardly less glowing.[84] At epist. 60. 5. 2 Jerome claims to have read it, but is much more likely to have got at it only through Cicero's Consolatio.[85]

It appears to have been this work of Cicero's, written to console himself on the death of his daughter Tullia in 45 BC, which above all transmitted to the Latin world the consolatory literature of the Greeks. It is now lost;[86] but much of its substance is preserved in the first and third books of the Tusculan Disputations, which deal with the problems of death and the alleviation of grief, and in which reference is made several times to the earlier work.[87] It was long thought that in composing his Consolatio Cicero kept very tightly to

was a kind of archetype for later consolations was happily disposed of by Kassel; subsequently only Johann has seriously sought to maintain the earlier position.

[82] By M. Pohlenz, De Ciceronis Tusculanis Disputationibus (Göttingen, 1909), 15–19, and by Johann (cf. esp. 127–36, and see the review of K. Abel, Gnomon, 42 (1970), 261–5). The fragments of Crantor's work are collected and discussed by F. Kayser, De Crantore academico dissertatio (Heidelberg, 1841) and F. W. A. Mullach, Fragmenta philosophorum Graecorum (3 vols., Paris, 1860–81), 3. 131–52, though how much of the surviving material can be ascribed to Crantor with certainty is doubtful: due scepticism is shown by K. Kuiper, 'De Crantoris fragmentis moralibus', Mnemosyne, 29 (1901), 341–62.

[83] Acad. prior. 2. 135; cf. also e.g. Tusc. 1. 115, 3. 71.

[84] Diog. Laert. 4. 27 θαυμάζεται δὲ αὐτοῦ μάλιστα βιβλίον τὸ Περὶ πένθους.

[85] Cf. comm. on 5. 2 legimus . . . Cicero and Platonis . . . percucurrimus.

[86] A reconstruction was attempted by J. van Wageningen, De Ciceronis libro Consolationis (Groningen, 1916), with hopelessly unsatisfactory results; see the excellent critique by R. Philippson, Berliner Philologischer Wochenschrift, 37 (1917), 496–504. The fact is that no work can be reconstructed on the basis of a few surviving fragments and the putative fragments of another author (Crantor, as perserved in the Ad Apollonium of pseudo-Plutarch). The best discussion of the Consolatio is that of Kumaniecki. E. T. Sage, The Pseudo–Ciceronian Consolatio (Chicago, 1910), is an intriguing study of a probable forgery of the Consolatio, published at Venice in 1583.

[87] Cic. Tusc. 1. 65, 76, 83; 3. 70, 76; also 4. 63. Buresch (1886), 96–9, sought to establish in some detail the connections between the two works, but his premises are not sound.

the lines of Crantor's treatise, chiefly on the strength of the elder Pliny's statement that 'in Consolatione filiae Crantorem, inquit [sc. Cicero], sequor'.[88] But the phrase 'Crantorem sequor' does not necessarily mean that Cicero copied Crantor verbatim; indeed, the view that Cicero followed Crantor exclusively or even principally is challenged by his own comment at *ad Att.* 12. 14. 3, written at the same time as the *Consolatio*, that there is not a work dealing with grief that he has not read, the statement at *Tusc.* 3. 76 'in Consolatione omnia in consolationem unam coniecimus', and the inclusion in Jerome's list of consolatory writers at *epist.* 60. 5. 2, which is almost certainly derived from the *Consolatio*,[89] of authors later than Crantor.[90] 'Crantorem sequor', it has been suggested,[91] may mean no more than 'I share Crantor's point of view'.

The Ciceronian corpus also contains a few examples of the consolatory letter, including perhaps the most famous (certainly one of the most beautiful) of all the *consolationes* of the ancient world, the masterpiece sent to Cicero on Tullia's death by Servius Sulpicius Rufus.[92] But for the richest instances of practical consolation in this period we must turn to the younger Seneca.[93] In the *Ad Marciam* and the *Ad*

---

[88] Plin. *nat.* pref. 22.   [89] Cf. comm. on 5. 2 *Platonis . . . percucurrimus.*

[90] It has also been argued by A. Grilli, 'Cicerone e l'*Eudemo*', *PP* 17 (1962), 96–128, that in the *Consolatio* Cicero drew directly on the *Eudemus* of Aristotle.

[91] By Kumaniecki, 378.

[92] Cic. *ad fam.* 4. 5, discussed by Kassel, 98–103. Of Cicero's own compositions the letter to Titius (*ad fam.* 5. 16) is the most noteworthy; cf. also *ad fam.* 5. 18, *ad Att.* 12. 10, 15. 1, *ad Brut.* 1. 9.

[93] Of the considerable literature on consolation in Seneca see esp. J. Dartigue-Peyrou, *Quae sit apud Senecam consolationum disciplina, vis ratioque* (Paris, 1897), Favez (1930*a*), G. de Vico, 'Premesse per una lettura delle "consolationes" di Seneca', *GIF* 8 (1955), 333–48, H.-H. Studnik, *Die consolatio mortis in Senecas Briefen* (Cologne, 1958), M. Coccia, 'La consolatio in Seneca', *Rivista di cultura classica e medioevale*, 1 (1959), 148–80, K. Abel, *Bauformen in Senecas Dialogen* (Bibliothek der klassischen Altertumswissenschaft, NF 2 R., Bd. 18; Heidelberg, 1967). There is a helpful commentary on the *Ad Helviam* by C. Favez, *L. Annaei Senecae dialogorum liber XII ad Helviam de consolatione* (Lausanne, 1918); on the *Ad Marciam* see Favez (1928), and C. C. Grollios, *Seneca's Ad Marciam: Tradition and Originality* (Athens, 1956). The *Ad Polybium* is usefully served by Grollios, Τέχνη ἀλυπίας: κοινοὶ τόποι τοῦ Πρὸς Πολύβιον τοῦ Σενέκα καὶ πηγαὶ αὐτῶν (Ἑλληνικά, παράρτημα 10; Thessaloniki, 1956), and Atkinson. Jerome was certainly familiar with at least some of Seneca's work (cf. Hagendahl (1958), 297), but attempts to establish a direct dependency have generally been unsuccessful. Hagendahl (1974), 223–5, rightly maintains that the parallels adduced by S. Jannaccone, 'S. Girolamo

Polybium (dial. 6 and 11) Seneca offers his addressee consolation on the death of a close relative, while in the *Ad
Helviam matrem (dial.* 12) he seeks to comfort his mother
about his exile. Pieces such as these, though directed to a
particular and personal situation, have the character rather
of an essay than of a letter; here, as elsewhere, the distinction
between letter and treatise becomes hard to define.[94] Among
the letters to Lucilius good specimens of the genre are
afforded by *epist.* 63 and 99.

The best known of consolations written in verse[95] is
probably the pseudo-Ovidian *Consolatio ad Liviam;*[96] others
which deserve mention are Ov. *Pont.* 4. 11 and Statius' poem
to Abascantus on the death of his wife Priscilla (*silv.* 5. 1), the
closest to a genuine consolation among Statius' works.[97]
Among later and lesser pagan writers we have letters from
Fronto, Apollonius of Tyana, the Emperor Julian, and
Libanius, the last of these also the author of two funeral
speeches on Julian,[98] the second written on a colossal scale;
the Plutarchian corpus contains three pieces, the *De exilio*
and the touching *Consolatio ad uxorem* by Plutarch himself,
and the *Consolatio ad Apollonium*, an unauthentic work
which draws to at least some extent on Crantor.[99]

---

e Seneca', *GIF* 16 (1963), 326–38, and by Trillitzsch, both of whom devote part of
their discussions to Jerome's consolatory writing, do not demonstrate a literary
relationship; nor does Guttilla (1977–9), 222–30, succeed in proving that *epist.* 60
displays a direct debt to the *Ad Marciam*. The two authors have so much
consolatory material in common, however, that it would be surprising if Jerome had
been completely unacquainted with Seneca's *consolationes*.

[94] The ancients faced the same problem of definition; cf. Mitchell, 299 n. 1.

[95] For which see in general J. Esteve-Forriol, *Die Trauer- und Trostgedichte in der
römischen Literatur* (Munich, 1962), which contains useful collections of material.

[96] On which see esp. J. Richmond, 'Doubtful Works Ascribed to Ovid', *ANRW*
II. 31. 4. 2744–83, at 2768–83.

[97] Other poems in the *Silvae* contain some consolation, but have in general rather
the character of *epicedia*: 2.1, 2.6, 3.3, 5.3, 5.5, and the mock-*epicedion* on a
friend's parrot, 2.4.

[98] *Orat.* 17 and 18. Isolated examples of the funeral speech may also be found
among the works of Libanius' contemporaries Himerius and Themistius, and
(earlier) of Dio Chrysostom and Aelius Aristides.

[99] It was thus critical to the attempted reconstructions of the Περὶ πένθους
referred to above (n. 82). Kassel, however, about half of whose book (49–98)
consists of notes on this text, demonstrates that there is little in it which can be
attributed to Crantor for certain (cf. esp. 35–6, 58, 68–9, 73), a position accepted by

The pagan tradition possessed a richness and variety
which stemmed from the different approaches to the treatment of grief employed by the different philosophical
schools. But practical consolation does not require—indeed,
it may be hindered by—adherence to a particular philosophical system, and from the time of Cicero a broad eclecti-
cism is apparent in the choice of *praecepta* and *solacia* to be
applied to the *consolandus*.[100] Certain topics recur with great
regularity: we are all born mortal; death frees us from the
miseries of life; time heals all griefs; we grieve not for those
who have died but for ourselves; and so forth. The major
areas of difference concerned the permissibility of grief and
the existence of the soul after the death of the body. Stoic
teaching, with its belief in the supremacy of reason, insisted
that powerful emotions had to be suppressed; grief was
irrational, and the wise man would never feel it. Others
accepted that grief was natural and proper, and should
merely be moderated, not indulged in: a far more practical
line when it came to offering consolation. The key problem
confronting pagan consolers, however, was that they had
little to offer the bereaved by way of hope for the continued
existence of the deceased. The Epicureans positively denied
that the soul outlived the body: a precept which could be
used to combat the fear of death but which will have been
cold comfort to those who had lost loved ones.[101] Belief in
some form of immortality was held in other quarters, but it
was vague and speculative.[102] The best Cicero can do, in

J. Hani, *Plutarque, Consolation à Apollonios* (Études et commentaires, 78; Paris,
1972), 43–9. Hani, 27–43, also argues for the authenticity of the work, but I remain
among the sceptics. I do not, all the same, find it quite so dismal reading as
Nisbet–Hubbard (1970), who refer to it (280) as 'a dreary congeries of all possible
topics'.

[100] Cicero states (*Tusc.* 3. 76) that he incorporated the various traditions in his
Consolatio; and even the Stoic Seneca, eschewing sectarian fundamentalism, made
use of ideas and arguments from other philosophical schools (cf. the succinct
discussion of Atkinson, 870–2).

[101] See the sensible comments of E. J. Kenney, *Lucretius: De rerum natura Book 3*
(Cambridge, 1971), 32–3, quoting Santayana and Cornford.

[102] The Stoics could not agree amongst themselves whether the soul survived the
death of the body or not, and if so for how long. In a famous passage of the *Ad
Marciam* (*dial.* 6. 25–6), partly coloured by Platonism, Seneca comforts Marcia
with the notion that her dead son continues to live among the blessed souls in

seeking to refute the proposition that death is an evil, is to argue an either-or case: whether the soul is mortal or immortal, death is no evil and may be despised.[103]

Christian belief in a single, benevolent, and loving God, and in the doctrine of resurrection, meant that Christian consolers did not face the same difficulty. Fellow-Christians who died would be resurrected to a new life, blissful and eternal, in heaven; this conviction must have been a comfort to the bereaved far beyond any which the pagan tradition could provide, and Christian consolatory writing displays, for the most part, a new warmth and (whether self-deceptive or not) a new certainty. The wealth of relevant Biblical material available also ensured that consolation would have a different kind of character in the hands of the Christians. But the τόποι which had been grounded in the philosophy of the pagans were not abandoned. Though some Christian *consolationes* were based wholly or very largely on the Scriptures and Christian doctrine generally, many used in addition materials which had long been available to non-Christians. There were plenty of stock τόποι, after all, which could be put equally well to pagan or to Christian use; the notion of death as an escape from ills, for example, or the idea that we should not mourn the loss of loved ones, rather be grateful for having once had them, do not remotely conflict with Christian belief. We shall see below, in connection with *Letter* 60, how Jerome intertwines the two traditions, and how he employs originally pagan ideas for a Christian end.

Already in Tertullian the beginnings of a Christian *consolatio* can be perceived;[104] but the first of the Fathers to give

---

heaven; but this life too will come to an end at the great conflagration which will consume the entire universe prior to its being created anew. Seneca's views, however, are themselves unsettled and inconsistent; for example, at *epist*. 54. 4 and 99. 29–30, and even elsewhere in the *Ad Marciam* (19. 5), he writes of death as complete extinction. On *dial*. 6. 25–6, and Stoic ideas on the soul after death generally, see now R. B. Rutherford, *The* Meditations *of Marcus Aurelius: A Study* (Oxford, 1989), 244–55; also E. Badstübner, *Beiträge zur Erklärung und Kritik der philosophischen Schriften Senecas* (Hamburg, 1901), 1–18, Favez (1928), pp. xxxvii–xxxix, Gregg, 42–4. For an interesting early fourth-century Christian account of Stoic belief on this point see Lact. *inst*. 7. 20. 8–9.

[103] This is the thrust of *Tusc*. 1; cf. *sen*. 66–7, and other passages cited by Powell, 239. Cicero's either-or position of course goes back to Plato, *apol*. 40c.

[104] Tert. *pat*. 9.

us an example of consolation in practice is Cyprian.[105] His treatise *De mortalitate*, in origin probably a sermon, addressed to a Christian congregation at Carthage in 252 in the wake of the Decian persecution and at a time when plague was sweeping across the Roman Empire, is aimed chiefly at putting heart and resolve into believers, and particularly backsliders; but it also offers comfort to those who had lost relatives and friends in the epidemic.[106] Much more remains from the fourth and early fifth centuries. In the Greek East the Cappadocian Fathers show their importance here as elsewhere. Nineteen letters of consolation are found among the works of Basil.[107] We have funeral orations from Gregory of Nyssa on Meletius, Pulcheria, and Flacilla, and from Gregory of Nazianzus on his father and his brother Caesarius;[108] the latter also furnishes a few letters.[109] Others who contribute to the genre are John Chrysostom[110] and Theodoret of Cyrus.

In the West, Paulinus of Nola provides a consolatory letter

[105] The fundamental study of the Christian *consolatio* in Latin is Favez (1937), which does not, however, consider the work of Augustine (an omission which the author later rectified; see n. 112 below). Some of the principal *consolationes* are re-examined in a diachronic way by Guttilla (1984–5). On the Greek side, Gregg on Basil and the Gregorys is thorough and important; but there is as yet no comprehensive study of the Greek contribution to Christian consolation.

[106] The text is not well served by the commentary of M. L. Hannan (Catholic University of America Patristic Studies, 36; Washington, DC, 1933), one of a disappointing series of commentaries on consolatory works emanating from the same institution around the same time (the others being those of Kelly and Mannix on Ambrose; see below, n. 115). Their focus is mainly linguistic and grammatical, and they bear the stamp of having followed a prescribed pattern: written, as it were, by numbers.

[107] Including six (*epist.* 139, 140, 238, 247, 256, 257) which are addressed not to individuals or communities who have in some way been bereaved but to churches and monastic centres persecuted by Arians; for their essential consolatory character see Gregg, 132. The consolatory letters of Basil are usefully discussed also by Mitchell.

[108] *Orat.* 18 and 7 respectively. The speeches on his sister Gorgonia (*orat.* 8) and on Basil (*orat.* 43), with which these are normally associated, are more straightforwardly panegyrical and have little to do with consolation.

[109] For which see again, in addition to Gregg, Mitchell.

[110] It is the consolatory writing of Chrysostom in particular that is examined in L. Malunowiczówna, 'Les Éléments stoïciens dans la consolation grecque chrétienne', *Studia Patristica*, 13. *Papers presented to the Sixth International Conference on Patristic Studies held in Oxford 1971, Part 2*, ed. E. A. Livingstone (Texte und Untersuchungen, 116; Berlin, 1975), 35–45.

in verse (*carm.* 31),[111] and another (*epist.* 13) in prose, addressed to the Christian senator Pammachius on the death of his wife Paulina; Jerome wrote to the same man on the same occasion (*epist.* 66). There are a few pieces by Augustine,[112] and one by Sulpicius Severus (*epist.* 2). The most important Christian consolers who write in Latin, however, are Ambrose and Jerome himself. Ambrose's contribution lies mainly in the field of the funeral oration, in the two speeches on the death of his brother Satyrus[113] and those on the deaths of the Emperors Valentinian II and Theodosius; also extant are two letters, *epist.* 15[114] and 39, and the treatise *De bono mortis*.[115] But it is among the works of Jerome that the Christian consolatory epistle is best represented.[116]

Ancient rhetorical precept concerning the composition of letters of consolation is not abundant.[117] Seneca tells us that it was normal practice to give precepts before *exempla*, but

[111] On which see C. Favez, 'A propos des "consolations": note sur la composition du *carmen* 31 de Paulin de Nole', *REL* 13 (1935), 266–8, G. Guttilla, 'Una nuova lettura del *carme* 31 di s. Paolino di Nola', *Koinonia*, 11 (1987), 69–97. One might also mention *carm.* 33, the *Obitus Baebiani*, which qualifies as a sort of consolation, though one of an idiosyncratic character; it is not, however, certainly the work of Paulinus.
[112] *Epist.* 92, 259, 263; *serm.* 172, 173. For consolation in Augustine see C. Favez, 'Les Epistulae 92, 259 et 263 de S. Augustin', *MH* 1 (1944), 65–8, and M. M. Beyenka, *Consolation in Saint Augustine* (Catholic University of America Patristic Studies, 83; Washington, DC, 1950), and 'Saint Augustine and the Consolatio Mortis', *CBull* 29 (1953), 25–8.
[113] At least the first of these was known to Jerome, and perhaps the second too; cf. comm. on 14. 1 *huiusce . . . gratius*, 14. 2 *multo . . . ad gloriam*.
[114] Cf. n. 69 above.
[115] For the consolatory writings of Ambrose see esp. Favez (1930b), and Duval (1977). The commentaries of M. D. Mannix on the *De obitu Theodosii* (Catholic University of America Patristic Studies, 9; Washington, DC, 1925), and T. A. Kelly on the *De obitu Valentiniani* (Catholic University of America Patristic Studies, 58; Washington, DC, 1940), have the weaknesses referred to at n. 106 above. Much better is that of W. T. Wiesner on the *De bono mortis* (Catholic University of America Patristic Studies, 100; Washington, DC, 1970). For the first speech on Satyrus there is the useful edition of Albers (1921). K. Schenkl, 'Zu Ciceros Consolatio', *Wiener Studien*, 16 (1894), 38–46, argues interestingly, though not conclusively, that the second speech on Satyrus is indebted to Cicero's *Consolatio*.
[116] Except in general studies of consolation (see nn. 75, 105 above), surprisingly little has been written on the consolatory letters of Jerome. The most detailed treatments are those of Guttilla (1977–9), (1980–1), and (1984–5), 129–47, 161–73 (on *epist.* 60), 190–209.
[117] See in general Mitchell, 299–304.

adds that it might be appropriate to deviate from this rule in certain circumstances.[118] The rhetorician Julius Victor prescribes that consolatory letters should be very brief.[119] We are fortunate to have sample letters of condolence in two treatises on epistolography, the Τύποι ἐπιστολικοί falsely attributed to Demetrius of Phalerum, and the Ἐπιστολιμαῖοι χαρακτῆρες ascribed to Libanius.[120] Though written at widely different times,[121] the examples given in these works have a similar content. The three principal elements of the letter they describe are sympathy, exhortation, and consolation itself. This certainly reflects much of ancient practice; but the whole epistolary genre is essentially informal,[122] and, as we shall see, Jerome's consolatory letters show great independence and freedom from constraint in both content and form.

Though it was denied by some that consolation should fall within the province of rhetoric at all,[123] there were, at least in late Antiquity, much more stringent rules governing epideictic oratory. Menander Rhetor, writing around AD 300, distinguished three types of funeral speech: ὁ παραμυθητικὸς λόγος, ὁ ἐπιτάφιος λόγος, and ἡ μονῳδία.[124] The differences between the types are largely differences of emphasis, not of content: in the first, consolation predominates, in the second, eulogy, in the third, lament. Scholarship has

---

[118] *Dial.* 6.2.1.   [119] *Rhet.* 27, p. 448 Halm.

[120] Demetr. *form. epist.* 5, [Liban.] *char. epist.* 21, 62 Weichert.

[121] The former probably belongs to the second or first century BC, the latter perhaps to the fifth century AD; cf. Mitchell, 301.

[122] This is not to deny that in certain letters of consolation a similarity in structure may be perceived. For Gregg, 54–62, this may be analysed as (*a*) an introduction expressing sympathy, (*b*) eulogy and lament, (*c*) consolation and exhortation, while Favez (1937), 44, divides the body of the letter into two main parts, the first devoted to the afflicted person, the second to the cause of the affliction. But to speak in terms of a *traditional plan*, as some (notably Favez) have done, is, in my view, greatly to overstate the case.

[123] At Cic. *de orat.* 2.50 Antonius asserts that *consolatio*, like *obiurgatio* and *cohortatio*, has no place in the categories of rhetoric, and that it does not call for theoretical guidelines. Q. Fabius Laurentius Victorinus, *in rhet. Cic.* 1.5, p. 174 Halm, takes issue with those who do classify consolation under rhetorical headings, maintaining that consolation is a matter for a friend, not for an orator.

[124] *Epid.* 2.9, 11, 16 Russell–Wilson; for a full examination see J. Soffel, *Die Regeln Menanders für die Leichenrede* (Beiträge zur klassischen Philologie, 57; Meisenheim am Glan, 1974).

devoted an inordinate amount of time to trying to match extant funeral speeches of the fourth century AD with the Menandrean patterns;[125] though Menander's is the only such manual to survive, it seems unlikely that it was unique, we cannot be certain that the orators knew it directly, and there is no reason to suppose that if they did they would have felt constrained to write to his prescription.[126] We can say, however, that Menander preserves a particular rhetorical tradition, and the funeral speeches we possess conform to it reasonably closely. This has a particular relevance to *Letter* 60 beyond the simple fact that rhetorical precept concerned with oratory is often applicable to other types of discourse as well.

Ten letters of Jerome may broadly be considered consolatory: 23, 39, 60, 66, 75, 77, 79, 108, 118, and 127. In length as in character they vary widely. *Letter* 23 covers about three pages in Hilberg's edition;[127] *Letter* 108, forty-five. In the latter the strictly consolatory element is very slight. Its avowed purpose is to console Eustochium on Paula's death (108. 2. 2), but Jerome's main concern is to celebrate the praises of her distinguished mother; the result is rather a memoir, or an obituary, with considerable biographical content, than anything else. *Letter* 127 performs, in fewer words, the same function for Marcella, and here a consolatory aim is still less apparent. The eulogistic element also features prominently in *Letter* 77, but before Jerome can turn to the *laudes* of Fabiola he has to make excuses for her

[125] Cf. esp. J. Bauer, *Die Trostreden des Gregorius von Nyssa in ihrem Verhältnis zur antiken Rhetorik* (Marburg, 1892), X. Hürth, *De Gregorii Nazianzeni orationibus funebribus* (Strasbourg, 1906), L. Méridier, *L'Influence de la seconde sophistique sur l'œuvre de Grégoire de Nysse* (Paris, 1906), 233–7, 251–74, F. Boulanger, *Grégoire de Nazianze: Discours funèbres en l'honneur de son frère Césaire et de Basile de Césarée* (Paris, 1908), pp. xxvi–xxxii, F. Rozynski, *Die Leichenreden des hl. Ambrosius* (Breslau, 1910), P. B. Albers, 'Über die erste Trauerrede des hl. Ambrosius zum Tode seines Bruders Satyrus', *Beiträge zur Geschichte des christlichen Altertums und der byzantinischen Literatur: Festgabe Albert Ehrhard zum 60. Geburtstag* (Bonn and Leipzig, 1922), 24–52, S. Ruiz, *Investigationes historicae et litterariae in sancti Ambrosii De obitu Valentiniani et De obitu Theodosii imperatorum orationes funebres* (Munich, 1971).
[126] The errors involved in trying to fit the funeral speeches of Ambrose in particular into the Menandrean categories are exposed by Duval (1977), supported (at 295–7) by A. Cameron and P. L. Schmidt.
[127] CSEL 54–6; see n. 141 below.

act of divorcing her first husband and remarrying, and emphasize that she herself was penitent. In *Letter* 39 he expends considerable energy in attacking the excesses of grief which Paula has displayed upon Blesilla's death; this letter offers rebuke no less than consolation. *Letter* 66 is remarkable for being devoted largely to praise not of the deceased but of the bereaved. *Letter* 118 is less concerned to comfort Julian for the loss of his wife and two daughters than to encourage him to adopt a new life of poverty. These few points give some indication of the flexibility of the genre and of Jerome's approach; he employs no stereotype, but writes each time in a manner suggested by the nature of the circumstances and of the persons involved.[128]

It may be that in writing to his great friend Heliodorus on the death of his nephew, Jerome felt that he ought to call upon all his considerable literary powers. For *Letter* 60 is certainly the greatest of his consolations. In length it is second only to *Letter* 108, a piece very different in nature, and substantially longer than most of the consolatory letters of other authors. Those of (for instance) Cicero, Fronto, Basil, and Augustine are on a very much smaller scale, and the contributions of Libanius and Theodoret in particular tend to be no more than notes, sometimes only a few lines long. Only the *Dialogues* of Seneca, if we can regard them as letters, can really compare. Nor can one fail to be struck by the scope of the piece, the movement beyond the normal bounds of consolation to reflections on wider matters (cc. 4, 17–18). Far from being fixed exclusively on deceased and *consolandus*, the focus undergoes changes. The combination of pagan and Christian materials, too, is much more marked than in any other of Jerome's *consolationes*; this characteristic will be considered further below, pp. 31–3.

Perhaps the most remarkable feature of *Letter* 60, however, lies in its exceptional affinity to funeral orations. Nearly all Jerome's consolations have something of the character of

---

[128] It is interesting to look at the letters chronologically, and to consider how the approach shifts from letter to letter; but I question whether we may proceed from there to trace a *development* in the character of Jerome's consolation (or of Christian Latin consolation in general) in any meaningful sense, as Guttilla (1980–1) and (1984–5) seeks to do.

a funeral oration in that they contain eulogy. For while eulogy is an important, often the most important, function of a funeral speech, it is, naturally enough, not a necessary constituent of the consolatory epistle.[129] In shorter letters there is in any case no room for a large laudatory element, and where it occurs it tends to consist of a few comments of a general nature; in longer pieces, too, praise of the deceased may be absent.[130] But of Jerome's consolatory letters only *Letter* 118 has a negligible eulogistic content, and the chief purpose of that letter is sufficient explanation of that. Even in the relatively short *Letter* 23 room is found for praise of the subject (cf. 23. 2. 2), and in certain of the letters, as has been indicated, it is the main ingredient.

By itself the presence of a *laudes* section, substantial and carefully defined as it is, does no more than demonstrate a relation between *Letter* 60 and funeral speeches of a kind apparent in many other letters of consolation. But in c. 1 Jerome has already made it clear that the affinity is closer. First, the letter—designated an *epitaphium*—is described in terms of a floral tribute upon Nepotianus' grave (1. 2). Then follows: 'moris quondam fuit ut super cadavera defunctorum in contione pro rostris laudes liberi dicerent et instar lugubrium carminum ad fletus et gemitus audientium pectora concitarent. en rerum in nobis ordo mutatus est et in calamitatem nostram perdidit sua iura natura: quod exhibere senibus iuvenis debuit, hoc iuveni exhibemus senes' (1. 3). There can be little doubt about the meaning of this. Jerome imagines himself upon the *rostra*, pronouncing an oration over Nepotianus' body, a task in which Heliodorus seems to be associated (cf. the plural *senes*, etc.). What we have is, in effect, a funeral oration in epistolary form,[131] a fact which easily explains the letter's unusual length.

---

[129] It may, of course, be regarded as an aid to consolation, particularly to Christians: to emphasize the virtues of the deceased is to reinforce the point that they are now in heaven. Augustine is explicit about this in his letter to Cornelius, where he writes of his correspondent desiring to be comforted by hearing the praises of his dead wife (*epist.* 259. 1).

[130] See comm. on 7. 3 *audias laudes eius.*

[131] As was observed by Vollmer, 475, and by W. Kierdorf, *Laudatio funebris: Interpretationen und Untersuchungen zur Entwicklung der römischen Leichenrede* (Beiträge zur klassischen Philologie, 106; Meisenheim am Glan, 1980), 65.

Comparison with the patterns laid down by Menander for the various kinds of funeral speech (see above, p. 26) is instructive. Broadly the letter most resembles—as we should expect—the paramythetic type of speech. The element of lamentation is relatively slight (mainly cc. 1 and 13), and to praise Nepotianus is not Jerome's main aim. But in form it does not adhere closely to Menander's pattern. The rhetor prescribes that the first part of the speech should consist of lamentation and encomium, and that consolation should follow. So too in his blueprint for the ἐπιτάφιος λόγος consolatory matter is left until the end. In *Letter* 60 there has already been a considerable amount of consolation by the time Jerome reaches the encomiastic part in c. 8. Jerome knew the rules of the rhetoricians, but was not going to be constrained by them—as he makes explicit, in regard to one particular point, at 8.1. The tradition represented by Menander did not for him possess such authority as to determine the structure of his consolation.

The tenor of the letter is of course thoroughly Christian. After an opening in which Jerome expresses his inadequacy to the task he has undertaken and his own grief at Nepotianus' death (c. 1), he plunges right to the heart of Christian doctrine: death has been destroyed by Christ, at whose resurrection the kingdom of heaven was opened to believing souls (cc. 2–3). Nepotianus is therefore now with God, a point made explicit at 7.1. This thought must be the ultimate consolation to Heliodorus, and strictly Jerome need go no further; but his purpose is not so bald. He wishes to sing the praises of Nepotianus, for one thing; for another, he has to confront a problem deriving from his Christian conviction that the young man now resides in heaven. Since this is so, he should not be mourned, but Jerome cannot help weeping: 'invito et repugnanti per genas lacrimae fluunt' (2.2). This dilemma, posed in c. 2, is then shelved until c. 7, where Jerome finds a solution: he and Heliodorus are grieving not for Nepotianus but for themselves, who lack his company and are conscious that they do not share with him in the joys of heaven. Such grief, when it springs from *pietas*, is quite legitimate; Jesus himself, after all, wept for Lazarus (7.2).

The eulogistic section of the letter (cc. 8–12) also has a

wholly Christian focus. Jerome consciously and pointedly rejects the rhetorical precept that a *laudatio* should begin by consideration of the subject's ancestry (8. 1); he will not consider this or any of Nepotianus' external advantages, for nothing is relevant but the merit of the individual soul. Nepotianus is praised in respect of his specifically Christian virtues, and these are considered principally from the time of his rebirth by baptism. As we should expect, the Christian thread persists to the end of the letter. Jerome urges Heliodorus to overcome his grief by appealing to his position as a bishop in the public eye (14. 5–6): 'ubertim fluentes lacrimas reprime, ne grandis pietas in nepotem apud incredulas mentes desperatio putetur in deum' (14. 6). The havoc wrought upon the Roman world by the barbarian invaders, described at 16. 2–5, is attributed to the anger of God engendered by Roman sin (c. 17). In a world lying in a state of general decay, in which human life grinds on towards inevitable death (c. 18), it is the love of Christ which prevents the lives of Heliodorus and Jerome from being utterly without purpose, and which binds them firmly to each other and to Nepotianus (c. 19).

It was natural that Jerome should include in his letter illustrative material from Scripture, and there are numerous quotations, *exempla*, and other references. The Bible, indeed, could have provided him with all he needed by way of consolatory precept, the proper attitude to grief, and parallels of various kinds. But he had no wish to restrict himself in this way. At 6. 2 he tells Heliodorus that in his letter consoling Paula on the death of Blesilla,[132] written in 384, he has already set out all the Scriptural material bearing on grief; now he wishes to do something different. He was fully aware of the riches offered by the pagan consolatory tradition, and by this time had no qualms about using pagan literature for Christian ends. Thus at 5. 2 he can claim, however untruthfully, to have read Crantor and the consolatory works of Plato, Diogenes of Sinope, Clitomachus, Carneades, and Posidonius. Cicero's *Consolatio* was at hand.[133] Illustrative passages are cited from Virgil, Horace,

---

[132] *Epist.* 39.   [133] See above, pp. 12–13.

and even Ennius and Naevius;[134] other classical authors are
mentioned in passing.[135] The Christian *exempla* are mingled
with others from pagan history and myth. The blending is
not complete or unconscious, for Jerome will at times move
from instances from the classical world to cases which he
claims as 'ours'.[136] But he is content to draw his examples of
fortitude in bereavement from Greek and Roman history
(5. 2–3), and in supplying parallels to Nepotianus' skill in
church adornment he moves easily from Fabius Pictor to the
Old Testament figures Bezalel and Hiram, and back to the
Greek philosopher Hippias of Elis (12. 3–4). The most
important debt to the pagan tradition, however, lies in
Jerome's reinforcement of the fundamental Christian consolation—that Nepotianus is with Christ—with topics of pagan
origin. As noted above, such topics rarely conflict with
Christian belief, but they are strictly superfluous to the
argument. The fact that Jerome incorporates them in his
letter doubtless has literary motivation; but it may also
suggest a sensitive understanding of the psychology of
bereavement. How much comfort words can actually bring
is questionable,[137] but if one is to make the attempt, it makes
sense to use all the weapons at one's disposal. Tragic death
can shake the religious conviction of even the most committed believer; thus in seeking to assuage Heliodorus' grief
Jerome's approach of suggesting other reflections on the
situation and on the advantages gained by Nepotianus by his
early death may have contained more than a grain of wisdom. The reflections that death is inevitable anyway (5. 1,
14. 3), that future ills should be prepared for (5. 1), that
Nepotianus has happily escaped from a world in a state of
collapse (15. 1, 17. 1), all lend strength to one who has lost
his beloved nephew. The exhortation Jerome offers his
friend also makes use of topics from the pagan world:

---

[134] Cf. 4. 1, 14. 4, 16. 1, 16. 3, 16. 5.
[135] Cf. 14. 2 (Plato again), 14. 4 (Hesiod?), 16. 5 (Thucydides and Sallust).
[136] Cf. 5. 3–6. 1, 12. 3.
[137] Our age perhaps understands better the resigned helplessness of the author of
P.Oxy. 115 (2nd century AD), who concludes her brief letter to a couple who have
lost their son with the words: ἀλλ' ὅμως οὐδὲν δύναταί τις πρὸς τὰ τοιαῦτα. παρηγορεῖτε
οὖν ἑαυτούς. εὖ πράττετε. See Kassel, 4, Gregg, 1–2.

remember the precept 'Nothing too much', and impose a limit on your grief (7. 3); do not grieve that you have lost him, rather be glad that you have had him at all (7. 3); do not grieve so much that false conclusions are drawn from that grief (14. 6, where see comm. on *ubertim . . . in deum*).

In *Letter* 60 Jerome does not seek to replace the kind of consolation offered by the pagans with a consolation that is wholly Christian in thought and substance. Nor does he simply attempt to blend the two. Rather, he starts with a thoroughly Christian perspective which he uses to transform an originally pagan genre. Pagan ideas and materials are not rejected out of hand but put to Christian use. The result is a work remarkable for the richness of its content, drawn from two contrasting traditions. Other works of Christian consolation are indebted in one way or another, and sometimes substantially, to pagan writing, but none has the breadth that Jerome's conscious and unabashed use of both classical and Biblical sources gives this letter. Ambrose, for example, though he displays knowledge of pagan texts and makes use of pagan consolatory topics such as that death is an escape from the ills of life, draws his historical *exempla* exclusively from the Bible.[138] Basil and the Gregorys too make use of pagan ideas and τόποι and belong much more to the Menandrean rhetorical tradition than either Jerome or Ambrose,[139] but their work betrays signs of deliberate Christianization: they eschew almost completely classical examples and quotations, substituting for them episodes and passages from Scripture.[140] In comparison, the Jerome of *Letter* 60, after he had come to terms with the acceptability of classical literature for a Christian author, stands out as a much more humanistic figure. His letter of consolation to Heliodorus is testimony to how an emergent culture can absorb and assimilate the history and literature of the culture it is supplanting.

---

[138] Cf. Favez (1930b), 86, 89.

[139] That the consolatory letters of Basil show the influence of the Menandrean tradition is argued by Gregg, 75–8.

[140] Cf. Gregg, 184–96. A notable exception is Greg. Naz. *epist.* 32, on which see Mitchell, 311–13. Basil draws his *exempla* from the OT exclusively (cf. Mitchell, 311), and nowhere in his consolations quotes, or even explicitly alludes to, pagan writings (cf. Gregg, 153, 191).

3. THE TEXT OF *LETTER* 60

The text of *Letter* 60 upon which the commentary is based is that of I. Hilberg in the Vienna corpus.[141] Hilberg's edition of the letters was the first to be established on truly critical principles, and has not been superseded. For *Letter* 60 Hilberg used nine MSS,[142] as follows:

G Naples, Bibl. Naz. VI. D. 59, s. vi.

Γ Lyons, Bibl. de la Ville 600 (517), s. vii–viii.

𝔄 Verona, Bibl. Capitolare XV (13), s. vii–viii.

K Épinal, Bibl. municipale 68 (149), s. viii.

𝔪 Cambridge (Mass.), Harvard University, Houghton Libr., fMS Typ. 6 (Phillipps 36185, *olim* 30499), s. viii.

D Vatican, Vat. lat. 355 + 356, s. ix–x.

Φ Wolfenbüttel, Herzogliche Bibl., Weissenb. 72 (4156), s. ix–x.

Ψ Autun, Bibl. du Séminaire 17A, s. x.

B Berlin, Deutsche Staatsbibl. 18 (Phillipps 1675), s. xii.

Of these, *Γ* is a florilegium containing only portions of the text, generally in paraphrase, while 𝔪 is merely a fragment, commencing at 14. 3 *onustus* and ending at 15. 1 *ago*. Brief descriptions of *G*, *Γ*, *𝔄*, *K*, and 𝔪 may conveniently be found in E. A. Lowe, *Codices Latini antiquiores: A Palaeographical Guide to Latin Manuscripts Prior to the Ninth Century* (11 vols. and supp., Oxford, 1934–71), under reference numbers 6. 781, 3. 405, 4. 486, 6. 762, and 2. 146 respectively.[143]

---

[141] CSEL 54. 548–75. Hilberg's complete edition of the letters, published between 1910 and 1918, takes up three volumes (CSEL 54–6); the first contains *epist.* 1–70, the second, *epist.* 71–120, the third, *epist.* 121–54. For the letters to Praesidius and Aurelius, which are not included by Hilberg, see above, n. 51.

[142] In the commentary (though not below) the phrase 'the MSS' refers to these nine only.

[143] Other references to discussions of *G*, *𝔄*, *K*, 𝔪, and *D* are supplied by Lambert, 1. 225, 303, 172, 158–9, 293 respectively; I draw attention in particular to the important investigation of 𝔪 by Z. Stewart, 'An Eighth-Century Fragment of Jerome', *HLB* 4 (1950), 254–8, and 'Insular Script without Insular Abbreviations: A Problem in Eighth-Century Palaeography', *Speculum*, 25 (1950), 483–90, to which I return below. In addition to the works cited by Lambert those who are interested might also consult (for *Γ*) E. A. Lowe, 'Codices Lugdunenses antiquis-

How Hilberg came to settle on these nine MSS, and how many he consulted before making his choice, is, however, unknown; the promised volume of prolegomena and indices[144] never saw the light of day. What we do know is that the nine represent a very small proportion of those which exist. Lambert's catalogue lists no fewer than 195 for *Letter* 60, of which seventeen are dated ninth-to-tenth century or earlier; and Lambert is fully aware that his list cannot be considered exhaustive.[145]

There is also some reason to question the accuracy of the collations which form the basis of Hilberg's edition. Z. Stewart[146] examined the fragment m and compared his findings with Hilberg's report of this MS in his apparatus criticus. His examination revealed three correcting hands, whereas Hilberg's apparatus gives no indication of more than one, and produced a total of fifteen additions and corrections to be made in the apparatus, most of which concern the text of the original hand before correction. Many of the additions are trivial, and, as Hilberg showed some concern not to make his edition too obese,[147] their absence from the apparatus need not imply that the readings

simi', *Bibliothèque de la ville de Lyon: documents paléographiques, typographiques, iconographiques*, fascicles 3–4 (also issued separately, Lyons, 1924), 47, plates 1 and 35, and (for *K*) H. C. Jameson, 'The Latin Manuscript Tradition of Jerome's *Vita sancti Malchi*', *Studies in the Text Tradition of St. Jerome's Vitae patrum*, ed. W. A. Oldfather (Urbana, Ill., 1943), 507–8. In assigning *G* to the sixth century, rather than the seventh, where Hilberg placed it, I follow Jameson, 491–2, who suggests that it might be even earlier; for the dates of the remainder I follow Lambert, whose dating differs significantly from that of Hilberg only in the case of *Γ*, which Hilberg put in the sixth century.

[144] Cf. CSEL 56, preface.

[145] Cf. 1, pp. vii–viii. The extent of Lambert's omissions may be gauged by the fact that the catalogue fails to mention MSS housed in libraries as important as the British Library and the Bodleian (e.g., for *epist.* 60, British Library MSS Harley 3044, Royal 6 C. XI, 6 D. I, 6 D. II, 6 D. III, and 8 A. XI, and Bodleian MSS Bodl. 702, Laud. Misc. 252 and 423; MS Laud. Misc. 252 belongs to the ninth century, and none of the rest postdates the early thirteenth), and that Lardet's edition of the *Adversus Rufinum* (CCSL 79) lists 198 MSS for that work, against Lambert's 169, no fewer than 80 of which were supplied by Lardet (cf. CCSL 79. 1*–3*) and appear in the addenda in the fourth volume.

[146] *HLB* 4 (1950), 257–8 (cf. n. 143 above).

[147] Cf. CSEL 54, preface: 'integram lectionum farraginem a me enotatam ut nimis prolixam salubribus lituris macrescere iussit Augustus Engelbrecht, cuius prudenti iudicio debetur, quod hoc volumen non in maiorem etiam ambitum crevit'.

had been missed altogether; but the presence in less than two pages of text of two certain errors and at least one important oversight, whether they are due to personal misreadings or to erroneous reports—Hilberg does not make it clear that all the collations are his own—must undermine confidence in the edition as a whole. In so far as we can trust the apparatus, it appears that the MSS are also of distinctly variable quality, though we can at least commend Hilberg for having been a generally judicious editor who made decisions between variants on fairly consistent principles.

It is plain that a great deal of work needs to be done on the MSS before a more authoritative text can be produced, and we may hope that someone will be prepared to undertake a comprehensive study of the manuscript tradition of the letters of the kind that P. Lardet has conducted for the *Adversus Rufinum*.[148] Such a study would naturally involve all the letters, and I have not thought it worth while to reap the very partial rewards to be gained by conducting a separate examination of the tradition of *Letter* 60 alone; I have therefore done no original work on the MSS.[149] I doubt, in any case, whether the text of *Letter* 60 would be significantly improved by such an investigation, though I would hesitate to make the same claim for other letters; we might obtain clues to the solving of one or two cruces, but I would hazard that in general improvements would be fairly trivial. I have, however, the reservations expressed above notwithstanding, given due attention to the variants presented by Hilberg's apparatus, and at a number of places offer a divergent text. The divergences are as follows:

---

[148] In CCSL 79. Lardet's discussion of the manuscript tradition of the *Adversus Rufinum* takes up nearly 200 pages, with a further 80 on incunabula and the most important of the later printed editions. His text is based on fourteen principal witnesses, including Hilberg's *B* (*g* in Lardet); this is the only MS used both by Lardet and by Hilberg for *epist.* 60.

[149] As I have not personally inspected the MSS employed by Hilberg, I have on occasion had to infer the readings of particular MSS where they are not made explicit in his apparatus. For example, at 10. 8, where Hilberg reads *et omne convivium* and in the apparatus prints *erat G* for *et*, it is reasonable to infer that all the MSS bar *G* read *et*, though it is impossible to be sure that where a MS is not mentioned as supporting a given variant it must support the text.

	This edition	Hilberg
1. 1	⟨nos⟩ reliquit senes	reliquit senes
2. 1	mutaret	inmutaret
5. 1	ordinem non tenes?	ordinem non tenes!
10. 8	per omne convivium	et omne convivium
10. 9	lectione adsidua	lectione quoque adsidua
11. 2	in recitando illo †ipso vel placere vel displicere† cotidie videretur	in recitando illo ipso vel placere vel displicere cotidie videretur
14. 4	[et in diversas bestias]	et in diversas bestias ⟨conversas alias ut Hecubam in canem⟩
14. 4	†Hesiodus†	Hesiodus
14. 4	regi	regio
17. 3	cernamus	cernimus
17. 3	cedere.	cedere?

All the above changes are discussed in the commentary; the list does not include differences in orthography or punctuation except in those two cases (5. 1, 17. 3) where the sense is affected.

Following the *editio princeps* of C. Sweynheym and A. Pannartz (Rome, 1468),[150] four important editions of the letters were published prior to Hilberg, all of them forming part of editions of the complete works of Jerome: those of D. Erasmus (Basle, 1516–20), M. Victorius (Rome, 1564–72), I. Martianay (Paris, 1693–1706), and D. Vallarsi (Verona, 1734–42).[151] Vallarsi's second edition (Venice, 1766–72) was reprinted by J.-P. Migne in PL 22–30.[152] While I have not

[150] The Strasbourg edition of J. Mentelin is probably earlier (1467?), but contains only 139 of the letters; the term *editio princeps* is therefore reserved for Sweynheym and Pannartz, the first complete edition.

[151] There are useful comments on all these editions by T. Trzciński, *Die dogmatischen Schriften des h. Hieronymus: eine literärhistorische Untersuchung* (Posen, 1912), 5–18, and by Lardet in CCSL 79. 219*–273* (mainly apropos the *Adversus Rufinum*). A list of fifteenth-century editions and translations of the works of Jerome may be found in *Bullettino di archeologia e storia dalmata*, 39 (1916), 158–63.

[152] On the editions of Vallarsi see G. Leiblinger, 'Domenico Vallarsi's Hieronymus-Ausgaben: eine bibliographische Studie', *Mitteilungen des österreichischen Vereins für Bibliothekwesen*, 11 (1907), 145–9, and 12 (1908), 34–46, 167–71, 247–57, who concludes that the second edition is less accurate than the first.

systematically examined the texts of *Letter* 60 presented by
these editions, I have consulted them for specific readings,
often with interest and not always without profit. In the
commentary the phrase 'the earlier editors' refers to all four
taken together. These are presumably the editions collect-
ively designated by Hilberg by the siglum ς, though he does
not specify them.[153]

A few words may usefully be said about the two most
readily available texts of the letters, the Budé and the Loeb.
J. Labourt's complete text in the Budé series (Paris,
1949–63), and F. A. Wright's selection (which includes *Letter* 60) in the Loeb Classical Library (Cambridge, Mass.,
and London, 1933), are both based on Hilberg, with occasional divergences. Labourt's edition, which was roundly
criticized on numerous grounds by reviewers,[154] is a poor
substitute for Hilberg; even the notes, where a useful contribution could have been made, are scanty and seldom of
much value. The Loeb volume, in turn, is less than perfect,[155] but Wright's translation deserves some favourable
comment. Though there are places where he misunder-
stands the Latin, there are others where he seems to me to hit
the mark exactly, and in such cases I have not, in my
translation, deliberately sought a different form of words for
the sake of it; such a debt ought to be acknowledged, though
for the most part it amounts to no more than a word here and
a phrase there. I have occasionally benefited also from
Labourt's translation.

The text I have printed represents Hilberg's in all respects
except for the significant changes listed above and some
points of orthography and punctuation. Concerning orthography, I have in a very few places deviated from Hilberg in

---

[153] In at least one place the siglum is used for a reading presented by only three of
the editions (see comm. on 16. 5 *alioquin . . . sunt*), but in general it seems to cover
all four.

[154] See esp. the review of the first volume by A. G. Amatucci, 'Per un'edizione
delle epistole di s. Gerolamo', *Arcadia: Accademia Letteraria Italiana: atti e
memorie*, ser. 3, vol. 2.3 (1950), 87–94, of the seventh and eighth by P. Antin,
Latomus, 21 (1962), 405–8, and 23 (1964), 99–101 (= Antin, *Recueil*, 411–17), and
of the eighth by M.-J. Rondeau, 'D'une édition des lettres de saint Jérôme', *REL* 42
(1964), 166–84.

[155] Particularly pernicious are the (not uncommon) misprints of a kind that can
be spotted only by comparing the text carefully with Hilberg's.

order to bring a word into line with the spelling that is now generally accepted; I have also preferred the letter v to u-consonantal. Changes in punctuation have been made with regard to both sense and the general colometry of the text; in particular, I have been concerned to assist the reader to grasp the sense of passages which might otherwise be confusing. I have not used quotation marks to indicate fragments of Scripture or other works where they are woven into the texture of the passage where they occur, but I have so indicated those passages that are meant to be thought of as direct speech, or are not embedded in the text to the same degree. Chapter and section numbers follow Hilberg.

TEXT AND TRANSLATION

HIERONYMI

Ad Heliodorum Epitaphium Nepotiani

1 GRANDES materias ingenia parva non sufferunt, et in ipso conatu ultra vires ausa succumbunt; quantoque maius fuerit quod dicendum est, tanto magis obruitur qui magnitudinem rerum verbis non potest explicare. Nepotianus meus, tuus, noster, immo Christi et, quia Christi, idcirco plus noster, ⟨nos⟩ reliquit senes et desiderii sui iaculo vulneratos intoler-
2 abili dolore confecit. quem heredem putavimus, funus tenemus. cui iam meum sudabit ingenium? cui litterulae placere gestient? ubi est ille ἐργοδιώκτης noster et cycneo canore vox dulcior? stupet animus, manus tremit, caligant oculi, lingua balbutit. quidquid dixero, quia ille non audiet, mutum videtur. stilus ipse quasi sentiens et cera subtristior vel rubigine vel situ obducitur. quotienscumque nitor in verba prorumpere et super tumulum eius epitaphii huius flores spargere, totiens inplentur oculi et renovato dolore totus in funere sum. moris quandam fuit ut super cadavera defun-
3 ctorum in contione pro rostris laudes liberi dicerent, et instar lugubrium carminum ad fletus et gemitus audientium pectora concitarent; en rerum in nobis ordo mutatus est, et in calamitatem nostram perdidit sua iura natura: quod exhibere senibus iuvenis debuit, hoc iuveni exhibemus senes.

2 Quid igitur faciam? iungam tecum lacrimas? sed apostolus prohibet, Christianorum mortuos dormientes vocans; et dominus in evangelio: 'non est', inquit, 'mortua puella, sed dormit.' Lazarus quoque, quia dormierat, suscitatus est. laeter et gaudeam, quod

JEROME

To Heliodorus: A Funeral Tribute for Nepotianus

MODEST talents cannot cope with lofty themes; when they make the attempt and venture beyond their powers they collapse, and the greater the subject to be dealt with, the more it overwhelms those who cannot unfold its greatness in words. Nepotianus, my Nepotianus, yours, ours—no, Christ's, and because Christ's, the more ours—has left us in our old age and plunged us, wounded with the stab of longing for him, into unbearable grief. We regarded him as our heir; instead, we hold his body in our hands. For whom shall my mind exert itself now? Whom shall my writings be eager to please? Where is he, the man who spurred me to my work, whose voice was sweeter than the song of a swan? My brain is numb, my hand trembles, a film covers my eyes, my tongue can only babble. Whatever I shall say seems voiceless, because he will not hear it. My very pen has grown rusty, as if it had feeling; my wax tablet has a sad look, its surface all mildewed. Every time I try to break into speech and scatter the flowers of this funeral tribute over his grave, my eyes fill with tears, my grief returns, and I am wholly absorbed in his death. It was once the custom that when people died their children should utter praises over their bodies in a public assembly, speaking from the platform, and, as though by means of dirges, rouse the hearts of the audience to weeping and wailing. In our case the order of things has been reversed, and to our misfortune nature has lost her privileges: the task which a young man such as he should have performed for his elders, we, his elders, are performing for him.

What then am I to do? Join my tears to yours? No: the apostle forbids it, calling the Christian dead 'those who sleep', and in the gospel the Lord says, 'The girl is not dead but asleep.' Lazarus too, because he had only fallen asleep, was roused to life again. Am I then to be glad and rejoice that

raptus sit ne malitia mutaret mentem eius, quia placuerit deo
2 anima illius? sed invito et repugnanti per genas lacrimae
fluunt, et inter praecepta virtutum resurrectionisque spem
credulam mentem desiderii frangit affectus. o mors, quae
fratres dividis et amore sociatos crudelis ac dura dissocias!
adduxit urentem ventum dominus de deserto ascendentem,
qui siccavit venas tuas et desolavit fontem tuum. devorasti
quidem Ionam, sed et in utero tuo vivus fuit. portasti quasi
mortuum, ut tempestas mundi conquiesceret et Nineve
3 nostra illius praeconio salvaretur. ille, ille te vicit, ille iugulavit fugitivus propheta, qui reliquit domum suam, dimisit
hereditatem suam, dedit dilectam animam suam in manus
quaerentium eam. qui per Osee quondam tibi rigidus mina-
batur, 'ero mors tua, o mors; ero morsus tuus, inferne', illius
morte tu mortua es, illius morte nos vivimus. devorasti et
devorata es, dumque adsumpti corporis sollicitaris inlecebra
et avidis faucibus praedam putas, interiora tua adunco dente
confossa sunt.

3 　　Gratias tibi, Christe salvator, tua agimus creatura, quod
tam potentem adversarium nostrum, dum occideris,
occidisti. quis ante te miserior homine, qui aeterno mortis
terrore prostratus vivendi sensum ad hoc tantum acceperat,
ut periret? regnavit enim mors ab Adam usque ad Moysen
etiam super eos qui non peccaverunt in similitudinem prae-
2 varicationis Adam. si Abraham, Isaac, et Iacob in inferno,
quis in caelorum regno? si amici tui sub poena offendentis
Adam, et qui non peccaverant alienis peccatis tenebantur
obnoxii, quid de his credendum est, qui dixerunt in
cordibus suis, 'non est deus', qui corrupti et abominabiles
facti sunt in voluntatibus suis, qui declinaverunt, simul
inutiles facti sunt; 'non est qui faciat bonum, non est usque
ad unum'? quod si Lazarus videtur in sinu Abraham locoque

he was snatched away to prevent wickedness changing his heart, because his soul was pleasing to God? The fact is, for all my resistance and opposition the tears still run down my cheeks, and though I know the teaching of the virtues and have the hope of the resurrection a feeling of longing is crushing my believing heart. O death, you who divide brother from brother and, harsh and cruel as you are, separate those who are united in love! The Lord brought a burning wind, rising from the desert, which dried up your veins and left your fountain desolate. You swallowed Jonah indeed, but even in your belly he remained alive. You carried him like a dead man, so that the tempest of the world might be quelled, and our Nineveh saved by his preaching. He it was who overcame you, he who slaughtered you, the fugitive prophet, who left his home, let his inheritance go, and delivered his soul, which he loved, into the hands of those who sought it. By the death of him who once, through the voice of Hosea, uttered against you the unyielding threat, 'Death, I shall be your death; hell, I shall be your smart', by his death you are dead, by his death we are alive. You swallowed and were swallowed up, and while you were seduced by the allurements of the flesh which he had assumed, and thought it prey for your greedy jaws, your guts were torn open by the curving hook.

Saviour Christ, we your creation thank you for having slain our mighty enemy in being slain yourself. Before you, was there anything more wretched than man, who, laid prostrate by the eternal fear of death, had received the sense of life for no other purpose than to die? For death held sway from Adam to Moses even over those who committed no sin after the manner of Adam's transgression. If Abraham, Isaac, and Jacob were in hell, who could have been in the kingdom of heaven? If your friends were subject to the penalty for Adam's offence, and those who had not sinned at all were held accountable for the sins of another, what are we to think of those who said in their hearts, 'There is no God', men who became corrupt and detestable in their desires, who left the straight and narrow path and made themselves worthless; 'there is none to do good, not a single one'? Even if Lazarus is seen in Abraham's bosom and a place of

2

3

3

2

3 refrigerii, quid simile infernus et regna caelorum? ante
Christum Abraham apud inferos; post Christum latro in
paradiso. et idcirco in resurrectione eius multa dormientium
corpora surrexerunt et visa sunt in caelesti Hierusalem.
tuncque conpletum est illud eloquium, 'surge, qui dormis, et
elevare, et inluminabit te Christus.' Iohannes Baptista in
heremo personat, 'paenitentiam agite; adpropinquavit enim
4 regnum caelorum.' a diebus enim Iohannis Baptistae regnum caelorum vim passum est et violenti diripuerunt illud.
flammea illa rumphea, custos paradisi, et praesidentia foribus cherubin Christi restincta et reserata sunt sanguine. nec
mirum hoc nobis in resurrectione promitti, cum omnes qui
in carne non secundum carnem vivimus municipatum
habeamus in caelo, et hic adhuc positis dicatur in terra,
'regnum dei intra vos est.'

4   Adde quod ante resurrectionem Christi notus tantum erat
in Iudaea deus, in Israhel magnum nomen eius, et ipsi qui
noverant eum tamen ad inferos trahebantur. ubi tunc totius
orbis homines ab India usque ad Britanniam, a rigida
septentrionis plaga usque ad fervores Atlantici oceani, tam
innumerabiles populi et tantarum gentium multitudines,
quam variae linguis, habitu tam vestis et armis? piscium ritu
ac locustarum et velut muscae et culices conterebantur;
absque notitia enim creatoris sui omnis homo pecus est.
nunc vero passionem Christi et resurrectionem eius cun-
2 ctarum gentium voces et litterae sonant. taceo de Hebraeis,
Graecis, et Latinis, quas nationes fidei suae in crucis titulo
dominus dedicavit. inmortalem animam et post dissolutionem corporis subsistentem, quod Pythagoras somniavit,
Democritus non credidit, in consolationem damnationis
suae Socrates disputavit in carcere, Indus, Persa, Gothus,
Aegyptius philosophantur. Bessorum feritas et pellitorum
turba populorum, qui mortuorum quondam inferiis homines
immolabant, stridorem suum in dulce crucis fregerunt melos,

refreshment, what similarity is there between hell and the kingdom of heaven? Before Christ, Abraham is among those in hell; after Christ, the robber is in paradise. And that is why at Christ's resurrection the bodies of many who were asleep arose and were seen in the heavenly Jerusalem. Then the saying was fulfilled, 'Up, sleeper, rise, and Christ will set you in the light.' John the Baptist cries out in the desert, 'Repent; for the kingdom of heaven is near.' And indeed from the days of John the Baptist the kingdom of heaven suffered assault and violent hands were laid upon it. The flaming sword which guarded paradise was quenched by the blood of Christ, the doors watched over by the cherubim unlocked by it. Nor is it surprising that this is promised to us at our resurrection, since all of us who live in the flesh but not according to the flesh have citizenship in heaven, and while we are still here on earth are told, 'The kingdom of heaven is within you.'

Besides this, before the resurrection of Christ, God was known in Judah and his name was great in Israel, but nowhere else; and even those who knew him were still dragged down to hell. Where in those days were the inhabitants of the whole world from India to Britain, from the frozen regions of the north to the raging Atlantic Ocean, countless peoples, multitudes of every nation, as different from each other in the way they dressed and the arms they bore as in the languages they spoke? Downtrodden like fishes and crustaceans, flies and gnats; for without knowledge of his creator every human being is no more than a beast. But now the voices and writings of all the nations ring out the suffering and resurrection of Christ. I say nothing about the Hebrews, Greeks, and Latins, peoples whom the Lord dedicated to his faith in the superscription on the cross. The immortality of the soul and its continued existence after the dissolution of the body, which Pythagoras dreamed about, Democritus did not believe, and Socrates debated in prison to console himself for his conviction, is become the philosophy of Indian, Persian, Goth, and Egyptian alike. The fierce Bessians, and all those skin-clad tribes who in former times used to perform human sacrifices at the funerals of the dead, have bent their shrill accents to the sweet music of the

et totius mundi una vox Christus est.

5   Quid agimus, anima? quo nos vertimus? quid primum adsumimus? quid tacemus? exciderunt tibi praecepta rhetorum, et occupata luctu, oppressa lacrimis, praepedita singultibus dicendi ordinem non tenes? ubi illud ab infantia studium litterarum et Anaxagorae ac Telamonis semper

2   laudata sententia, 'sciebam me genuisse mortalem'? legimus Crantorem, cuius volumen ad confovendum dolorem suum secutus est Cicero, Platonis, Diogenis, Clitomachi, Carneadis, Posidonii ad sedandos luctus opuscula percucurrimus, qui diversis aetatibus diversorum lamenta vel libris vel epistulis minuere sunt conati, ut etiamsi nostrum areret ingenium de illorum posset fontibus inrigari. proponunt innumerabiles viros et maxime Periclen et Xenophontem Socraticum, quorum alter amissis duobus filiis coronatus in contione disseruit, alter, cum sacrificans filium in bello audisset occisum, deposuisse coronam dicitur et eandem capiti reposuisse postquam fortiter in acie dimicantem rep-

3   perit concidisse. quid memorem Romanos duces quorum virtutibus quasi quibusdam stellis Latinae micant historiae? Pulvillus Capitolium dedicans mortuum, ut nuntiabatur, subito filium se iussit absente sepeliri; Lucius Paulus septem diebus inter duorum exequias filiorum triumphans urbem ingressus est. praetermitto Maximos, Catones, Galos, Pisones, Brutos, Scaevolas, Metellos, Scauros, Marios, Crassos, Marcellos atque Aufidios, quorum non minor in luctu quam in bellis virtus fuit et quorum orbitates in Consolationis libro Tullius explicavit, ne videar aliena potius quam nostra quaesisse; quamquam et haec in suggillationem nostri breviter dicta sint, si non praestet fides quod exhibuit infidelitas.

cross, and the only sound heard throughout the world is 'Christ'.

What shall we do, my soul? Where shall we turn? Where **5**
begin? What omit? Have the teachings of the rhetoricians escaped you, and are you so beset by grief, overwhelmed by tears, impeded by sobs, that you cannot maintain order in your discourse? Where is that enthusiasm for literature that has been yours from childhood, and that saying of Anaxagoras and Telamon that everybody praises, 'I knew that I had begotten a mortal'? I have read Crantor, whose book Cicero **2**
used as a model when he was seeking to comfort his own distress, I have gone through the consolatory works by Plato, Diogenes, Clitomachus, Carneades, and Posidonius, writers who at different periods tried by treatise or letter to lessen the sorrows of various people, so that even if my own mind were barren, I could water it from their fountains. They lay before us the examples of a great many men, most notably Pericles and Xenophon, the follower of Socrates. After Pericles had lost his two sons, he put on a garland and delivered a speech at a public assembly. Xenophon was performing a sacrifice when he heard that his son had been killed in battle. It is said that he then laid his sacrificial garland aside, only to replace it on his head after learning that he had fallen fighting courageously in the fray. Why **3**
should I call to mind those Roman leaders whose virtues flash out of the annals of Roman history like so many stars? Pulvillus was dedicating the Capitol when he received the news that his son had suddenly died; his response was to give orders that the burial should take place without him. Lucius Paulus made his triumphal entry into Rome during the week that separated the funerals of his two sons. I pass over the Maximi, the Catones, the Gali, Pisones, Bruti, Scaevolae, Metelli, Scauri, Marii, Crassi, Marcelli, Aufidii, who displayed no less courage in time of grief than in time of war, and whose bereavements Cicero has handled in his *Consolation*. I do not want it to seem that I have sought my examples from outside rather than from within our own community. And yet these cases too must be briefly mentioned, to make us feel ashamed if faith should fail to provide what unbelief afforded them.

6   Igitur ad nostra veniamus. non plangam cum Iacob et David filios in lege morientes, sed cum Christo in evangelio suscipiam resurgentes. Iudaeorum luctus Christianorum gaudium est. ad vesperum demorabitur fletus et ad matutinum laetitia. nox praecessit, dies autem adpropinquavit.

2   unde et Moyses moriens plangitur, Iesus absque funere et lacrimis in monte sepelitur. quidquid de scripturis super lamentatione dici potest, in eo libro quo Paulam Romae consolati sumus breviter explicavimus. nunc nobis per aliam semitam ad eundem locum perveniendum est, ne videamur praeterita et obsoleta quondam calcare vestigia.

7   Scimus quidem Nepotianum nostrum esse cum Christo, et sanctorum mixtum choris, quod hic nobiscum eminus rimabatur in terris et aestimatione quaerebat, ibi videntem comminus dicere, 'sicut audivimus, ita et vidimus in civitate domini virtutum, in civitate dei nostri.' sed desiderium absentiae eius ferre non possumus, non illius sed nostram vicem

2   dolentes. quanto ille felicior, tanto nos amplius in dolore, quod tali caremus bono. flebant et sorores Lazarum, quem resurrecturum noverant; et, ut veros hominis exprimeret affectus, ipse salvator ploravit quem suscitaturus erat. apostolus quoque eius, qui dixerat, 'cupio dissolvi et esse cum Christo', et alibi, 'mihi vivere Christus est et mori lucrum', gratias agit quod Epafras de mortis sibi vicinia redditus sit, ne haberet tristitiam super tristitiam, non incredulitatis metu sed

3   desiderio caritatis. quanto magis tu, et avunculus et episcopus, hoc est et in carne et in spiritu pater, aves viscera tua et quasi a te divulsa suspiras. sed obsecro ut modum adhibeas in dolore, memor illius sententiae, 'ne quid nimis', obligatoque parumper vulnere audias laudes eius cuius semper virtute laetatus es; nec doleas quod talem amiseris, sed gaudeas quod

Let us come, then, to what is ours. I shall not join Jacob   **6**
and David in mourning sons who died under the Law, but
receive with Christ those who rise again under the Gospel.
What is sorrow for Jews is joy for Christians. Weeping shall
linger until evening; in the morning there will be gladness.
The night has passed, day is at hand. For this reason even   2
Moses is lamented when he dies, while Joshua is buried on a
mountain without funeral and tears. All the Scriptural
material there is on lamentation I have briefly set out in the
letter in which I consoled Paula while we were at Rome.
Now I must strike through to the same goal by a different
path, so as not to seem to be treading a beat that is long worn
out and done with.

We know full well that our Nepotianus is with Christ, and   **7**
mingles with the saintly bands; and that he can see there at
close hand what, with us here on earth, he could only
scrabble around for and seek by blind approximation, so that
he can say, 'As I have heard, so too have I seen in the city of
the Lord of virtues, in the city of our God.' But we cannot
bear our longing at his absence, and it is not his situation that
we mourn, but ours. The happier he is, the deeper the grief   2
we feel, because we do not share in his prosperity. Lazarus'
sisters, too, wept for their brother, though they knew he was
going to rise again, and, to demonstrate that he had true
human feelings, our saviour himself grieved over the man he
was about to restore to life. Again, his apostle, who had said,
'I wish to die and to be with Christ', and in another place,
'For me, to live is Christ, and to die is gain', gives thanks that
Epaphroditus has been restored to him from the very edge of
death, so that he might not have sadness upon sadness; and
this he does not in the fear engendered by unbelief but in the
longing caused by love. How much more must you, Nepotia-   3
nus' uncle and his bishop too, that is to say his father both in
the flesh and in the spirit, yearn for this vital part of yourself
and sigh over it, torn, as it were, from your insides. But I
urge you to put a limit to your grief, and to remember the
famous maxim, 'Nothing too much'. Bind up your wound
for a while and listen to the praises of the man whose
virtue always caused you such delight. Do not grieve that
you have lost such a one as him, but be glad that you have

talem habueris, et sicut hi qui in brevi tabella terrarum situs
pingunt, ita in parvo isto volumine cernas adumbrata, non
expressa, signa virtutum suscipiasque a nobis non vires sed
voluntatem.

8   Praecepta sunt rhetorum ut maiores eius qui laudandus est
et eorum altius gesta repetantur, sicque ad ipsum per gradus
sermo perveniat, quo videlicet avitis paternisque virtutibus
inlustrior fiat et aut non degenerasse a bonis aut mediocres
ipse ornasse videatur. ego carnis bona, quae semper et ipse
contempsit, in animae laudibus non requiram, nec me ia-
ctabo de genere, id est de alienis bonis, cum et Abraham et
Isaac, sancti viri, Ismahelem et Esau peccatores genuerint, et
e regione Iephte in catalogo iustorum apostoli voce numera-
2   tus de meretrice sit natus. 'anima', inquit, 'quae peccaverit,
ipsa morietur'; ergo et quae non peccaverit ipsa vivet. nec
virtutes nec vitia parentum liberis inputantur; ab eo tempore
censemur, ex quo in Christo renascimur. Paulus, persecutor
ecclesiae et mane lupus rapax Beniamin, ad vesperam dedit
escam, Ananiae ovi submittens caput. igitur et Nepotianus
noster quasi infantulus vagiens et rudis puer subito nobis de
Iordane nascatur.

9   Alius forsitan scriberet quod ob salutem illius orientem
heremumque dimiseris et me, carissimum sodalem tuum,
redeundi spe lactaveris, ut primum, si fieri posset, sororem
cum parvulo viduam, dein, si consilium illa respueret, saltim
nepotem dulcissimum conservares. hic est enim ille de quo
tibi quondam vaticinatus sum, 'licet parvulus ex collo pendeat
2   nepos'. referret, inquam, alius, quod in palatii militia sub
chlamyde et candenti lino corpus eius cilicio tritum sit, quod

had him at all. Like those who paint maps on small tablets, in this little book you will see indications of his virtues drawn in outline, not depicted in detail. Accept from me my willingness to undertake this task, even if my powers are inadequate to it.

The rhetorical precept is that one should begin by going **8** some way back to the ancestors of the subject of the eulogy and their accomplishments, and in this way come to the subject himself by stages. The purpose of this is to make him more distinguished by reason of his inherited virtues, and to show either that he has not fallen short of his ancestors' high standards or, if his family is a mediocre one, that he himself has added some distinction to it. For my part, in praising Nepotianus' soul I shall not concern myself with physical advantages, which he himself always despised, nor shall I boast about his family, that is, about other people's qualities, since Abraham and Isaac, who were holy men, were the fathers of the sinners Ishmael and Esau, and conversely Jephthah, who is included by the apostle in the list of the righteous, was the son of a whore. Scripture says, 'The soul **2** which sins shall itself die'; it must therefore also be the case that the soul which does not sin shall live. Neither the virtues nor the vices of parents are ascribed to their children; our reckoning begins from the time when we are reborn in Christ. Paul, the persecutor of the Church, who in the morning was a plundering wolf, a Benjamin, in the evening gave food to eat, and bowed his head before the sheep Ananias. And so let our Nepotianus too, like a crying baby or a young boy, be born to us directly out of the Jordan.

Somebody else might perhaps describe how for his safety **9** you abandoned the East and the desert, and beguiled me, your dearest friend, with the hope of your return. Your intention was, if it proved possible, to maintain your widowed sister with her little child, or, if she rejected the idea, at least to look after your sweet little nephew. Yes, Nepotianus is the person of whom I once said prophetically to you, 'though your little nephew hang about your neck'. Someone else, I say, might record that while he was serving **2** in the palace, beneath his tunic and shirt of gleaming linen his body was chafed by the rough fabric of goats' hair, that

stans ante saeculi potestates lurida ieiuniis ora portaverit, quod adhuc sub alterius indumentis alteri militarit et ad hoc habuerit cingulum, ut viduis, pupillis, oppressis, miseris subveniret. mihi non placent dilationes istae inperfectae servitutis dei, et centurionem Cornelium, ut lego iustum, statim audio baptizatum.

10   Verumtamen velut incunabula quaedam nascentis fidei conprobemus, ut, qui sub alienis signis devotus miles fuit, donandus laurea sit postquam suo regi coeperit militare. balteo posito habituque mutato quidquid castrensis peculii fuit in pauperes erogavit. legerat enim, 'qui vult perfectus esse, vendat omnia quae habet et det pauperibus et sequatur me', et iterum, 'non potestis duobus dominis servire, deo et

2   mamonae'. excepta vili tunica et operimento pari, quod tecto tantum corpore frigus excluderet, nihil sibi amplius reservavit. cultus ipse provinciae morem sequens nec munditiis nec sordibus notabilis erat. cumque arderet cotidie aut ad Aegypti monasteria pergere aut Mesopotamiae invisere choros vel certe insularum Dalmatiae, quae Altino tantum freto distant, solitudines occupare, avunculum pontificem deserere non audebat, tota in illo cernens exempla virtutum

3   domique habens unde disceret. in uno atque eodem et imitabatur monachum et episcopum venerabatur. non, ut in plerisque accidere solet, adsiduitas familiaritatem, familiaritas contemptum illius fecerat, sed ita eum colebat quasi parentem, ita admirabatur quasi cotidie novum cerneret.

    Quid multa? fit clericus et per solitos gradus presbyter ordinatur. Iesu bone, qui gemitus, qui heiulatus, quae cibi interdictio, quae fuga oculorum omnium! tum primum et

4   solum avunculo iratus est. querebatur se ferre non posse, et

while he stood before the powers of this world, his face was
pale with fasting, that while he was still in the uniform of one
master, he was actually in the service of another, and wore
his belt of office for the purpose of assisting widows and
orphans, the oppressed and the unfortunate. But I do not
care for these deferrals of God's service, which are the mark
of an incomplete commitment, and no sooner do I read that
the centurion Cornelius was a just man than I hear of him as
being baptized.

Nevertheless, let us approve of all this as the cradle of an   **10**
embryonic faith, seeing that the man who has been a devoted
soldier under foreign standards will deserve to be presented
with the laurel when he has begun to serve his own king.
Putting aside his belt and changing his attire, Nepotianus
gave away all his service money to the poor. For he had read,
'The man who wishes to be perfect must sell all he has and
give to the poor and follow me', and again, 'You cannot serve
two masters, God and mammon'. Apart from a cheap tunic   **2**
and cloak, designed simply to clothe his body and shut out
the cold, he kept back nothing for himself. He dressed in the
ordinary fashion of the province and did not make himself
conspicuous by being either particularly smart or particularly shabby. Every day he burned to go to the monasteries
of Egypt, or visit the communities of monks in Mesopotamia, or at least settle in the desolate islands of Dalmatia,
which are separated from Altinum by nothing more than a
strait; but he did not dare to abandon his uncle, the Bishop,
for in him he could see patterns of virtue that were complete
in themselves, and had someone at home that he could learn
from. In one and the same man there was a monk for him to   **3**
imitate and a bishop to revere. It did not happen, as it so
often does with many people, that constant association with
his uncle bred familiarity, and familiarity contempt; on the
contrary, he respected him like a father, and admired him as
if each day he saw him afresh.

To be brief, he took holy orders, and, passing through the
customary stages, was ordained priest. Dear Jesus, all that
wailing and groaning! How he refused to eat, how he avoided
seeing anyone! Then, for the first and only time, he was
angry with his uncle. He complained that he could not bear   **4**

iuvenalem aetatem incongruam sacerdotio causabatur. sed
quanto plus repugnabat, tanto magis omnium in se studia
concitabat, et merebatur negando, quod esse nolebat, eoque
dignior erat, quod se clamabat indignum. vidimus Timo-
theum nostri temporis et canos in Sapientia electumque a
Moysi presbyterum quem ipse sciret esse presbyterum.
5   igitur clericatum non honorem intellegens sed onus primam
curam habuit ut humilitate superaret invidiam, deinde ut
nullam obsceni in se rumoris fabulam daret, ut qui mordebantur ad aetatem eius stuperent ad continentiam. subvenire
pauperibus, visitare languentes, provocare hospitio, lenire
blanditiis, gaudere cum gaudentibus, flere cum flentibus;
caecorum baculus, esurientium cibus, spes miserorum, solamen lugentium fuit. ita in singulis virtutibus eminebat quasi
6   ceteras non haberet. inter presbyteros et coaequales primus
in opere, extremus in ordine. quidquid boni fecerat ad
avunculum referebat; si quid forte aliter evenerat quam
putarat, illum nescire, se errasse dicebat. in publico episcopum, domi patrem noverat. gravitatem morum hilaritate
frontis temperabat. gaudium risu, non cachinno, intelle-
7   geres. viduas et virgines Christi honorare ut matres, hortari
ut sorores, cum omni castitate. iam vero, postquam domum
se contulerat et relicto foris clerico duritiae se tradiderat
monachorum, creber in orationibus, vigilans in precando,
lacrimas deo, non hominibus, offerebat. ieiunia in aurigae
modum pro lassitudine et viribus corporis moderabatur.
mensae avunculi intererat et sic adposita quaeque libabat ut
8   et superstitionem fugeret et continentiam reservaret. sermo
eius per omne convivium de scripturis aliquid proponere,
libenter audire, respondere verecunde, recta suscipere,

the load, and alleged that his youth made him unsuitable for
the priesthood. But the more he resisted, the more he
stimulated everyone's enthusiasm for him; his refusal merely
earned him the position he did not want, and his cry that he
was unworthy proved him all the worthier. We have seen a
Timothy in our own time, and the grey hairs mentioned in
the book of Wisdom, and a priest chosen by Moses whom
Moses himself knew to be a priest. And so regarding the   5
ministry not as an honour but as a burden, his first consideration was to overcome envy by humility, his second, to
give no ground for rumours of indecent behaviour against
himself, so that those who were aggrieved at his youth might
be astonished at his chastity. He helped the poor, visited the
sick, challenged others by his hospitality, soothed people
with gentle words, rejoiced with those who rejoiced and wept
with those who wept; he was a staff to the blind, food to the
hungry, the hope of the wretched, a comfort to those who
mourned. Every virtue stood out in him as if it were the only
one he had. Among the priests and those of his own age he   6
was foremost in action, last in line. All the good he did he
ascribed to his uncle; if it happened that anything turned out
contrary to his expectation, he maintained that his uncle
knew nothing about it and that the mistake was entirely his.
In public he acknowledged him as his bishop, at home as his
father. He was of a serious disposition, but lightened the
tone by a cheerful expression. You would know that something had delighted him not from a coarse guffaw but from a
chuckle. Widows and virgins of Christ he honoured as   7
mothers, encouraged as sisters, in a perfectly chaste way. But
when he returned home, he left his clerical role outside and
submitted to the harsh life of a monk; frequent in supplica-
tion, vigilant in prayer, he offered tears not to men but to
God. Like a charioteer carefully controlling his horses, he
adjusted his fasting according to his state of tiredness and his
physical strength. He sat at his uncle's table and tasted just
enough of everything that was put before him to avoid
superstition and at the same time maintain restraint. His talk   8
throughout the entire meal was to bring forward something
from Scripture, listen willingly to what was said about it,
give modest answers to any questions he was asked, support

prava non acriter confutare, disputantem contra se magis
docere quam vincere, et ingenuo pudore qui ornabat aetatem, quid cuius esset simpliciter confiteri; atque in hunc
modum eruditionis gloriam declinando eruditissimus habe-
9   batur. 'illud', aiebat, 'Tertulliani, istud Cypriani, hoc La-
ctantii, illud Hilarii est. sic Minucius Felix, ita Victorinus, in
hunc modum est locutus Arnobius.' me quoque, quia pro
sodalitate ✶ avunculi diligebat, interdum proferebat in
medium. lectione adsidua et meditatione diuturna pectus
suum bibliothecam fecerat Christi.
11   Quotiens ille transmarinis epistulis deprecatus est ut aliquid ad se scriberem! quotiens nocturnum de evangelio
petitorem et interpellatricem duri iudicis mihi viduam exhibuit! cumque ego silentio magis quam litteris denegarem, et
pudore reticentis pudorem suffunderem postulantis, avunculum mihi opposuit precatorem, qui et liberius pro alio
2   peteret et pro reverentia sacerdotii facilius inpetraret. feci
ergo quod voluit, et brevi libello amicitias nostras aeternae
memoriae consecravi; quo suscepto Croesi opes et Darii
divitias se vicisse iactabat. illum oculis, illum sinu, illum
manibus, illum ore retinebat; cumque in strato frequenter
evolveret, super pectus soporati dulcis pagina decidebat. si
vero peregrinorum, si amicorum quispiam venerat, laetabatur super se nostro testimonio, et quidquid minus in opusculo erat distinctione moderata et pronuntiationis varietate
pensabat, ut in recitando illo †ipso vel placere vel displicere†
3   cotidie videretur. unde hic fervor, nisi ex amore dei? unde
legis Christi indefessa meditatio, nisi ex desiderio eius qui
legem dedit? alii nummum addant nummo et, marsuppium
suffocantes, matronarum opes venentur obsequiis; sint
ditiores monachi quam fuerant saeculares, possideant opes

what was right, refute what was wrong without being sharp, teach rather than crush his opponent, and with that disarming modesty that was the jewel of his youth, simply state the source of each interpretation; and in this way by disclaiming a reputation for learning he became regarded as the most learned of all. 'This', he would say, 'is Tertullian's opinion, that Cyprian's; this comes from Lactantius, that from Hilary. This is what Minucius Felix said, Victorinus put it this way, Arnobius' teaching was along these lines.' I too was sometimes brought into the discussion, because he loved me for my friendship with his uncle. By continual reading and long meditation he had made his mind a library of Christ.

9

Time and again, in his letters from across the sea, he begged me to write something for him, repeatedly playing the part of the man in the gospel who came at night with a request, or the widow who kept interrupting the stern judge. And when I declined to comply, not in so many words but by saying nothing, and overspread the modesty of the request with the modesty of the refusal, he got his uncle to intercede with me, since he could make the request more freely on behalf of a third party, and more easily obtain it because of my respect for the episcopate. So I did what he wanted, and dedicated our friendships to everlasting memory in a little book; and when he had received it, he boasted that he had outdone the riches of Croesus and the wealth of Darius. He kept it before his eyes, in his pocket, in his hands, on his lips; and when he unrolled it when he was in bed, as he often did, he would fall asleep with the cherished page across his chest. If a stranger or friend came by, he used to take delight in the evidence of my regard for him; and whatever shortcomings there were in my work he compensated for by well-regulated articulation and variety in tone, so that in reading out those very parts he seemed each day to please or displease [?]. Where did this fervour come from, if not from the love of God? What was the source of his unwearied meditation on the law of Christ, if not the longing for him who gave the law? Let others accumulate money and—while keeping a tight grip on their purses—hunt with their flattery the wealth of married women; let them be richer as monks than they were as men of the world, let them possess wealth while they

11

2

3

sub Christo paupere quas sub locuplete diabolo non habuer-
ant, et suspiret eos ecclesia divites quos tenuit mundus ante
mendicos; Nepotianus noster aurum calcans scedulas consectatur, sed, sicut sui in carne contemptor est et paupertate
incedit ornatior, ita totum ecclesiae investigat ornatum.

12   Ad conparationem quidem superiorum modica sunt quae
dicturi sumus, sed et in parvis idem animus ostenditur. ut
enim creatorem non in caelo tantum miramur et terra, sole et
oceano, elefantis, camelis, equis, bubus, pardis, ursis, leoni-
bus, sed et in minutis quoque animalibus, formica, culice,
muscis, vermiculis et istius modi genere, quorum magis
corpora scimus quam nomina, eandemque in cunctis venera-
mur sollertiam, ita mens Christo dedita aeque et in maioribus
et in minoribus intenta est, sciens etiam pro otioso verbo
2   reddendam esse rationem. erat ergo sollicitus si niteret altare,
si parietes absque fuligine, si pavimenta tersa, si ianitor
creber in porta, vela semper in ostiis, si sacrarium mundum,
si vasa lucentia; et in omnes caerimonias pia sollicitudo disposita non minus, non maius neglegebat officium. ubicumque
3   eum in ecclesia quaereres, invenires. nobilem virum Quintum
Fabium miratur antiquitas, qui etiam Romanae scriptor historiae est, sed magis ex pictura quam litteris nomen invenit;
et Beselehel nostrum plenum sapientia et spiritu dei scriptura
testatur, Hiram quoque, filium mulieris Tyriae, quod alter
tabernaculi, alter templi supellectilem fabricati sunt. quomodo enim laetae segetes et uberes agri interdum culmis
aristisque luxuriant, ita praeclara ingenia et mens plena
4   virtutibus in variarum artium redundat elegantiam. unde
et apud Graecos philosophus ille laudatur, qui omne quod
uteretur usque ad pallium et anulum manu sua factum
gloriatus est. hoc idem possumus et de isto dicere, qui
basilicas ecclesiae et martyrum conciliabula diversis floribus et arborum comis vitiumque pampinis adumbraret,

serve a poor Christ which they did not have while an opulent
devil was their master, and let the Church sigh over the
riches of men who were destitute when the world was their
home; our Nepotianus stamps on gold and goes after bits of
paper, but, just as he despises himself in the flesh and
proceeds all the more adorned by reason of his poverty, so he
seeks out every adornment for the Church.

Compared with the above, the details I am about to give 12
are of only moderate importance, but even in little things the
same spirit is displayed. We admire the creator not only in
heaven and earth, sun and ocean, elephants, camels, horses,
oxen, leopards, bears, and lions, but also in tiny animals, the
ant, the gnat, flies, worms, and species of this sort, which we
can better identify than give names to, and in all cases we
revere the same skill. In the same way, a mind dedicated to
Christ is attentive in great things and small alike, since it
knows that account must be rendered even for an idle word.
Nepotianus, therefore, was anxious that the altar should be 2
shining, the walls free from soot, the floors swept, the
doorkeeper continually at the entrance, the hangings always
in place over the doors, the sanctuary tidy and the vessels
gleaming; and his respectful concern, devoted to all religious
rites, neglected no duty, great or small. Whenever you
looked for him in church, you would find him. In ancient 3
times people admired the noble Quintus Fabius, who was
also a historian of Rome, but derived his name from his
painting rather than his writing; and Scripture bears witness
to our Bezalel, a man full of wisdom and the spirit of God,
and Hiram too, the son of a woman from Tyre, because the
one manufactured the furnishings for the tabernacle, the
other for the temple. For just as bountiful crop-land and
fertile fields are from time to time a mass of stalks and ears of
corn, so brilliant talents and minds packed with virtues
stream over into a range of elegant arts. That is also why 4
among the Greeks praise is bestowed on that philosopher
who boasted that everything he wore, down to his cloak and
his ring, had been made by his own hands. We can say the
same about Nepotianus as well, seeing that he shaded the
basilicas of the church and the assembly-halls of the martyrs
with a variety of flowers, and the foliage of trees, and vine-

ut quidquid placebat in ecclesia tam dispositione quam visu
laborem presbyteri et studium testaretur.

13   Macte virtute! cuius talia principia, qualis finis erit? o
miserabilis humana condicio, et sine Christo vanum omne
quod vivimus! quid te subtrahis, quid tergiversaris, oratio?
quasi enim mortem illius differre possimus et vitam facere
longiorem, sic timemus ad ultimum pervenire. omnis caro

2 faenum et omnis gloria eius quasi flos faeni. ubi nunc decora
illa facies, ubi totius corporis dignitas, quo veluti pulchro
indumento pulchritudo animae vestiebatur? marcescebat,
pro dolor, flante austro lilium, et purpura violae in pallorem
sensim migrabat. cumque aestuaret febribus et venarum
fontes hauriret calor, lasso anhelitu tristem avunculum consolabatur. laetus erat vultus et universis circa plorantibus
solus ipse ridebat. proicere pallium, manus extendere, videre
quod alii non videbant, et quasi in occursum se erigens
salutare venientes: intellegeres illum non emori sed migrare,

3 et mutare amicos, non relinquere. volvuntur per ora lacrimae
et obfirmato animo non queo dolorem dissimulare quem
patior. quis crederet in tali illum tempore nostrae necessitu-
dinis recordari et luctante anima studiorum scire dulcedi-
nem? adprehensa avunculi manu, 'hanc', inquit, 'tunicam,
qua utebar in ministerio Christi, mitte dilectissimo mihi,
aetate patri, fratri collegio, et, quidquid a te nepoti debebatur affectus, in illum transfer quem mecum pariter diligebas.' atque in talia verba defecit, avunculum manu, me
recordatione contrectans.

14   Scio quod nolueris amorem in te civium sic probare, et
affectum patriae magis quaesisse in prosperis. sed huiusce
modi officium in bonis iucundius est, in malis gratius. tota
hunc civitas, tota planxit Italia. corpus terra suscepit, anima
Christo reddita est.

leaves, so that everything in the church that gave pleasure by
its arrangement or innate appearance testified to the hard
work and enthusiasm of the priest.

Bless you for your virtue! When the beginnings are like   **13**
this, how will the end be? How wretched is the human
condition, how meaningless our whole life without Christ!
Why do you draw back and hesitate, my words? We are
afraid to come to the end, as if we could put off his death and
make his life longer. All flesh is grass, and all its glory like the
flower of the grass. Where now is that handsome face, the   **2**
impressive bearing of his whole body, in which the beauty of
his soul was clad as if in a beautiful garment? O grief! As the
south wind blew, the lily withered, and the purple of the
violet faded, little by little, into paleness. And though he was
raging with fever, the heat draining the founts of his veins,
yet amid his weary, gasping breaths he sought to console his
grieving uncle. His face was full of joy and, while everyone
around him wept, he alone wore a smile. He threw off his
cloak and held out his hands: he could see what the rest could
not, and, raising himself up as though to meet them, greeted
those who were coming to him. You would have thought he
was not dying but moving on, exchanging friends, not
leaving them behind. Tears roll down my face, and though   **3**
my mind is resolute I cannot disguise the pain I feel. Who
would believe that at such a time he would remember our
friendship and, as his soul battled for life, call to mind the
pleasures of study? Taking his uncle's hand, he said, 'This
tunic which I wore in the service of Christ: send it to my
dearest friend, my father in years, my brother in the priesthood, and whatever debt of affection you owe to your
nephew, transfer to him whom you love as much as I do.'
And with those words he died, holding his uncle by the
hand, and me in his thoughts.

I know that you did not want to prove the love of the   **14**
citizens for you in this way, but rather to have gained
expression of your country's affection under prosperous
circumstances. But courtesies like this, though more
pleasant when times are good, are more welcome when they
are bad. The whole city, the whole of Italy mourned him.
The earth received his body, his soul was returned to Christ.

tu nepotem quaerebas, ecclesia sacerdotem. praecessit te successor tuus. quod tu eras, ille post te iudicio omnium merebatur. atque ita ex una domo duplex pontificatus egressa est dignitas: dum in altero gratulatio est quod tenuerit, in altero maeror quod raptus sit ne teneret.

2　Platonis sententia est omnem sapienti vitam meditationem esse mortis. laudant hoc philosophi et in caelum ferunt, sed multo fortius apostolus: 'cotidie', inquit, 'morior per vestram gloriam.' aliud est conari, aliud agere; aliud vivere moriturum, aliud mori victurum. ille moriturus ex gloria est;

3　iste moritur semper ad gloriam. debemus igitur et nos animo praemeditari quod aliquando futuri sumus et quod, velimus nolimus, abesse longius non potest. nam si nongentos vitae excederemus annos, ut ante diluvium vivebat humanum genus, et Mathusalae nobis tempora donarentur, tamen nihil esset praeterita longitudo quae esse desisset. etenim inter eum qui decem vixit annos et illum qui mille, postquam idem vitae finis advenerit et inrecusabilis mortis necessitas, transactum omne tantundem est, nisi quod magis senex onustus peccatorum fasce proficiscitur.

4　　　optima quaeque dies miseris mortalibus aevi
　　　prima fugit; subeunt morbi tristisque senectus
　　　et labor, et durae rapit inclementia mortis.

Naevius poeta: 'pati', inquit, 'necesse est multa mortalem mala.' unde et Niobam, quia multum fleverit, in lapidem [et in diversas bestias] commutatam finxit antiquitas, et †Hesiodus† natales hominum plangens gaudet in funere. prudenterque Ennius:

　　　'plebes', ait, 'in hoc regi antestat: loco licet
　　　lacrimare plebi, regi honeste non licet.'

5　ut regi, sic episcopo, immo minus regi quam episcopo. ille enim nolentibus praeest, hic volentibus; ille terrore subicit, hic servitute dominatur; ille corpora custodit ad mortem, hic animas servat ad vitam. in te omnium oculi diriguntur, domus tua et conversatio

You felt the loss of a nephew, the Church of a priest. Your successor went before you: everybody judged him to be worthy of your position after your day. And thus a single house has had the distinction of two episcopates: one member of the family was congratulated on having attained it, the other lamented, for he was snatched away before he could attain it.

There is a saying of Plato's that for a wise man the whole of life is a preparation for death. Philosophers are most effusive in their praise of this maxim, but what the apostle says has much more force: 'Every day I die, by my glorying in you.' It is one thing to try, quite another to do; one thing to live, about to die, another to die, about to live. The philosopher's death will take him from glory; the Christian always dies to glory. And so we too should reflect beforehand on what we are some day going to be, and what— whether we like it or not—cannot be very far away. Should we live more than nine hundred years, as people used to do before the Flood, and be granted a life as long as Methuselah's, yet that length of time, once past, would be nothing, since it had ceased to be. Indeed, between the ten-year-old child and the man who has lived a thousand years, when the end of life and the inevitable constraint of death have come to both alike, there is no difference—it is all the same— except that the old man goes off more heavily laden with sins. 'The best days of life are the first to fly from poor mortals; diseases creep up on us, and gloomy age and travail, and harsh, unyielding death takes hold.' The poet Naevius says, 'A mortal must of necessity suffer many ills.' It is for this reason that the ancients made up the story that Niobe was turned into stone as the price of her heavy weeping, and Hesiod [?] bewails the births of men and rejoices at their deaths. Ennius, too, shows wisdom when he says, 'In this respect ordinary people are better off than a king: at the appropriate moment the people may weep, but a king may not honourably do so.' As with a king, so with a bishop; in fact it is more true for a bishop than for a king. A king commands unwilling subjects, a bishop willing ones; a king subdues by terror, a bishop governs by service; the one guards bodies for death, the other saves souls for life. All have their eyes fixed on you; your house and conduct,

quasi in specula constituta magistra est publicae disciplinae.
6 quidquid feceris, id sibi omnes faciendum putant. cave ne
committas quod aut qui reprehendere volunt digne lacerasse
videantur, aut qui imitari cogantur delinquere. vince quantum potes, immo etiam plus quam potes, mollitiem animi
tui, et ubertim fluentes lacrimas reprime, ne grandis pietas in
nepotem apud incredulas mentes desperatio putetur in
deum. desiderandus tibi est quasi absens, non quasi mortuus, ut illum expectare, non amisisse videaris.

15   Verum quid ago medens dolori quem iam reor et tempore
et ratione sedatum, ac non potius replico tibi vicinas regum
miserias et nostri temporis calamitates, ut non tam plangen-
dus sit qui hac luce caruerit, quam congratulandum ei quod
2 de tantis malis evaserit? Constantius, Arrianae fautor hereseos, dum contra inimicum paratur et concitus fertur ad
pugnam, in Mopsi viculo moriens magno dolore hosti reliquit
imperium. Iulianus, perditor animae suae et Christiani iugulator exercitus, Christum sensit in Media quem primum in
Gallia denegarat, dumque Romanos propagare vult fines,
3 perdidit propagatos. Iovianus gustatis tantum regalibus bonis
fetore prunarum suffocatus interiit, ostendens omnibus quid
sit humana potentia. Valentinianus vastato genitali solo et
inultam patriam derelinquens vomitu sanguinis extinctus est.
huius germanus Valens Gothico bello victus in Thracia eundem locum et mortis habuit et sepulchri. Gratianus ab exer-
citu suo proditus et ab obviis urbibus non receptus ludibrio
hosti fuit, cruentaeque manus vestigia parietes tui, Lu-
4 gdune, testantur. adulescens Valentinianus et paenae puer post
fugam, post exilia, post recuperatum multo sanguine imperium, haut procul ab urbe fraternae mortis conscia necatus
est, et cadaver exanimis infamatum suspendio. quid loquar

placed, as it were, on a height, instruct the community in how to behave. Whatever you do, they all believe it will be proper for them to do. Make sure you do not perform any act   6 which those who wish to find fault with you may seem to have been right in censuring, or which would compel those who wish to imitate you to do wrong. Overcome to the best of your ability, or even beyond your ability, the softness of your heart, and suppress those freely flowing tears, or your great love for your nephew will be construed by unbelieving minds as despair of God. You must miss him as one that is absent, not dead, so that you may appear to be waiting to see him again, not to have lost him completely.

But what am I doing, applying remedies to a grief that I   **15** am sure has already been mitigated by time and reason? Why do I not rather recount for you the recent misfortunes of kings and the disasters of our time, considering that Nepotianus is not so much to be mourned for having been deprived of the light of this world as congratulated for having escaped from such great evils? Constantius, the   2 supporter of the Arian heresy, was preparing to meet his enemy and advancing at speed to battle when he died in Mopsus' village and—to his great chagrin—left his empire to his opponent. Julian, destroyer of his own soul, slayer of the Christian army, first denied Christ in Gaul, then felt his reality in Media, and while he sought to extend the Roman territories, lost what had already been built up. Jovian had   3 merely tasted the advantages of kingship when he was suffocated by fumes from a coal fire, giving everyone a demonstration of what human power really is. Valentinian died from a discharge of blood, leaving his fatherland unavenged, his native soil devastated. His brother Valens suffered defeat in the war against the Goths, and found his burial in Thrace, where he fell. Gratian, betrayed by his troops and denied admittance by the cities along the road, became an object of derision to his enemy; your walls, Lyons, attest the traces of that bloody hand. The young   4 Valentinian, still virtually a boy, after flight and exile, after recovering his empire at great cost of blood, was murdered not far from the city that was privy to his brother's death, and his lifeless corpse disgraced by hanging. Why should I

de Procopio, Maximo, Eugenio, qui utique dum rerum potirentur terrori gentibus erant? omnes capti steterunt ante ora victorum et, quod potentissimis quondam miserrimum est, prius ignominia servitutis quam hostili mucrone confossi sunt.

16 Dicat aliquis, 'regum talis condicio est, feriuntque summos fulgura montes.' ad privatas veniam dignitates, nec de his loquar qui excedunt biennium; atque, ut ceteros praetermittam, sufficit nobis trium nuper consularium diversos exitus scribere. Abundantius egens Pityunte exulat; Rufini caput pilo Constantinopolim gestatum est et abscissa manus dextera ad dedecus insatiabilis avaritiae ostiatim stipes mendicavit; Timasius praecipitatus repente de altissimo dignitatis gradu evasisse se putat quod in Oase vivit inglorius. non

2 calamitates miserorum sed fragilem humanae condicionis narro statum; horret animus temporum nostrorum ruinas prosequi. viginti et eo amplius anni sunt quod inter Constantinopolim et Alpes Iulias cotidie Romanus sanguis effunditur. Scythiam, Thraciam, Macedoniam, Thessaliam, Dardaniam, Daciam, Epiros, Dalmatiam cunctasque Pannonias Gothus, Sarmata, Quadus, Alanus, Huni, Vandali, Marco-

3 manni vastant, trahunt, rapiunt. quot matronae, quot virgines dei et ingenua nobiliaque corpora his beluis fuere ludibrio! capti episcopi, interfecti presbyteri et diversorum officia clericorum, subversae ecclesiae, ad altaria Christi stabulati equi, martyrum effossae reliquiae; ubique luctus, ubique gemitus et plurima mortis imago. Romanus orbis

4 ruit et tamen cervix nostra erecta non flectitur. quid putas nunc animi habere Corinthios, Athenienses, Lacedaemonios, Arcadas cunctamque Graeciam, quibus imperant barbari? et certe paucas urbes nominavi, in quibus olim fuere regna non modica. inmunis ab his malis videbatur oriens et tantum nuntiis consternatus: ecce tibi anno praeterito ex

mention Procopius, Maximus, Eugenius, who—as long as they were in power at any rate—brought terror to the nations? All of them stood captive before the gaze of their conquerors, and—the most galling thing for men who were once supremely powerful—suffered the ignominious pang of slavery before being run through by the enemy sword.

Someone may say, 'This is what happens to kings; light- **16** ning strikes the tops of mountains.' I shall come, then, to men of private office, citing cases from within the last two years only; and to pass over the rest, it will be enough for me to describe the various ends of three who recently possessed consular rank. Abundantius lives in impoverished exile at Pityus. The head of Rufinus was carried to Constantinople on javelin-point, and his severed right hand begged for alms from door to door to disgrace his unquenchable avarice. Timasius was suddenly flung from a position of the highest rank, and thinks that he has got off lightly to be living in dishonour in the Oasis. What I am recounting is not the 2 disasters that befall wretched individuals but the fragility of the human situation; my mind shudders to come to the ruins of our age. For twenty years and more, Roman blood has been spilt every day between Constantinople and the Julian Alps. Scythia, Thrace, Macedonia, Thessaly, Dardania, Dacia, the Epirus provinces, Dalmatia, and all the Pannonias have been laid waste, pillaged, and plundered by Goth and Sarmatian, Quadian and Alan, Huns, Vandals, and Marco- manni. How many married women, how many virgins of 3 God, freeborn people and people of high birth, have been outraged by these brutes! Bishops have been taken prisoner, priests and clerics of various orders put to death, churches destroyed, horses stabled at the altars of Christ, the relics of martyrs dug up; grief and lamentation are everywhere, and the image of death in its many forms. The Roman world is collapsing, and yet we do not bend our haughty necks. What 4 do you suppose the Corinthians are thinking now, and the Athenians, Spartans, Arcadians, and the whole of Greece, over whom the barbarians now hold sway? And I have named only a few cities, that once were the seat of mighty kingdoms. The East seemed immune from these troubles, and alarmed only by news of them. And then last year from

ultimis Caucasi rupibus inmissi in nos non Arabiae sed
septentrionis lupi tantas brevi provincias percucurrerunt.
quot monasteria capta, quantae fluviorum aquae humano
5 cruore mutatae sunt! obsessa Antiochia et urbes reliquae,
quas Halys, Cydnus, Orontes Eufratesque praeterfluunt.
tracti greges captivorum; Arabia, Phoenix, Palaestina,
Aegyptus timore captivae.

> non, mihi si linguae centum sint oraque centum,
> ferrea vox,
> omnia poenarum percurrere nomina possim.

neque enim historiam proposui scribere, sed nostras breviter
flere miserias. alioquin ad haec merito explicanda et Thucydides et Sallustius muti sunt.

17   Felix Nepotianus, qui haec non videt; felix, qui ista non
audit. nos miseri, qui aut patimur aut patientes fratres nostros
tanta perspicimus; et tamen vivere volumus, eosque qui his
carent flendos potius quam beandos putamus. olim offensum
sentimus nec placamus deum. nostris peccatis barbari fortes
sunt, nostris vitiis Romanus superatur exercitus; et quasi non
hoc sufficeret cladibus, plus paene bella civilia quam hostilis
2 mucro consumpsit. miseri Israhelitae, ad quorum conparationem Nabuchodonosor servus dei scribitur; infelices nos,
qui tantum displicemus deo ut per rabiem barbarorum illius
in nos ira desaeviat. Ezechias egit paenitentiam, et centum
octoginta quinque milia Assyriorum ab uno angelo una nocte
deleta sunt; Iosaphat laudes domino concinebat, et dominus
pro laudante superabat; Moyses contra Amalech non gladio
3 sed oratione pugnavit. si erigi volumus, prosternamur. pro
pudor et stolida usque ad incredulitatem mens! Romanus
exercitus, victor orbis et dominus, ab his vincitur, hos
pavet, horum terretur aspectu, qui ingredi non valent, qui,
si terram tetigerint, se mortuos arbitrantur, et non intellegimus prophetarum voces, 'fugient mille uno persequente',

the furthest crags of the Caucasus wolves were set upon us, not wolves of Arabia but of the north, who overran vast provinces in no time at all. How many monasteries were taken, how many rivers transformed by human blood! Antioch was besieged; so too the other cities which lie on the Halys, Cydnus, Orontes, and Euphrates. Prisoners were hauled off in throngs; Arabia and Phoenicia, Palestine and Egypt were held captive by fear. 'Not even if I had a hundred tongues and a hundred mouths, a voice of iron, could I recount the names of all the punishments suffered.' Besides, I did not intend to write a history, but briefly to lament our misfortunes. And in any case, to deal with these matters as they deserve even a Thucydides and a Sallust would be dumb. 5

Happy is Nepotianus, who neither sees nor hears these things. We are the wretched ones, who either suffer the torments ourselves, or else see our brothers suffering them. And yet we want to carry on living, and hold that those who are free from all this should be mourned rather than reckoned fortunate. We have long felt that God is offended, but we do nothing to placate him. It is because of our sins that the barbarians are strong, through our vices that the Roman army is defeated; and as if this were not enough of disaster, almost as much destruction has been wreaked by civil wars as by the sword of the enemy. Wretched were the Israelites, in comparison with whom Nebuchadnezzar is described as a servant of God; unhappy are we, who displease God so much that his anger rages against us through the fury of the barbarians. Hezekiah repented, and one hundred and eighty-five thousand Assyrians were wiped out by one angel in a single night. Jehoshaphat sang praises to the Lord, and the Lord repaid him with victory. Moses fought Amalek not with a sword but with prayer. If we want to be raised up, let us cast ourselves down. For shame! How unbelievably stupid we are! The Roman army, conqueror and master of the world, is overcome by these barbarians, trembles before them, is terrified to look at them, when they cannot even walk properly and think themselves good as dead as soon as they touch the ground; and we do not understand the words in the prophets, 'A thousand shall flee with one in pursuit', 17 2 3

nec amputamus causas morbi, ut morbus pariter auferatur statimque cernamus sagittas pilis, tiaras galeis, caballos equis cedere.

18 Excessimus consolandi modum et, dum unius mortem flere prohibemus, totius orbis mortuos planximus. Xerxes, ille rex potentissimus, qui subvertit montes, maria constravit, cum de sublimi loco infinitam hominum multitudinem et innumerabilem vidisset exercitum, flesse dicitur, quod post centum annos nullus eorum quos tunc cernebat super-**2** futurus esset. o si possemus in talem ascendere speculam, de qua universam terram sub nostris pedibus cerneremus! iam tibi ostenderem totius mundi ruinas, gentes gentibus et regnis regna conlisa; alios torqueri, alios necari, alios obrui fluctibus, alios ad servitutem trahi; hic nuptias, ibi planctum; illos nasci, istos mori; alios affluere divitiis, alios mendicare; et non Xerxis tantum exercitum sed totius mundi homines qui nunc vivunt in brevi spatio defuturos. vincitur sermo rei magnitudine, et minus est omne quod dicimus.

19 Redeamus igitur ad nos, et quasi e caelo descendentes paulisper nostra videamus. sentisne, obsecro te, quando infans, quando puer, quando iuvenis, quando robustae aetatis, quando senex factus sis? cotidie morimur, cotidie commutamur, et tamen aeternos esse nos credimus. hoc ipsum quod dicto, quod scribitur, quod relego, quod emendo, de vita mea trahitur. quot puncta notarii, tot meorum damna **2** sunt temporum. scribimus atque rescribimus, transeunt maria epistulae et findente sulcos carina per singulos fluctus aetatis nostrae momenta minuuntur. solum habemus lucri quod Christi nobis amore sociamur. caritas patiens est, benigna est; caritas non zelatur, non agit perperam, non inflatur, omnia sustinet, omnia credit, omnia sperat, omnia patitur; caritas numquam excidit. haec semper vivit in pectore; ob hanc Nepotianus noster absens praesens est, et per tanta terrarum spatia divisos utraque conplectitur

nor do we excise the causes of the disease, so that the disease can be carried off with it and we can immediately see arrows yield to javelins, soft caps to helmets, pack-horses to chargers.

I have gone beyond the bounds of consolation, and in **18** forbidding you to lament the death of one man I have mourned the dead of the whole world. That most powerful of kings, Xerxes, who demolished mountains and paved the sea, once reviewed from a lofty height an infinite multitude of men and an army beyond number, and is said to have wept, because within a hundred years not one of those he could see would still be alive. If only we could climb to an 2 observation-post like that, from which we could see the earth in its totality under our feet! Then I would show you the ruins of the whole world, peoples clashing with peoples and kingdoms with kingdoms; some being tortured, others killed, some overwhelmed by the waves, others dragged off to slavery; here a wedding, there weeping; births on this side, deaths on that; these awash with riches, those begging; and not just Xerxes' army, but every person now alive, destined in a short space of time to die. The theme is too great to be put into words, and everything I say falls short of its goal.

Let us come back to ourselves, then, and as it were coming **19** down from heaven let us look for a minute at our own situation. Let me ask you this: are you aware of the actual moment when you reached infancy, childhood, youth, middle age, old age? Every day we are dying and in the process of change, and yet we think we will go on for ever. These words that I dictate and the scribe writes down, that I read through and correct, amount to something taken from my life. Every mark the scribe makes means a loss of my time here on earth. We write and we write back, letters cross the seas, and as the 2 ship cleaves furrows on its course, with every wave the moments of our life tick away. Our only gain is that we are united with each other in the love of Christ. Love is longsuffering and kind; love is not envious or boastful or pompous; it bears everything, believes everything, is full of hope, endures everything; love never passes away. It always lives in the heart; through it, our Nepotianus, though absent, is present, and grasps us, separated as we are by such vast

3 manu. habemus mutuae obsidem caritatis. iungamur spiritu, stringamur affectu, et fortitudinem mentis quam beatus papa Chromatius ostendit in dormitione germani, nos imitemur in filio. illum nostra pagella decantet, illum cunctae litterae sonent. quem corpore non valemus, recordatione teneamus, et cum quo loqui non possumus, de eo numquam loqui desinamus.

tracts of the earth, with either hand. In him we have a   3
guarantee of our love for each other. Let us join together in
spirit, bind ourselves in the bonds of affection, and, in the
case of our son, copy that strength of mind which Father
Chromatius displayed at the death of his brother. Let our
pages sing of him, let every letter sound his praise. Though
we cannot have him in the flesh, let us keep him in our
memory, and though we cannot speak with him, let us never
cease to speak about him.

COMMENTARY

AD HELIODORUM EPITAPHIUM NEPOTIANI: though *epitaphium* does not appear in the title in all the MSS, it is Jerome's own word for the letter; cf. 1. 2, *epist.* 77. 1. 1, and esp. *epist.* 112. 3. 2, amid discussion of the proper title of *De viris illustribus*: 'epitaphium autem proprie scribitur mortuorum, quod quidem in dormitione sanctae memoriae Nepotiani presbyteri olim fecisse me novi'. This does not mean, however, that Jerome is attempting to represent the piece as an ἐπιτάφιος λόγος according to the Menandrean categories; see Introduction, p. 30.

c. 1. Jerome expresses doubt in his own ability to write an *epitaphium* on Nepotianus, because his *ingenium* is inadequate to the task. In Nepotianus, too, he has lost his source of inspiration, and his mind is clouded by the shock and grief which the young man's death has caused him. Attempts to compose the tribute are defeated by tears, as Jerome seeks to utter praises over Nepotianus, who by rights should have lived to perform this same duty for his elders.

1. 1. Grandes . . . explicare: normally one might expect a writer to choose a field in which his abilities would not be overwhelmed (cf. Hor. *ars* 38–9 'sumite materiam vestris, qui scribitis, aequam / viribus'); but Jerome's implicit claim that he is incapable of doing justice to his subject has the clear purpose of magnifying the importance of that subject. In an oratorical context Isocrates had been quite explicit more than seven centuries before: τοὺς μὲν γὰρ ἄλλους ἐν τοῖς προοιμίοις ὁρῶ καταπραΰνοντας τοὺς ἀκροατὰς καὶ προφασιζομένους ὑπὲρ τῶν μελλόντων ῥηθήσεσθαι, καὶ λέγοντας τοὺς μὲν ὡς ἐξ ὑπογυίου γέγονεν αὐτοῖς ἡ παρασκευή, τοὺς δ' ὡς χαλεπόν ἐστιν ἴσους τοὺς λόγους τῷ μεγέθει τῶν ἔργων ἐξευρεῖν (*Panegyricus*, 13); from the same period cf. e.g. Isoc. *panath.* 36, Dem. *Phil.* 2. 11.

Such self-depreciation, or affected modesty, had indeed become part of the stock-in-trade of the classical author long since. Its purposes were various. In the judicial situation rhetorical theory saw it as a means of making the jurors favourable to the pleader; cf. Cic. *inv.* 1. 22, Quint. *inst.* 4. 1. 8 'ut praecipua in hoc dicentis auctoritas, si omnis in subeundo negotio suspicio sordium aut odiorum aut ambitionis afuerit, ita quaedam in his commendatio tacita, si nos infirmos, inparatos, inpares agentium contra ingeniis dixerimus'. It could, equally, have a eulogistic function, the object of praise being made more distinguished by the writer's avowed inability to tell fittingly of his praiseworthy qualities. Jerome writes thus of Evagrius of Antioch: 'cuius ego pro Christo laborem si arbitrer a me dici posse, non sapiam, si penitus tacere velim, voce in gaudium erumpente non possim' (*epist.* 1. 15. 2), and, more colourfully, of Paula: 'si cuncta mei corporis membra verterentur in linguas et omnes artus humana voce resonarent, nihil dignum sanctae ac venerabilis Paulae virtutibus dicerem' (*epist.* 108. 1. 1, perhaps an adaptation of Virg. *Aen.* 6. 625–7; cf. on 16. 5 *non . . . possim*); cf. also *epist.* 23. 2. 2, Greg. Naz. *orat.* 43. 1. This connection between praise and self-depreciation also has a basis in rhetoric; cf. *Rhet. Her.* 3. 11 'ab eius persona, de quo loquemur, si laudabimus: vereri nos ut illius facta verbis consequi possimus'.

The self-depreciatory expression of incompetence could be taken further, and have another end in view. The author might express reluctance, or even make an initial refusal, to undertake the task at all. This *recusatio* topic is particularly common in literary prefaces from the time of Cicero on (for the characteristics of which see T. Janson, *Latin Prose Prefaces: Studies in Literary Conventions* (Studia Latina Stockholmiensia, 13; Stockholm, 1964), and, for the Middle Ages, G. Simon, 'Untersuchungen zur Topik der Widmungsbriefe mittelalterlicher Geschichtsschreiber bis zum Ende des 12. Jahrhunderts', parts 1–2, *Archiv für Diplomatik*, 4 (1958), 52–119, and 5 (1959), 73–153). Cases normally involve a request from another person that the task be attempted, and regularly result in the author's doubts being overcome by his desire to comply. In this way responsibility for the work's being written is transferred to the person who requested it, providing the author with a kind of escape-clause should the work prove a failure; cf. Janson, 124, Simon, 2. 113. A classic instance is the preface to Cicero's *Orator*, fully discussed by Janson, 40 ff.: 'utrum difficilius aut maius esset negare tibi saepius idem roganti an efficere id quod rogares diu multumque, Brute, dubitavi. nam et negare ei quem unice diligerem cuique me carissimum esse sentirem . . . durum admodum mihi videbatur; et suscipere tantam rem . . . vix arbitrabar esse eius qui vereretur reprehensionem doctorum atque prudentium . . . quod quoniam me saepius rogas, aggrediar non tam perficiendi spe quam experiendi voluntate; malo enim, cum studio tuo sim obsecutus, desiderari a te prudentiam meam quam, si id non fecerim, benevolentiam' (*orat.* 1–2). Cf.

also e.g. Quint. *inst.* 1 pref. 1–3, *Paneg.* 3. 1. 2, Lact. *epit.* pref.,
Jer. *epist.* 1. 1–2 'saepe a me, Innocenti carissime, postulasti, ut
de eius miraculo rei, quae in nostram aetatem inciderat, non
tacerem. cumque ego id verecunde et vere, ut nunc experior,
negarem meque adsequi posse diffiderem . . . tu e contrario
adserebas in dei rebus non possibilitatem inspici debere, sed
animum . . . quid igitur faciam? quod inplere non possum,
negare non audeo. super onerariam navem rudis vector inponor
. . . hortaris, ut tumida malo vela suspendam, rudentes explicem,
clavum regam. pareo iam iubenti et, quia caritas omnia potest,
spiritu sancto cursum prosequente confidam, habiturus in utraque parte solacium: si me ad optatos portus aestus adpulerit,
gubernator putabor; si inter asperos orationis anfractus inpolitus
sermo substiterit, facultatem forsitan quaeras, voluntatem certe
flagitare non poteris', and, among many other instances in
Jerome, *epist.* 130. 1. 1–2, *pref. in psalm., pref. in Ezram, in
Ezech. lib.* 3 pref. (CCSL 75. 91 = PL 25. 76), *in Ioel* pref.
(CCSL 76. 160 = PL 25. 949–50). For examples from the
Middle Ages see Simon, 1. 68–9.

   Other manifestations of the self-depreciatory theme, which
became more common (and the author's self-abasement more
extreme) under the influence of changing social conditions
during the Empire, and, to some extent, of Christianity, include
the use by the author of terms such as *mediocritas mea* to describe
himself, the use of diminutives, and the author's apology for his
defective style even when there is nothing defective about it at
all. There are countless examples in Jerome; cf. e.g. *epist.* 75. 4. 2
'quo ille desiderio nostra opuscula flagitavit . . . non nos
honorans, qui parvuli et minimi Christianorum omnium sumus
. . . sed Christum', 85. 3. 2 'non debeas turbidos nostri ingenioli
rivos quaerere' (diminutive), 142. 1. 1 'nostra . . . parvitate' (in
reference to himself), *in Zach.* pref. (CCSL 76A. 748 = PL 25.
1418) 'tuae benevolentiae erit, non eruditionem nostram, quae
vel nulla vel parva est, sed pronam in te suspicere voluntatem',
and, particularly interesting in view of his recognition of affected
modesty in St Paul, *epist.* 29. 7. 2 'nos, ut scis, Hebraici sermonis
lectione detenti in Latina lingua rubiginem obduximus in tantum, ut loquentibus quoque nobis stridor quidam non Latinus
interstrepat. unde ignosce ariditati: etsi inperitus sum, inquit,
sermone, apostolus, sed non scientia [cf. 2 Cor. 11: 6]. illi
utrumque non deerat, et unum humiliter rennuebat; nobis
utrumque deest'. See further Janson, 124–49, Simon, 1. 108–19,
Curtius, 91–3, 411–16.

   ultra vires ausa: for the expression cf. Manil. 3. 1–3 'in nova surgentem maioraque viribus ausum [sc. me] . . . ducite, Pierides'.

Nepotianus meus, tuus, noster: for Nepotianus see Introduction, p. 15. At *epist.* 3. 4. 1 Jerome describes his childhood friend Bonosus, who had now adopted the harsh life of the religious hermit, in similar terms: 'Bonosus tuus, immo meus et, ut verius dicam, noster'; and Marcella is described almost identically at *epist.* 127. 1. 3. Favez (1937), 131, points out that in Christian consolation the consoler sometimes implicitly expresses sympathy with the bereaved by referring to the departed as *meus* or *noster*; see further on ⟨*nos*⟩ . . . *confecit* below. In this letter Nepotianus is only once mentioned by name without *noster* being added (17. 1).

⟨**nos**⟩ . . . **confecit:** Jerome is plainly thinking of Heliodorus and himself, both *senes*: Jerome was approaching fifty at this time (see Introduction, p. 1, and Appendix 1), and it is probable that Heliodorus was a contemporary of his at the rhetor's school in Rome (cf. Cavallera, 1. 14 n. 1). But I doubt whether it is sufficient merely to understand *nos* with *senes* and *vulneratos*—the sentence reads very awkwardly—and I have therefore supplied it; it could easily have fallen out of the text after *noster*, and its insertion here results in a desirable double-cretic clausula (see Appendix 2, esp. p. 237). I am grateful to Dr Winterbottom for this suggestion. For what it is worth, *Γ*, beginning a new extract at *reliquit*, reads *nos caros* in place of *senes*.

In thus linking himself with his friend, and especially in indicating his own grief at Nepotianus' death, Jerome forges a close association with Heliodorus and offers him sympathy, in itself a kind of consolation (cf. Greg. Naz. *epist.* 165. 3 τὸ . . . γὰρ συναλγεῖν ἱκανόν εἰς παραμυθίαν). Expressions of this kind occur frequently in Christian writers; cf. e.g. Jer. *epist.* 39. 1. 2 'quis enim siccis oculis recordetur viginti annorum adulescentulam tam ardenti fide crucis levasse vexillum . . . ?', 75. 1. 1 'lugubri nuntio consternatus super sancti et venerabilis mihi dormitione Lucini vix brevem epistulam dictare potui', Ambr. *epist.* 15. 1 'dum semper affixum tenere animo desidero virum sanctum, atque omnes actus eius quasi in specula positus exploro, hausi, nimia indagine sollicitudinis, amaritudinem nuntii celerioris', *obit. Valent.* 26, Bas. *epist.* 301 *ad init.*, 302 *ad init.* ὅσον μὲν ἐστενάξαμεν ἐπὶ τῇ ἀγγελίᾳ τοῦ πάθους τοῦ κατὰ τὸν ἄριστον τῶν ἀνδρῶν Βρίσωνα τί χρὴ καὶ λέγειν; Basil, indeed, writing to the church of Ancyra on the death of Athanasius, says that he does so οὐ παρακλήσεως ἕνεκεν . . . ἀλλὰ τὴν ὀδύνην τῆς καρδίας ἡμῶν, καθ᾽

ὅσον δυνατόν, ἐκ τῆς φωνῆς ταύτης ὑμῖν διασημαίνοντες (*epist.* 29).
Among pagans, too, the consoler may indicate that he shares
in the grief of the bereaved; and as in the case of Christian
consolationes, such expressions normally occur at the beginning
of the piece, following rhetorical precept (on which see Nisbet–Hubbard (1970), 280–1, Kassel, 51, 98 n. 1). Cicero and
Sulpicius Rufus both claim to be so grief-stricken as to require
consolation themselves (Cic. *ad fam.* 4. 5. 1 (Sulpicius), 5. 16. 1,
5. 18. 1). Seneca sympathizes with Lucilius (*epist.* 63. 1 'moleste
fero decessisse Flaccum, amicum tuum'), and pseudo-Plutarch
with Apollonius (*ad Apoll.* 1 (101E) καὶ πάλαι σοι συνήλγησα καὶ
συνηχθέσθην); cf. also Julian, *epist.* 201 Bidez–Cumont (37 Hertlein) οὐκ ἀδακρυτί σου τὴν ἐπιστολὴν ἀνέγνων, ἣν ἐπὶ τῷ τῆς
συνοικούσης θανάτῳ πεποίησαι, τοῦ πάθους τὴν ὑπερβολὴν ἀναγγείλας,
Liban. *epist.* 1473. 1 καὶ γὰρ ἐστενάξαμεν καὶ ἐδακρύσαμεν καὶ
παρήλθομεν σοῦ τὴν λύπην. Generally, however, expressions of
sympathy play a smaller part in pagan than in Christian consolation; among pagans it is reason which is held to be of the greatest
importance, and Seneca, for example, while never devoid of
feeling, maintains a cooler, more detached approach to the task
of alleviating someone else's grief (cf. Favez (1930*a*), and
(1930*b*), 84).

desiderii . . . vulneratos: the use of *vulnerare* and *vulnus* in
reference to the mental effect of emotions such as grief and love,
generally poetic in the Late Republic and Early Empire, later
becomes frequent in prose. In Jerome cf. e.g. *epist.* 66. 1. 1
'vereor, ne nunc inportunius loquar et adtrectans vulnus pectoris tui . . . commemoratione exulcerem [sc. id]', 107. 7. 2
'caritatis iaculo vulnerata' (a probable reminiscence of S. of S. 2:
5, τετρωμένη ἀγάπης ἐγώ in LXX), *hom. Orig. in cant.* (PL 23.
1138) 'alius iaculum carnei amoris excepit, alius ex terrena
cupidine vulneratus est'. Jerome also employs the wound-image
in another important way, namely, to denote the effect of
committing a sin; cf. e.g. *epist.* 79. 10. 2 'cavendum est vulnus,
quod dolore curatur', 122. 1. 4 'Samuhel quondam plangebat
Saul, quia superbiae vulnera paenitentiae medicamine non cura-
bat'.

iaculum does not appear to be used in a metaphorical sense
before Tertullian (e.g. *nat.* 1. 9. 4 'opinor, ut contemptores
deorum vestrorum haec iacula [sc. omnem cladem publicam vel
iniuriam] eorum p⟨rovo⟩camus'), and in association with *desiderium, amor*, and the like, not until the late fourth century (cf.
Rufin. *Orig. in cant.* 3 (PG 13. 162) 'se vulneratam sentit esse
iaculis caritatis', and the cases quoted above); cf. *TLL* 7. 1. 78–9.

1. 2. quem . . . tenemus: for the notion that the natural order of things has been reversed, implicit here, cf. 1. 3 *rerum . . . senes* with n.

cui iam . . . in funere sum: the picture is of course exaggerated. Jerome can hardly have been so overwhelmed by grief at a time when Heliodorus' own grief has subsided (cf. 15. 1), and that he is incapable of writing the *epitaphium* is quickly disproved. But this description of his condition, however imaginary, vividly emphasizes his genuine sorrow.

meum sudabit ingenium: *sudare* = 'exert oneself' is not unusual, but I do not think it is commonly found with *ingenium*. Cf., however, Jer. *epist.* 27. 1. 3, 39. 8. 1 'illam [sc. Blesillam] mea lingua resonabit, illi mei dedicabuntur labores, illi sudabit ingenium', 114. 3. 1 'tibi enim meum sudavit ingenium et facundiam Graecam Latinae linguae volui paupertate pensare'.

litterulae: in the sense of *epistulae*, *TLL*, 7. 2. 1534, records no instances of the diminutive between Cicero and Jerome, who uses it several times (cf. *epist.* 52. 5. 7, 85. 1. 1, 143. 2. 3). In reference to individual characters, the tradition is fuller; Jerome employs the word thus at *epist.* 7. 1. 1, and perhaps at *epist.* 128. 1. 3, though here it probably refers to literature generally. In the present case it seems to mean, quite simply, 'writings'. The diminutive perhaps continues the self-depreciation begun at 1. 1 *ingenia parva*; cf. on 1. 1 *Grandes . . . explicare*.

ἐργοδιώκτης: a problem for the copyists, with very confused readings in 𝔄𝐾Ψ, but certainly correct, as at *epist.* 28. 1 (where it also caused the scribes some difficulty). Labourt held *G*'s *epidioctes* to be similar in meaning to ἐργοδιώκτης, and therefore possible; but the only instance of ἐπιδιώκτης recorded by LSJ occurs in the *Corpus glossariorum Latinorum*, ed. G. Goetz (7 vols., Leipzig, 1888–1923), 2. 307. 57, as equivalent to *persecutor*. ἐργοδιώκτης, for which there is in any case better MS support, gives excellent sense ('taskmaster', 'inspirer of my labours' (Wright)), and is much better attested elsewhere; cf. e.g. LXX Exod. 3: 7, Philo, *quis rer. div. heres* 255. There is no need to consider seriously Vallarsi's conjectured ὀροσπίζης (probably 'blue-throat'; cf. D. W. Thompson, *A Glossary of Greek Birds* (2nd edn., London and Oxford, 1936), 213–14, on ὀρόσπιζος), which seems to have caused the printers of the various editions as much trouble as the true reading caused the copyists of the MSS.

cycneo . . . dulcior: it was an ancient notion that the swan sang immediately before its death and that this song was particularly sweet, and expressions such as this became proverbial; cf. e.g. Aes. *Agam.* 1444–5, Plato, *Phaedo* 84E, Sen. *Phaedr.* 302 'dulcior vocem moriente cygno', Aelian, *nat. anim.* 2. 32, Ambr. *hex.* 5. 12. 39, Prud. *c. Symm.* 1. 62–3 'blandosque susurros / in morem recinens suave inmorientis oloris', Otto, 105, sect. 497, with the *Nachträge*. At *de orat.* 3. 6 Cicero, telling of L. Licinius Crassus' last speech in the senate before his death, says, 'illa tamquam cycnea fuit divini hominis vox et oratio'. Here there is certainly a conscious connection between the dying swan and the dead Nepotianus. Jerome uses the image again at *epist.* 52. 3. 5 'ad poetas venio, Homerum, Hesiodum, Simonidem, Stesichorum, qui grandes natu cygneum nescio quid et solito dulcius vicina morte cecinerunt'. It is possible that it occurred in Cicero's *Consolatio*, and it was this which reminded Jerome of it in the present case; cf. Cic. *Tusc.* 1. 73, and for Jerome's debt to the *Consolatio* in this letter, and its connections with the *Tusculans*, Introduction, pp. 13 (with n. 50), 19.

On the veracity of the legend see W. G. Arnott, 'Swan Songs', *G&R* 24 (1977), 149–53; and for further observations, Nisbet–Hubbard (1978), 342.

stupet ... balbutit: typical effects of shock; cf. e.g. Sen. *contr.* 1. 1. 16 'non potui, inquit, sustinere illud durum spectaculum. offensam mihi putas tantum excidisse? mens excidit, non animus mihi constitit, non in ministerium sustinendi corporis suffecerunt pedes, oculi subita caligine obtorpuerunt', 7. 1. 17, Quint. *inst.* 9. 2. 43, [Quint.] *decl. min.* 286. 9 Winterbottom, Ambr. *obit. Valent.* 3 'oculi non solum corporis, sed etiam mentis hebetati sunt, et quadam caecitate omnis sensus obductus est, quoniam ereptus est mihi'. Jerome claims to have been similarly affected in writing his *epitaphium* on Paula: 'quotienscumque stilum figere volui et opus exarare promissum, totiens obriguerunt digiti, cecidit manus, sensus elanguit' (*epist.* 108. 32). Other kinds of emotion may also provoke such responses; cf. e.g. (fear) Lucr. 3. 152–6 'verum ubi vementi magis est commota metu mens, / consentire animam totam per membra videmus / sudoresque ita palloremque exsistere toto / corpore et infringi linguam vocemque aboriri, / caligare oculos, sonere auris, succidere artus', (passion) Catull. 51. 9–12 'lingua sed torpet, tenuis sub artus / flamma demanat, sonitu suopte / tintinant aures, gemina teguntur / lumina nocte' (from Sappho fr. 31 Lobel–Page).

balbutit (or *balbuttit*; for the form see *TLL* 2. 1695): a favourite word of Jerome's; cf. *epist.* 22. 29. 6, 79. 6. 3, 107. 1. 3, 107. 13. 6, 108. 26. 5, 128. 1. 1, *vita Malchi* 9 (PL 23. 58), *adv. Pelag.* 3. 17 (PL 23. 587), *hom. Orig. in Ier.* 1 (PL 25. 591). In most of these cases it refers to the stammering, ill-formed words of a little child; here it must mean 'babbles', or perhaps 'stutters'. The earliest instances recorded by *TLL* are in Cicero (*acad. prior.* 137, *Tusc.* 5. 75, *div.* 1. 5, always in reference to philosophers), but the word seems onomatopoeic, and may be very old.

quidquid . . . videtur: 'whatever I shall say . . . seems voiceless'; the present *videtur* suggests that Jerome's words appear voiceless now, even in advance of his speaking them. *mutus* of something said is unusual; but cf. perhaps Lucan 1. 247 'tacito mutos volvunt in pectore questus', Claud. *rapt. Pros.* 3. 160 'abrumpit mutas in fila querellas'.

stilus . . . obducitur: *obducitur* must be taken with both *stilus* and *cera*. *B*'s *idcirco*, in place of *cera*, looks like an attempt to establish concord, but it is not unusual for a plural subject to take a singular verb, where the subject consists of two parts, each in the singular.

Jerome seems to be suggesting that he has been so affected by grief that he has been unable to write anything for a long time. We may believe him when, writing to Theophilus of Alexandria a few months after the death of Paula (for the date see Cavallera, 2. 43), he says, 'ita enim sanctae et venerabilis Paulae dormitione confectus sum, ut absque translatione huius libri [i.e. Theophilus' Paschal Epistle for 404] usque in praesentiarum nihil aliud divini operis scripserim' (*epist.* 99. 2. 2). But plainly there is exaggeration in the present claim, with the images of the rusty pen and the wax tablet dulled by mildew, doubtless designed to show how much Jerome shares Heliodorus' sorrow (cf. above on *cui iam . . . in funere sum*). Catullus too uses the image of rust to exaggerated effect, though for a quite different purpose, at 64. 42, where a single day's holiday produces rust on ploughs. For the notion that rust or mould is caused by lack of use cf. Sen. *benef.* 3. 2. 3 'quae in usu sunt et manum cottidie tactumque patiuntur, numquam periculum situs adeunt', Apul. *flor.* 17 pp. 31. 24–32. 1 Helm 'gladius usu splendescit, situ robiginat', and esp. (noting the rhetorical context) Sen. *contr.* 2. 2. 8 'memini Latronem in praefatione quadam dicere quod scholastici quasi carmen didicerunt: non vides ut immota fax torpeat, ut exagitata reddat ignes? mollit viros otium, ferrum situ carpitur et rubiginem ducit, desidia dedocet'.

quasi sentiens: 'as if it had feeling'; 'as though it felt his loss' (Wright).

subtristior: a very rare word, occurring elsewhere, according to Forcellini, only at Ter. *Andr.* 447, Cypr. *epist.* 11. 4, and Jer. *epist.* 107. 9. 3. This is the only instance of the comparative

form, and the only case where the word is applied to an
inanimate object. It would be a dubious matter, however, to
represent the word as an archaism recalled to use in the third
century AD and later. Adjectives compounded with *sub-* could
easily be formed when required, and it is probably due to little
more than chance that the extant occurrences of *subtristis* fall
centuries apart.

in verba prorumpere: cf. e.g. Tac. *ann.* 11. 2, Apul. *met.* 6.
17 'turris prorumpit in vocem subitam', [Quint.] *decl. mai.* 19. 6
pp. 377. 21–378. 1 Håkanson, and many instances in Jerome,
e.g. *epist.* 21. 5. 1 'in verba prorumpimus', 46. 4. 1 (Paula and
Eustochium). For *erumpere* used similarly cf. e.g. *epist.* 1. 12. 2,
43. 3. 3.

super . . . spargere: the metaphor comes from the Roman
practice of scattering flowers over the tomb of the deceased; cf.
e.g. Virg. *Aen.* 5. 79 'purpureosque iacit flores [sc. Aeneas]' (over
Anchises' tomb), 6. 884–5 'purpureos spargam flores animam-
que nepotis / his saltem accumulem donis', Tib. 2. 4. 48, Auson.
epit. 31. 1–4 'sparge mero cineres bene olentis et unguine nardi, /
hospes, et adde rosis balsama puniceis. / perpetuum mihi ver
agit inlacrimabilis urna / et commutavi saecula, non obii', Jer.
epist. 66. 5. 3 'ceteri mariti super tumulos coniugum spargunt
violas, rosas, lilia floresque purpureos et dolorem pectoris his
officiis consolantur: Pammachius noster sanctam favillam ossa-
que veneranda elemosynae balsamis rigat', Lattimore, 135–6,
Toynbee, 62–4.

epitaphii huius is a defining genitive— 'the flowers consisting
of this *epitaphium*'—but Jerome may also have in mind the *flores
verborum* or *eloquentiae* which the *epitaphium* contains. For *flos*
used by Jerome in this sense cf. e.g. *in Zach. lib.* 3 pref. (CCSL
76A. 848 = PL 25. 1497) 'nimio verborum flore luxuriat', *adv.
Iovin.* 1. 1 (PL 23. 212) 'verborum floribus ornatus', 1. 3 (PL 23.
212) 'eloquentiae suae flore', *epist.* 52. 1. 2 'calentibus adhuc
rhetorum studiis atque doctrinis quaedam scolastico flore depinximus'.

For other types of flower-imagery in Jerome see on 13. 2
marcescebat . . . migrabat.

inplentur oculi: cf. 2. 2, 13. 3, *epist.* 39. 1. 4 'lacrimis ora
conplentur, singultus occupant vocem'; and for the same kind of
exaggeration in different contexts, Cic. *Cael.* 60 'haec facta illius
clarissimi ac fortissimi viri mentio et vocem meam fletu debilita-
vit et mentem dolore impedivit', Jer. *epist.* 45. 6. 1 'haec . . . flens
dolensque conscripsi', 46. 1. 3 (Paula and Eustochium), 123. 15.
4 'non possum absque lacrimis Tolosae facere mentionem'.

totus in funere sum: 'I am wholly absorbed in his death'. The use of *totus* qualifying the verb, where an adverb would be used in English, is found as early as Plautus (cf. *Cist.* 535), and there are many later instances (cf. e.g. Cic. *Cluent.* 72, Hor. *sat.* 1. 9. 1–2, Ov. *fast.* 6. 251 'in prece totus eram'). In Jerome cf. e.g. *epist.* 3. 4. 3, 49. 13. 5 'totus in certamine positus est', 98. 19. 2 (tr. from Theophilus) 'toti ad terrena conversi'. *omnis* can be used similarly (cf. e.g. Hor. *epist.* 1. 1. 11 'omnis in hoc sum'); and other words, such as *multus* and *frequens*, may follow the same construction (cf. KS 1. 236). The use of ὅλος in Greek is comparable; cf. e.g. Dem. *fals. leg.* 127 ὅλος πρὸς τῷ λήμματι, Lucian, *Hermot.* 2 ὅλος εἶ ἐν τῷ πράγματι.

1. 3. moris . . . concitarent: for the construction *moris . . . fuit*, with the genitive, see LHS 2. 62; for the expression itself, in the form *moris est* or *mos est*, cf. e.g. Virg. *Aen.* 7. 601 'mos erat Hesperio in Latio . . . ', Val. Max. 2. 8. 6 'moris est ab imperatore ducturo triumphum consules invitari ad cenam', Plin. *epist.* 3. 21. 3 'fuit moris antiqui, eos qui vel singulorum laudes vel urbium scripserant, aut honoribus aut pecunia ornare', Jer. *epist.* 147. 5. 2. Sometimes it introduces a kind of ἔκφρασις, as here; one may compare the use of *est locus* (cf. e.g. Virg. *Aen.* 1. 159, Ov. *met.* 8. 788).

The practice here mentioned—the *laudatio funebris*—is described more fully by Polybius 6. 53. 1–3; cf. also Cic. *de orat.* 2. 341, Liv. 2. 47. 11, Dion. Hal. 5. 17. 2–6, Tac. *ann.* 3. 5. The tribute was of course awarded only to people of distinction. O. C. Crawford, 'Laudatio funebris', *CJ* 37 (1941), 17–27, gives a good brief account of the practice; its history is outlined by Vollmer. On Roman funerary rites generally see Toynbee, 43–61. It is worth noting that among Christians mourning at funerals was strictly suppressed (contrast *instar . . . concitarent*, Polybius 6. 53. 3), though of course it was impossible to stamp out spontaneous outbreaks of lamentation altogether; cf. P. Brown, *The Cult of the Saints: Its Rise and Function in Latin Christianity* (London, 1981), 70, 157–8, Alexiou, 29–31.

Taken in conjunction with *en rerum . . . senes* following, this passage makes it clear that Jerome conceived of this letter as a sort of *laudatio funebris*; see Introduction, p. 29.

instar lugubrium carminum: 'as though by means of dirges'. For this use of *instar* cf. *in Ezech.* 25. 8–11 (CCSL 75. 340 = PL 25. 236–7) 'quidquid in saeculo dogmatum perversorum est, quidquid ad terrenam scientiam pertinet et putatur esse robustum, hoc dialectica arte subvertitur et instar incendii

in cineres favillasque dissolvitur', Cassian, *c. Nest.* 4. 6. 7 'bene
apostolus instar divinorum verborum docens . . . ipsum de-
scendisse dicit quem ascendisse'.

rerum . . . senes: Jerome has already expressed the feeling
that the natural order of things has been reversed (cf. 1. 2 *quem
heredem putavimus, funus tenemus*), and does so again at 14. 1
praecessit te successor tuus. For the idea that it is natural and
proper for people to outlive their elders cf. e.g. Cic. *sen.* 84
'[Cato, filius meus] cuius a me corpus est crematum, quod contra
decuit, ab illo meum', *amicit.* 15 'cum illo quidem . . . actum
optime est, mecum incommodius, quem fuerat aequius, ut prius
introieram, sic prius exire de vita' (Laelius of Scipio Aemilia-
nus), Virg. *Aen.* 11. 160–1, [Plut.] *ad Apoll.* 34 (119E) σὲ ἔδει ὑπ'
ἐκείνου [sc. υἱοῦ σου] τελείου γενομένου κηδευθῆναι μεταλλάξαντα τὸν
βίον· τοῦτο γὰρ εἶναι κατὰ φύσιν, Ambr. *exc. Sat.* 1. 37 'haec tu,
frater, mihi iustius exhiberes, haec ego a te expectabam, haec ego
officia desiderabam', Auson. *parent.* 11. 15–16; the wish of
parents that their children should survive them is a regular form
of this theme (cf. e.g. Plaut. *Asin.* 16–17, Sen. *contr.* 1. 1. 6
'aliquis peribit fame qui filium suum optat superstitem?', Sen.
dial. 6. 1. 2, Quint. *inst.* 9. 2. 98 'ita mihi contingat herede filio
mori', Lact. *inst.* 4. 28. 13). The notion is found also in
sepulchral epigrams; cf. e.g. *Anth. Pal.* 7. 261 ἠιθέῳ γὰρ σῆμα
Βιάνορι χεύατο μήτηρ / ἔπρεπε δ' ἐκ παιδὸς μητέρα τοῦδε τυχεῖν,
Buecheler 164 'quod par parenti fuerat facere filium, / mors
immatura fecit ut faceret pater', 165–78, 556. 2–3, 1153 'et quas
exsequias debebat nata parenti, / has pater adversis casibus ipse
dedit', 1479 'si non fatorum praepostera iura fuissent, / mater in
hoc titulo debuit ante legi', 1480–5, Engström 31–4, Lier (1903),
456–60, Lattimore, 187–91, E. Griessmair, *Das Motiv der Mors
Immatura in den griechischen metrischen Grabinschriften* (Commentationes Aenipontanae, 17; Innsbruck, 1966), 44–7. See
further E. Courtney, *A Commentary on the Satires of Juvenal*
(London, 1980), 477 (on Juv. 10. 240–1), T. Wiedemann, *Adults
and Children in the Roman Empire* (London, 1989), 40–1.

in calamitatem . . . natura: 'to our misfortune, nature has
lost her privileges' (according to which the old die first).

c. 2. Jerome now confronts the problem of grief which faces
Christians when they lose a loved one. He knows that he should
not weep over Nepotianus, who is not dead but asleep, but finds it
impossible not to do so. At this stage, however, he does no more
than hint at a solution to the problem, presenting it in full only in
c. 7. Instead, in a complex and allusive passage he describes the

destruction of death by Christ, creating a mood of hope after the sorrow and near-despair of c. 1, and explaining more fully why grief is inappropriate.

2. 1. Quid igitur faciam?: cf. e.g. *epist.* 1. 2. 1, 84. 4. 1, 130. 1. 2, where Jerome also uses the question in articulating a dilemma or difficulty. Quintilian includes the expression as an example in his section on rhetorical questions (*inst.* 9. 2. 11).

iungam . . . suscitatus est: Jerome rejects the idea that he should mourn Nepotianus' death. The Bible clearly indicates that for Christians death is merely a falling asleep, which will be followed by resurrection into heaven; it is therefore inappropriate to grieve when they die. The same point is made at *epist.* 39. 4. 6 'nos vero, qui Christum induimus . . . non debemus super mortuos [sc. Christianos] contristari'; elsewhere cf. e.g. *const. apol.* 6. 30, Cypr. *mort.* 20, Ambr. *exc. Sat.* 1. 70, Bas. *grat. act.* 6. Conversely it is appropriate enough to mourn those who at their death will not go to be with Christ; cf. e.g. *epist.* 39. 3. 2 'lugeatur mortuus, sed ille, quem gehenna suscipit, quem tartarus devorat, in cuius poenam aeternus ignis exaestuat', Aug. *serm.* 302. 18, John Chrys. *epist.* 197, *de morte* (PG 63. 809).

The three pieces of evidence from Scripture which Jerome presents in answer to his question seem to show a gradual progression in importance. First comes Paul's prohibition, with his opinion that the Christian dead are only asleep; then a saying of Jesus himself, to the effect that a girl (in Mark and Luke, the daughter of Jairus) who appears to be dead is in reality not dead at all; and finally the case of Lazarus, whose raising by Jesus is physical proof that he was only asleep all along. Jerome does not mention that Jesus raised up the girl too, perhaps to allow a climax in the third piece of evidence. The cases of Lazarus and the girl, instances of resurrection in this world, appear to indicate to Jerome the reality of celestial resurrection, which all Christians will experience.

The conception of death as a sleep in Christian writers owes most to the Bible; in addition to the passages adduced by Jerome here cf. e.g. Matt. 27: 52, Acts 13: 36, 1 Cor. 15: 6, and, from the OT, 1 Kgs. 1: 21, 2: 10, 2 Chr. 16: 13, Ps. 87: 6. The Hebrew tradition, evident also in late Jewish apocalyptic literature, had far more influence on the Fathers than the classical, where the image occurs as early as Homer (*Il.* 11. 241, 14. 482–3); cf. M. B. Ogle, 'The Sleep of Death', *MAAR* 11 (1933), 81–117, who argues, *inter alia*, that among classical writers the conception does not reflect popular belief but represents a literary convention. For classical examples see also Albers (1921), 52, Nis-

bet–Hubbard (1970), 284; in pagan consolation cf. e.g. [Plut.] *ad
Apoll*. 12 (107D) εἰ γὰρ δὴ ὕπνος τίς ἐστιν ὁ θάνατος καὶ περὶ τοὺς
καθεύδοντας μηδέν ἐστι κακόν, δῆλον ὡς οὐδὲ περὶ τοὺς τετελευτηκό-
τας εἴη ἄν τι κακόν. ἀλλὰ μήν γ' ὅτι ἥδιστός ἐστιν ὁ βαθύτατος τί δεῖ
καὶ λέγειν;

iungam . . . lacrimas?: for the expression cf. *in Ezech. lib.* 3
pref. (CCSL 75. 91 = PL 25. 75) 'quis crederet ut totius orbis
exstructa victoriis Roma corrueret . . . ut cotidie sancta Beth-
leem, nobiles quondam utriusque sexus atque omnibus divitiis
affluentes, susciperet mendicantes? quibus, quoniam opem ferre
non possumus, condolemus, et lacrimas lacrimis iungimus'.

apostolus . . . vocans: cf. 1 Thess. 4: 13–14 'nolumus autem
vos ignorare, fratres, de dormientibus, ut non contristemini
sicut et ceteri qui spem non habent. si enim credimus quod Iesus
mortuus est et resurrexit, ita et deus eos qui dormierunt per
Iesum adducet cum eo'. For the passage used by Jerome in
similar contexts cf. *epist.* 3. 3. 2, 39. 3. 7, and esp. 75. 1. 3 'adversum mortis ergo duritiam . . . hoc solacio erigimur, quod brevi
visuri sumus eos, quos dolemus absentes. neque enim mors, sed
dormitio et somnus appellatur. unde et beatus apostolus vetat de
dormientibus contristari, ut, quos dormire novimus, suscitari
posse credamus'. The text also forms the basis of Aug. *serm.* 172,
173.

non est . . . dormit: Matt. 9: 25 (Vulg.: 'non est enim mortua
puella sed dormit'), Mark 5: 39 (Vulg.: 'puella non est mortua
sed dormit'), Luke 8: 52 (Vulg.: 'non est mortua [some
MSS: + puella] sed dormit'). Jerome will not have been thinking of any one of these gospels in particular.

Lazarus . . . suscitatus est: cf. John 11: 1–44, esp. 11
'Lazarus amicus noster dormit; sed vado, ut a somno exsuscitem
eum'.

laeter . . . illius?: the alternative course, with the answer 'yes'
implied; but as Jerome goes on to say, he cannot but weep.

For *raptus . . . illius* cf. Wisd. 4: 11–14 'raptus est ne malitia
mutaret intellectum illius . . . placita enim erat deo anima illius';
mutaret is overwhelmingly preferred to *inmutaret* in patristic
citations of this passage (cf. VL Beuron ad loc.), and in printing
it I follow the majority of the MSS against Hilberg. The passage
is highly appropriate to Nepotianus, as the author of Wisdom is
speaking of the *iustus morte praeoccupatus* (cf. Wisd. 4: 7). It is
frequently employed in Christian consolation, providing a comforting explanation of someone's death; cf. e.g. Cypr. *mort.* 23,
Paul. Nol. *epist.* 13. 6, Jer. *epist.* 39. 3. 1, 75. 2. 1, 79. 2. 4
(together with the present case, the only instances in Jerome

where the passage is cited, according to the list of testimonia in
VL Beuron), and Ambrose's adaptation, *exc. Sat.* 1. 30 'nam si
pacato saeculo bellisque cessantibus raptum Enoc nemo deflevit,
sed magis propheta laudavit [cf. Gen. 5: 22–4, Hebr. 11: 5], sicut
de illo scriptura dixit: raptus est, ne malitia mutaret cor eius,
quanto magis nunc iure dicendum est, cum ad saeculi lubricum
vitae accedat ambiguum: raptus est, ne in manus incideret
barbarorum, raptus est, ne totius orbis excidia, mundi finem,
propinquorum funera, civium mortes, postremo ne sanctarum
virginum atque viduarum, quod omni morte acerbius est, conlu-
vionem videret'. For the idea of death as an escape from ills
generally see on 15. 1 *ut . . . evaserit.*

2. 2. sed invito . . . fluunt: *invito et repugnanti*, sc. *mihi*. So
Sulpicius Severus writes to the deacon Aurelius, 'sciam virum
illum non esse lugendum, cui post evictum mundum triumpha-
tumque saeculum nunc demum reddita est corona iustitiae. sed
tamen ego non possum mihi imperare, quin doleam' (*epist.* 2. 7).
Cf. Sen. *epist.* 99. 18–19 'cum primus nos nuntius acerbi funeris
perculit, cum tenemus corpus e complexu nostro in ignem
transiturum, lacrimas naturalis necessitas exprimit et spiritus
ictu doloris inpulsus quemadmodum totum corpus quatit, ita
oculos, quibus adiacentem umorem perpremit et expellit. hae
lacrimae per elisionem cadunt nolentibus nobis: aliae sunt
quibus exitum damus cum memoria eorum quos amisimus
retractatur': Jerome continues to write as if in the first flush of
grief. For his exaggeration cf. on 1. 2 *cui iam . . . in funere sum*
and *inplentur oculi.*

praecepta virtutum: 'the teaching of the virtues'; presumably, that one's mind ought not to be overcome by grief. The
idea has a Stoic flavour, but it seems improbable that Jerome was
thinking of the doctrines of any particular philosophical school.
Cf. perhaps Cic. *Tusc.* 2. 43 'vide, ne, cum omnes rectae animi
adfectiones virtutes appellentur, non sit hoc proprium nomen
omnium, sed ab ea, quae una ceteris excellebat, omnes nomina-
tae sint. appellata est enim ex viro virtus; viri autem propria
maxime est fortitudo, cuius munera duo sunt maxima, mortis
dolorisque contemptio'.

credulam . . . affectus: cf. *epist.* 108. 21. 4 'cum os stoma-
chumque signaret et matris dolorem crucis niteretur inpressione
lenire, superabat affectus et credulam mentem parentis viscera
consternabant'.

credulus is most often used of persons, but it is not rare with
words such as *mens*, which are essentially personal in nature; cf.
e.g. [Sen.] *Herc. O.* 965 'mens credula', Sen. *Tro.* 3 'animum . . .

credulum', *Thy.* 962–3 'credula . . . pectora', *Cod. Theod.* 16. 6. 4 'credulas mentes', and, in a Christian sense (= 'believing in God'), Apring. *in apoc.* 21. 22 'credul[a]e . . . mentes', Drac. *laud. dei* 1. 466 'credula corda'. Cf. also 14. 6 *incredulas mentes* with n.

mens, animus, etc., are also frequently found with *frangere*; for *mens* cf. e.g. Sen. *dial.* 11. 5. 4, Lucan 1. 353–5 'pietas patriique penates / quamquam caede feras mentes animosque tumentes / frangunt', Auson. *ecl.* 2. 20.

Jerome's recognition that it is *desiderium*, his own longing for the dead Nepotianus, that lies at the back of his uncontrollable grief (cf. 1. 1), adumbrates what he is to say at 7. 1 *desiderium . . . dolentes,* where the idea is conceptualized much more clearly.

o mors . . . dissocias!: cf. *epist.* 75. 1. 2 (quoted below at 2. 2–3 *adduxit . . . confossa sunt*), with Hos. 13: 15 (quoted in part in the same n., at (*a*)).

Although Jerome does not hold Nepotianus to be *mortuus* (cf. 2. 1), he now appears to be unable to shake off the idea of the cruelty of earthly *mors.* The feeling behind this sentence, however, is that its cruelty lies in its effect on those who survive: as in *credulam . . . affectus* above and in c. 7, the focus is not on the deceased but on the bereaved.

The personification of death here probably owes most to Hos. 13: 14 (quoted in the text at 2. 3), but it occurs in Scripture also at e.g. Job 28: 22, 1 Cor. 15: 55, Rev. 6: 8. In classical literature the same personification is widespread, going back at least as far as Hom. *Il.* 14. 231; see Nisbet–Hubbard (1970), 67, for further examples.

2. 2–3. adduxit . . . confossa sunt: a very difficult passage, designed to show that God has triumphed over death; the implication is, again, that as far as Nepotianus is concerned there is no need to grieve. Jerome is addressing *mors* throughout. It is illuminating to compare *epist.* 75. 1. 2–3 (AD 399), where Jerome uses much of the same material and expresses the same fundamental idea:

verum est illud super necessitate mortis prophetale vaticinium, quo fratres dividat et carissima inter se nomina crudelis et dura dissociet. sed habemus consolationem, quod domini sermone iugulatur et dicitur ad eam: ero mors tua, o mors, ero morsus tuus, inferne; et in consequentibus: adducet urentum ventum dominus de deserto ascendentem, qui siccabit omnes venas eius et desolabit fontem illius. exivit enim virga de radice Iesse et flos de virginali frutice pullulavit, qui loqueretur in Cantico canticorum: ego flos campi et lilium convallium. flos noster mortis interitus; ideoque et mortuus est, ut mors illius morte moreretur. quod autem de deserto dicitur adducendus, virginalis uterus demonstratur, qui absque coitu et semine viri deum nobis fudit infantem, qui calore spiritus sancti exsiccaret fontes libidinum et caneret in psalmo: in terra deserta et invia et sine aqua, sic in sancto apparui tibi.

In the following analysis the passage is divided into five sections, (*a*) to (*e*).

(*a*) *adduxit . . . fontem tuum*: cf. Hos. 13: 15 'adducet urentem ventum dominus de deserto ascendentem et siccabit venas eius et desolabit fontem eius', where 'eius' refers to the figure of Ephraim, representing all the tribes of northern Israel. Hos. 13 presents many problems of interpretation, but is concerned essentially with the firm stand taken by God against the wickedness of Ephraim. At 13: 15 Ephraim's destruction is foretold in these images of drought.

Jerome applies the verse to the destruction of death, which has already been mentioned at Hos. 13: 14 (for Jerome's misunderstanding of this verse see on (*d*)). At *epist.* 75. 1. 3 he clearly understands the *ventus* to be Christ, and the same interpretation occurs at *in Os.* 13. 14–15 (CCSL 76. 150–1 = PL 25. 939–40) (AD 406):

superest ut ventum urentem quem adducet dominus de deserto ascendentem, illum intellegamus, de quo et in Abacuc legimus: deus ab Austro veniet, et sanctus de monte Pharan . . . hunc itaque ventum urentem, qui siccet venas mortis, et fontes eius arefaciat, adducet dominus de deserto ascendentem; de deserto autem humani generis, in quo et diabolus quaerens requiem, invenire non potuit. sive desertum intellegimus sanctae Mariae uterum virginalem, quod absque semine humano nullo frutice pullulaverit; sed virga simplex atque purissima et unione fecunda ediderit eum florem qui dicit in Cantico canticorum: ego flos campi et lilium convallium. et pulchre tam in Esaia quam in praesenti loco, flos ascendens et ventus ascendens dicitur, quia de humilitate carnis ad excelsa conscendit, et nos secum duxit ad patrem, dicens in evangelio: cum exaltatus fuero, omnia traham ad me. ipse quasi radix ascendet de terra inhabitabili, et nequaquam mors in eum, sed ipse morti superveniet, neque enim mors in eo ullam suae potestatis viam repperit, et hoc est quod in Proverbi⟨i⟩s dicitur: impossibile est super petram serpentis invenire vestigia. et ipsa [*leg.* ipse] loquitur in evangelio: ecce veniet princeps mundi huius et inveniet in me nihil. iste siccabit venas mortis, et desolabit fontes eius. venae mortis et fontes et aculeus, peccata ab apostolo nominantur; quibus arefactis, mors quoque ipsa siccabitur.

That Jerome has the same idea in mind in the present passage seems certain, as will be shown.

At (*b*) *devorasti . . . salvaretur* the image is changed, and death

presented in the guise of the great fish which swallowed Jonah
(cf. Jonah 2: 1). This notion recurs at *in Ion.* 2. 1 (CCSL
76. 393 = PL 25. 1131), which also belongs to AD 396: 'et prae-
paravit dominus piscem grandem, ut deglutiret Ionam. LXX: et
praecepit dominus ceto magno, et devoravit Ionam. morti et
inferno praecepit dominus, ut prophetam suscipiat. quae avidis
faucibus [cf. (*e*)] praedam putans, quantum in devoratione
laetata est, tantum luxit in vomitu. tuncque completum est illud
quod legimus in Osee: ero mors tua, o mors: ero morsus tuus,
inferne [cf. (*d*)]'. Although Jonah appears to have succumbed to
death, he is released on praying to God (cf. Jonah 2: 2–11); death
is thus defeated. He subsequently preaches in Nineveh and the
people of the city repent (3: 4–5). For the quelling of the storm
cf. Jonah 1: 15; it is of no concern to Jerome that in the Biblical
account the storm ceases after Jonah has been thrown into the
sea but before he is swallowed by the fish. *mundi* suggests that
Jerome understands the storm allegorically, referring to the
trouble which arises out of the world's disregard for God, a
disregard which Jonah shares (cf. Jonah 1: 3), and which in-
directly causes his being cast into the sea; cf. *in Ion.* 1. 4 (CCSL
76. 384–5 = PL 25. 1124) 'dominus autem misit ventum magnum in mare, et facta est tempestas magna in mari et navis
periclitabatur conteri . . . potest fuga prophetae [sc. Ionae] et ad
hominis referri in communi personam, qui dei praecepta con-
temnens, recessit a facie eius, et se mundo tradidit, ubi postea
malorum tempestate, et totius mundi contra se saeviente naufragio, compulsus est sentire deum, et reverti ad eum quem
fugerat'. In this letter, however, Jonah's own sins, having no
place in the argument, are suppressed.

The story of Jonah, then, is seen as an indication that death is
not all-powerful. But there is more to the reference than this.
Jonah is a type of Christ; cf. e.g. *in Ion.* 2. 2–3 (CCSL
76. 394 = PL 25. 1131–2) 'si Ionas refertur ad dominum, et ex eo
quod tribus diebus ac noctibus in utero ceti fuit, passionem
indicat salvatoris, debet et oratio illius typus esse orationis
dominicae'. The parallel comes from the words of Jesus himself
at Matt. 12: 39–41 and Luke 11: 29–30, where he uses the Jonah
story as a symbol for his own death and resurrection, his descent
into hell being represented by Jonah's being swallowed by the
fish. At *epist.* 53. 8. 10 Jerome again refers to the parallel,
understanding Nineveh as a symbol for the Gentiles: 'Ionas,
columba pulcherrima, naufragio suo passionem domini praefi-
gurans mundum ad paenitentiam revocat et sub nomine Nineve
salutem gentibus nuntiat'; hence, perhaps, *Nineve nostra* here.

The *tempestas mundi* was quelled by Christ's passion; cf. *in Ion.*
1. 15 (CCSL 76. 392 = PL 25. 1130) 'consideremus ante passionem Christi, errores mundi, et diversorum dogmatum flatus
contrarios, et naviculam totumque humanum genus, id est
creaturam domini periclitantem, et post passionem eius tranquil⟨l⟩itatem fidei, et orbis pacem, et secura omnia, et conversionem ad deum, et videbimus quomodo post praecipitationem
Ionae steterit mare a furore suo'.

(*c*) *ille, ille . . . quaerentium eam* may at first glance appear still
to refer to Jonah (*fugitivus propheta, qui reliquit domum suam*),
and indeed at *in Ion.* 4. 3 (CCSL 76. 412 = PL 25. 1145–6) Jonah
is made to say 'dimisi domum meam, reliqui haereditatem
meam'. But in fact it is not so much Jonah as Jeremiah who is
meant; cf. Jeremiah 12: 7 'reliqui domum meam, dimisi hereditatem meam, dedi dilectam animam meam in manu inimicorum
eius'. The mental leap from one figure to the other will have
been quite easy. Again the point of the allusion is to express the
overcoming of death. Jeremiah 11 tells that a plot has been laid
against Jeremiah's life; in c. 12 Jeremiah prays to God to destroy
the wicked (12: 7 is part of the prayer), and God promises to do
so unless they repent. Death is overcome, presumably, by
Jeremiah's escape from the plotters and God's promise to crush
them.

Jeremiah, like Jonah, is later definitely viewed by Jerome as
a *persona* of Christ; cf. *in Ier.* 11. 18–20 (CCSL 74.
117 = PL 24. 756) (*c*. AD 414–16) 'omnium ecclesiarum iste consensus est, ut sub persona Hieremiae a Christo haec dici intellegant', 12. 7–8 (CCSL 74. 123 = PL 24. 760) 'qui in evangelio
locutus est: surgite, abeamus hinc, et iterum: relinquetur vobis
domus vestra deserta, hic etiam in propheta eadem comminatur
et, quod facturus est, fecisse se dicit'. At *in Ier.* 12. 7–8 the
hereditas of Jeremiah is also taken as a symbol of the *hereditas* of
Christ. Less concretely, but hardly less significantly, a connection is also established in 396 by the application to Christ of part
of Jeremiah 12: 7 (in paraphrase); cf. *in Ion.* 1. 3 (CCSL
76. 382 = PL 25. 1122) 'de domino autem et salvatore nostro
possumus dicere, quod dimiserit domum et patriam suam'. In
the light of the rest of the present passage the parallel must hold
good here too. The interpretation may owe something to Origen,
as often; cf. the latter's *hom. in Ier.* 10. 7 (translated by Jerome in
381), on Jeremiah 12: 7, with Duval (1985), 341.

quaerentium eam is not derived from Jeremiah 12: 7, where
VL, Vulgate, and the quotation of the verse at Jer. *in Ier.* ad loc.

all have 'inimicorum eius'. It comes from conflation with other
passages in Jeremiah, e.g. 19: 7, 21: 7, 22: 25, 34: 20.

At (*d*) *qui per Osee . . . vivimus* Jerome returns to Hosea, and
states the overthrow of death with absolute clarity. In the OT
the speaker of *ero mors . . . inferne* (Hos. 13: 14; text as Vulg.) is
dominus deus tuus (13: 4). To Jerome this is none other than
Christ; cf. *in Os.* 13. 14–15 (CCSL 76. 148 = PL 25. 937) 'libera-
vit autem omnes dominus, et redemit in passione crucis et
effusione sanguinis sui, quando anima eius descendit in infernum, et caro eius non vidit corruptionem; et ad ipsam mortem
atque infernum locutus est: ero mors tua, o mors. idcirco enim
mortuus sum, ut tu mea morte moriaris. ero morsus tuus,
inferne, qui omnes tuis faucibus devorabas'. The allusion to
Christ in *illius morte tu mortua es, illius morte nos vivimus* is in any
case quite apparent. The florilegium *Γ* makes it explicit: *de morte
xp̄i mors mortua est o mors xp̄i morte nos vivimus.*

It is noteworthy that *ero mors . . . inferne*, which represents
Jerome's translation, arises from a misunderstanding of the
Hebrew text. The passage is indeed difficult, and LXX, Symmachus, and Aquila all give slightly different versions (see Jer. *in
Os.* ad loc.). The nature of the problem is fully explained by
W. R. Harper, *A Critical and Exegetical Commentary on Amos
and Hosea* (Edinburgh, 1905), 404–5. Briefly, to make sense of
the passage in its context, it is necessary to take the preceding
clauses, 'de manu mortis liberabo eos, de morte redimam eos', as
questions, to which the implied answer is in the negative; and
then to translate what follows not by *ero mors . . . inferne* but
rather, keeping more closely to LXX, by something like 'ubi est
causa tua, mors? ubi est aculeus tuus, inferne?' (Jerome's translation from LXX in his commentary), meaning not 'Your
judgement has been done away with, death', as Paul understands
the words at 1 Cor. 15: 55, but 'Come with your judgement,
death'. Only thus may the sense of Hos. 13 be retained: God
resolute against those who have spurned him.

(*e*) *devorasti . . . confossa sunt* brings the section to a triumphant, climactic end: death is ripped apart. The connection
between Jonah and Christ is finally made clear. Death is still
envisaged in terms of the great fish (cf. *faucibus, praedam,
interiora tua, adunco dente*; and *devorasti*, repeated from 2. 2),
but its prey is now Christ, God become man (*adsumpti corporis;
adsumere* is frequently found with *corpus, caro*, and the like, in
reference to the incarnation of Christ (cf. *TLL* 2. 933–4)).
devorata es follows easily after *morsus*; and cf. Tert. *resurr.*

54. 4–5 'ceterum mors merito in interitum devoratur, quia et ipsa in hoc devorat. devoravit, inquit, mors invalescendo, et ideo devorata est in contentionem. ubi est, mors, aculeus tuus? ubi est, mors, contentio tua? proinde et vita, mortis scilicet aemula, per contentionem devorabit in salutem quod per contentionem [tuam] devoraverat mors in interitum'. For the image of the hook cf. *in Ion.* 1. 12 (CCSL 76. 390 = PL 25. 1129) 'me cupit devorare mors, ut vos pariter occidat, et non intellegit quia velut in hamo escam capit, ut mea morte moriatur', with Duval (1985), 359.

It is evident, then, that the figure of Christ underlies the whole passage, and that Jonah and Jeremiah are, to Jerome's mind, symbolic *personae* of him. Christ's work in overcoming death was adumbrated long before it was finally achieved.

For further discussion of the passage, particularly its relation to the *Commentary on Jonah*, see Y.-M. Duval, *Le Livre de Jonas dans la littérature chrétienne grecque et latine: sources et influence du Commentaire sur Jonas de saint Jérôme* (2 vols., Paris, 1973), 1. 283–6. On typology generally see the bibliography in *ODCC* s.v. 'Types'.

2. 2. deserto: the singular *desertum* is found only from the time of Tertullian and almost exclusively in Biblical and ecclesiastical Latin, apparently reflecting LXX ἔρημος; cf. *TLL* 5. 1. 686–8.

desolavit fontem tuum: for *desolare* used with words like *fons* cf. also Isa. 11: 15 'desolabit dominus linguam maris Aegypti', 19: 5 'fluvius desolabitur atque siccabitur'.

2. 3. iugulavit: the verb is quite natural, given the personification of *mors*, and *iugulare* is occasionally used with abstracts in any case; cf. e.g. Cic. *Phil.* 13. 38 'causa . . . iugulata', Mart. 1. 106. 9 'durum iugules mero dolorem', Jer. *epist.* 75. 1. 2 (quoted at 2. 2–3 *adduxit . . . confossa sunt*), 143. 1. 2 'heresis Caelestina iugulata est'.

o mors . . . inferne: at *in Os.* 13. 14–15 (CCSL 76. 149 = PL 25. 938) Jerome carefully distinguishes between *mors* and *infernus*: 'inter mortem autem et inferos, hoc interest: mors est quo anima separatur a corpore; infernus, locus in quo animae recluduntur, sive in refrigerio, sive in poenis, pro qualitate meritorum'. By *inferne* here Jerome understands 'hell' in the broad sense, referring to the time before Christ opened the gates of heaven; see on 3. 2 *si Abraham . . . regno?*.

avidis faucibus: for the *fauces* of death, envisaged as a beast, cf. e.g. Arnob. *nat.* 2. 78 'mortis reperiamur in faucibus', Claud. *paneg. IV cons. Hon.* 58 'leti rapuit de faucibus urbes'; and of other personified abstractions, e.g. Cic. *Catil.* 3. 1 'urbem . . . paene ex faucibus fati ereptam', *Arch.* 21 'belli ore ac faucibus'.

interiora: = *viscera*; cf. e.g. Sen. *nat.* 3. 1. 3, Plin. *nat.* 20. 101, Aug. *serm.* 277. 8. 8 'viscera nostra, interiora nostra, quae dicuntur intestina'.

c. 3. By Christ's death and resurrection death itself was overcome. In consequence the kingdom of heaven was opened to all those who had followed God in time past and to all believing Christians: an obvious consolation to Heliodorus as he grieved for his nephew.

With this chapter it is instructive to compare *epist.* 39. 4, which uses much of the same material, but is aimed more directly at showing that the bereaved has no reason to grieve. Prominent among other writers who use the prospect of resurrection as a τόπος of consolation is Theodoret; cf. Gregg, 207–8, who points out that only one of Theodoret's consolatory letters omits to employ the τόπος, and that no less than half of his *epist.* 47 (43) (Codex Patmensis; Sources chrétiennes, 40) is devoted to the resurrection theme.

3. 1. salvator: a Christian neologism, = σωτήρ. For full discussion of its origins and usage see C. Mohrmann, 'Les Emprunts grecs dans la latinité chrétienne', *VChr* 4 (1950), 193–211, at 201–5 (= Mohrmann, *Études*, 3. 127–45, at 135–9).

creatura: also a Christian formulation, a frequent Biblical equivalent to κτίσις or κτίσμα. It may refer either to the act of creation (cf. e.g. Rom. 1: 20, Jer. *epist.* 123. 11. 1), or to what is created, as here and at e.g. Rom. 1: 25, Jer. *epist.* 64. 18. 10. See *TLL* 4. 1115–17.

adversarium: Jerome is referring to *mors*, of course, but there may be a loose mental connection with Satan, to whom the word *adversarius* is often specifically applied; cf. e.g. Tert. *anim.* 35. 3 'in diabolum transfertur adversarii mentio' (i.e. 'the word "adversary"'), Jer. *in Eph.* 4. 27 (PL 26. 511) 'diabolus Graecum verbum est, quod Latine dicitur criminator: lingua vero Hebraea Satan appellatur, id est, adversarius, sive contrarius'.

periret: a clever ambiguity; not only 'die' in the natural sense, but also 'die' in the sense of 'enter *infernus*' (cf. 3. 2), thus not gaining eternal life.

regnavit . . . praevaricationis Adam: Rom. 5: 14 (Vulg.: 'sed regnavit mors ab Adam usque ad Mosen etiam in eos qui non peccaverunt in similitudinem praevaricationis Adae'). The passage is cited with full regard to its Pauline context. Paul is dealing with the reconciliation of man to God through Christ: through Adam's sin death held sway over all men, but through Christ came eternal life. Paul's point about Moses is not that with the coming of the Mosaic Law death ceased to reign, but that it held sway even before the Law, when strictly there could

be no sin as there was no set standard to sin against, because of
the transmitted effect of Adam's sin in violating an express
command of God. Quoting the verse here enables Jerome to
introduce easily Abraham, Isaac, and Jacob, who preceded
Moses, and to say that until Christ opened heaven even these
great patriarchs were trapped in *infernus* (3. 2); how great then
was the work of Christ in overcoming death.

   praevaricationis: originally a technical term, meaning collu-
sion between advocates in legal cases; cf. e.g. Cic. *Cael.* 24 'at
praevaricatione est Asicius liberatus'. In Christian Latin, however, it is used to denote a transgression or breach of law in a
Christian sense, 'sin'; cf. e.g. Rom. 4: 15, Heb. 9: 15, Jer. *epist.*
121. 8. 15. The verb *praevaricari* occurs in the sense of 'to sin' as
early as Tert. *fug.* 7. The terms may be stronger than *peccatio,
peccare*, etc.; cf. H. Goelzer, *Étude lexicographique et grammati-
cale de la latinité de saint Jérôme* (Paris, 1884), 237.

3. 2. si Abraham . . . regno?: in pagan Latin *infernus* was
frequently used as an adjective referring to the underworld.
Christian writers took over the word and fitted it into their own
theology. Often it means the place of punishment for the wicked
after death (cf. e.g. *epist.* 96. 12. 1 (tr. from Theophilus) 'quis
enim infernus haec mala suscipere potest, qui tartarus de rebus
istius modi cogitare?'), but it may also refer to the abode of all
the dead, of which the place of punishment is a part (cf. e.g. Aug.
in psalm. 85. 18). Augustine indicates that there was a controversy over what the word ought to mean; cf. *quaest. hept.*
1. 126 'solet esse magna quaestio, quomodo intellegatur infernus: utrum illuc mali tantum an etiam boni mortui descendere
soleant'.

   In terms of normal Christian eschatology, at least from the
fourth century, *infernus* in its broader sense could be used only
of the time before Christ harrowed Hades (Ἅιδης, = *infernus*; cf.
Ambr. *bon. mort.* 10. 45) and brought out the souls of all the
faithful. (In the second and third centuries a different, though
not certainly dominant, eschatology is apparent, according to
which all departed souls, with a few exceptions—martyrs, for
example—remained in Hades until the General Resurrection; on
this see A. Stuiber, *Refrigerium interim: die Vorstellungen vom
Zwischenzustand und die frühchristliche Grabeskunst* (Theopha-
neia: Beiträge zur Religions- und Kirchengeschichte des Altertums, 11; Bonn, 1957), with the review of J. M. C. Toynbee,
JThS 9 (1958), 141–9.) It is to this time that Jerome here refers.
The sense of the chapter as a whole is that until the resurrection
of Christ the souls of all the dead were in *infernus*, which
admitted of degrees of comfort and discomfort (cf. on *quod si . . .*

caelorum? below). At the resurrection the gates of heaven were opened, and the souls of the dead went either to heaven or to hell, as everyone subsequently did directly they died (cf. 7. 1: Nepotianus is *cum Christo*). In effect there is both a 'Virgilian' and a Christian eschatology here. Jerome identifies *regnum caelorum* and *paradisus* (cf. 3. 3), though a distinction came to be drawn between them: after the harrowing of hell, the souls of the blessed went to paradise and would only later, after the Last Judgement, when all the souls in purgatory had been purged, go to heaven. In Jerome's time, however, the doctrine of purgatory had not been fully developed, and Jerome here implies nothing about the Last Judgement.

The same idea occurs elsewhere in Jerome, with much of the same Biblical material employed; cf. *epist.* 129. 2. 1, *in Eccl.* 3. 18–21 (CCSL 72. 281 = PL 23. 1041) 'hoc autem dicit . . . quod ante adventum Christi omnia ad inferos pariter ducerentur. unde et Iacob ad inferos descensurum se dicit. et Iob pios et impios in inferno queritur retentari. et evangelium, chasmate interposito, apud inferos et Abraham cum Lazaro et divitem in suppliciis esse testatur. et revera, antequam flammeam illam rotam, et igneam romphaeam, et paradisi fores Christus cum latrone reseraret, clausa erant caelestia et spiritum pecoris hominisque aequalis vilitas coarctabat', and, in consolation, *epist.* 39. 4. 1–2 'quomodo me lugere prohibes, cum et Iacob Ioseph in sacco fleverit. . . ? perfacilis ad ista responsio est: luxisse Iacob filium, quem putabat occisum, ad quem et ipse erat ad infernum descensurus dicens: descendam ad filium meum lugens in infernum, quia necdum paradisi ianuam Christus effregerat, necdum flammeam illam romphaeam et vertiginem praesidentium cherubin sanguis eius extinxerat—unde et Abraham, licet in loco refrigerii, tamen apud inferos cum Lazaro scribitur'. Cf. also *in Os.* 13. 14–15 (quoted at 2. 2–3 *adduxit . . . confossa sunt* (*d*)), where *infernus* is clearly the abode of the souls of all the dead; and, for possible influence on Jerome, Orig. *hom. in 1 Sam.* 28 : 3–25, esp. c. 9: πρὸ τῆς τοῦ κυρίου μου Ἰησοῦ Χριστοῦ ἐπιδημίας ἀδύνατον ἦν τινα παρελθεῖν ὅπου τὸ ξύλον τῆς ζωῆς . . . διὰ τῆς φλογίνης ῥομφαίας Σαμουὴλ οὐκ ἠδύνατο διελθεῖν, οὐκ Ἀβραάμ. διὰ τοῦτο καὶ Ἀβραὰμ βλέπεται ὑπὸ τοῦ κολαζομένου . . . περιέμενον οὖν τὴν τοῦ κυρίου μου Ἰησοῦ Χριστοῦ ἐπιδημίαν καὶ πατριάρχαι καὶ προφῆται καὶ πάντες ἵν' οὗτος τὴν ὁδὸν ἀνοίξῃ (for Jerome's attitude to Origen see Introduction, pp. 6–7).

On Jerome's eschatology in general see the useful study of J. P. O'Connell, *The Eschatology of Saint Jerome* (Mundelein, Ill., 1948).

dixerunt . . . ad unum: cf. Ps. 13: 1, 3 (LXX) 'dixit insipiens in corde suo: non est deus. corrupti sunt et abominabiles facti sunt in studiis suis . . . omnes declinaverunt, simul inutiles facti sunt; non est qui faciat bonum, non est usque ad unum', (Hebr.) 'dixit stultus in corde suo: non est deus. corrupti sunt et abominabiles facti sunt studiose . . . omnes recesserunt, simul conglutinati sunt; non est qui faciat bonum, non est usque ad unum'. The fact that the quotations more closely resemble the text of the Gallican (LXX) Psalter than that of the version from the Hebrew, which had been completed by this time (see Introduction, p. 10), probably indicates no more than that Jerome was quoting from memory.

quod si . . . caelorum?: for the story of Lazarus and the rich man see Luke 16: 19–31. On this passage Jerome wrote a homily (CCSL 78. 507–16) in which he again makes the point that until the resurrection of Christ no one was in paradise (CCSL 78. 515. 269–72). The souls of the dead were all in *infernus*, but this was divided between a place of refreshment and comfort, the nearest thing to paradise (cf. 510. 92–6 'paradisus pauperis, sinus erat Abrahae. Abraham a longe, et Lazarum in sinu eius. dicat mihi aliquis: in inferno est paradisus? ego hoc dico, quia sinus Abrahae paradisi veritas ⟨non⟩ est: sed et sancti sinum paradisum fateor'), and a place of torment, giving indications of the ultimate torment which would be suffered after the Judgement (cf. 514. 247–515. 268). But the *locus refrigerii*, Jerome says here, is nothing in comparison with heaven itself.

The allusion to the story of Lazarus and the rich man suggests an answer to the question posed immediately above: if even those who had done no sin were held liable for Adam's wrongdoing, and so entered *infernus*, what is one to believe of the wicked? Answer: that they entered a part of *infernus* that was far worse.

quod si: 'even if'; cf. Cic. *ad Q. fr.* 1. 1. 27 'quod si te sors Afris aut Hispanis aut Gallis praefecisset, immanibus ac barbaris nationibus, tamen esset humanitatis tuae consulere eorum commodis et utilitati salutique servire'.

locoque refrigerii: for *refrigerium* and its complexity of meaning see C. Mohrmann, 'Locus refrigerii', in B. Botte and C. Mohrmann, *L'Ordinaire de la messe* (Paris and Louvain, 1953), 123–32 (= Mohrmann, *Études*, 2. 81–91). In the context of the rich man, Lazarus, and Abraham, the expression is probably derived from Luke 16: 24 'mitte Lazarum . . . ut refrigeret linguam meam'.

3. 3. ante . . . paradiso: for the *latro* cf. Luke 23: 39–43. Jerome brings the redeeming work of Christ into the sharpest possible focus. Before his resurrection even Abraham was in *infernus*, and the implied answer to the question above, *si Abraham . . . regno?*, is of course 'no one'. But at his resurrection Christ opened heaven even to a *latro*. The contrast between Abraham and the robber, between the time before and the time after, is made greater by the fact that Jerome does not mention the robber's repentance, a point he stresses in *hom. in Luc. 16: 19–31* (CCSL 78. 515. 274 ff., esp. 275–6 'magnitudo enim fidei meruit magnitudinem praemiorum').

inferos: *inferi* = the inhabitants of the *infernus locus*, in either the Christian or the pagan sense (see on 3. 2 *si Abraham . . . regno?*); and sometimes, by metonymy, = the *infernus locus* itself (cf. e.g. [Sen.] *Herc. O.* 15, Ambr. *in psalm.* 40. 30 'caelum aperuit, inferos clausit').

paradiso: a borrowing from Greek, derived ultimately from Persian. The fundamental meaning is 'fruit-garden'; cf. e.g. Gell. 2. 20. 4 'vivaria autem quae nunc vulgus dicit . . . παραδείσους Graeci appellant', Aug. *serm.* 343. 1 'conscripta sunt verba eius, quae habuit in paradiso; hoc est in viridario suo'. Among Christians it meant particularly the Garden of Eden (cf. e.g. Gen. 2–3 *passim*, Tert. *adv. Iud.* 2. 11, Jer. *epist.* 52. 5. 4), and was often used, as here, for heaven, the place of the faithful after death. Paul's words at 2 Cor. 12: 2–4 gave rise to some dispute whether *paradisus* and *caelum* should or should not be identified; cf. esp. Aug. *gen. ad. litt.* 12. 1. Epiphanius of Salamis explicitly differentiates between them at Jer. *epist.* 51. 5. 7 (tr. from Epiphanius); but Jerome here clearly identifies the two (see on 3. 2 *si Abraham . . . regno?*).

et idcirco . . . Hierusalem: cf. Matt. 27: 50–3 'Iesus autem iterum clamans voce magna emisit spiritum . . . et monumenta aperta sunt, et multa corpora sanctorum qui dormierant surrexerunt, et exeuntes de monumentis post resurrectionem eius venerunt in sanctam civitatem et apparuerunt multis'. Matthew is clearly talking about an earthly resurrection, the purpose of which seems to have been to give a sign that Jesus had actually been resurrected. At *epist.* 46. 7. 6 Paula and Eustochium (in fact probably Jerome himself; see Introduction, p. 13 n. 51) strongly assert that this resurrection must have been terrestrial: 'nec statim Hierosolyma caelestis, ut plerique ridicule arbitrantur, in hoc intellegitur, cum signum nullum esse potuerit apud homines domini resurgentis, si corpora sanctorum in caelesti Hierusalem visa sunt'. Here, however, Jerome introduces *caelesti*, thus giving a different sense to Matthew's account: the *dormientium corpora* must refer to those in *infernus* who were released upon Christ's resurrection (for *dormientium* see on 2. 1 *iungam . . .*

suscitatus est). Significantly, at *in Matt.* 27. 53 (CCSL
77. 276 = PL 26. 213) Jerome expresses uncertainty whether the
earthly or the heavenly Jerusalem should be understood: 'sanctam
autem civitatem in qua visi sunt resurgentes aut Hierusalem
caelestem intellegamus aut hanc terrenam quae ante sancta
fuerit'. The present interpretation of Matthew's words is found
also at *epist.* 120. 8. 8 'monumenta quoque . . . ideo sunt aperta,
ut egrederentur de his, qui prius in fidelitate mortui erant, et
cum resurgente Christo atque vivente viverent et ingrederentur
caelestem Hierusalem et haberent municipatum nequaquam in
terra, sed in caelo [cf. 3. 4], morientesque cum terreno Adam
resurgerent cum Adam caelesti'. For a similar application to the
heavenly Jerusalem of a Biblical detail about the earthly Jerusalem cf. *epist.* 22. 41. 3 'tunc vere super asinam dominus ascendet
et caelestem ingredietur Hierusalem'.

corpora, being taken directly from the gospel account, implies
nothing about Jerome's view of the substance of persons in
infernus or in heaven. In fact he shared the orthodox view of his
time, that in heaven people had some kind of physical body; cf.
e.g. *epist.* 75. 2. 4, 84. 5. 1, *c. Ioh.* 23–36 (PL 23. 373–89).

eloquium: 'saying', in this sense found almost exclusively
among Christian writers; the only certain non-Christian case is
[Cic.] *in Sall.* 16 (cf. *TLL* 5. 2. 415), though for *eloquium* = 'ut-
terance' generally cf. also Mela 3. 91, Juv. 7. 19.

surge . . . Christus: Eph. 5: 14 (Vulg.: 'surge, qui dormis, et
exsurge a mortuis, et inluminabit tibi Christus'). In quoting the
verse elsewhere Jerome (who was not responsible for the Vulgate
text of Ephesians; see Introduction, p. 9) sometimes writes
'exsurge' where he writes *elevare* here (cf. e.g. *epist.* 119. 10. 6,
in Eph. 5. 14 (PL 26. 525–6), *in Ier.* 29 (36). 8–9 (CCSL
74. 279 = PL 24. 859)), sometimes 'elevare' (cf. e.g. *in Ier.* 1. 17A
(CCSL 74. 10 = PL 24. 686), 31 (38). 25–6 (CCSL 74. 316 = PL
24. 882), *in Abd.* 1 (CCSL 76. 356 = PL 25. 1102)). 'exsurge' is
more usual in the Old Latin versions; cf. the testimonia in VL
Beuron ad loc. The Greek is ἀνάστα ἐκ τῶν νεκρῶν. The preference for *elevare* in this and other instances, if there is any good
reason for it at all, may be attributable to desire for stylistic
variety after *surge* (so at *in Ier.* 29 (36). 8–9 Jerome writes
'elevare . . . exsurge'); otherwise it may reflect a wish to
emphasize Christ's part in the action: 'be raised up' rather than
'rise'.

In applying these words to those released from *infernus* and
admitted to heaven at Christ's resurrection Jerome employs
them differently from the author of Ephesians, who uses them in

reference to the living. But Jerome knew the passage to be a quotation from an unknown document—probably a liturgical formula or hymn (cf. T. K. Abbott, *A Critical and Exegetical Commentary on the Epistles to the Ephesians and to the Colossians* (Edinburgh, 1897), 158); Jerome himself held it to be some liturgical work (cf. *in Eph.* 5. 14 (PL 26. 525))—and he will have felt no difficulty in investing it with this new meaning.

Iohannes . . . adpropinquavit enim regnum caelorum: cf. Matt. 3: 1–2 'in diebus autem illis venit Iohannes Baptista praedicans in deserto Iudaeae et dicens: paenitentiam agite; adpropinquavit enim regnum caelorum'. That Jerome should call to mind John's prophecy at this point is natural enough; but the sentence is rather abruptly introduced, and its place in the context is settled only at 3. 4 *a diebus . . . illud*, where see n.

(*h)eremus* (= ἔρημος) first appears in Latin with Tertullian (e.g. *idol.* 5. 3, *adv. Marc.* 5. 3. 8); cf. *TLL* 5. 2. 747–8.

3. 4. a diebus . . . illud: cf. Matt. 11: 12 'a diebus autem Iohannis Baptistae usque nunc regnum caelorum vim patitur et violenti rapiunt [*al.* diripiunt; so also Jer. *in Matt.* 11. 12 (CCSL 77. 80 = PL 26. 72)] illud'. The Matthew passage is difficult, not least because it is not clear whether it is an editorial comment by Matthew himself or a continuation of Jesus' words in vv. 7–11. A further problem is whether the violence mentioned is to be understood as violence directed against the kingdom of heaven in the persons of John the Baptist and other Christian preachers, or as that of the resolute, who alone can press into the kingdom. In the present case Jerome clearly understands it in the latter sense, as he does elsewhere; cf. *in Matt.* 11. 12 (CCSL 77. 80 = PL 26. 72) 'grandis est enim violentia in terra nos esse generatos et caelorum sedem quaerere possidere per virtutem quod non tenuimus per naturam', *epist.* 22. 40. 3 'regnum caelorum vim patitur et violenti diripiunt illud. nisi vim feceris, caelorum regna non capies'. From the time of John heaven was no longer inaccessible to men, but could be stormed by the righteous: not that Jerome believed that anyone actually did burst into heaven until after Christ's resurrection; he will have held that the assault was only begun in John's time.

The force of *enim*, if it has not simply slipped into the text by repetition after *adpropinquavit enim* above (it is omitted by *D Ψ* and the original hand of *K*), is somewhat obscure. *a diebus . . . illud* cannot be taken as explaining the previous sentence. Logically it should be explained by it: it was from the time of John that the kingdom of heaven suffered violence, because John was the first to preach repentance and the imminent coming of the kingdom. In his commentary ad loc. Jerome indeed sets out this explanation. Equally, *enim* here cannot bear an adversative sense, = *autem*, a function it gradually develops in late-antique and early medieval Latin (cf. Löfstedt (1911), 34) (and it is not likely that Jerome is citing the verse without properly marrying it into his own context, and substituting the one particle for the other). *enim* must, I think, be understood either as continuing the thought of the previous sentence ('and indeed'), binding it more tightly into the context of resurrection, or as explaining why Jerome has introduced the previous sentence, i.e. 'I have introduced this comment about John preaching the coming of the kingdom in this connection because it was from that time on that the kingdom was assaulted and men were enabled to enter it by storm'.

Jerome's thoughts are clearly no longer focused on the souls of the righteous which are in *infernus*; he is, rather, looking at the opening of heaven from the point of view of Christians on earth.

flammea . . . sanguine: cf. Gen. 3: 24, where, after the expulsion of Adam from Eden, the cherubim and a flaming sword are stationed on guard before paradise. There is no mention of gates; but it seems an easy addition to the picture here, and there may have been some influence on Jerome's thought from Gen. 28: 17, where Jacob, after his dream, describes Bethel as the gate of heaven, or perhaps from the idea of the gates of hell (cf. e.g. Isa. 38: 10, Matt. 16: 18; for the corresponding image in classical thought, Nisbet–Hubbard (1970), 288). Cf. also *epist.* 108. 9. 3 'diligit dominus portas Sion . . . portas, quibus infernus non praevalet, per quas credentium ad Christum ingreditur multitudo'. *restincta* refers properly to the *flammea rumphea*, *reserata* to the gates of heaven; grammatically, however, *reserata* agrees with *cherubin*. Jerome has mentally reconstructed *praesidentia foribus cherubin* with *fores* as the subject, but keeps *reserata* neuter to preserve grammatical harmony.

Jerome use the same images, with minor changes, such as breaking down rather than unlocking the gate, at *epist.* 39. 4. 2 (quoted at 3. 2 *si Abraham . . . regno?*).

rumphea: = ῥομφαία; spelled variously in Latin. It denotes some kind of weapon, sometimes apparently a lance or spear (cf. e.g. Liv. 31. 39. 11), more often a sword (cf. e.g. Isid. *orig.* 18. 6. 3), and seems to be associated particularly with the Thracians (cf. Liv. 31. 39. 11, Plut. *Aem.* 18. 5, Gell. 10. 25. 4). It is found a number of times in LXX and Greek NT; cf. e.g. 1 Sam. 17: 51, Luke 2: 35, where it is rendered in the Vulgate by *gladius*.

In its Latin form it appears in the Vulgate only in Ecclus. and (once) Rev., which do not represent Jerome's work (see Introduction, pp. 8–9). Its presence here, from LXX Gen. 3: 24 ῥομφαίαν (Vulg.: 'gladium') may be explained by the fact that Jerome had not yet begun his revision of the Latin Octateuch on the basis of the Hebrew (see Introduction, p. 10); the word will have stuck in his mind from the LXX or an Old Latin text.

praesidentia . . . cherubin: *cherub* is normally masculine, but *TLL*, Onomasticon, 2. 390, notes a few instances where it is found in the neuter; cf. e.g. Tert. *adv. Marc.* 2. 22. 1. Some years later Jerome certainly held it to be masculine; cf. *in Ezech.* 9. 2–3 (CCSL 75. 105 = PL 25. 87) (AD 410–14) 'quamquam plerique τὰ χερουβεὶμ neutrali genere numeroque plurali dici putent, nos scire debemus singulari numero esse cherub, generis masculini, et plurali eiusdem generis cherubim, non quo sexus in ministris dei sit, sed quo unumquodque iuxta linguae suae proprietatem diversis appelletur generibus', 28. 11–19 (CCSL 75. 395 = PL 25. 272).

hoc: i.e. entry into heaven.

omnes . . . in caelo: this clause draws on three passages of Scripture: 2 Cor. 10: 3, where a distinction is drawn between *in carne* and *secundum carnem*; Rom. 8: 12–13 'debitores sumus non carni, ut secundum carnem vivamus; si enim secundum carnem vixeritis, moriemini; si autem spiritu facta carnis mortificatis, vivetis'; and Phil. 3: 20 'nostra autem conversatio [πολίτευμα; Jerome's *municipatus*] in caelis est'. The combination of these ideas found here seems entirely natural.

municipatus is a rare word. *TLL*, 8. 1648, records one case where it means 'township'. Normally it means 'the condition of being a citizen', and, except at *CIL* 3. 268, always in relation to heaven (from Phil. 3: 20); cf. e.g. Tert. *adv. Marc.* 3. 24, 5. 20, Jer. *epist.* 14. 3. 1, 58. 2. 3, *in Ier.* 17. 12–13 (CCSL 74. 168 = PL 24. 790). Jerome does not, however, use it consistently when citing or alluding to Phil. 3: 20 (cf. the testimonia in VL Beuron ad loc.), and it seems probable that he was equally familiar with *municipatus* and *conversatio* in the Latin text.

hic . . . intra vos est: the quotation *regnum . . . est* is from Luke 17: 21 (text as Vulg.). The words are addressed by Jesus to the Pharisees. In the Greek, the meaning of ἐντὸς ὑμῶν, here rendered by *intra vos*, is not clear. The most obvious meaning is 'within you', i.e. 'within your hearts', but this does not seem appropriate to the Pharisees; 'among you', i.e. in the persons of Jesus and the disciples, is a possibility; and Cyr. Alex. *in Luc.* 17. 20–1 suggests 'within your grasp'. Now although *intra* was sometimes confused with *inter* (cf. *TLL* 7. 2. 34. 43 ff., s.v. *intra*), *intra vos* ought naturally to mean 'within you'; and this is the sense required in the present context. Jerome is not interested here in the problem of how Jesus could have made such a statement to the Pharisees; but if it was applicable to them it must, by extension, have been applicable to all good Christians, and thus quite appropriate here.

c. 4. A further consequence of Christ's resurrection is that knowledge of God has spread throughout the whole terrestrial world. There is some exaggeration here, of course; but Jerome creates a mood of triumph and exhilaration which may have been of some help to Heliodorus in his grief. It is, however, only an apparent consolation. Jerome has glided from giving cogent reasons why there is no need to lament Nepotianus' death (death itself is overcome, and faithful Christians enter heaven) into something very much more general, which really has nothing to do with Nepotianus at all.

4. 1. notus . . . nomen eius: cf. Ps. 75: 2 (Vulg.: (LXX) 'notus in Iudaea deus, in Israhel magnum nomen eius', (Hebr.) 'cognoscetur [*al.* cognoscitur] in Iudaea deus, in Israhel magnum nomen eius'). If Jerome was consciously quoting from the LXX version here, when his translation from the Hebrew was complete (see Introduction, p. 10), it may have been to avoid the awkwardness of what he took to be a future tense in the Hebrew; but he is probably quoting from memory, with no thought of the textual difficulty. The psalm is concerned with the victorious power of God, but Jerome is not interested in the context, only in this particular verse, which enables him, with the insertion of *tantum*, to compare the extent of knowledge about God before and after Christ's resurrection. The limitation of the field of this knowledge to Judah and Israel, though not implied in the psalm, is natural for Jerome, who will have believed that the OT gave a full account of God's relations with man before the coming of Christ.

The same contrast is drawn elsewhere, in the same terms; cf. *epist.* 58. 3. 2 'postquam siccato Iudaeae vellere universus orbis caelesti rore perfusus est et multi de oriente et de occidente venientes recubuerunt in sinu Abraham, desiit notus esse tantum in Iudaea deus et in Israhel magnum nomen eius, sed in omnem terram exiit sonus apostolorum et in fines orbis terrae verba eorum', *tract. in psalm.* 75. 2 (CCSL 78. 49) 'antequam inluminaret crux mundum, antequam videretur dominus in terra, notus erat in Iudaea deus, in Israhel autem magnum nomen eius: quando autem venit salvator, in omnem terram exivit sonus eius, et in fines orbis terrae verba eius'.

ipsi . . . trahebantur: see nn. on 3. 1–3.

totius . . . oceani: Jerome describes the extent of the world by looking at it first in an east–west, and then in a north–south, direction.

In ancient writers India, and in particular the Ganges, was often regarded as the eastern boundary of the world, or at least of 'pars nostra terrarum', while the western boundary was generally held to be Spain, especially Cadiz and the Pillars of Hercules; cf. e.g. Plin. *nat.* 2. 242 'pars nostra terrarum . . . ambienti, ut dictum est, oceano velut innatans longissime ab ortu ad occasum patet, hoc est ab India ad Herculis columnas Gadibus sacratas', Sen. *nat.* 1 pref. 13, Juv. 10. 1–2 with the notes of J. E. B. Mayor, *Thirteen Satires of Juvenal* (2 vols., London, 1888), 2. 65, and nearer Jerome's own time, Ambr. *Abr.* 2. 7. 40 'ab Indiae quoque litoribus usque ad Herculis ut aiunt columnas', Sidon. *carm.* 5. 286–7. For Cadiz see also Otto, *Nachträge*, 167, Nisbet–Hubbard (1978), 96. On the western (or north-western) side, however, the distance of Britain from the centre of the Roman world also became a standard topic; cf. e.g. Catull. 29. 4 'ultima Britannia', Hor. *carm.* 1. 35. 29–30, Claud. *paneg. Manl. Theod.* 51. Heges. 2. 9. 1 refers to Britain as 'extra orbem posita'. Here Jerome ignores the Spain-tradition and, like Catull. 11. 1–12, puts Britain with India at the ends of the earth.

For ancient notions of the geography of India see A. Dihle, 'The Conception of India in Hellenistic and Roman Literature', *PCPhS* 10 (1964), 15–23, who points out that among Christian writers part of India was conceived of as bordering on Ethiopia; in this connection cf. Jer. *epist.* 53. 5. 2 'de Aethiopia, id est de extremis mundi finibus, venit', though it is possible that Jerome is thinking here not of the far east but of the far south. (Confusion between India and Ethiopia, or Indians and Ethiopians, is also evident in Virgil and other pagan authors; cf. J. Y. Nadeau, 'Ethiopians', *CQ* 20 (1970), 339–49, and 'Ethiopians Again, and Again', *Mnemosyne*, 30 (1977), 75–8.) Generally the Christian conception of India was wider than the pagan conception at the same period and accorded better with the geographical details known since the second century AD, often embracing the whole of modern India and as far as and including Indo-China.

By *septentrionis plaga* Jerome means the region of the far north; he is not necessarily thinking of the northernmost climatic zone in the technical sense, according to which the earth was divided into five zones corresponding to zones in the heavens, as described e.g. by Virg. *georg.* 1. 233 ff., Macr. *somn.* 2. 5. 11–12. (On this technical usage see K. Abel, 'Zone', *RE* supp. 14. 989–1188.) In contrast *fervores Atlantici oceani* must refer to the southern extremity of the known inhabited world. Jerome is probably thinking of the sea to the west and south-west of Europe, as he seems to be when he uses the phrase *Atlanticus oceanus* at *in Is.* 21. 13–17 (CCSL 73. 208 = PL 24. 193); but it is not inconceivable that he has in mind the Arabian Sea and the Indian Ocean, which Strabo, for example, regarded as part of the Atlantic (cf. *A Dictionary of Greek and Roman Geography*, ed. W. Smith (2 vols., London, 1873–8), 1. 312, s.v. 'Atlanticum mare'; the whole article contains a valuable survey of the evidence for the use of the term 'Atlantic'). *fervores* is taken by both Labourt and Wright to mean 'heat', as often, thus contrasting with the idea of cold in *rigida . . . plaga*; but with *oceani* the phrase is perhaps more naturally understood to mean 'the motion of the Atlantic', i.e. of the tides, etc., as at Cic. *nat. deor.* 3. 24 (cf. e.g. Lucr. 6. 436–7, Lucan 4. 461). I suspect that Jerome was in fact thinking of the movement of the water, the primary contrast being one not of temperature but of mobility; the *rigida septentrionis plaga* would include the elder Pliny's 'mare concretum' beyond Thule (*nat.* 4. 104). *rigida*, 'stiff with cold' (cf. e.g. Lucr. 2. 521 'rigidis . . . pruinis', Virg. *georg.* 2. 316), is thus much better than *frigida B*, which is in any case the *lectio facilior*; the variety of readings—some of them nonsensical—offered by the MSS indicate the difficulty Jerome's expression caused the scribes.

tantarum: common for *tot* in late Latin; cf. LHS 2. 206.

quam . . . armis: Virg. *Aen.* 8. 723. The quotation comes from the description of that part of Aeneas' shield which depicts Augustus reviewing the peoples he has conquered. It is thus very appropriate here, for what Jerome goes on to say is effectively that Christ has now 'conquered' all the peoples of the world. It is even possible that Jerome is alluding to the idea, which he will have met in Eusebius at least (cf. e.g. Euseb. *praep. evang.* 1. 4. 3–4), that the reign of Augustus, with the establishment of the *pax Romana*, enabled Christianity to spread; cf. *in Mich.* 4. 1–7 (CCSL 76. 469–70 = PL 25. 1187–8), *in Is.* 2. 4 (CCSL 73. 30 = PL 24. 46), with K. Sugano, *Das Rombild des Hieronymus* (Europäische Hochschulschriften, 15 R., Bd. 25; Frankfurt am Main, 1983), 97–101, and the review of E. D. Hunt, *CR* 34 (1984), 323–4, at 323.

ritu: often of animals; cf. e.g. Lucr. 4. 1265, Cic. *amicit.* 32,

Liv. 3. 47. 7, Jer. *epist.* 98. 3. 5 (tr. from Theophilus) 'in ritum
brutorum animalium'. Jerome also uses the word of peoples
whose behaviour he would have considered bestial; cf. *epist.*
69. 3. 6 'Scottorum et Aticottorum ritu ac de Re publica Platonis
promiscuas uxores, communes liberos habeant'.

locustarum: I am grateful to Mr Reynolds for pointing out
that, in view of its close conjunction with *piscium*, and given the
similar pairing of two kinds of insect in the next phrase, this
word is much more likely here to refer to marine crustaceans
than to locusts.

conterebantur: 'trodden down', 'crushed'; i.e. they were no
better off than the lowest of the animals.

passionem: *passio* in the sense of 'suffering' is common in
Christian writings, rare elsewhere; cf. *TLL* 10. 1. 619–22. For
discussion of the term see C. Mohrmann, 'Pascha, passio,
transitus', *Ephemerides liturgicae*, 66 (1952), 37–52 (= Mohrmann, *Études*, 1. 205–22).

4. 2. taceo de . . . : on *praeteritio* see Lausberg, 1. 436–7, sects.
882–6. The device is frequently employed by Jerome; cf. e.g.
epist. 52. 2. 2, 112. 2. 5 ('taceo de . . . '); 4. 1. 2, 92. 6. 1 (tr. from
Theophilus), 112. 2. 5 ('praetermitto . . . '); 100. 9. 1 (tr. from
Theophilus), 108. 20. 7 ('quid memorem . . . ?'); c. 15. 4 ('quid
loquar . . . ?').

Hebraeis . . . dedicavit: cf. Luke 23: 38 'erat autem et
superscriptio inscripta super illum litteris Graecis et Latinis et
Hebraicis, hic est rex Iudaeorum', John 19: 20. The other
evangelists do not mention in what languages the superscription
was written; cf. Matt. 27: 37, Mark 15: 26. It is not clear in what
sense Jerome regarded the superscription as instrumental in
dedicating these peoples to the Christian faith.

inmortalem . . . philosophantur: the immortality of the
soul, a question that exercised the minds of the great pre-
Christian philosophers, who held varying opinions on the matter, is now held to be true even by barbarian peoples from
remote lands: such has been the power of Christ's resurrection.

Courcelle (1948), 55 n. 1, suggests that this passage is derived
from Cicero's *Consolatio*, which is the probable source of nearly
all of c. 5, including the list of Greek philosophers at 5. 2 (see nn.
on c. 5). This is certainly arguable: the *Consolatio* is closely
related to the *Tusculans* (see Introduction, p. 19), where reference is made to the views of Pythagoras and Democritus on the
soul's immortality and to Socrates' discussion of the matter in
prison (e.g. *Tusc.* 1. 38, 1. 82, 1. 72). But it is also true that
Jerome knew about Pythagoras' doctrines from other sources

(see below on *Pythagoras somniavit*); he may well have known
the basic line of the *Phaedo* from elsewhere, even if, as is
probable, he did not read it at first hand (see on 14. 2 *Platonis . . .
mortis*), and it is not implausible that he had found Democritus'
view too in other writers.

philosophor is intransitive, and *esse* must be understood with
inmortalem . . . subsistentem; *quod* is the relative pronoun after
the virtual acc. + inf. clause, i.e. 'That the soul is immortal . . . a
thing which Pythagoras dreamed about . . . is the philosophy of
the Indian . . . '.

dissolutionem corporis: *dissolutio* (*corporis*) as a synonym
for *mors* is found in both pagan and Christian authors; cf. e.g.
Cic. *fin.* 2. 101 'dissolutione, id est morte, sensus omnis ex-
stinguatur', Sen. *epist.* 77. 9, Ambrosiast. *in Rom.* 5. 12 'mors
autem dissolutio corporis, cum anima a corpore separatur', Hil.
in psalm. 119. 18. It is the Latin equivalent of διάλυσις (cf. e.g.
Plato, *Phaedo* 88B).

Pythagoras somniavit: for Pythagoras' belief in metempsy-
chosis, and his doctrines generally, see Guthrie, 1. 146–340.
Jerome knew of his philosophy through a number of later
writers, including Cicero, Seneca, Origen, and Porphyry; cf.
adv. Rufin. 3. 39–40 (CCSL 79. 107–11 = PL 23. 484–7), with
Courcelle (1948), 54, 61.

The phrase recalls Hor. *epist.* 2. 1. 52 'somnia Pythagorea'. By
using *somniare* here Jerome may have wished to suggest that
Pythagoras' thoughts on the soul's immortality were never more
than a dream: as a pagan he would never have experienced the
reality.

Democritus: with Leucippus, one of the founders of Greek
atomism. He considered the soul to be as perishable as the body.
For fragments of his work see H. Diels and W. Kranz, *Die
Fragmente der Vorsokratiker* (6th edn., 3 vols., Berlin, 1951–2),
2. 130–207; and for the philosophy of the atomists, Guthrie,
2. 382–507.

in consolationem . . . carcere: the story is told in full by
Plato in the *Phaedo*, which Jerome had probably not read
directly (see on 14. 2 *Platonis . . . mortis*).

Indus . . . Aegyptius: Jerome is of course aiming at an
impressionistic picture, and he would not have pretended that
Christianity had absorbed the whole of these peoples. But it had
certainly penetrated them all by this time. The Church appears
to have reached the Malabar coast of India by the end of the
second century; its foundation in Egypt was traditionally
ascribed to St Mark the Evangelist, and Alexandria was an

important Christian centre very early; it existed in Persia, or more precisely, Armenia, from the late third century, when it was brought by Gregory the Illuminator; and the Visigoths were converted around AD 382–95. For details see *ODCC* s.vv. 'Armenia, Christianity in', 'Coptic Church', and 'India, Christianity in', with appended bibliographies, A. S. Atiya, *A History of Eastern Christianity* (London, 1968), and E. A. Thompson, *The Visigoths in the Time of Ulfila* (Oxford, 1966), 78–93.

With this impression of the wide extent of Christianity one might compare *epist.* 46. 10. 2 (Paula and Eustochium) (AD 386), where mention is made of pilgrims to Jerusalem from Gaul, Britain, Armenia, Persia, India, Ethiopia, Egypt, Pontus, Cappadocia, Coele-Syria, and Mesopotamia, and *epist.* 107. 2. 3 (AD 401 or 402) 'de India, Perside et Aethiopia monachorum cotidie turbas suscipimus; deposuit faretras Armenius, Huni discunt psalterium, Scythiae frigora fervent calore fidei; Getarum rutilus et flavus exercitus ecclesiarum circumfert tentoria'.

Bessorum feritas: i.e. *Bessi feri*; a Thracian tribe, known to Herodotus (7. 111. 2). They are noted as brigands by Strabo 7. 5. 12. For details of their involvement in the Graeco–Roman world see *RE* s.n. Bessoi. Their conversion to Christianity is likely to have been recent, for in AD 400 Paulinus of Nola writes of it as if it is still topical: 'nam simul terris animisque duri / et sua Bessi nive duriores / nunc oves facti duce te gregantur / pacis in aulam. / quasque cervices dare servituti / semper a bello indomiti negarunt, / nunc iugo veri domini subactas / sternere gaudent' (*carm.* 17. 205–12).

pellitorum . . . populorum: the expression is vague; Jerome is probably thinking loosely of the northern barbarian peoples, such as the Goths and Huns, whose incursions into the Roman world had been frequent in recent years (cf. 16. 2–5 with nn.). The conversion of the Huns is referred to at *epist.* 107. 2. 3 (quoted above at *Indus . . . Aegyptius*).

mortuorum . . . inferiis: 'at the funerals of the dead'; *inferiis* is virtually a locative. *inferis* $K^{ac\ m^2}D\Psi$—i.e. 'sacrificed men to the dead'—can hardly be right: it renders *mortuorum* redundant, and the phrase, of which I have noticed no other instances, seems highly unnatural.

melos: = μέλος, one of the many words which are attested in early Latin literature and appear frequently in late authors, but are found rarely, and in some cases not at all, in between. To this category belong, for example, *confovere* (5. 2), *demorari* used intransitively (6. 1, where, however, the word may not be

Jerome's own but reflect the language of VL), *lactare* = 'beguile', 'deceive' (9. 1), *marsuppium* (11. 3), and *offirmare* (13. 3).
These words presumably survived in the spoken language
during a long period when their use was avoided in literature; in
some cases their revival in the literary language may be attributable partly to the fondness for archaism shown by authors of the
second century AD such as Apuleius. For *melos* see *TLL* 8. 625–7;
Jerome employs the word also at *in Is.* 16. 11–13 (CCSL
73. 264 = PL 24. 238), *tract. in psalm.* 136. 2 (CCSL 78. 296–7).

   totius . . . est: a triumphant ending, with a powerful double-
cretic clausula. For the exaggeration cf. e.g. *epist.* 65. 12. 3 'his
sagittis [sc. dei] totus orbis vulneratus et captus est', 78. 14. 3 'ad
apostolos quoque . . . descenderit spiritus sanctus et divisis
linguis credentium totus evangelica praedicatione mundus
expletus sit', Tert. *apol.* 37. 4–8; and see further on 14. 1 *tota
hunc . . . Italia.*

c. 5. Having made the points he has made in cc. 2–3, Jerome need
strictly go no further in his attempt to console Heliodorus, as he
has made it quite clear that Nepotianus, being a Christian, must be
in heaven, which is the ultimate consolation. But the purpose of
the letter is not merely consolatory, as is evident particularly from
the inclusion of the long eulogistic section at cc. 8–12 (on which see
esp. Introduction, pp. 28–9, and on 7. 3 *audias laudes eius*), and on
the consolatory side itself Jerome has not yet tapped the great well
of material available to him from predecessors, who form a
tradition in which he plainly feels himself to stand; this material,
though logically superfluous to his consolatory argument, can at
least reinforce it. He therefore carries on, first encouraging both
Heliodorus and himself in their grief by quoting examples from
pagan history of staunch fortitude in bereavement.

5. 1. Quid agimus, anima?: the phrase recurs at *epist.* 108. 27. 1.
For the device of addressing one's own heart or soul, which goes
back to Homer, see G. Williams, *Tradition and Originality in
Roman Poetry* (Oxford, 1968), 461–2.

   exciderunt . . . non tenes?: *praecepta rhetorum* here is a
vague, general phrase; *dicendi ordinem* indicates that Jerome is
thinking mainly about the *dispositio* of his material, on which see
Lausberg, 1. 241–7, sects. 443–52. In his exhortatory *consolatio*
to Julian he professes a rather different attitude: 'extemporalis
est epistula absque ordine sensuum, sine lenocinio et conposi-
tione sermonum, ut totum in illa amicum, nihil de oratore
repperias . . . nos leporem artis rhetoricae contemnentes et
puerilis atque plausibilis eloquii venustatem ad sanctarum scri-

pturarum gravitatem confugimus, ubi vulnerum vera medicina est' (*epist.* 118. 1. 2–3). But this claim is not without exaggeration: while the style of the piece is fairly low-key, its organization is not entirely haphazard.

Hilberg took this sentence not as a question but as an exclamation, implausibly in the context: Jerome is not despairing of his ability to write the piece, but encouraging himself to do so. There is no necessity, however, to follow the earlier editors in adding *-ne* to *exciderunt*.

Anaxagorae . . . mortalem: Jerome means that he knew quite well that Nepotianus was mortal and would inevitably die, and so should not be so overwhelmed with grief.

At *Tusc.* 3. 28 ff. Cicero discusses the view, which he attributes to the Cyrenaic school, that it is the unexpected evil which causes distress. Future ills should therefore be anticipated; cf. *Tusc.* 3. 29 'haec igitur praemeditatio futurorum malorum lenit eorum adventum, quae venientia longe ante videris'. (Such *praemeditatio* was also a typically Stoic practice; cf. I. Hadot, *Seneca und die griechisch-römische Tradition der Seelenleitung* (Quellen und Studien zur Geschichte der Philosophie, 13; Berlin, 1969), 60–1, and Cicero's reference to Chrysippus at *Tusc.* 3. 52.) In his account he quotes the saying of the philosopher Anaxagoras on hearing of the death of his son in exactly the same words as Jerome uses here, and at 3. 28 quotes three lines spoken by Telamon, father of Ajax, in a play now lost but generally considered to be Ennius' *Telamo* (but perhaps Pacuvius' *Teucer*; cf. Jocelyn, 394): 'ego cum genui, tum morituros scivi et ei rei sustuli. / praeterea ad Troiam cum misi ob defendendam Graeciam, / scibam me in mortiferum bellum, non in epulas mittere'. Both sayings illustrate the principle that *praemeditatio* mitigates the distress caused when evils befall. It seems highly probable that Jerome draws the references here from this section of the *Tusculans*, or, more likely still, from Cicero's *Consolatio*, from which most of c. 5 is derived (cf. on 5. 2 *Platonis . . . percucurrimus* and 5. 2–3 *proponunt . . . explicavit*). Admittedly the dicta are known to other authors (cf. e.g. (for Anaxagoras) Val. Max. 5. 10. 3, Plut. *cohib. ira* 16 (463D), *tranq. anim.* 16 (474D), [Plut.] *ad Apoll.* 33 (118D), Symm. *epist.* 3. 6. 3, (for Telamon) Sen. *dial.* 11. 11. 2, Fronto p. 217 Naber), but the fact that they are found in combination in Cicero (who refers to them again at *Tusc.* 3. 58), and that Anaxagoras' words are presented by Jerome in precisely the same form as they are given by Cicero (which is not true of Valerius Maximus, or of Symmachus, who merely alludes to them), makes the probability of a Ciceronian source overwhelming. It is in any case highly likely that Cicero was the source for Valerius and Symmachus too; cf. on 5. 2–3 *proponunt . . . explicavit*.

The notion that grief may be alleviated by advance consideration of potential misfortune is frequently found in consolation; cf. e.g. Cic. *ad fam.* 5. 16. 2 'est autem consolatio pervulgata quidem illa maxime, quam semper in ore atque in animo habere debemus, homines nos ut esse meminerimus ea lege natos, ut omnibus telis fortunae proposita sit vita nostra', Sen. *epist.* 63. 15 'tunc ego debui dicere, minor est Serenus meus: quid ad rem pertinet? post me mori debet, sed ante me potest. quia non feci inparatum subito fortuna percussit', [Plut.] *ad Apoll.* 21 (112C) ἀλλ' οὐ γὰρ ἤλπιζον φησί ταῦτα πείσεσθαι, οὐδὲ προσεδόκων. ἀλλ' ἐχρῆν σε προσδοκᾶν . . . καὶ οὐκ ἂν νῦν ἀπαράσκευος ὥσπερ ὑπὸ πολεμίων ἐξαίφνης ἐπελθόντων ἐλήφθης, Ambr. *exc. Sat.* 1. 35 'cuius [sc. Satyri] ego casum, quo esset tolerabilior, nec praemeditari potui: ita pavebat animus de illo tale aliquid cogitare', Theodoret, *epist.* 14 (Collectio Sirmondiana; Sources chrétiennes, 98).

As most consolations deal with the grief engendered by someone's death, the *praemeditatio* τόπος is often closely related to the notion that death is inescapable, which is itself frequently employed as a means of consoling the bereaved. In pagan consolation cf. e.g. Cic. *ad fam.* 4. 5. 4 (Sulpicius) 'si hoc tempore non diem suum obisset, paucis post annis tamen ei moriendum fuit, quoniam homo nata fuerat', Sen. *epist.* 93. 12, 99. 8 'omnis eadem condicio devinxit: cui nasci contigit mori restat', *dial.* 6. 10. 5, 11. 1. 4 'maximum ergo solacium est cogitare id sibi accidisse quod omnes ante se passi sunt omnesque passuri', *Cons. ad Liv.* 357–60, Petron. 111. 8 (where the soldier comforts the widow of Ephesus), [Plut.] *ad Apoll.* 6 (104A), Demetr. *form. epist.* 5; discussing the παραμυθητικὸς λόγος Menander Rhetor writes φιλοσοφῆσαι δὲ ἐπὶ τούτοις οὐκ ἀπειρόκαλον καθόλου περὶ φύσεως ἀνθρωπίνης . . . ὅτι πέρας ἐστὶν ἅπασιν ἀνθρώποις τοῦ βίου ὁ θάνατος (*epid.* 2. 9 (414. 2–5) Russell–Wilson). The idea is taken up by Christian writers and sometimes, naturally enough, connected with their belief in resurrection; cf. e.g. Jer. *epist.* 39. 3. 1 'dolemus quemquam mortuum: ad hoc enim nati sumus, ut maneamus aeterni?', 75. 1. 3 'adversum mortis ergo duritiam et crudelissimam necessitatem hoc solacio erigimur, quod brevi visuri sumus eos, quos dolemus absentes', 108. 27. 3, Ambr. *epist.* 39. 5 'caro enim nostra perpetua esse ac diuturna non potest; necesse est occidat, ut resurgat', *obit. Valent.* 48 'nihil ergo habetis, quod gravissime doleatis in fratre:

homo natus est, humanae fuit obnoxius fragilitati', *exc. Sat.* 1. 4,
2. 3, Paul. Nol. *epist.* 13. 6 'commune enim tibi cum omnibus
amisisse mortalem', Bas. *epist.* 6. 2 ἀνάβλεψον πρὸς τὸν οὐρανόν· καὶ
οὗτος ποτε λυθήσεται· πρὸς τὸν ἥλιον· οὐδὲ οὗτος διαμενεῖ. οἱ ἀστέρες
σύμπαντες, ζῷα χερσαῖα καὶ ἔνυδρα, τὰ περὶ γῆν κάλλη, αὐτὴ ἡ γῆ,
πάντα φθαρτά, πάντα μικρὸν ὕστερον οὐκ ἐσόμενα. ἡ τούτων ἔννοια
παραμυθία ἔστω τοῦ συμβεβηκότος.
   For detailed discussion of these τόποι see Johann, 63–84.
5. 2. legimus ... Cicero: for Crantor and his influential treatise
Περὶ πένθους see Introduction, pp. 18–19. That Cicero used this
work in composing his *Consolatio* on the death of his daughter
Tullia in 45 BC is corroborated by Plin. *nat.* pref. 22, but the
extent of his debt to it has generally been exaggerated (see
Introduction, pp. 19–20). It is most improbable that Jerome had
himself read Crantor's work, despite his claim here; see below on
Platonis . . . percucurrimus.
   confovendum: for *confovere* see on 4. 2 *melos.* It appears in
extant literature first at Afran. *com.* 143, and thereafter not until
Apul. *met.* 8. 7; cf. *TLL* 4. 252. In Jerome cf. e.g. *epist.* 66. 5. 3,
85. 6. 1, *c. Ioh.* 22 (PL 23. 373), *in Ion.* 4. 6 (CCSL 76.
415 = PL 25. 1148).
   Platonis ... percucurrimus: among Plato's writings consolatory elements are found in the *Apology*, the funeral oration in
the *Menexenus*, and the *Phaedo* (with the pseudo-Platonic *Axiochus*, considered spurious certainly by the time of Diogenes
Laertius (first half of third century AD?); cf. Diog. Laert. 3. 62).
Whether Jerome knew any of these works at first hand is
doubtful. Courcelle (1948), 53–9, discusses the evidence for
Jerome's knowledge of Plato and shows that, for all his claims to
have read him, his references and allusions to Platonic writings
rarely presuppose personal acquaintance with the Greek text.
He never alludes to the *Apology* or the *Menexenus*, and his
knowledge of the *Phaedo* may be entirely second-hand (cf. on
14. 2 *Platonis . . . mortis*). If he had read them, it may have been
very quickly (cf. *percucurrimus*), and with the aid of a Latin
translation; he certainly knew of the *Protagoras* through Cicero's
version (cf. Courcelle (1948), 56).
   It is still less likely that he had read directly the consolatory
writings of the other philosophers here mentioned (Diogenes,
founder of the Cynic school; Clitomachus, pupil of Carneades,
founder of the New Academy; and Posidonius, historian and
philosopher, who greatly influenced many Latin writers, Cicero
and Seneca among them), if indeed consolatory writings there
were; from Cicero we know of a book by Clitomachus, 'quem ille

eversa Karthagine misit consolandi causa ad captivos cives suos'
(*Tusc.* 3. 54), but Kassel, 26 n. 2, is rightly wary of believing in
the existence of specifically consolatory works by the rest.
Courcelle (1948), 54–5, argues cogently that Jerome derived
what he knew of these authors from Cicero's *Consolatio*, and that
the same is true of his knowledge of Crantor (the same view had
been expressed long before by Buresch (1886), 47–8). Elsewhere
Jerome certainly exaggerates his first-hand knowledge of Greek
philosophers (cf. *epist.* 84. 6. 2, *adv. Rufin.* 3. 39 (CCSL
79. 107–8 = PL 23. 484)), while the *Consolatio* is the source for
the rest of this chapter (cf. on 5. 2–3 *proponunt . . . explicavit*),
and is closely connected with the *Tusculans* (see Introduction,
p. 19), in which reference is made to all these writers (cf. 1. 104
(Diogenes), 2. 61 (Posidonius), 3. 54 (Clitomachus and Carneades; quoted in part above)). Jerome may of course have come
across scattered references to them in other writers too;
Diogenes, for example, is mentioned a number of times by
Seneca.

There is nothing surprising in Jerome's exaggerated claim to
have read Crantor and the rest. For one thing, it will have helped
to convince Heliodorus that he was well equipped to undertake
his task. Jerome was in any case prone to exaggerate; one might
compare his claim that 'novum testamentum Graecae reddidi
auctoritati' (*epist.* 71. 5. 3; see also *vir. ill.* 135 (PL 23. 717)),
whereas in fact it is unlikely that he revised any of the NT other
than the gospels (see Introduction, p. 9).

vel libris vel epistulis: at times Jerome draws an explicit
contrast between *libri* and *epistulae*; cf. e.g. *epist.* 28. 1 'epistulae
brevitatem causati sumus et rem libri non posse explicari litteris
praetexuimus', *epist. ad Praesidium* p. 55. 51–2 Morin 'longam
orationem conpendio breviem—epistola quippe librum redolere
non debet'. In these cases the difference is one of scale; Jerome
was highly conscious of the precept that a letter (*epistula*) should
be short, though he often admits to having failed to observe the
due limit (cf. Arns, 96–8, Bartelink (1980), 89–90, 120–1, and his
fuller discussion, 'Een gemeenplaats uit de briefliteratuur bij een
christelijk auteur: brevitas epistolaris bij Hieronymus', *Lampas*,
10 (1977), 61–5; for the precept in general see e.g. Demet. *de
eloc.* 228, Jul. Vict. *rhet.* 27 p. 448 Halm, and the unknown
author in the same volume, p. 589). Here the distinction, such as
it is, may equally be between consolatory treatises of an essentially general nature and more personal pieces.

etiamsi . . . inrigari: for this use of *arere* cf. Ennod. *epist.* 2. 7
'nos ab scolarum gymnasiis sequestrati, arentis ingenii guttis

quaedam oceani fluenta provocamus', Paul. Nol. *carm.* 15. 41 'in quorum arentes animas pia gratia fluxit'. *fontibus* suggests not only sources of supply for a dry *ingenium*, but original sources of supply. The word is often used in reference to philosophers; cf. e.g. Cic. *acad. post.* 1. 8 'sed meos amicos in Graeciam mitto . . . ut ea a fontibus potius hauriant quam rivulos consectentur', *nat. deor.* 1. 120 'Democritus . . . cuius fontibus Epicurus hortulos suos inrigavit', *de orat.* 1. 42, where there is a metaphor of Socrates as *fons*.

5. 2–3. proponunt . . . explicavit: this group of men who have displayed great fortitude in the face of bereavement, and are thus examples to Jerome and Heliodorus (and particularly appropriate ones at that, given that—in the cases of the four specifically identified, and also of others (see on 5. 3 *Maximos . . . Aufidios*)—their fortitude was shown at the deaths of sons, and that in different ways Nepotianus was a son to both Jerome and Heliodorus (cf. 7. 3, with n. on *in carne . . . pater*, 13. 3, 19. 3)), is particularly interesting in that the same *exempla* are found in other authors to illustrate the same quality:

- (a) Cic. *Tusc.* 3. 70: Q. Maximus, L. Paulus, M. Cato, and 'reliqui, quos in Consolatione conlegimus';
- (b) Cic. *ad fam.* 4. 6. 1: Q. Maximus, L. Paulus, Galus, M. Cato;
- (c) Val. Max. 5. 10: Horatius Pulvillus, Aemilius Paulus, Q. Marcius Rex, Pericles, Xenophon, Anaxagoras;
- (d) Sen. *dial.* 6. 13: Xenophon (not named), Pulvillus, Paulus; in c. 12 Sulla is mentioned, in c. 14 Bibulus and Caesar;
- (e) [Plut.] *ad Apoll.* 33 (118C–119D): Anaxagoras, Pericles, Xenophon, Dion of Syracuse, Demosthenes, Antigonus (Gonatas);
- (f) Symm. *epist.* 3. 6. 3: Pericles, Anaxagoras, M. Horatius (Pulvillus).

It is possible that some of these *exempla* were proverbial by Jerome's time, and earlier; but Kunst, 124–31, makes a strong case that they are all derived by Jerome from Cicero's *Consolatio*, which he mentions here as containing a wealth of *exempla* which he does not trouble to detail. (Kunst's view is attacked by J. Doignon, 'Lactance intermédiaire entre Ambroise de Milan et la *Consolation* de Cicéron?', *REL* 51 (1973), 208–19, who holds (218) that Jerome is not dependent on the *Consolatio* itself but on Cicero's evidence on the *Consolatio*; that, in fact, he is relying on Cic. *Tusc.* 3. 70, adding names taken from Valerius Maximus,

Seneca, and certain of Cicero's letters to Atticus. Given that Jerome mentions the *Consolatio* in this chapter, and that at *Tusc.* 3. 70 Cicero makes it plain that the *exempla* he cites there are merely a few of those to be found in the *Consolatio*, this hypothesis seems extraordinary.) Cicero will in turn probably have drawn the Greek *exempla* from Crantor's Περὶ πένθους, which we may suppose, with a fair degree of certainty, to have been pseudo-Plutarch's source too (for the debt of the *Ad Apollonium* to Crantor see Introduction, p. 21). It appears extremely likely that Valerius Maximus, Seneca, and Symmachus were also dependent on the *Consolatio*, as maintained by R. Helm, 'Valerius Maximus, Seneca und die "Exemplasammlung"', *Hermes*, 74 (1939), 130–54, at 132–7, arguing against the view that Valerius and Seneca were dependent on some specially-tailored collection of examples.

The occurrence of the case of Anaxagoras in Valerius and Symmachus among other examples of fortitude suggests that it played a similar part in the *Consolatio*; it certainly did so in Crantor, to judge from the pseudo-Plutarch passage. Jerome, however, has just used the Anaxagoras story to illustrate the principle of *praemeditatio futurorum malorum* (see on 5. 1 *Anaxagorae . . . mortalem*), which is how Cicero treats it in the *Tusculans*. Jerome may of course have used both the *Tusculans* and the *Consolatio* as sources for this chapter; but it seems quite possible that in the *Consolatio* the case of Anaxagoras was used twice, as illustrative both of fortitude in bereavement and of the *praemeditatio* principle.

To display fortitude at times of loss was regularly considered virtuous and the notion is often found in consolation (the only one of the passages mentioned above which has nothing directly to do with consolation is (*c*)). Cf. also Sen. *contr.* 4 pref. 6 'o magnos viros, qui fortunae succumbere nesciunt et adversas res suae virtutis experimenta faciunt! declamavit Pollio Asinius intra quartum diem quam filium amiserat: praeconium illud ingentis animi fuit malis suis insultantis', Sen. *epist.* 99. 6 'innumerabilia sunt exempla eorum qui liberos iuvenes sine lacrimis extulerint, qui in senatum aut in aliquod publicum officium a rogo redierint et statim aliud egerint. nec inmerito; nam . . . supervacuum est dolere si nihil dolendo proficias', *dial.* 11. 14. 4–16. 3 (with further *exempla*). The elder Seneca, however, considered it possible to be too thick-skinned; cf. *suas.* 2. 15.

For the use of historical *exempla* by ancient authors see Nisbet–Hubbard (1970), 157, and the bibliography there given.

Quintilian boasts of the wealth and utility of Roman *exempla*: 'quae sunt tradita antiquitus dicta ac facta praeclare et nosse et animo semper agitare conveniet. quae profecto nusquam plura maioraque quam in nostrae civitatis monumentis reperientur. an fortitudinem, iustitiam, fidem, continentiam, frugalitatem, contemptum doloris ac mortis melius alii docebunt quam Fabricii, Curii, Reguli, Decii, Mucii aliique innumerabiles? quantum enim Graeci praeceptis valent, tantum Romani, quod est maius, exemplis' (*inst.* 12. 2. 29–30). On Jerome's use of pagan as well as Christian *exempla* see Bartelink (1980), 36–7; and for *exempla* as a feature of rhetoric see the evidence in Lausberg, with his index, 2. 699, s.v. 'exemplum'.

5. 2. Periclen . . . concidisse: these stories about Pericles, the great Athenian statesman, and Xenophon, the author and follower of Socrates, are not found in any extant contemporary sources (except, in the case of Pericles, for the passage from Protagoras quoted by pseudo-Plutarch (see below)). The details about Pericles occur at Val. Max. 5. 10 ext. 1; Symm. *epist.* 3. 6. 3 merely says 'Pericles amissis recens filiis venit in curiam'. Of sources not dependent on Cicero's *Consolatio*, Plut. *Per.* 36. 6–8, and Aelian, *var. hist.* 9. 6, make reference to Pericles' great fortitude in the face of losing his sons (and other members of his family, according to Plutarch) during the plague early in the Peloponnesian War, but do not mention this particular incident. The origins of this story may lie with Protagoras, whose account is quoted by [Plut.] *ad Apoll.* 33 (118E–F); it is quite likely that Crantor had excerpted Protagoras' words first, and that pseudo-Plutarch took them from him.

The story of Xenophon as told by [Plut.] *ad Apoll.* 33 (118F–119A) and Val. Max. 5. 10 ext. 2 tallies closely with what Jerome says here. Sen. *dial.* 6. 13. 1 presents only slight variations. Aelian, *var. hist.* 3. 3, is very close, and is probably indebted either to the *Ad Apollonium* or to Crantor himself (at the same point in his work he also gives the stories of Anaxagoras, Dion, and Antigonus, all of which occur in pseudo-Plutarch). Diogenes Laertius knows the story (cf. 2. 54), but is somewhat muddled about it. He declares that Ephorus is his source for the incident of the death of Xenophon's son Gryllus at Mantinea, but when he mentions the announcement about it made to Xenophon, uses the vague φασί. He also (2. 55) attributes to Xenophon the famous phrase of Anaxagoras at the news of his son's death (see on 5. 1 *Anaxagorae . . . mortalem*), perhaps following confused sources. The anecdote may well have originated with a fourth-century historian or perhaps a eulogy of

Gryllus (cf. Diog. Laert. 2. 55 φησὶ δ' Ἀριστοτέλης ὅτι ἐγκώμια καὶ
ἐπιτάφιον Γρύλλου μυρίοι ὅσοι συνέγραψαν, τὸ μέρος καὶ τῷ πατρὶ
χαριζόμενοι), from either of which Crantor could have derived it.

Jerome may have drawn the phrase *Xenophontem Socraticum*
from Cicero, who at *Tusc.* 2. 62 wrote 'Socraticum Xenophontem', and perhaps expressed himself similarly in the *Consolatio*;
but it is an easy shorthand phrase, found in Julius Paris' epitome
of Valerius Maximus (5. 10 ext. 2), where Valerius himself wrote
'Xenophon . . . quod ad Socraticam disciplinam adtinet . . .'.

   coronatus: cf. Protagoras ap. [Plut.] *ad Apoll.* 33 (118F)
ἐστεφανωμένον κατὰ τὸ πάτριον ἔθος (of Pericles).

5. 3. quid memorem . . . ?: for *praeteritio* see on 4. 2 *taceo de* . . . .

   Pulvillus . . . sepeliri: the story is found also at Val. Max.
5. 10. 1, Sen. *dial.* 6. 13. 1–2, and Symm. *epist.* 3. 6. 3, of whom
only Symmachus gives the detail that Pulvillus gave orders for
the corpse to be taken away for burial. Julius Paris' epitome of
Val. Max. 5. 10. 1 presents Pulvillus as saying 'tolle . . . cadaver',
though our text of Valerius contains nothing of the kind; it
seems likely that Valerius originally included the detail, and that
it fell out in the course of transmission. Its absence, however,
does not destroy the value of the episode as an example of
fortitude in bereavement, as long as it is made clear that
Pulvillus continued to perform the rite of dedicating the temple
in spite of the news, and both Seneca and Valerius do this.

   For historical accounts of the dedication of the temple of
Jupiter on the Capitol (*Capitolium* can mean either the hill or the
temple only), which traditionally took place in 509 BC, see
Liv. 2. 8. 6–8 and Plut. *Public.* 14, both of which mention
Pulvillus' order. The story appears to have been famous, and is
touched on by Cicero at *dom.* 139.

   For details of what is known about M. Horatius Pulvillus see
RE s.n. Horatius 15.

   Capitolium dedicans: Sen. *dial.* 6. 13. 1 has 'Capitolium
dedicanti', and Kunst, 127 n. 1, says, 'eum [sc. Hieronymum]
Senecam hoc imitari putes breviloquio'. This is possible, if
Jerome had a text of the *Ad Marciam* before him as well as one of
the *Consolatio*; but the expression need hardly be derivative at
all, in view of the liking of fourth-century writers for the present
participle, and of the fact that Jerome is clearly aiming for
brevity in all his *exempla* here.

   Lucius . . . ingressus est: the bereavement of L. Aemilius
Paulus, who defeated Perseus of Macedonia at Pydna in 168 BC,
is mentioned also by Cic. *Tusc.* 3. 70, *ad fam.* 4. 6. 1, *amicit.* 9,
Sen. *dial.* 6. 13. 3–4, and Val. Max. 5. 10. 2. Of these only the

Cicero letter specifically records the detail of seven days, but
Valerius states that the one son died four days before Paulus'
triumph (celebrating the victory over Perseus), the other three
days after it (Julius Paris' epitome is slightly different here). The
story of Paulus' loss appears to have been very famous; cf. also
Liv. 45. 40. 7–8, Diod. 31. 11. 1, Vell. 1. 10. 3–5, Plut. *Aem.* 35,
App. *Mac.* 19, most of which note that the sons died within a
matter of days of each other, on either side of Paulus' triumph.
Polybius does not make much of it, mentioning only that his
sons predeceased him (31. 28. 2).

For details of the life of Paulus see *RE* s.n. Aemilius 114.

praetermitto . . . quaesisse: with this instance of *praeteritio*
(for which see on 4. 2 *taceo de . . .*) Jerome leaves behind his
pagan *exempla* and suggests that he is about to draw others from
the Christian world. In similar fashion, and in a similar context,
he passes from examples from Biblical history to one from the
contemporary world (Melanium) at *epist.* 39. 5. 4 'quid vetera
replicem? praesentia exempla sectare'.

Maximos . . . Aufidios: such as Q. Fabius Maximus Cunctator, M. Porcius Cato the censor, and C. Sulpicius Galus, *cos.*
166 BC, all of whom displayed great fortitude at the deaths of
their sons; cf. Cic. *ad fam.* 4. 6. 1 (all three), *Tusc.* 3. 70 (Maximus, Cato), *sen.* 12 (Maximus), 84 (Cato), *amicit.* 9 (Cato,
Galus), Plut. *Fab.* 24. 4 (Maximus). For the form *Galus* (not
Gallus) see *Der kleine Pauly: Lexikon der Antike*, eds. K. Ziegler
and W. Sontheimer (5 vols., Munich, 1975), 5. 424, s.n. Sulpicius.

The fact that *Maximos* heads the list suggests that Jerome may
be indulging in a pun here.

Consolationis libro: see Introduction, pp. 19–20, and previous nn. on this chapter.

ne videar . . . quaesisse: *aliena* = 'examples from the pagan
world', *nostra* = 'examples from the Christian world'. For the
idea cf. *epist.* 52. 2. 1 'quod ne de gentili tantum litteratura
proferre videamur, divinorum voluminum sacramenta co-
gnosce'; and for the *aliena/nostra* distinction, Paul. Nol. *epist.*
7. 3 'paucis tamen et ad ipsum loquamur, ne neget sibi scriptum
quod de se tibi scriptum est; Aeschino enim dicitur quod audit
Micio [cf. Ter. *Ad.* 96–7]. sed quid de alienis loquar, cum de
proprio cuncta possimus et aliena loqui non soleat esse sani
capitis, quo dei gratia sano et salvo sumus quibus caput Christus
est?'.

quamquam . . . infidelitas: for the construction of the
sentence cf. *epist.* 123. 7. 1 'quod [i.e. restrictions on marriage]

quidem observat et gentilitas in condemnationem nostri, si hoc
non exhibeat veritas Christo, quod tribuit mendacium diabolo'.

c. 6. After 5. 3 *ne videar . . . quaesisse* and the opening sentence of
c. 6 one expects Jerome to give instances of Jewish (OT) and
Christian fortitude in bereavement, as he does at *epist.* 39. 5. 3–5.
Instead, however, he uses relevant examples from the Bible to
show that while before the redeeming work of Christ grief at
someone's death was appropriate, as the prospect was then *infernus*
(cf. 3. 1–2), it is certainly not appropriate now, when the prospect
for Christians is heaven (cf. 3. 3–4). This idea has been implied
throughout cc. 2–3. Suddenly, however, he breaks off, and says
that he has already, in *epist.* 39, used all the relevant Scriptural
material on the subject of the expression of grief, and intends now
to tread a different path.

6. 1. non plangam . . . resurgentes: for Jacob cf. Gen. 37: 33–5,
where he weeps for Joseph when he thinks he has been devoured
by a wild beast; for David cf. 2 Sam. 18: 33, where he weeps for
Absalom. Both examples recur, and at greater length, at *epist.*
39. 4. 1–2, where Jerome anticipates Paula's using them in
objection to his criticism of her weeping, and makes it clear that
there was nothing inappropriate in the actions of Jacob and
David, since their sons would inevitably have entered *infernus*,
and Absalom in any case had sinned, rebelling against David
(cf. 2 Sam. 15–18).

   resurgentes is general, and does not refer to the *filios*; 'those
who rise again'. *evangelio* = 'the Gospel dispensation' (Wright),
as opposed to the Law.

   For *morientes,* = *mortuos,* cf. below on 6. 2 *et Moyses . . .
plangitur.*

Iudaeorum: i.e. Jacob, David, etc. Death, of course, is still a
matter of grief for the Jews, who do not accept the resurrection
of Jesus; cf. *epist.* 39. 4. 6 'flent usque hodie Iudaei et nudatis
pedibus in cinere volutati sacco incubant . . . nos vero, qui
Christum induimus et facti sumus iuxta apostolum genus
regium ac sacerdotale, non debemus super mortuos contristari'.

ad vesperum . . . laetitia: Ps. 29: 6 (so Vulg. LXX (and VL);
Hebr.: 'ad vesperum commorabitur fletus et in matutino laus').
Again the quotation follows the LXX version (cf. on 3. 2
dixerunt . . . ad unum, 4. 1 *notus . . . nomen eius*), this time possibly
because *laetitia* (ἀγαλλίασις) makes better sense here than *laus*;
otherwise it may just be a question of memory, as often.

   In Ps. 29 the psalmist thanks God for deliverance. In its
context the meaning of this verse seems to be that the joy

occasioned by God's favour will supersede the weeping caused
by his anger, which will endure only briefly. Jerome finds it easy
to apply the verse to the situation before and after Christ's
resurrection.

demorabitur = 'linger'; as often, without any idea of delay or
hesitation. The intransitive use of *demoror* is attested first at
Plaut. *Rud.* 440, and then only rarely until the third century AD;
cf. *TLL* 5. 1. 510–11. See on 4. 2 *melos*.

nox . . . adpropinquavit: Rom. 13: 12 (Vulg.: 'adpropiavit'
for *adpropinquavit*, though many MSS have the latter form). An
appropriate verse; Paul is talking about the *dies salutis*. There is,
however, a slight difference. In talking of the *dies salutis* Paul
appears to be thinking of the second coming of Christ, though
his words will also fit the case of any individual Christian to
whom death comes, bringing salvation. In any case, Paul is
looking forward; it is clear that for him the day has not yet
dawned. But for Jerome that day has already arrived, both for
Christians generally, because of the opening of heaven at
Christ's resurrection, and for Nepotianus in particular, who will
now have entered heaven.

For imagery this verse is particularly well chosen after the
previous quotation.

6. 2. et Moyses . . . plangitur: cf. Deut. 34: 8, where the children
of Israel weep for the death of Moses for thirty days; understandably so, for as yet there had been no redemption, and even
so good and great a man as Moses (*et Moyses*) would not be able
to enter heaven immediately.

moriens plangitur is a good example of the use, common in late
Latin, of the present participle when the action it depicts should
strictly be represented in the past; Moses is lamented not *moriens*
but *mortuus*. See LHS 2. 386–7. *morientes* above (6. 1) is similar.

Iesus . . . sepelitur: the death and burial of Joshua 'in monte
Ephraim' are recorded at Josh. 24: 29–30. Jerome infers that the
burial was *absque funere et lacrimis* from the fact that they are
unmentioned in the Bible account; cf. *epist.* 39. 4. 5, quoted
below. Joshua is of course here meant to be understood as a type
of Christ, the point being that grief at someone's death was
appropriate only in the days before Christ.

The same contrast between Moses and Joshua/Jesus is found
at *epist.* 39. 4. 5, which greatly illuminates this passage: 'nequeo
scripturae satis laudare mysteria et divinum sensum in verbis
licet simplicibus admirari, quid sibi velit, quod Moyses plangitur et Iesus Nave, vir sanctus, sepultus refertur et tamen fletus
esse non scribitur; nempe illud, quod in Moysi, id est in lege

veteri, omnes sub peccati Adam tenebantur elogio et ad inferos descendentes consequenter lacrimae prosequebantur secundum apostolum, qui ait: et regnavit mors ab Adam usque ad Moysen etiam super eos qui non peccaverunt [cf. 3. 1]; in Iesu vero, id est in evangelio, per quem paradisus est apertus, mortem gaudia prosequuntur'. Cf. also *epist.* 78. 36. 4 'Aaron plangitur, Iesus non plangitur. in lege descensus ad inferos, in evangelio ad paradisum transmigratio', (for the contrast put to a different use) *adv. Iovin.* 1. 22 (PL 23. 240–1). At *epist.* 53. 8. 4 Joshua is expressly declared to be a type of Jesus, 'non solum in gestis, verum etiam in nomine' (it may well be that his typological significance is derived primarily from his name, especially as the far less important OT figure, Joshua the son of Jehozadak (*Iesus Iosedech*), is also regarded by Jerome, and other Fathers, as a type of Christ; cf. *adv. Iovin.* 2. 4 (PL 23. 288), *in Agg.* 2. 2–10 (CCSL 76A. 730 = PL 25. 1403), J. Lécuyer, 'Jésus, fils de Josédec, et la sacerdoce du Christ', *RecSR* 43 (1955), 82–103). For an illuminating discussion of Joshua/Jesus typology in the early Church see J. Daniélou, *Sacramentum futuri: études sur les origines de la typologie biblique* (Paris, 1950), 203–16.

quidquid . . . vestigia: having just touched on the cases of Jacob, David, Moses, and Joshua, Jerome now tells Heliodorus that he has already set out, in *epist.* 39 (*eo libro*), written in 384 to Paula on the death of her daughter Blesilla, all the Scriptural material which deals with lamentation. By this he seems to be referring to those passages which suggest guidelines for right behaviour in cases of bereavement, and which he discusses mainly at *epist.* 39. 4–5. These include, indeed, the examples already mentioned briefly in this chapter (see on 6. 1 *non plangam . . . resurgentes*, 6. 2 *Iesus . . . sepelitur*). Jerome does not wish simply to repeat himself in the present letter and says he will approach his task of indicating the proper reaction to Nepotianus' death differently (though in fact he subsequently does bring up further Biblical material on lamentation, some of which has already appeared in *epist.* 39 (see on 7. 2 *flebant . . . caritatis*)). Whether Heliodorus was actually in a position to read *epist.* 39, and see the difference in approach, one cannot tell (for the circulation of Jerome's letters see Introduction, pp. 13–15).

Jerome's letter of 409 to Geruchia, urging her not to remarry, is prefaced by a similar statement of intent: 'in veteri via novam semitam quaerimus et in antiqua detritaque materia rudem artis excogitamus elegantiam, ut nec eadem sint et eadem sint. unum iter et perveniendi, quo cupias, multa conpendia' (*epist.* 123. 1. 1).

c. 7. Jerome now for the first time specifically states that Nepotianus is in heaven. Grief is therefore quite inappropriate; but it is difficult not to grieve, because he and Heliodorus miss Nepotianus, and regret that they cannot enjoy the blessings he now enjoys. Even Paul and Jesus himself were capable of grief at the death of people who would be resurrected, and indeed to display such grief is an indication of love. However, restraint should be exercised, and Heliodorus should now listen to the praises of his nephew.

7. 1. Scimus . . . dei nostri: Nepotianus has not been mentioned by name since 1. 1, and not at all since 2. 1. What Jerome has said about the destruction of death and the opening of heaven, about fortitude in bereavement and the inappropriateness of grief, has of course been inspired by the death of Nepotianus and would naturally have been understood by Heliodorus as applying to his case, but it has all been couched in rather general terms. As he is dealing with a deeply personal matter, Jerome now takes it in hand to particularize the points he has already made.

Shift from general to particular, and the notion that the general principle is more important, is very common in rhetorical precept and practice; cf. e.g. Cic. *orat.* 45 'nam quoniam, quicquid est quod in controversia aut in contentione versetur, in eo aut sitne aut quid sit aut quale sit quaeritur: sitne, signis; quid sit, definitionibus; quale sit, recti pravique partibus; quibus ut uti possit orator, non ille vulgaris sed hic excellens, a propriis personis et temporibus semper, si potest, avocet controversiam; latius enim de genere quam de parte disceptare licet, ut quod in universo sit probatum id in parte sit probari necesse', Sen. *contr.* 9. 4. 9 'nondum de propria sed de communi causa loquor. si efficio ut qui cecidit patrem possit absolvi, pro hoc animosius agam', [Quint.] *decl. min.* 244. 5, 288. 1 Winterbottom. M. L. West, *Hesiod: Works and Days* (Oxford, 1978), 142–3, lists instances in Greek poetry going back to Homer.

To declare that someone is with Christ, or in heaven, is the most obvious τόπος of Christian consolation; for other instances cf. e.g. *epist.* 39. 6. 1 'parce filiae iam cum Christo regnanti', 75. 2. 1 'obsecro te . . . ut Lucinum tuum desideres quidem ut fratrem, sed gaudeas regnare cum Christo', Ambr. *epist.* 15. 2 'inter angelorum ministeria Christo adhaereret', 15. 4 'est igitur iam superiorum incola, possessor civitatis aeternae illius Hierusalem, quae in caelo est'. The absence of similar convictions among most pagans meant that the notion of an afterlife expressed in any but the vaguest or most non-committal terms rarely figured in the armoury of pagan consolers, though rhetorical lip-service was sometimes paid to the idea of the deceased living with the gods, or in the Elysian Fields (cf. Menand. Rhet. *epid.* 2. 9 (414. 16 ff.) Russell–Wilson, with their note).

sanctorum: 'saints' in the broad sense, i.e. all those in heaven.

rimabatur: Wright's 'groped after' gets the sense of attempting to apprehend something unseen, but misses the point of *in terris*, which not only means 'on earth' as opposed to in heaven, but suggests the idea of the soil; *rimari* is often used in agricultural contexts, meaning to turn up the ground, as at Virg. *georg.* 3. 534. 'Scrabbled around for' is perhaps nearer the mark.

aestimatione: the idea is a general one of estimation or judgement, without any technical sense of valuation; almost 'guess-work' (Wright). Cf. e.g. *epist.* 119. 7. 3 'erravit Paulus et humana aestimatione deceptus est'. Tert. *anim.* 9. 3 is helpful: 'sed nos corporales quoque illi inscribimus lineas, non tantum ex fiducia corporalitatis per aestimationem, verum et ex constantia gratiae per revelationem'. Here *aestimatione* contrasts with *videntem* below.

sicut ... dei nostri: Ps. 47: 9 (Vulg.: (LXX) 'sicut audivimus sic vidimus in civitate domini virtutum, in civitate dei nostri', (Hebr.) 'sicut audivimus ita vidimus in civitate dei exercituum, in civitate dei nostri'). Most likely another quotation from memory (hence *domini virtutum*); cf. on 3. 2 *dixerunt ... ad unum*, 4. 1 *notus ... nomen eius*, 6. 1 *ad vesperum ... laetitia*. The psalm is concerned with the glory of God and its manifestation, so the use of the verse here does not remove it far from its original context (it is used similarly at *epist.* 108. 21. 1). But Jerome conveniently interprets *civitate domini* as referring to the celestial kingdom of heaven, whereas in the psalm it actually refers to the earthly Jerusalem.

desiderium ... dolentes: Jerome now finds a solution to the problem presented at 2. 1–2: he knows he should not weep for Nepotianus, who is in heaven, but cannot help it. The explanation here put forward is that the grief experienced is grief not for the condition of the deceased, but for that of the bereaved themselves, who are by his death separated from him. This idea occurs frequently in consolation; cf. e.g. *epist.* 39. 1. 1 'non quo lugenda sit illa, quae abiit, sed quod nobis inpatientius sit dolendum, quod talem videre desivimus', 75. 1. 1 'non quo eius vicem doleam, quem scio ad meliora transisse . . . sed quo torquear desiderio non meruisse me eius viri videre faciem', 108. 30. 2 (quoted below at 7. 2 *quanto . . . bono*), Ambr. *epist.*

39. 5 'verum forte asseras securum te de meritis eius ac fide; nequire tamen ferre desiderium, quod eam iam non videas secundum carnem, idque tibi summo dolori sit', *obit. Valent.* 46. There is a similar emphasis on the bereaved, rather than on the deceased, at Jer. *epist.* 77. 9. 1 'nos hoc tantum dolemus, quod pretiosissimum de sanctis locis monile perdidimus'. The question whether one's grief is really grief for oneself or for the dead occurs also in pagan consolation; cf. e.g. Sen. *dial.* 6. 12. 1 'dolor tuus . . . utrum sua spectat incommoda an eius qui decessit?', 11. 9. 1, [Plut.] *ad Apoll.* 19 (111E) οἱ πενθοῦντες τοὺς οὕτως ἀποθανόντας [i.e. those who have died young] ἑαυτῶν ἕνεκα πενθοῦσιν ἢ τῶν κατοιχομένων; The same kind of notion occurs at Sen. *dial.* 12. 14. 1, although the grief of the consoland there is caused by something other than someone's death. See further Johann, 92–9. For the question of the legitimacy of grieving for oneself see below on 7. 2 *flebant . . . caritatis.*

Kunst, 132, points out that *alicuius vicem dolere* and *desiderium ferre* are very Ciceronian phrases.

7. 2. quanto . . . bono: the grief occasioned by the sense of loss and separation when someone dies is aggravated for Christians by the knowledge that they do not share with him in the joys of heaven. But it is important that the emotion underlying the grief should not be envy; cf. *epist.* 108. 30. 2 'nos nostram vicem dolemus et invidere potius gloriae eius videbimur, si voluerimus diutius flere regnantem'. Similarly, Cicero makes Laelius say of Scipio, who is imagined to have gone to be with the gods, 'quocirca maerere hoc eius eventu vereor ne invidi magis quam amici sit' (*amicit.* 14).

flebant . . . caritatis: Jerome now introduces two cases from the NT which give evidence that grief may be proper even when the person lamented has passed to a new life in heaven; in other words, when grief is felt by the bereaved for their own condition. In so doing he contradicts his assertion at 6. 2 that he has already used up in *epist.* 39 all the Scriptural material which deals with grief and intends to tread a new path (see on 6. 2 *quidquid . . . vestigia*): the case of Lazarus is mentioned at *epist.* 39. 2. 1, and that of Paul and Epaphroditus is a Biblical item not found in that letter.

These examples also show in what sense it is legitimate for a bereaved person to grieve for his own condition. It would be possible to lament the loss of the usefulness to oneself of a friend who has died, but this would be selfish and quite wrong; Cicero makes the point: 'si id dolemus, quod eo iam frui nobis non licet, nostrum est id malum quod modice feramus, ne id non ad amicitiam sed ad domesticam utilitatem referre videamur' (*Brut.* 5). Grief is legitimized, however, when its stimulus is love, or *pietas*, towards the deceased. So here, the sorrow which Paul anticipates he will feel if Epaphroditus dies comes *desiderio caritatis*, and Jesus' tears for Lazarus are said to have been shed *ut veros hominis exprimeret affectus*. This kind of grief is often found mentioned, with the writer's tacit approval, in Christian consolation; cf. e.g. *epist.* 75. 2. 1 (quoted above at 7. 1 *Scimus . . . dei nostri*), 79. 1. 3 'mortem iuvenis mariti sic flevit, ut exemplum coniugii dederit', Ambr. *exc. Sat.* 1. 10 'non omnis infidelitatis aut infirmitatis est fletus . . . pietatis indices', 2. 14, *obit. Theod.* 54 'fles, Honori, germen augustum, et lacrimis pium testificaris adfectum', Paul. Nol. *epist.* 13. 4. Paulinus of Nola crisply delineates the conflict between the demands of *pietas* and those of Christian faith; cf. *carm.* 31. 7–10 'heu! quid agam? dubia pendens pietate laboro, / gratuler an doleam? dignus utroque puer; / cuius amor lacrimas et amor mihi gaudia suadet, / sed gaudere fides, flere iubet pietas'.

flebant . . . suscitaturus erat: for the story of the raising of Lazarus see John 11: 1–44. John does not in fact mention Martha weeping, though it is understandable that Jerome should include her with Mary here (*sorores*), especially as she plays a considerable part in the story as a whole. *ut . . . affectus* may owe something to vv. 35–6 'et lacrimatus est Iesus. dixerunt ergo Iudaei, ecce quomodo amabat eum', though it would in any case have been a reasonable assumption that Jesus' tears were caused by his love for Lazarus.

The case of Jesus weeping is used elsewhere by consolers to legitimize a certain amount of grief. Even in *epist.* 39, where he strongly criticizes Paula's excessive mourning for Blesilla, Jerome uses the incident to justify his own grief at the girl's death: 'matris prohibituri lacrimas ipsi plangimus. confiteor affectus meos, totus hic liber fletibus scribitur. flevit Iesus Lazarum, quia amabat eum' (39. 2. 1). Cf. also e.g. Ambr. *exc. Sat.* 1. 10, Paul. Nol. *epist.* 13. 4, Aug. *epist.* 263. 3 (where Mary and Martha are also mentioned). The author of the letter to Turasius (CSEL 3. 3. 274–82), a piece without parallel in the depth of its feeling that grief is inappropriate for Christians, takes a contrary position, arguing absurdly that Jesus wept because he was about to restore Lazarus to life.

For *salvator* see on 3. 1.

apostolus . . . caritatis: although Paul knows that for a Christian death is a good thing, he would still have grieved, out of love, if Epaphroditus had died: another good precedent for regarding grief of a certain kind as permissible.

   cupio . . . cum Christo: Phil. 1: 23 (Vulg. (giving the context): 'coartor enim e duobus, desiderium habens dissolvi et cum Christo esse; multo magis melius. [24] permanere autem in carne magis necessarium est . . . '). *cupio,* which Jerome regularly employs in citing this verse (cf. e.g. *epist.* 3. 5. 1, 22. 17. 1, 108. 1. 3; he never uses a phrase with *habens,* to judge from the testimonia in VL Beuron), probably reflects his good sense of Latinity; it is clearly superior to the 'desiderium habens' of the Vulgate (which for Philippians is not Jerome's work; cf. Introduction, p. 9), a literal rendering of the Greek τὴν ἐπιθυμίαν ἔχων. Tertullian too writes 'cupio' at *pat.* 9. 5. *mihi . . . lucrum:* Phil. 1: 21 (text as Vulg.). These texts are cited by Ambrose in consolation at *exc. Sat.* 2. 40–1, *obit. Valent.* 46.

   For Epaphroditus cf. Phil. 2: 27 'infirmatus est [sc. Epaphroditus] usque ad mortem, sed deus misertus est eius, non solum autem eius verum etiam et mei, ne tristitiam super tristitiam haberem'. There is no explicit mention of *gratiae,* but it was reasonable for Jerome to infer it from the context. Where Jerome derived the form *Epafras* from is not clear; the Greek is Ἐπαφρόδιτος, rendered in the Vulgate by 'Epafroditus' (Phil. 2: 25). It may simply be a slip.

   incredulitas nearly always appears, as here, in the sense of *religious* unbelief; cf. *TLL* 7. 1. 1040–2.

7. 3. **episcopus:** = ἐπίσκοπος, 'bishop', the head of a Christian community. On the use of the term, and of parallel terms, in the early Church, see C. Mohrmann, 'Episkopos-Speculator', in her *Études,* 4. 231–52. For grades of the clergy at Jerome's time see on 10. 3 *fit . . . ordinatur.*

   in carne . . . pater: not strictly *in carne,* of course, but *pater* is a fairly loose word which can be applied to anyone who fulfils a father's function or inspires fatherly respect (cf. e.g. Virg. *Aen.* 5. 348), or is simply of a father's years (cf. 13. 3 with n. on *aetate . . . collegio*). As Nepotianus' father was dead, Heliodorus was in any case the nearest thing he had to a real father.

   aves . . . suspiras: the metaphor in *viscera,* boldly sustained in *divulsa,* is vivid but not too harsh after *pater:* *viscera* sometimes = 'flesh and blood', usually in reference to a child, the product of the womb and virtually a part of oneself; cf. *OLD* s.v. *viscus* 1, sect. 5, and esp. Ov. *met.* 8. 478, *Cons. ad Liv.* 263–4 'spes quoque multorum flammis uruntur in isdem; / iste rogus miserae viscera matris habet', Quint. *inst.* 6 pref. 3 'unum igitur optimum fuit, infaustum opus et quidquid hoc est in me infelicium litterarum super inmaturum funus consumpturis viscera mea flammis inicere'. In each of these instances, interestingly, the context concerns death, and the *viscera* are imagined on a pyre; more significantly still, the second of the three occurs in consolation, the *mater* being the *consolanda*, while the Quintilian passage deals with the author's grief at the death of his son. For *viscera* more generally, as the object of one's affection, cf. *epist.* 89. 1. 1 (Theophilus to Jerome) 'noluit ante proficisci, nisi te et sanctos fratres qui tecum sunt in monasterio quasi sua viscera amplexaretur et inviseret', Ambr. *obit. Valent.* 58, where the author speaks of the dead Valentinian as his *viscera*. The word is clearly very emotive when used in this kind of sense.

aves, which was printed by Hilberg, following Φ and the original hand of *B*, is certainly correct; the reading is supported by *habes* ΚΨ (*aveo* and *habeo* were frequently confused; cf. *TLL* 2. 1313–14), and is much more potent than *doles GD* (or the *doles abesse* of the earlier editors, which is in any case unattested in the MSS).

suspiras + acc., = 'sigh over', 'long after', seems very elevated; it occurs mainly in poetry.

obsecro . . . nimis: although grief is understandable and permissible when a loved one has died, it must still be kept under restraint. The notion is common in Christian consolation; cf. e.g. Ambr. *epist.* 39. 8 'nec nimio maerore tuam in dubium adducas sententiam', *exc. Sat.* 2. 11 'non enim mediocre malum est inmoderatio doloris aut metus mortis', Paul. Nol. *epist.* 13. 10 'his . . . et verborum et exemplorum caelestium auctoritatibus ut ad pietatem lacrimarum usus es, ita etiam ad earum modum utere . . . scriptura divina, quae producere nos lacrimas quasi evaporando dolore permittit, terminos quoque designato praescribit tempore, cum dicit amaritudinem luctus uno ferendam die', Aug. *epist.* 263. 3, Bas. *epist.* 28. 1, 62 καιρὸς ἡμῖν . . . μὴ λυπεῖσθαι ὡς καὶ οἱ λοιποί, οἱ μὴ ἔχοντες ἐλπίδα [1 Thess. 4: 13], οὐ μὴν οὐδ' ἀπαθῶς ἔχειν πρὸς τὸ συμβάν, ἀλλὰ τῆς μὲν ζημίας αἰσθάνεσθαι, ὑπὸ δὲ τῆς λύπης μὴ καταπίπτειν, Greg. Naz. *epist.* 165. 2 οὔτε τὸ λίαν ἀπαθὲς ἐπαινῶ, οὔτε τὸ ἄγαν περιπαθές· τὸ μὲν γὰρ ἀπάνθρωπον, τὸ δὲ ἀφιλόσοφον. ἀλλὰ δεῖ τὴν μέσην βαδίζοντα, τῶν μὲν ἄγαν ἀσχέτων φιλοσοφώτερον φαίνεσθαι, τῶν δὲ φιλοσοφούντων ἀμέτρως ἀνθρωπικώτερον, John Chrys. *epist.* 197, and above all Jer. *epist.* 39, where he is especially anxious to restrain Paula's grief, e.g. 5. 2 'ignoscimus matris lacrimis, sed modum quaerimus in dolore', 6. 4 'detestandae sunt istae lacrimae plenae sacrilegio, incredulitate plenissimae, quae non habent modum, quae usque ad vicina mortis accedunt'. Alexiou, 27–9, shows how the Greek Fathers attempted similarly to moderate, but not to suppress completely, the often excessive ritual lamentation of the bereaved in the Greek world.

Christians, of course, had good reasons for not mourning the deaths of other Christians. Excessive grief would suggest that faith was lacking (cf. e.g. Jer. *epist.* 39. 6. 4, quoted above), and hence give a handle to unbelievers, which Jerome is at pains to avoid at 14. 6, where see n. on *ubertim . . . in deum.* The notion that grief should be moderated, however, appears frequently in pagan consolation too. Behind it lies principally the idea that to express grief is natural, but to over-indulge it, weak, an attitude which exercised some influence on Christian consolers (cf. esp. the passage from Gregory of Nazianzus quoted above). Good examples are Plato, *Menex.* 247C–248C, Cic. *ad Att.* 12. 10 'tuus autem dolor humanus is quidem, sed magno opere moderandus', *ad fam.* 5. 18. 2, Sen. *epist.* 63. 1 'moleste fero decessisse Flaccum . . . plus tamen aequo dolere te nolo', 99. 16, *dial.* 6. 7. 1 'at enim naturale desiderium suorum est. quis negat, quam diu modicum est?', 11. 18. 6 'fluant lacrimae, sed eaedem et desinant', 12. 16. 1 'non prohibuerunt [sc. maiores] luctus sed finierunt; nam et infinito dolore, cum aliquem ex carissimis amiseris, adfici stulta indulgentia est, et nullo inhumana duritia', Plut. *ad uxor.* 2 (608B–C), [Plut.] *ad Apoll.* 3–4 (102C–E) τὸ δὲ πέρα τοῦ μέτρου παρεκφέρεσθαι καὶ συναύξειν τὰ πένθη παρὰ φύσιν εἶναί φημι . . . οὔτ᾽ ἀπαθεῖς ἐπὶ τῶν τοιούτων συμφορῶν ὁ λόγος ἀξιοῖ γίγνεσθαι τοὺς εὖ φρονοῦντας οὔτε δυσπαθεῖς· τὸ μὲν γὰρ ἄτεγκτον καὶ θηριῶδες, τὸ δ᾽ ἐκλελυμένον καὶ γυναικοπρεπές, 28 (116C). Only occasionally does the notion occur that one ought to let one's grief have full rein; cf. e.g. Stat. *silv.* 2. 6. 1–2, Hor. *carm.* 1. 24. 1–2 (both *epicedia* rather than *consolationes*), and in these poems too a sterner position is taken at the end.

The philosophical view that such μετριοπάθεια was the proper means of dealing with grief—as opposed to ἀπάθεια and to complete submission to it—appears to have been held by Crantor (cf. Kunst, 133, Gregg, 83–5), and may have had a place in Cicero's *Consolatio* (for Cicero's debt to Crantor in this work see on 5. 2 *legimus . . . Cicero*, and Introduction, pp. 19–20). The notion is so widespread, however, and so understandable for Christians to hold, that it would be rash to suppose that Jerome is directly indebted to the *Consolatio* for what he says here, as Kunst seems to do.

The concept of the value of moderation, in all things, not merely in grief, is of course originally Greek, the saying μηδὲν ἄγαν (*ne quid nimis*) being attributed by Aristotle to Chilon (Arist. *rhet.* 1389ᵇ). It appears early in Latin; cf. e.g. Ter. *Andr.* 61. Jerome quotes the saying and the doctrine elsewhere; cf. *epist.* 108. 21. 4 (in connection with Paula's extremely hard life in the convent), 130. 11. 1–2 (on moderation in fasting).

obligatoque . . . vulnere: for *vulnus* used to denote the mental effect of grief see on 1. 1 *desiderii . . . vulneratos*. The metaphor is easily sustained by *obligato*, a word commonly used of wounds (cf. *TLL* 9. 2. 89).

audias laudes eius: it was by no means essential, according to the tradition, that a letter of consolation should contain eulogy of the deceased. There is none, for example, in Sen. *epist.* 63, or in *dial.* 11, and neither of these works is directed to giving consolation on the death of a child, when it might have been difficult to devote a section to praise. But the close relationship between letters of consolation and funeral orations (see Introduction, pp. 16–17), which regularly contained panegyric, meant that the former often had a partially encomiastic function. This is particularly true of the present letter, which Jerome conceived as a funeral oration in epistolary form (see Introduction, p. 29); the lengthy eulogistic section which he is about to introduce thus fits naturally into his scheme for the piece.

The rhetorical handbooks, in their discussions of epideictic oratory, give clear indications of the kind of things which would have been expected in eulogy; cf. e.g. *Rhet. Her.* 3. 10 'laus igitur potest esse rerum externarum, corporis, animi. [The classification goes back to Plato and Aristotle; cf. H. Caplan, [*Cicero*] *ad C. Herennium* (London and Cambridge, Mass., 1954), 174.] rerum externarum sunt ea, quae casu aut fortuna . . . accidere possunt: genus, educatio, divitiae, potestates, gloriae, civitas, amicitiae, et quae huiusmodi sunt et quae his contraria . . . corporis sunt ea, quae natura corpori attribuit . . . velocitas, vires, dignitas, valetudo, et quae contraria sunt. animi sunt ea, quae consilio et cogitatione nostra constant: prudentia, iustitia, fortitudo, modestia, et quae contraria sunt', Cic. *inv.* 2. 177–8, Quint. *inst.* 3. 7. 10–18. Much later Menander Rhetor, discussing the ἐπιτάφιος λόγος, says much the same: ἐγκωμιάσεις δὲ ἀπὸ πάντων τῶν τόπων τῶν ἐγκωμιαστικῶν, γένους, γενέσεως, φύσεως, ἀνατροφῆς, παιδείας, ἐπιτηδευμάτων, τεμεῖς δὲ τὴν φύσιν δίχα, εἴς τε τὸ τοῦ σώματος κάλλος, ὅπερ πρῶτον ἐρεῖς, εἴς τε τὴν τῆς ψυχῆς εὐφυΐαν (*epid.* 2. 11 (420. 10–14) Russell–Wilson).

External qualities were not valued purely for their own sake but for the use to which the possessor put them; cf. e.g. Cic. *inv.* 2. 178 'videre autem in laudando et in vituperando oportebit non

tam, quae in corpore aut in extraneis rebus habuerit is, de quo
agetur, quam quo pacto his rebus usus sit', *Rhet. Her.* 3. 13,
Quint. *inst.* 3. 7. 13. In an interesting passage Statius regards
them as of relatively little importance: 'laudantur proavis aut
pulchrae munere formae, / quae morum caruere bonis, falsoque
potentes / laudis egent verae: tibi quamquam et origo niteret / et
felix species multumque optanda maritis, / ex te maior honos,
unum novisse cubile, / unum secretis agitare sub ossibus ignem'
(*silv.* 5. 1. 55–6). In Christian writers, particularly in the Latin
West but also in the Greek East, *res externae* and *corpus* are
normally minimized or omitted altogether as subjects for praise
(as in this letter; cf. c. 8), in accordance with the Christian
emphasis on personal responsibility and spiritual qualities, and
while *prudentia, modestia,* and other aspects of *animus* still find a
place in eulogy, specifically Christian virtues such as faith,
prayer, and humility have greater importance; see, for example,
the sort of things Jerome praises in Nepotianus in c. 10. Only
rarely are features such as physical beauty praised by Christians;
when Ambrose does so at *obit. Valent.* 58 ff. it is by way of
quotations from the Song of Songs, and the body is regarded as
the home of the soul, which is what is really important (cf. Favez
(1937), 108; also 13. 2 *ubi totius corporis dignitas, quo veluti
pulchro indumento pulchritudo animae vestiebatur?*). Generally,
eulogy is seen as a means of glorifying not man but God; cf. e.g.
Paul. Nol. *epist.* 13. 13 'non enim hominis, sed divina per
hominem opera laudamus'. See further Favez (1937), 106–26.

cuius . . . laetatus es: the transposition of *semper* and *virtute*
from the normal word-order results in a fine double-cretic
clausula. For the influence of prose-rhythm on word-order in
Jerome see Appendix 2, pp. 240–1.

nec doleas . . . habueris: the τόπος belongs to both Christian
and pagan consolation; closely related is the idea that one
received the other person as a gift from God or from fortune in
the first place. Cf. e.g. Jer. *epist.* 108. 1. 2 'non maeremus, quod
talem amisimus, sed gratias agimus, quod habuimus, immo
habemus', 118. 4. 2 'non contristor, quod recepisti, sed ago
gratias, quod dedisti', Ambr. *exc. Sat.* 1. 3 'laetandum enim
magis est, quod talem fratrem habuerim, quam dolendum, quod
fratrem amiserim; illud enim munus, hoc debitum est', Paul.
Nol. *epist.* 13. 6, Bas. *epist.* 5. 2 οὐκ ἀπεστερήθημεν τοῦ παιδός, ἀλλ'
ἀπεδώκαμεν τῷ χρήσαντι, 269. 2 μὴ οὖν, ἐπειδὴ ἀφηρέθημεν αὐτόν,
ἀγανακτῶμεν, ἀλλ', ὅτι τὴν ἀρχὴν συνῳκήσαμεν, χάριν ἔχωμεν τῷ
συζεύξαντι; Cic. *Tusc.* 1. 93, Sen. *epist.* 63. 7 'desine beneficium
fortunae male interpretari: abstulit, sed dedit', 99. 3 'si amicum

perdidisses, danda opera erat ut magis gauderes quod habueras
quam maereres quod amiseras', *dial.* 6. 12. 2, 11. 10. 1 'illud
quoque . . . necesse est te adiuvet cogitantem non iniuriam tibi
factam quod talem fratrem amisisti, sed beneficium datum quod
tam diu tibi pietate eius uti fruique licuit', Plut. *ad uxor.* 8
(610E), [Plut.] *ad Apoll.* 28 (116A–B), Liban. *epist.* 1473. 3 τοιαῦτα
γὰρ τὰ τῆς Τύχης· ἔδωκεν, εἶτα ἀφείλετο; and, for contrast, Plin.
epist. 8. 5. 2 'habet quidem Macrinus grande solacium, quod
tantum bonum tam diu tenuit, sed hinc magis exacerbatur quod
amisit; nam fruendis voluptatibus crescit carendi dolor'. The
similarity in wording between our passage and Ambr. *exc. Sat.*
1. 3 has caused some to think that both Jerome and Ambrose
may have been drawing on a phrase in Cicero's *Consolatio* (so
Buresch (1886), 104, G. Madec, *Saint Ambroise et la philosophie*
(Paris, 1974), 156); alternatively it might be argued that Jerome
is directly indebted to Ambrose here, as at 14. 1 *huiusce . . .
gratius*, where see n.; but attributions to particular sources are
dangerous in the case of common τόποι such as this, and we
should observe that Seneca expresses himself in exactly the same
kind of way at *epist.* 99. 3.

The general balance of the clauses *nec . . . amiseris* and *sed . . .
habueris*—the rhythm, the equal number of syllables—and their
rhyme are most striking.

sicut . . . virtutum: there is a slight anacoluthon here. The
true comparison is between the map-makers and Jerome himself; but, after *sicut . . . pingunt*, which would properly be
followed by some expression like 'so I have delineated his
virtues', Jerome recalls that Heliodorus has been the subject of
every clause after *obsecro ut*, and, wishing to preserve the
construction (though the force of *obsecro* is very weak by the time
we get to *cernas* and *suscipias*), he is forced to break from the
logical arrangement imposed by *sicut . . . pingunt*. The sense is
nevertheless quite plain.

On maps in the Later Empire see J. O. Thomson, *History of
Ancient Geography* (Cambridge, 1948), 378–81, O. A. W. Dilke,
Greek and Roman Maps (London, 1985), 112–22, 167–70.
Whether Jerome is here thinking of maps of the world or of a
smaller area is not clear; probably just maps generally.

For the image of the *brevis tabella* cf. *epist.* 73. 5. 1, 123. 13. 1
'quasi in brevi tabella latissimos terrarum situs ostendere volui,
ut pergam ad alias quaestiunculas . . .', 147. 12, *in Is.* 66. 22–3
(CCSL 73A. 796 = PL 24. 675).

terrarum situs is a well-established phrase; cf. e.g. Cic. *div.*
2. 97, Hor. *epist.* 2. 1. 262.

cernas . . . virtutum: a borrowing from Cic. *Cael.* 12 (on Catiline): 'habuit enim ille, sicuti meminisse vos arbitror, permulta maximarum non expressa signa sed adumbrata virtutum'; cf. *Tusc.* 3. 3. Jerome is of course merely interested in the expression; he does not intend to draw a parallel between Catiline and Nepotianus. That he knew the speech well is clear from his numerous reminiscences of it; see J. F. Gilliam, 'The *Pro Caelio* in St. Jerome's Letters', *HThR* 46 (1953), 103–7. This particular passage is imitated also by Ambr. *fug. saec.* 3. 14 'habemus haec genera non adumbrata sed expressa virtutum', Symm. *or.* 3. 7 'agnosco in te non adumbrata vestigiis sed expressa veterum signa virtutum'.

non vires sed voluntatem: for the self-depreciation cf. 1. 1 *Grandes . . . explicare* with n.; the same contrast between ability and intention is made in several of the passages there cited, three of them (*pref. in psalm., in Ezech. lib.* 3 pref., *in Ioel* pref.) using the same terms (*vires* and *voluntas*; cf. Ov. *Pont.* 3. 4. 79). For the notion that the intention is more important cf. also [Quint.] *decl. min.* 281. 2 Winterbottom 'numquam mens exitu aestimanda est' (with Winterbottom's note), *decl. mai.* 5. 10 pp. 94. 27–95. 1 Håkanson 'non fortunam tibi debeo sed affectum, non exitum sed voluntatem', Jer. *epist.* 68. 1. 1 'in amicis . . . non res quaeritur, sed voluntas, quia alterum ab inimicis saepe praebetur, alterum sola caritas tribuit', 153. 1. 3, (in legal contexts) Cic. *Mil.* 19 'nisi vero, quia perfecta res non est, non fuit punienda, proinde quasi exitus rerum, non hominum consilia legibus vindicentur', Call. *dig.* 48. 8. 14 'divus Hadrianus in haec verba rescripsit: in maleficiis voluntas spectatur, non exitus'.

c. 8. The eulogistic section opens with a rejection of the precept that one should begin with consideration of the subject's ancestors. Family, like physical attributes, is unimportant and irrelevant. What matters is the individual soul, and Jerome proposes to praise Nepotianus simply with regard to his own merits, starting from the time of his baptism, when he was reborn in Christ.

8. 1. Praecepta . . . videatur: ancestors belong to the category of *res externae*; see on 7. 3 *audias laudes eius.* What Jerome says here about the handling of the theme accords closely with the rhetorical handbooks; cf. [Arist.] *rhet. ad Al.* 35. 6–9 (1440^b–1441^a), *Rhet. Her.* 3. 13 'ab externis rebus: genus, in laude, quibus maioribus natus sit; si bono genere, parem aut excelsiorem fuisse; si humili genere, ipsum in suis, non in maiorum virtutibus habuisse praesidium', Quint. *inst.* 3. 7. 10 'ante hominem patria ac parentes maioresque erunt, quorum

duplex tractatus est: aut enim respondisse nobilitati pulchrum
erit aut humilius genus inlustrasse factis'. Jerome also clearly
knows of the principle of beginning the eulogy with *res externae*
(cf. *Rhet. Her.* 3. 13, where this is put first in the order of the
three categories from which praise is to be drawn, Quint. *inst.* 3.
7. 10 'primum dividitur [sc. laus hominum] in tempora, quodque
ante eos fuit quoque ipsi vixerunt, in iis autem qui fato sunt
functi etiam quod est insecutum', Empor. *rhet.* p. 567. 25–6
Halm 'laudatur autem aliquis aut reprehenditur ex his quae sunt
ante ipsum, quae in ipso quaeque post ipsum', Menand. Rhet.
epid. 2. 11 (419. 15–18) Russell–Wilson; Polybius, by contrast,
describes the *laudator* recounting the deeds of the ancestors only
after the deceased himself has been eulogized (6. 54. 1)). The
connections between this passage (and as far as *genere*) and
Quint. *inst.* 3. 7. 10 ff. are not, however, so close verbally as to
indicate a direct debt on Jerome's part, as argued by Hagendahl
(1974), 225–6.

For *avitis . . . videatur* cf. also Greg. Naz. *orat.* 43. 8 (on Basil)
εἰ γὰρ μέγα τοῖς ἄλλοις τὸ προσλαβεῖν τι παρὰ τῶν ἄνωθεν εἰς
φιλοτιμίαν, μεῖζον ἐκείνῳ τὸ προσθεῖναι τοῖς ἄνω παρ' ἑαυτοῦ, καθάπερ
ῥεύματος ἀνατρέχοντος.

eorum . . . repetantur: with *repetere*, *alte* or *altius* often has
a temporal sense; cf. e.g. Cic. *orat.* 11, *Cluent.* 66, Jer. *epist.*
108. 3. 1 (quoted below at *nec . . . genere*). This is also the
obvious meaning here. The transposition of *altius* from its
more natural position before the verb is likely to be due less
to a wish of Jerome to suggest in addition the greatness of
the ancestors' deeds (*altius gesta*) than to a wish to improve
the rhythm: though *altius repetantur* makes a flawless clausula
accentually, metrically it gives a hexameter-type (dactyl–
spondee) ending, which Jerome may well have wanted to
avoid. *gesta repetantur* is acceptable either way. For Jerome's
attention to rhythm see Appendix 2.

avitis paternisque: a very common formula for 'ancestral'.

carnis . . . non requiram: *carnis bona* = 'physical advantages', in contrast to qualities of soul—the category of *corpus* in
the rhetoricians (see on 7. 3 *audias laudes eius*). Nepotianus'
disregard of the flesh is made quite clear in the following
chapters.

nec . . . genere: for Jerome's refusal to praise his subject's
lineage cf. *epist.* 77. 2. 3, 79. 2. 1, 108. 3. 1 'alii altius repetant et
ab incunabulis eius ipsisque, ut ita dicam, crepundiis matrem
Blesillam et Rogatum proferant patrem . . . nos nihil laudabimus, nisi quod proprium est', 127. 1. 3 'neque vero Marcellam

tuam . . . institutis rhetorum praedicabo, ut exponam inlustrem familiam, alti sanguinis decus et stemmata per consules et praefectos praetorio decurrentia. nihil in illa laudabo, nisi quod proprium est'. Only personal qualities are of any account. At *epist.* 130. 3. 1 he writes: 'rhetorum disciplina est abavis et atavis et omni retro nobilitate ornare, quem laudes, ut ramorum sterilitatem radix fecunda conpenset et, quod in fructu non teneas, mireris in trunco', and then goes on briefly to praise Demetrias' father, before recalling himself (4. 1): 'verum quid ago? oblitus propositi, dum admiror iuvenem, laudavi aliquid bonorum saecularium, cum in eo mihi virgo magis nostra laudanda sit, quod haec universa contempserit'. Gregory of Nazianzus explicitly passes over his father's ancestry (and *res externae* in general) at *orat.* 18. 5, while at *orat.* 43. 4 he justifies praise of Basil's ancestors by saying that the qualities which he intends to eulogize were inherited by Basil and characterized his life; these qualities are also for the most part essentially Christian (cf. *orat.* 43. 5–10). Paulinus of Nola justifies beginning a eulogy of the elder Melania with reference to her ancestry by appealing not to rhetorical practice, which he rejects, but to Biblical precedent in the gospel accounts of the family origins of John the Baptist and Jesus himself (*epist.* 29. 7–8).

A striking manifestation of the Christian view that ancestry was unimportant was the redefinition of the concept of *nobilitas* in Christian terms. Among Christians people came to be regarded as *nobilis* less by reason of their consular (or prefectorial; cf. T. D. Barnes, 'Who were the Nobility of the Roman Empire?', *Phoenix*, 28 (1974), 444–9) ancestry than by reason of their Christian virtues; cf. e.g. Jer. *epist.* 1. 9. 2, 107. 13. 4, 108. 1. 1 'nobilis genere, sed multo nobilior sanctitate [sc. Paula]', 127. 1. 3 'opibus et nobilitate contempta facta est paupertate et humilitate nobilior [sc. Marcella]', 130. 7. 11, [Jer.] *epist.* 148. 21. 1 'nescit religio nostra personas nec condiciones hominum sed animos inspicit, servum et nobilem de moribus pronuntiat', Prud. *perist.* 10. 123–5 'absit ut me nobilem / sanguis parentum praestet aut lex curiae: / generosa Christi secta nobilitat viros' (the following verses are also illuminating), Bede, *hist. abb.* 1.

cum . . . natus: Jerome uses three examples from the Bible to show that considerations of *genus* are irrelevant when someone's personal qualities are being assessed; ancestry can be quite misleading.

For Ishmael cf. Gen. 16: 1–12, esp. 11–12, where the angel declares to Hagar that he will be a 'ferus homo, manus eius contra omnes et manus omnium contra eum'. He is not, however, a particularly happy choice as a sinner son of a father who is *sanctus*, for elsewhere in Genesis God blesses him (17: 20) and says that he will make of him a great nation (21: 18). For Esau's birth cf. Gen. 25: 25; his sin must be his intention to kill Jacob (cf. Gen. 27: 41). For Jephthah cf. Judg. 11: 1 (the son of a *meretrix*), Heb. 11: 32 ff. (inclusion in a list of faithful men). *apostoli voce* may indicate that Jerome shared Origen's belief (cf. Euseb. *hist. eccl.* 6. 25. 11–14) that Hebrews was not written directly by Paul but composed by someone else on the basis of what he had heard Paul say.

   e regione: 'on the other hand', as at e.g. *epist.* 54. 5. 4, 107. 6. 3, *adv. Iovin.* 2. 7 (PL 23. 295). The usage is derived by extension from the more literal meaning, 'opposite', which occurs at e.g. Caes. *Gall.* 7. 36. 5, Cic. *nat. deor.* 2. 103, Jer. *epist.* 108. 13. 2, Exod. 19: 2 'castrametati sunt in eodem loco, ibique Israhel fixit tentoria e regione montis'.

8. 2. anima . . . vivet: Jerome draws on Ezekiel for further evidence that ancestral vices and virtues are irrelevant to the individual soul; the stress is entirely on one's own actions. The quotation, *anima . . . morietur*, comes from Ezek. 18: 4, repeated at 18: 20 (text as Vulg.). The converse idea, *quae non peccaverit, ipsa vivet*, while not necessarily entailed by what precedes, as *ergo* would suggest, is an obvious corollary found also at Ezek. 18: 19. It receives support in the gospels; cf. e.g. John 8: 51, 11: 26 'omnis qui vivit et credit in me [sc. Iesum] non morietur in aeternum' (both passages quoted by Jerome at *in Ezech.* 18. 3–4 (CCSL 75. 230 = PL 25. 170)).

   Ezekiel is consciously rejecting the Mosaic view that sin is transmitted from one generation to another, the basis of which is the commandment-passage at Exod. 20: 5 'ego sum dominus deus tuus, fortis, zelotes, visitans iniquitatem patrum in filiis in tertiam et quartam generationem eorum qui oderunt me'; the case of the Gibeonites and the descendants of Saul at 2 Sam. 21 is an instance where God is said to have put his threat into operation. At *epist.* 39. 2. 3–4 Jerome accepts both Ezekiel's view and the Mosaic view as possible for the present time, but with his continual emphasis on personal action and responsibility seen, for example, in the rigorous ascetic life he often prescribes and his critical attitude towards worldly people, he must generally have adhered to the Ezekiel line. This is the view he holds at *epist.* 107. 6. 2–3, where it is, however, modified in the case of young children, who cannot be held wholly responsible for their actions.

   inquit: almost 'it is written', without a conscious subject.

ab eo tempore . . . renascimur: i.e. all that matters for the individual is how he lives after baptism, which washes away all past sins and is essential for salvation. That baptism is implied in *renascimur* is clear from John 3: 5 'respondit Iesus: amen, amen dico tibi, nisi quis renatus fuerit ex aqua et spiritu, non potest introire in regnum dei' and from the reference to the Jordan which follows; see also 9. 2. Cyprian's biographer Pontius takes the same approach: 'unde igitur incipiam? unde exordium bonorum eius adgrediar, nisi a principio fidei et nativitate caelesti? siquidem hominis dei facta non debent aliunde numerari, nisi ex quo deo natus est' (*vita Cypr.* 2).

Paulus . . . caput: the example of Paul is introduced to show the irrelevance of one's life before baptism to the assessment of one's vices and virtues. Nepotianus is also set off in a splendid light by the implicit comparison with the great apostle (cf. the direct comparison with Timothy at 10. 4).

The image of the *lupus rapax* is drawn from Gen. 49: 27; Jacob, prophesying the future of each of the twelve tribes, says of Benjamin, 'Beniamin lupus rapax; mane comedet praedam, et vespere dividet spolia' (VL (significantly): ' . . . mane manducabit [*al.* comedet] adhuc et ad vesperam dabit [*al.* dividet] escam'; Jerome had not yet done the Vulgate translation of Genesis (cf. Introduction, p. 10)). Paul was of the tribe of Benjamin; cf. Rom. 11: 1, Phil. 3: 5. The figure of the wolf is well suited to Paul before his conversion, and Jerome uses it elsewhere; cf. e.g. *epist.* 38. 1 'Paulus, lupus rapax et Beniamin adulescentior, in extasi caecatur, ut videat'. For his persecution of the Church cf. Acts 7: 59, 8: 3, 9: 1 ff.

mane and *ad vesperam* are of course to be taken metaphorically, referring to the time before and after Paul's conversion (for the imagery cf. 6. 1 *ad vesperum . . . adpropinquavit* with nn.). The story of Ananias' hospitality towards Paul, and of the latter's baptism just a few days after his blinding on the Damascus road, is told at Acts 9: 10–19. The only reference to food (9: 19), however, indicates Paul and not Ananias as the recipient; *Ananiae* cannot, therefore, be indirect object after *dedit escam* (so Wright), which must be taken absolutely as an extension of the image of the wolf (cf. the VL text of Gen. 49: 27, quoted above). Whereas previously Paul was *rapax*, he now *provides* food—in physical or spiritual form, to the needy, presumably. *Ananiae ovi* forms a phrase, as at *epist.* 69. 6. 7 'Paulus, persecutor ecclesiae et lupus rapax Beniamin, Ananiae ovi submittit caput'.

The metaphor of Paul as a wolf contrasts easily with that of

Ananias as a sheep, an image derived ultimately from the Biblical picture of Christians as sheep (cf. e.g. John 21: 15–17), and perhaps from the idea of the sheep led to the slaughter (cf. Isa. 53: 7), where the emphasis is on the mildness of the animal.

igitur . . . nascatur: as with Paul, so with Nepotianus; Jerome says that he will consider only his life after baptism. The images of the *infantulus vagiens* and the *rudis puer* perhaps remind us that, though Nepotianus himself had not been baptized until adulthood (cf. 9. 2), a swing back to infant baptism, to which there had been resistance in the years following the recognition of Christianity as the official religion of the Empire, is observable from *c*.365; cf. J. Jeremias, *Die Kindertaufe in den ersten vier Jahrhunderten* (Göttingen, 1958), 110–13. The Jordan is named simply because it was the river in which Jesus was baptized by John (cf. Matt. 3: 13 ff., Mark 1: 9).

Jerome takes up a similar position in the case of Fabiola; cf. *epist.* 77. 2. 2 'novis mihi est efferenda praeconiis et ordine rhetorum praetermisso tota de conversionis ac paenitentiae incunabulis adsumenda', after which he says that he will not go on to boast of her ancestors.

c. 9. After c. 8 it is a surprise to find that Jerome does not immediately begin his account of Nepotianus' life post-baptism. Instead, by means of two instances of *praeteritio* (for which see on 4. 2 *taceo de . . .*), he touches first on Heliodorus' return to Altinum from the East many years before, undertaken for the sake of Nepotianus and his mother, and then describes Nepotianus' life in the *palatii militia* before he became a fully committed, baptized Christian.

9. 1. Alius . . . nepos: during his stay at Antioch, *c*.373–5 (for which see Introduction, pp. 2–3), Jerome tried to persuade Heliodorus, who had arrived there separately, to accompany him to the Syrian desert, where they would take up the hermit life. But after much soul-searching Heliodorus declined and decided to return to Altinum, saying, however, that when Jerome had settled in the desert, he should write inviting him to join him. See Kelly, 40, 44.

It is to Heliodorus' departure from the East that Jerome here refers. The incident would seem to have little to do with the *laudes Nepotiani*; but plainly Jerome regards it as one which a eulogist less rigorous than himself, one who felt less strongly about including details of Nepotianus' pre-baptismal life in the eulogy, might call on. The point must be that Heliodorus' return to Altinum is thought of as marking the start of Nepotianus' spiritual career; the influence of his uncle on the young man was pronounced, to judge particularly from Jerome's comments at 10. 2–3.

Though, as the context demands, Jerome seeks to present Heliodorus' abandonment of the East in a favourable light, undertaken *ob salutem illius . . . ut . . . nepotem dulcissimum conservares*, it plainly still rankles after more than twenty years. *lactaveris*, as Labourt saw, must mean not so much 'nourished' as 'beguiled', 'led on', almost 'deceived', which gives greater point to *carissimum sodalem tuum*; for *lactare* in this sense cf. e.g. Plaut. *Cist.* 215–18, Ter. *Andr.* 647–8 'non[ne] tibi sat esse hoc solidum visumst gaudium, / nisi me lactasses amantem et falsa spe produceres', Jer. *epist.* 82. 8. 1 'nos usque ad praesentem diem ficta pacis ostensione lactaverit', *c. Ioh.* 36 (PL 23. 388), *in Os.* 7. 11 (CCSL 76. 77 = PL 25. 878) 'ab Aquila et Symmacho θελγομένη vel ἀπατωμένη dicitur, id est lactata, sive decepta', and see on 4. 2 *melos* (*TLL* 7. 2. 855 gives only one instance between Accius and the fourth century AD). Again, the quotation *licet . . . nepos* is drawn from the letter which Jerome actually wrote to Heliodorus from the desert, in which he is sharply critical of his friend's action: 'recordare tirocinii tui diem, quo Christo in baptismate consepultus in sacramenti verba iurasti: pro nomine eius non te matri parciturum esse, non patri. ecce adversarius in pectore tuo Christum conatur occidere; ecce donativum, quod militaturus acceperas, hostilia castra suspirant. licet parvulus ex collo pendeat nepos, licet sparso crine et scissis vestibus ubera, quibus nutrierat, mater ostendat, licet in limine pater iaceat, per calcatum perge patrem, siccis oculis ad vexillum crucis vola! pietatis genus est in hac re esse crudelem' (*epist.* 14. 2. 2–3; for the military metaphors cf. on 9. 2 *sub alterius . . . militarit*). Sensitivity was never Jerome's strong point.

The fact that Jerome can quote verbatim from a letter he wrote so long before is a sure indication that he retained copies of at least some of his correspondence; cf. *epist.* 35. 1. 2 (Damasus), where it is made clear that in 384 Jerome had a collection of letters which he had written during his time in the desert. Augustine recognizes that Jerome may have preserved copies of letters which he had sent Augustine; cf. Aug. *epist.* 71. 2 (= Jer. *epist.* 104. 2. 1), 82. 30 (= Jer. *epist.* 116. 30. 1). The practice was not unusual; cf. e.g. J. F. Matthews, 'The Letters of Symmachus', *Latin Literature of the Fourth Century*, ed. J. W. Binns (London, 1974), 58–99, at 64, on Symmachus. It is no surprise that Jerome should have preserved in his archive a literary piece like *epist.* 14, of which he later (AD 394) wrote:

'dum essem adulescens . . . scripsi ad avunculum tuum, sanctum Heliodorum, exhortatoriam epistulam plenam lacrimis querimoniisque et quae deserti sodalis monstraret affectum. sed in illo opere pro aetate tunc lusimus et calentibus adhuc rhetorum studiis atque doctrinis quaedam scolastico flore depinximus' (*epist.* 52. 1. 1–2). Fabiola, who had spent time with Jerome in the Holy Land, is said to have known it inside out (*epist.* 77. 9. 2: 'tenebat memoriter'), and it may have circulated widely, as certain of Jerome's letters are known to have done; see Introduction, pp. 13–15.

heremum: see on 3. 3 *Iohannes . . . adpropinquavit enim regnum caelorum.*

sororem . . . viduam: nothing is known about Heliodorus' sister or the circumstances of her widowing. As Nepotianus served for a time in the *palatii militia* (cf. 9. 2), her husband was presumably a man of some standing.

hic . . . nepos: *hic* = Nepotianus, the subject of the discussion; *vaticinatus sum* = 'said, with visionary insight'. The words *licet . . . nepos* proved prophetic in that they predicted the close relationship which was to develop between Heliodorus and Nepotianus; *vaticinatus sum* cannot be satisfactorily understood in any other way.

The image of the child around an adult's neck is a favourite of Jerome's; cf. *epist.* 107. 4. 8 'cum avum viderit, in pectus eius transiliat, e collo pendeat', 128. 1. 3 'de matris pendeat collo'.

For *nepos* = 'nephew' cf. e.g. Ven. Fort. *carm.* 6. 2. 16 'non cecidit patruus, dum stat in orbe nepos'.

9. 2. referret . . . baptizatum: this second instance of *praeteritio* enables Jerome to point out that Nepotianus lived a good and Christian life before he was baptized, when in the *palatii militia*; he cannot say so by direct means because he has ruled out as irrelevant consideration of his life before baptism. At the end of the passage he indeed expresses dissatisfaction with Nepotianus' lack of total commitment. In itself the fact that Nepotianus was in the *palatii militia* does not seem to have mattered much to Jerome; cf. *epist.* 79. 2. 4, where he says of Nebridius, 'nihil nocuit militanti [sc. Nebridio] paludamentum et balteus et apparitorum catervae, quia sub habitu alterius alteri militabat'. For early Christian attitudes to military service (if that is what *palatii militia* here implies; see below) see Harnack, 46–92 (Engl. tr. 65–104), with Gracie's introduction to the English translation, 9–18, J. Helgeland, 'Christians and the Roman Army from Marcus Aurelius to Constantine', *ANRW* II. 23. 1. 724–834, with his bibliography.

palatii militia: it is possible that this was not the army but the civil service. Most civil servants ranked as soldiers from the time of Diocletian, and Constantine completed the system by granting military privileges and status to the palatine offices. Civil servants were issued with a uniform, and wore a *cingulum*; and although the duties entailed were different from those of real soldiers, service in a government department was still called *militia* (*officialis*, as opposed to *armata*). An official could be called a *miles*, and the other military language of 10. 1—*alienis signis, castrensis peculii*, etc.—would not be out of place in a civil service context, especially when a deliberate contrast is being drawn between Nepotianus as a *miles* serving the Emperor or the state, and Nepotianus as a *miles Christi*. On the superficial military character of the civil service see Jones, *LRE*, 1. 566; and on *palatini* generally Jones's index, and *RE* s.v. 'Palatini'. Heliodorus too had been in the *militia*; cf. *epist.* 14. 6. 4.

chlamyde . . . lino: the Roman military uniform seems to have comprised three garments, *pallium* (cloak), *chlamys* (tunic), and *sticharium* (shirt), the last of which is probably represented by *candenti lino* here; cf. Jones, *LRE*, 1. 624–5.

cilicio: *cilicium* = κιλίκιον, material made originally from the hair of Cilician goats. For its various uses see *RE* s.v. 'Cilicium'. Christians used it for ascetic purposes—hair-shirts, or rough mattresses; cf. e.g. *epist.* 130. 4. 4 'aiunt . . . eam . . . ciliciolum in nuda humo habuisse pro stratu'. To wear it was a mark of penitence, for which there was Biblical authority; cf. e.g. *epist.* 147. 8. 1 'hortatus sum, ut ageres paenitentiam et in cilicio et cinere volutareris', 1 Kgs. 21: 27 'cum audisset Ahab sermones istos, scidit vestem suam et operuit cilicio carnem suam ieiunavitque et dormivit in sacco', Isa. 22: 12 (these two passages quoted by Jerome at *epist.* 122. 3. 5 and 122. 1. 5 respectively). See further P. Antin, 'Le Cilice chez saint Jérôme', *La Vie spirituelle*, supp. 1 (1947), 58–61 (= Antin, *Recueil*, 305–9), R. Grégoire, 'Cilicium induere', *Homenaje a Fray Justo Pérez de Urbel* (2 vols., Abadia de Silos, 1976–7; = *Studia Silensia*, 3–4 (1976–7)), 2. 299–320, who traces the practice through the Middle Ages up to modern times.

lurida . . . portaverit: in referring to a person's fasting Jerome often comments on his or her consequent paleness (cf. e.g. *epist.* 22. 7. 2 'pallebant ora ieiuniis', 54. 6. 2 'pallor ex ieiuniis'); this may reflect the common τόπος associating paleness with hunger or emaciation, for which see F. Bömer, *P. Ovidius Naso: Metamorphosen: Buch 8–9* (Heidelberg, 1977), 253 (on Ov. *met.* 8. 801). For Jerome's views and those of other patristic writers on fasting see on 10. 7 *ieiunia . . . moderabatur*.

For the rare use of *portare* with parts of the body see *TLL* 10.

2. 51, which cites no other instances with *os*; in Jerome cf. *epist.* 22. 17. 2, *in Is.* 58. 3–4 (CCSL 73A. 663 = PL 24. 564) ('vacuum portare ventrem' in both cases).

sub alterius . . . militarit: cf. *epist.* 79. 2. 4 (quoted above at *referret . . . baptizatum*). *alteri*, of course, is Christ.

The depiction of the Christian life as military service is common in Christian literature. It doubtless owes most to the NT (cf. e.g. Rom. 6: 13, 2 Cor. 6: 7, and esp. Eph. 6: 11–17 'induite vos arma dei . . . '), though the metaphor is not originally or exclusively Christian (cf. Gracie's introduction to his translation of Harnack, 19–20); it finds, for example, parallels in the worship of Isis, whose initiates were regarded as soldiers (cf. W. W. Tarn and G. T. Griffith, *Hellenistic Civilisation* (3rd edn., London, 1952), 358), and of Mithras, where one of the seven grades of initiation bestowed the title *miles* (cf. Jer. *epist.* 107. 2. 2, Harnack, 38 (Engl. tr. 58)). The whole Christian body is sometimes represented as an army, with Christ as its commander; cf. e.g. Tert. *orat.* 29. 3, Cypr. *mort.* 15, Jer. *epist.* 14. 2. 1, 58. 1. 3, 107. 4. 8, c. 15. 2 with n. on *Iulianus . . . propagatos*. For the basic metaphor of fighting for God in Jerome cf. e.g. *epist.* 14. 7. 1, 22. 39. 4, 130. 5. 3. See in general Harnack, 1–46 (Engl. tr. 27–64), *Dict. spir.*, 10. 1210–23, s.v. 'Militia Christi'.

habuerit cingulum: i.e. 'undertook military (or public) service'. *cingulum* is often used symbolically in this way; cf. *TLL* 3. 1068–9, and esp. Rufin. *hist.* 10. 33 'militiae cingulum non dari nisi immolantibus iubet [sc. Iulianus]', *Cod. Theod.* 6. 30. 18, Aug. *epist.* 151. 8 'ne . . . susciperet cingulum militiae Christianae', Prud. *perist.* 1. 32 'ad perenne cingulum Christus vocat [sc. milites martyres]'.

mihi . . . baptizatum: for *centurionem . . . baptizatum* cf. Acts 10, which recounts the story of the calling and baptism of the centurion Cornelius, 'vir iustus et timens deum' (v. 22). Jerome means that one becomes *iustus* through baptism; cf. Rom. 6: 1–11, esp. v. 4, and 5: 19. Nepotianus' dedication to God's service was incomplete while he was still unbaptized.

c. 10. Jerome now passes to the time when Nepotianus left the *militia* and began to devote himself fully to the service of Christ. Though anxious to become a monk, he would not leave his uncle Heliodorus, who provided him with a pattern for his life, and consequently he became a *clericus*, though claiming that he was unworthy. He had many virtues: he cared for others, was humble and sexually continent, prayed regularly and vigilantly, fasted in

moderation, and possessed a masterly knowledge of Scripture and
of the writings of the Fathers. Favez (1937), 109–26, collects many
instances in Christian letters of consolation and funeral speeches
where the deceased is eulogized in respect of qualities such as
these.

The descriptive parts of the passage, particularly from 10. 5, are
kept stylistically very simple: Jerome allows the facts to speak for
themselves.

10. 1. Verumtamen . . . erogavit: Jerome makes no mention of
baptism here; but as what follows is clearly, in Jerome's terms,
legitimate praise of Nepotianus, one must assume that the latter
was baptized around the same time as he left the *militia*. Jerome
does not seem to have felt that to leave the *militia* was an
essential part of the total dedication to Christ which baptism
symbolized, but complete renunciation of worldly things was an
ideal encouraged by Christ's words at Matt. 19: 21 (quoted
below in the text), and right for a *clericus* (cf. *epist.* 52. 5. 2),
which Nepotianus soon became. It did not matter that Nebri-
dius was in the *militia* (cf. *epist.* 79. 2. 4, quoted at 9. 2 *referret . . .
baptizatum*), indeed he could not effect a total renunciation as he
had a young family (cf. *epist.* 79. 4. 1), and Jerome praises him
without any suggestion that he lacked full commitment; he must
have been baptized, especially as he 'dormivit in domino' (*epist.*
79. 6. 1).

  incunabula . . . fidei: the image is familiar; cf. e.g. Cic. *de
orat.* 1. 23 'repetamque non ab incunabulis nostrae . . . doctrinae
quendam ordinem praeceptorum', Jer. *epist.* 52. 4. 3 'ab incunabulis fidei', 77. 2. 2 'de conversionis ac paenitentiae incunabulis',
Salv. *eccl.* 4. 42 'quasi exordia et quasi incunabula conversionis
suae'.

  ut . . . sit: the clause is best taken as causal, i.e. 'seeing that
. . .'; for *ut* in this sort of sense see LHS 2. 647–8.

  donandus laurea sit: Jerome is thinking of the laurel as a
symbol of military victory, borne at triumphs. For the image
applied to a member of the army of Christ cf. e.g. Prud. *perist.* 5.
537–40 'tu solus, o bis inclyte, / solus bravii duplicis / palmam
tulisti, tu duas / simul parasti laureas'. For the expression cf.
Hor. *carm.* 4. 2. 9 'laurea donandus Apollinari'.

  balteo: probably the same item as the *cingulum* of 9. 2; at *epist.*
64. 12. 1, when discussing the vestments of priests, Jerome takes
the words to be synonymous.

  castrensis peculii: a technical phrase, explained by the
jurists; cf. e.g. Paul. *sent.* 3. 4A. 3 'castrense . . . peculium est,
quod in castris adquiritur vel quod proficiscenti ad militiam

datur', Macer *dig.* 49. 17. 11 'castrense peculium est, quod a parentibus vel cognatis in militia agenti donatum est vel quod ipse filius familias in militia adquisiit, quod, nisi militaret, adquisiturus non fuisset'.

in pauperes erogavit: so too Paula and others praised by Jerome gave their possessions to the poor; cf. e.g. *epist.* 75. 4. 1 (Lucinus), 79. 4. 1 (Nebridius), 108. 5. 1 (Paula) 'quid ergo referam amplae et nobilis domus et quondam opulentissimae omnes paene divitias in pauperes erogatas?'. At *epist.* 120. 1. 4 Jerome suggests that the Christian poor should be helped above all: 'haec dicimus, non quo in pauperes Iudaeos sive gentiles et omnino cuiuslibet gentis sint pauperes prohibeamus faciendam elemosynam, sed quo Christianos et credentes pauperes incredulis praeferamus'.

To give to the poor was obviously an important Christian duty, but was not by itself sufficient for the perfect Christian life; cf. e.g. *epist.* 66. 8. 4, 71. 3. 2–3, *in Matt.* 19. 21 (CCSL 77. 170–1 = PL 26. 137).

legerat . . . sequatur me: *qui . . . me* is adapted, from the second person to the third, from Matt. 19: 21 'ait illi [i.e. the rich young ruler] Iesus: si vis perfectus esse, vade, vende quae habes [VL: vende omnia tua] et da pauperibus, et habebis thesaurum in caelo, et veni, sequere me'. Nepotianus' action reveals his obedience to God, who speaks to men through Scripture.

non potestis . . . mamonae: cf. Matt. 6: 24 'nemo potest duobus dominis servire; aut enim unum odio habebit et alterum diliget, aut unum sustinebit et alterum contemnet. non potestis deo servire et mamonae', Luke 16: 13 'nemo servus potest duobus dominis servire; aut enim unum odiet et alterum diliget, aut uni adherebit et alterum contemnet. non potestis deo servire et mamonae'; the words are Jesus'.

At *in Matt.* 6. 24 (CCSL 77. 39 = PL 26. 44) Jerome explains 'mamonae': 'mammona sermone syriaco divitiae nuncupantur'.

10. 2. excepta . . . reservavit: for the idea that clothes should be simply practical, worn to keep out the cold, cf. e.g. *epist.* 66. 5. 1, 107. 10. 1 'spernat bombycum telas, Serum vellera et aurum in fila lentescens. talia vestimenta paret, quibus pellatur frigus, non quibus corpora vestita nudentur', 127. 3. 4 'nostra vidua [sc. Marcella] talibus usa est vestibus, quibus obstaret frigus, non membra nudaret'. Normally, as in these cases, the topic occurs where Jerome is making a contrast, implicit or explicit, between Christian and worldly women, who over- (or under-) dress and over-adorn themselves, a practice which Jerome saw as sexually provocative and corrupting (cf. e.g. *epist.* 38. 3. 2, 54. 7. 1) and which comes in for some of his bitterest satire (cf. Wiesen, 113–65). For both this attitude and that evinced in the present passage, where a quite different point is being made, support could be found in Scripture; cf. e.g. Matt. 6: 25 'ne solliciti sitis . . . corpori vestro quid induamini', (against female adornment) 1 Tim. 2: 8–10, Rev. 17: 4 (quoted in support of non-adornment by Cyprian at *hab. virg.* 12).

cultus . . . erat: *cultus* = 'dress'; for parallels see Nisbet–Hubbard (1970), 115. For the avoidance of any kind of ostentation in dress cf. e.g. Sen. *epist.* 5. 1–3, Greg. Naz. *orat.* 18. 23, Jer. *epist.* 22. 27. 3 'vestis nec satis munda nec sordida et nulla diversitate notabilis [sc. sit]', 52. 9. 1 (Jerome advising Nepotianus) 'vestes pullas aeque vita ut candidas; ornatus et sordes pari modo fugiendae, quia alterum delicias, alterum gloriam redolet', 125. 7. 1 (a slightly different view) 'sordes vestium candidae mentis indicio sint, vilis tunica contemptum saeculi probet, ita dumtaxat, ne animus tumeat, ne habitus sermoque dissentiat'.

Ostentation was of course to be avoided by the Christian in all things, being contrary to the virtue of *humilitas*, and it was important that the practice of virtue itself did not become ostentatious; cf. e.g. *epist.* 23. 2. 2 'inculta vestis, vilis cibus, neglectum caput, ita tamen ut, cum omnia faceret, ostentationem fugeret singulorum', 24. 5. 1 'ita pallor in facie est, ut cum continentiam indicet non redoleat ostentationem', 58. 2. 2 'nihil est . . . grande tristi et lurida facie vel simulare vel ostentare ieiunia'.

aut . . . aut . . . vel: such a combination of disjunctive particles is by no means rare; cf. e.g. Quint. *inst.* 3. 6. 72 'ut aut de nomine aut scripto et sententia vel ratiocinatione quaeratur', 8. 6. 68–9.

Aegypti . . . choros: Christian monasticism is generally held to have originated in Egypt around the beginning of the fourth century, St Antony traditionally being regarded as its founder (though no fourth-century sources call Antony the founder of monasticism, and in *Vita Pauli* Jerome makes a case for the priority of Paul of Thebes). There is reason to believe, however, that the practice first developed in Syria and Mesopotamia; cf. R. Murray, 'The Features of the Earliest Christian Asceticism', *Christian Spirituality: Essays in Honour of Gordon Rupp*, ed. P. Brooks (London, 1975), 63–77, at 65, and esp. A. Vööbus, *History of Asceticism in the Syrian Orient: A Contribution to the History of Culture in the Near East* (Corpus scriptorum Christianorum orientalium, 184, Subsidia 14, 17; 2 vols., Louvain, 1958–60), 1. 138–69. At any rate, the practice will have been well

established in both Egypt and Mesopotamia by this time. At
epist. 22. 34–6 Jerome discusses the three classes of monks in
Egypt.

Early monasticism in general has been the subject of a wealth
of literature; in addition to the above see esp. P. de Labriolle,
'Les Débuts du monachisme', *Histoire de l'Église depuis les
origines jusqu'à nos jours*, ed. A. Fliche and V. Martin (21 vols.,
Paris, 1934–52), 3. 299–369, with his bibliography, D. J. Chitty,
*The Desert a City: An Introduction to the Study of Egyptian and
Palestinian Monasticism under the Christian Empire* (Oxford,
1966), O. Chadwick, *John Cassian* (2nd edn., Cambridge, 1968),
1–36, G. D. Gordini, 'Origine e sviluppo del monachesimo a
Roma', *Gregorianum*, 37 (1956), 220–60, K. Lorenz, 'Die
Anfänge des abendländischen Mönchtums im 4. Jahrhundert',
ZKG 77 (1966), 1–61. For the testimony of Jerome see P. Antin,
'Le Monachisme selon saint Jérôme', *Mélanges bénédictins pu-
bliés à l'occasion du 14ᵉ centenaire de la mort de S. Benoît* (S.-
Wandrille, 1947), 71–113 (= Antin, *Recueil*, 101–33).

monasterium = μοναστήριον. In origin the word referred to the
dwelling of a single monk, as Isidore later noted: 'monasterium
unius monachi habitatio est. μόνος enim apud Graecos solus,
στηριον statio; id est solitarii habitatio' (*orig.* 15. 4. 5); in this
sense it appears at e.g. *Itin. Eg.* 4. 6, 16. 2, Jer. *vita Hilar.* 24 (PL
23. 40) 'exemplo . . . eius per totam Palaestinam innumerabilia
monasteria esse coeperunt', *tract. in psalm.* 119 (CCSL 78. 259)
'in monasteriis et maxime in coenobiis solent ista esse vitia'. The
plural therefore sometimes denotes the group of individual cells
and consequently the monastery; cf. e.g. Greg. Naz. *orat.* 43. 62,
Mac. Aeg. *perf.* 9, Ambr. *epist.* 15. 12. Generally, however,
monasterium indicates the dwelling of a colony of monks (*monachi*; *monachae*, if women), or simply the colony itself, without the
associated idea of a building. See *TLL* 8. 1402–4. *monachus*
showed a similar extension of its original meaning; cf. on 10. 3 *in
uno . . . venerabatur.*

insularum . . . solitudines: *insularum Dalmatiae* presumably refers to the archipelago extending along the east coast of
the Adriatic, with *freto* referring not to a narrow strait but to the
whole width of that sea. In comparison with Egypt or Mesopotamia these islands are very close indeed to Altinum. Jerome can
hardly mean the small islands of the lagoon on which Altinum
stood, to which the inhabitants of the city moved after the
destruction of Altinum itself by Attila in 452 (cf. *RE* s.n.
Altinum); *Dalmatiae* would then be rendered pointless.

Jerome is almost certainly thinking of the same islands when he writes to Julian in 407: 'extruis monasteria, multus a te per insulas Dalmatiae sanctorum numerus sustentatur' (*epist.* 118. 5. 6); and it was probably to one of them that Bonosus withdrew around 374 (cf. *epist.* 3. 4, Kelly, 35).

avunculum . . . non audebat: the references to Heliodorus in the third person in this part of the letter (cf. 10. 3, 6–9, 11. 1, 13. 2–3) are distinctly functional. They help to fix the focus very much on Nepotianus and away from Heliodorus, giving the *laudes* section an appropriately general context, and allowing Heliodorus to view with greater objectivity and better perspective the character-portrait of Nepotianus which is being drawn.

pontificem: the word is from the fourth century occasionally used of a bishop, as at e.g. *epist.* 108. 6. 1. See the comments of C. Mohrmann, 'L'Étude du grec et du latin de l'Antiquité chrétienne', in her *Études*, 4. 91–110, at 99–100.

tota . . . exempla virtutum: 'representations of virtue that were quite complete in themselves'. For this use of *tota* see D. R. Shackleton Bailey, *Propertiana* (Cambridge, 1956), 93.

Jerome readily seizes the opportunity to flatter Heliodorus.

domique . . . disceret: for the idea cf. Sen. *contr.* 1. 1. 3 'quid porro tam longe exempla repeto, tamquam domi [Bursian's conjecture for MSS 'modo'] desit?', [Quint.] *decl. min.* 287. 4 Winterbottom 'iam domi habet exemplum'. The expression here, however, appears to be proverbial, as Otto, 120, sect. 573, notes; cf. Ter. *Ad.* 413 'domi habuit unde disceret', and esp. Sidon. *epist.* 7. 9. 19 'ut proverbialiter loquar, domi habuit unde disceret'.

10. 3. in uno . . . venerabatur: cf. *epist.* 52. 7. 6 'esto subiectus pontifici tuo et quasi animae parentem suspice . . . plura tibi in eodem viro observanda sunt nomina: monachus, pontifex, avunculus'.

A *monachus* (μοναχός) was properly a Christian who for his religion's sake chose to live in isolation; cf. e.g. Rut. Nam. 1. 441–2 'ipsi se monachos Graio cognomine dicunt / quod soli nullo vivere teste volunt', Jer. *epist.* 58. 5. 1 'monachus, id est solus', and esp. 14. 6. 1 (addressing Heliodorus) 'interpretare vocabulum monachi, hoc est nomen tuum: quid facis in turba, qui solus es?'. Augustine too recognizes that, strictly speaking, the word should not be applied to ascetics living in communities; cf. *in psalm.* 132. 6. In practice, however, it came to be used for members of the various ascetic sects irrespective of whether they lived in groups (like the cenobites) or as solitaries (like the anchorites). Orosius is altogether broader in his definition: 'monachi, hoc est Christiani, qui ad unum fidei opus dimissa

saecularium rerum multimoda actione se redigunt' (*hist.* 7. 33.
1). In Greek at least the word also possesses connotations of
uniqueness and of perfection; cf. e.g. Arist. *metaph.* 1040ª, Plot.
6. 8. 7, Dion. Ar. *eccl. hier.* 6. 1. 3 οἱ θεῖοι καθηγεμόνες ἡμῶν
ἐπωνυμιῶν αὐτοὺς ἱερῶν ἠξίωσαν, οἱ μὲν θεραπευτὰς, οἱ δὲ μοναχοὺς
ὀνομάζοντες, ἐκ τῆς τοῦ θεοῦ καθαρᾶς ὑπηρεσίας . . . καὶ τῆς ἀμερίστου
καὶ ἑνιαίας ζωῆς, ὡς ἐνοποιούσης αὐτοὺς . . . εἰς θεοειδῆ μονάδα καὶ
φιλόθεον τελείωσιν.

A distinction is frequently drawn between *monachi* and *clerici*
(for which see below on *fit . . . ordinatur*); cf. e.g. Jer. *epist.* 14. 8.
1 'alia . . . monachi causa est, alia clericorum'. Monks could
nevertheless be ordained and the roles of *monachus* and *clericus*
combined: there is nothing odd in Heliodorus' being described
as both monk and bishop. On the relationship between the
monastic and clerical ways of life see K. Heussi, *Der Ursprung
des Mönchtums* (Tübingen, 1936), 182–6.

episcopum: see on 7. 3, and below on *fit . . . ordinatur*.

non . . . adsiduitas . . . fecerat: cf. *epist.* 45. 2. 2 'adsiduitas
familiaritatem, familiaritas fiduciam fecerat'.

'Familiarity breeds contempt' was certainly a Latin proverb in
the Middle Ages; cf. Otto, 132, sect. 641, citing [Aug.] *scal.
parad.* 8 'vulgare proverbium est, quod nimia familiaritas parit
contemptum'—a work apparently written by Guigo, a twelfth-
century Carthusian prior (cf. PL 40. 997–8, 153. 785–6). I know
of no instances earlier than the present one, however.

ita admirabatur . . . cerneret: i.e. his admiration for him
never faded through over-exposure, picking up *adsiduitas . . .
fecerat*.

fit . . . ordinatur: a *clericus* (κληρικός) was an ordained
minister of the Church, as opposed to a member of the laity
(*laicus*). For fourth- and fifth-century views of the origin of the
title, and of what the word actually covered, cf. e.g. Jer. *epist.* 52.
5. 1 'clericus, qui Christi servit ecclesiae, interpretetur primum
vocabulum suum et nominis definitione praelata nitatur esse,
quod dicitur. si enim κλῆρος Graece sors Latine appellatur,
propterea vocantur clerici, vel quia de sorte sunt domini vel quia
dominus ipse sors, id est pars, clericorum est', Aug. *in psalm.* 67.
19 'et cleros et clericos hinc appellatos puto, qui sunt in
ecclesiastici ministerii gradibus ordinati, quia Matthias sorte
electus est, quem primum per apostolos legimus ordinatum',
Cod. Theod. 16. 2. 2 (AD 319) 'qui divino vultui ministeria
religionis impendunt, id est hi, qui clerici appellantur'.

Within the ordained ministry were various orders or grades,
membership of any of which qualified a man as a *clericus*.

Isidore, writing in the early seventh century, recognized a definite hierarchy of nine grades (cf. *orig.* 7. 12. 2 'generaliter autem clerici nuncupantur omnes qui in ecclesia deserviunt, quorum gradus et nomina haec sunt: ostiarius, psalmista, lector, exorcista, acolythus, subdiaconus, diaconus, presbyter, episcopus'), but there were variations on this pattern (cf. *ODCC* s.v. 'Orders and Ordination'). The minor orders began to be established from the third century (they are first found mentioned by Cornelius, Bishop of Rome, in a letter written to Fabius of Antioch in 252 and quoted by Euseb. *hist. eccl.* 6. 43. 11; of those on Isidore's list only the psalmist is missing), but were never of great importance; only *episcopi, presbyteri,* and *diaconi* had major sacerdotal and liturgical functions (which were limited in the case of *diaconi*—in particular they were forbidden by the Council of Nicaea to celebrate the eucharist—and it is not clear whether or not they could strictly be called *sacerdotes* (see on 10. 4 *sacerdotio*)), the lesser clergy merely attending them and carrying out less important duties. Jerome sometimes writes as if there were only three grades—bishops, presbyters, and deacons—altogether (cf. e.g. *epist.* 14. 8. 4–5, 49. 21. 3), but it is clear that he knew of others (cf. e.g. *epist.* 51. 2. 1 (tr. from Epiphanius) 'diaconos et hypodiaconos', 52. 5. 6 'lector . . . acolythus . . . psaltes'; the 'archipresbyteri' and 'archidiaconi' mentioned at *epist.* 125. 15. 1, however, refer not so much to separate grades as to the principal presbyter and deacon in each church). Exactly what grades Nepotianus had to pass through to become a presbyter, other than that of deacon (as we may presume), is uncertain. Paulinian seems to have started off by being ordained deacon; cf. below on 10. 3–4 *Iesu . . . indignum.*

For the organization of the early Church and its offices the first three books of Bingham are still invaluable; the differences in the functions of bishops and presbyters who were under episcopal authority are discussed in bk. 2, c. 3. Hatch too is helpful on such matters. For Jerome's view that in apostolic times the terms 'bishop' and 'presbyter' were synonymous, referring to the same office, cf. *in Tit.* 1. 5 (PL 26. 562–3), *epist.* 146, with Kelly, 147.

ordinatur: Christian writers adopted *ordinare* to mean 'appoint to an office in the ministry' (cf. *TLL* 9. 2. 945), but there are pagan antecedents for this kind of usage; cf. e.g. Suet. *Vesp.* 23. 2 'candidatum ad se vocavit; exactaque pecunia . . . sine mora ordinavit', *Iul.* 76. 3, *Cod. Theod.* 2. 12. 7 'si in rem quoque suam cognitor vel procurator quis fuerit ordinatus'.

10. 3–4. Iesu . . . indignum: resistance to ordination, as either

presbyter or bishop, was typical of the fourth century. Ambrose
and Augustine were effectively forced to be ordained; cf. Paul.
Med. *vita Ambr.* 6–9, Possid. *vita Aug.* 4, Aug. *serm.* 355. 2.
John Chrysostom recounts his own efforts to avoid the priesthood at *sacerd.* 1. 6, Paulinus of Nola his at *epist.* 1. 10; other
instances are collected and discussed by P.-H. Lafontaine, *Les
Conditions positives de l'accession aux ordres dans la première
législation ecclésiastique (300–492)* (Ottawa, 1963), 72–91. The
most fascinating illustration of the phenomenon is perhaps the
account by Epiphanius of Salamis of the ordination of Jerome's
brother Paulinian in a letter written to John of Jerusalem in 394
and translated by Jerome, = Jer. *epist.* 51. 1. 5–6: 'cum igitur
celebraretur collecta in ecclesia villae, quae est iuxta monasterium nostrum, ignorantem eum [sc. Paulinianum] et nullam
penitus habentem suspicionem per multos diaconos adprehendi
iussimus et teneri os eius, ne forte liberare se cupiens adiuraret
nos per nomen Christi, et primum diaconum ordinavimus
proponentes ei timorem dei et conpellentes, ut ministraret;
valdeque obnitebatur indignum esse se contestans. vix ergo
conpulimus eum et suadere potuimus testimoniis scripturarum
et propositione mandatorum dei. et cum ministrasset in sanctis
sacrificiis, rursus cum ingenti difficultate tento ore eius ordinavimus presbyterum'. From the third century cf. the case of
Cornelius: 'non . . . vim fecit ut episcopus fieret, sed ipse vim
passus est ut episcopatum coactus exciperet' (Cypr. *epist.* 55. 8).

    Close connections can be observed between resistance of this
kind and reluctance or 'refusal' to accept the Principate; cf. J.
Béranger, *Recherches sur l'aspect idéologique du Principat*
(Schweizerische Beiträge zur Altertumswissenschaft, 6; Basle,
1953), 137–69, who (139–40) collects cases of emperors 'refusing' office from Augustus to Magnus Maximus. In this context it
becomes clear that, though resistance to ordination may reflect
the view that the priesthood, and especially the episcopate, is a
great office which can be exercised worthily only with difficulty,
and may at times have been motivated simply by a wish to avoid
sacerdotal responsibility, the response was to a greater or lesser
extent conventional. Refusal proved one's worth; so Pliny could
say of Trajan, 'recusabas enim imperare, recusabas, quod erat
bene imperaturi. igitur cogendus fuisti' (*Paneg.* 1. 5. 5–6), and
Porphyrius of Gaza, like Nepotianus and Paulinian, resisted
ordination—as bishop, in this case—on the claim that he was
unworthy (cf. Mark the deacon, *vita Porph.* 16). The continuing
tradition associated with the appointment of a new Speaker in
the House of Commons illustrates the tenacity of the theme.

10. 3. Iesu bone: for the oath cf. *epist.* 77. 7. 1 'Iesu bone, quo illa fervore, quo studio intenta erat divinis voluminibus', 130. 6. 2.

10. 4. sacerdotio: the term *sacerdos* (priest) certainly covered both bishops and presbyters (but cf. on 11. 1 *sacerdotii*); whether deacons could strictly be called *sacerdotes* or not is a vexed question (cf. Bingham, bk. 2, c. 20, sects. 1–2, who sets out evidence on both sides). At *epist.* 108. 28. 3 Jerome seems to imply that in his view deacons were not *sacerdotes*: 'aderant . . . episcopi et sacerdotum inferioris gradus ac Levitarum innumerabilis multitudo', where 'Levitarum' refers, as often, to deacons.

clamabat indignum: the emphatic position of *indignum* at the end helps to stress the contrast with *dignior*, and at the same time allows a superior clausula (cf. the more natural *indignum clamabat*). For Jerome's attention to prose-rhythm see Appendix 2.

vidimus . . . esse presbyterum: although Nepotianus was young he was fitted to be a priest by reason of his wisdom and lifestyle. Cf. *epist.* 58. 1. 2 'noli igitur . . . annorum aestimare nos numero nec sapientiam canis reputes, sed canos sapientia Salomone teste: cani hominis prudentia eius. nam et Moyses septuaginta presbyteros iubetur eligere, quos ipse sciret esse presbyteros, utique non aevo, sed prudentia iudicandos, et Danihel adhuc puer et longaevos iudicat, atque inpudicos senes aetas lasciva condemnat'.

For Timothy cf. 1 Tim. 4: 12 'nemo adulescentiam tuam contemnat, sed exemplum esto fidelium in verbo, in conversatione, in caritate, in fide, in castitate'. Nepotianus of course gains in stature by being compared with his Biblical predecessor. Sidonius Apollinaris couches in similar terms a parallel drawn between Lupus, Bishop of Troyes, and St James the Less: 'alter saeculi tui Iacobus' (*epist.* 6. 1. 1). For *nostri temporis* cf. Bartelink (1980), 111.

canos in Sapientia alludes to Wisd. 4: 8–9 'senectus enim venerabilis est non diuturna, neque numero annorum conputata; cani sunt autem sensus hominibus, et aetas senectutis vita immaculata'; *electum . . . presbyterum* to Num. 11: 16–17 'et dixit dominus ad Mosen: congrega mihi septuaginta viros de senibus Israel, quos nosti quod senes populi sint ac magistri . . . ut sustentent tecum onus populi et non tu solus graveris'. It is clear from *epist.* 58. 1. 2 (quoted above) that Jerome understands Moses to have chosen *presbyteri* (πρεσβύτεροι, = *senes*) by reason not of their age but of their wisdom; the case is therefore a very good parallel to that of Nepotianus.

Although the sentence is wholly dependent on Scriptural

sources, the notion of a young man possessing wisdom or other qualities associated with age was also a τόπος of pagan literature; cf. Curtius, 106–9. For the image of grey hairs in this connection see the examples collected by Powell, 233 (on Cic. *sen.* 62).

10. 5. clericatum . . . onus: cf. *epist.* 69. 8. 3 'si quis episcopatum desiderat, bonum opus desiderat: opus, non dignitatem, laborem, non delicias'. The play on *honos/onus* is a well-established pun; see the many instances collected by Otto, 167, sect. 828, and the *Nachträge*. Jerome employs it again, in a like context, at *epist.* 82. 8. 1 'fratrem meum causam dicit esse discordiae, hominem, qui quiescit in monasterii cellula et clericatum non honorem interpretatur, sed onus'. Sidonius and Stephen of Tournai (late twelfth century) push it to the limit; cf. Sidon. *epist.* 8. 8. 3 'is profecto inveniere, quem debeat sic industrium quod latentem non tam honorare censor quam censetor onerare', Steph. Torn. *epist.* 146 (PL 211. 432) 'eum sic honorastis et onerastis, ut et honor non deficiat ex onere, et onus proficiat ex honore'.

clericatum = the office of a *clericus*, for which see on 10. 3 *fit . . . ordinatur*.

humilitate: one should not of course be *too* humble; cf. e.g. *epist.* 22. 27. 4 'ne satis religiosa velis videri nec plus humilis quam necesse est, ne gloriam fugiendo quaeras'. For the importance of avoiding ostentation in the practice of virtue see on 10. 2 *cultus . . . erat*.

nullam . . . fabulam: a second possible reminiscence of Cicero's *Pro Caelio*, though much less certain than that at 7. 3 *cernas . . . virtutum*, where see n.; cf. *Cael.* 69 'hic etiam miramur, si illam commenticiam pyxidem obscenissima sit fabula consecuta?'. Jerome uses the same expression at *epist.* 79. 5. 2 'in primo aetatis flore tantae verecundiae fuit, ut virginalem pudorem vinceret et ne levem quidem in se obsceni rumoris fabulam daret' and *adv. Iovin.* 1. 41 (PL 23. 272) 'obsceni rumoris . . . fabulam'; it is a sort of personal cliché (cf. on 11. 1 *interpellatricem . . . iudicis*).

mordebantur: there seems no reason to regard this as a deponent usage, as Wright and Labourt suggest ('railed against his youth', 'auraient critiqué sa jeunesse'). *mordeor* can, at least in late Latin, mean 'be aggrieved', 'be envious' (cf. *invidiam* above)—rather more than the regular 'be hurt', 'be vexed'— though it is rare in this sense. *TLL*, 8. 1486–7, gives as parallels Hesych. *in lev.* 19. 17 'non invidere operantibus iustitiam, nec morderi quando alii secundum Christum glorificantur', and Cassiodorus' Latin version of Josephus' *Jewish Antiquities* 10. 14

'Daniel . . . invidiae apud ceteros crimine laborabat: mordentur enim, qui quosdam . . . plus quam se valere conspiciunt', where Josephus' original Greek gives βασκαίνουσι . . . οἱ . . . ἑτέρους . . . βλέποντες (*ant. Iud.* 10. 250).

stuperent ad continentiam: *continentia* in the sexual sphere, a virtue highly prized in early Christian thought (virginity was normally held up as the ideal), was naturally considered to be more difficult to achieve in youth, the time of giving free rein to one's passions (cf. e.g. Cic. *Cael.* 39–42). Nebridius and Valentinian II are also said, again in eulogistic passages, to have been very much in control of their sexuality in their youth; cf. Jer. *epist.* 79. 5. 1–2, Ambr. *obit. Valent.* 17.

subvenire . . . fuit: Jerome paints in these few strokes a clear picture of Nepotianus' social actions. The sequence of historic infinitives imparts a sense of timelessness, continuity, and vividness; the device is regularly used in bright descriptive passages (cf. KS 1. 135–8, LHS 2. 367–8) and, most significantly here, commonly forms part of the technique of the character-sketch (cf. e.g. Sall. *Catil.* 14. 6, 16. 2–3, Liv. 21. 4. 2, 21. 4. 4). At *epist.* 52. 15. 1–2 Jerome has similar thoughts on Nepotianus' duty as a *clericus*: 'officii tui est visitare languentes, nosse domos, matronas ac liberos earum . . . consolatores potius nos in maeroribus suis quam convivas in prosperis noverint'. Furia is instructed in much the same way; cf. *epist.* 54. 12. 2 'nudum vesti, esurientem ciba, aegrotantem visita'. Fabiola went to enormous lengths to help the sick and the poor, founding a hospital and giving out money lavishly (cf. *epist.* 77. 6); and Paula too took it upon herself to assist those who needed help of this kind (cf. *epist.* 108. 5). To succour the needy was to succour Christ; cf. *epist.* 130. 14. 7–8 'tibi [sc. Demetriae] aliud propositum est: Christum vestire in pauperibus, visitare in languentibus, pascere in esurientibus, suscipere in his, qui tecto indigent'.

blanditiis: 'gentle words', without any notion of flattery or allurement.

gaudere . . . flentibus: Rom. 12: 15 (text as Vulg.), part of a list of instructions to Christians; the passage slots easily into the infinitive sequence, and may even have inspired it.

caecorum . . . lugentium: the chiastic order slightly relieves the monotony.

caecorum baculus: so Jerome says to Pammachius, 'caecorum oculus sis, manus debilium, pes claudorum' (*epist.* 66. 13. 1). The metaphor of the staff is an obvious one; cf. e.g. Tobit 10: 4 'baculum senectutis nostrae, solacium vitae nostrae' (of a son), [Ambr.] *act. Seb.* 2. 7 'o filii, meae baculum senectutis'.

baculus, the masculine form, appears alongside the neuter *baculum* from the third century AD; prior to that there are no certain masculine instances. See *TLL* 2. 1670–2.

esurientium cibus: the primary meaning must be that Nepotianus literally provided food for the hungry (cf. Jerome's instructions at *epist.* 52. 5. 3 'mensulam tuam pauperes et peregrini et cum illis Christus conviva noverit'), but the notion of spiritual food, which occurs at e.g. Ezek. 34: 2–3, John 21: 15, may not be entirely absent from Jerome's mind.

solamen: words in -*men*, where they do not belong to the living language, are a feature of poetic or elevated style; cf. Löfstedt (1956), 2. 297. *solamen*, which first appears in Virgil (cf. J. Perrot, *Les Dérivés latins en -men et -mentum* (Études et commentaires, 37; Paris, 1961), 39), is highly poetic; in the context we might have expected the more prosaic *solacium*.

10. 6. extremus in ordine: this should mean that Nepotianus put himself in the lowest place: a positive virtue rather than a simple fact of rank. He may have been guided partly by the idea that the first would be last and the last first (cf. Matt. 19: 30, 20: 16, Mark 10: 31, Luke 13: 30).

in publico . . . noverat: showing respect in both situations. Heliodorus is referred to as Nepotianus' *pater* also at 7. 3, where see n. on *in carne . . . pater*.

gaudium . . . intellegeres: for the undesirability of immoderate or coarse laughter cf. Ecclus. 21: 23 'fatuus in risu inaltat vocem suam; vir autem sapiens vix tacite ridebit', Cic. *off.* 1. 103 'ipsumque genus iocandi non profusum nec immodestum, sed ingenuum et facetum esse debet'. *cachinnus* and *cachinnare* are often used of laughter uttered to deride or humiliate; cf. e.g. Catull. 56. 2, Cic. *Verr.* 2. 3. 62.

intellegeres: for the imperf. subj. of potentiality in the past see LHS 2. 334. Address to the reader is, like the historic infinitive, common in character-sketch; cf. e.g. Sall. *Catil.* 25. 3, Liv. 21. 4. 3.

10. 7. viduas . . . castitate: a *clericus* was naturally expected to be very careful in his relations with women; cf. *epist.* 52. 5. 4–6 'omnes puellas et virgines Christi aut aequaliter ignora aut aequaliter dilige. ne sub eodem tecto manseris; ne in praeterita castitate confidas . . . si propter officium clericatus aut vidua tibi visitatur aut virgo, numquam domum solus introeas'. By *virgines Christi* Jerome means women and girls who had dedicated themselves, or had been dedicated, to a life of virginity in the service of Christ, such as Eustochium, Asella, the younger Paula, and Pacatula (see *epist.* 22, 24, 107, 128 respectively); on this practice see esp. H. Koch, *Virgines Christi* (Texte und Untersuchungen, 31. 2; Leipzig, 1907), whose discussion is, however, limited to the first three centuries AD.

For the historic infinitives see on 10. 5 *subvenire . . . fuit.*

relicto . . . monachorum: i.e. while his duties as a *clericus* were pastoral, involving him in practical work with other people, he could when at home live a monastic type of life, with the emphasis on inward activities such as prayer.

creber . . . precando: the quality of prayerfulness is praised also in other subjects of Jerome's eulogy (cf. e.g. *epist.* 23. 2. 2 (Lea), 39. 1. 2 (Blesilla), 79. 2. 3 (Nebridius)), and in Valentinian (cf. Ambr. *obit. Valent.* 32). Prayer and the reading of Scripture were the cornerstones of the religious life, and there are numerous instances in Jerome of exhortation to pray and read and of the precept put into practice; cf. e.g. *epist.* 39. 5. 1, 43. 1, 58. 6. 2, 79. 9. 2, 107. 9. 3, 125. 11. 1.

orare and *precari* are synonymous. The adoption of *orare* and *oratio* by the early Christians as the regular words for 'pray' and 'prayer' is particularly interesting; see Löfstedt (1956), 2. 463–4.

lacrimas . . . offerebat: tears, a sign of contrition, are a usual part of the patristic experience of prayer. See B. Steidle, 'Die Tränen, ein mystisches Problem im alten Mönchtum', *Benediktinische Monatsschrift*, 20 (1938), 181–7, and esp. I. Hausherr, *Penthos: la doctrine de la componction dans l'Orient chrétien* (Orientalia Christiana analecta, 132; Rome, 1944).

ieiunia . . . moderabatur: cf. Jerome's advice to Nepotianus at *epist.* 52. 12. 1 'tantum tibi ieiuniorum impone, quantum ferre potes. sint pura, casta, simplicia, moderata, non superstitiosa ieiunia'. Fasting, which was both practised by Jesus (cf. Matt. 4: 2) and encouraged by him (cf. Matt. 6: 16–18, Mark 2: 18–20), held a position of great importance in patristic thought. Athanasius and Ambrose, for example, extol it in glowing terms (Athan. *virg.* 6–7, Ambr. *Hel.* 2. 2), while Basil regards restraint in eating as essential for salvation (*renunt. saec.* 7 καὶ, ἵνα πάντα συνελὼν εἴπω, εἰ κρατήσεις γαστρός, οἰκήσεις τὸν παράδεισον· εἰ δὲ οὐ κρατήσεις, γέγονας θανάτου παρανάλωμα). Its great virtue is that it counteracts lust, which is stimulated by too much food; cf. e.g. *epist.* 22. 11. 1, 79. 9. 5, Ambr. *virg.* 3. 2. 5, Aug. *epist.* 211. 8, Evagr. *sent. virg.* p. 149. 59–60 Wilmart. Satiety also blunts the mind (cf. e.g. *epist.* 52. 11. 4 'pulchre dicitur apud Graecos, sed nescio utrum apud nos aeque resonet: pinguis venter non gignit sensum tenuem', *adv. Iovin.* 2. 12 (PL 23. 302)), and so fasting is a good preparation for prayer and study; it is in fact 'non perfecta virtus, sed ceterarum virtutum fundamentum' (*epist.*

130. 11. 2), and Jerome regards it as one of the characteristics of paradise before the Fall (cf. *adv. Iovin.* 2. 15 (PL 23. 305)), and one of the requirements if man is to return to that state.

Although Jerome held that fasting should be continual, he was also very concerned that it should not be overdone; cf. e.g. *epist.* 22. 17. 2 'sint tibi cotidiana ieiunia et refectio satietatem fugiens. nihil prodest biduo triduoque transmisso vacuum portare ventrem, si pariter obruitur, si conpensatur saturitate ieiunium', 107. 10. 2, 125. 7. 1, 130. 11. 1–2 'neque vero inmoderata tibi imperamus ieiunia et inormem ciborum abstinentiam . . . sic debes ieiunare, ut non palpites et respirare vix possis et comitum tuarum vel porteris vel traharis manibus, sed ut fracto corporis appetitu nec in lectione nec in psalmis nec in vigiliis solito quid minus facias'. Other Fathers agreed (cf. e.g. Athan. *virg.* 8, Evagr. *sent. virg.* pp. 148. 13–149. 15 Wilmart 'ne dixeris: hodie non edam et crastino manducabo, quia non in sapientia facis istud; erit enim haec inaequalitas noxia corpori tuo et dolor stomacho tuo'); Nilus believed that immoderate fasts were prompted by the devil (Nilus, *epist.* 3. 46).

Marcella too is praised for her restrained fasting (cf. *epist.* 127. 4. 2); Paula, by contrast, was over-strict with herself (cf. *epist.* 108. 17. 3). Ambrose praises Valentinian for indulging in the practice; cf. *obit. Valent.* 16.

The parallel with the charioteer who does not push his horses too hard when they are weak or tired will have occurred readily to Jerome, who was fond of metaphors and similes with *auriga*. Cf. e.g. *epist.* 52. 13. 3 (Nepotianus as Christ's *auriga*), 64. 21. 2 (God as *auriga* of the chariot of the universe), 66. 2. 2 (Jesus as *auriga* of the chariot pulled by Paula, Eustochium, Paulina, and Pammachius), 69. 6. 1 'solus spiritus dei in aurigae modum super aquas ferebatur', 107. 10. 3 'in quadragesima continentiae vela pandenda sunt et tota aurigae retinacula equis laxanda properantibus', *adv. Iovin.* 2. 10 (PL 23. 299) 'sensus corporum quasi equi sunt, sine ratione currentes, anima vero in aurigae modum retinet frena currentium' (cf. Plato, *Phaedr.* 246A–256E).

sic . . . reservaret: in addition to the continual fast, Jerome sometimes recommends—at least for those who are to live a life of chastity—the complete avoidance of foods which were thought to foment the passions, in particular meat, but also certain vegetables; cf. e.g. *epist.* 54. 10. 2 'in ipsis cibis calida quaeque devita; non solum de carnibus loquor . . . sed etiam in ipsis leguminibus inflantia quaeque et gravia declinanda sunt', 79. 7. 7 'quarum uteri portant fetus, earum et intestina carnibus inpleantur'. Wine was allowed for health reasons, but was otherwise to be avoided on the same ground (cf. e.g. *epist.* 22. 8.

1–3, 107. 8. 2); Jerome warns Nepotianus against it at *epist.* 52.
11. 3 'numquam vinum redoleas, ne audias illud philosophi: hoc
non est osculum porrigere, sed propinare. vinolentos sacerdotes
et apostolus damnat et vetus lex prohibet'. Superstitious abstinence, however, was different, and quite contrary to Christian
teaching; the Jewish law contained a long list of food prohibi-
tions (cf. Lev. 11), but the early Christians lifted these restrictions, except for a very few (cf. Acts 15: 29), presumably on the
ground that the whole of God's creation was good (cf. 1 Tim. 4:
1–7 and *epist.* 121. 10. 23). For this reason Nepotianus ate a
small amount of everything on the table; while wishing to
exercise restraint (*continentia*) in his eating, he did not want it to
seem that he was cutting out items for the wrong reasons (cf.
Jerome's advice to him at *epist.* 52. 12. 1, quoted above at *ieiunia
. . . moderabatur*).

10. 8. sermo . . . habebatur: Marcella too liked to discuss
Scriptural questions (cf. *epist.* 127. 7. 1), and showed great
modesty in the answers she gave (cf. *epist.* 127. 7. 3).

per omne convivium is not read by any of the MSS; but it was
printed by the earlier editors and argued for, though somewhat
tentatively, by C. Schäublin, 'Textkritisches zu den Briefen des
Hieronymus', *MH* 30 (1973), 55–62, at 59–60. The alternatives
seem intolerably difficult. Hilberg, following all the MSS bar *G*,
read *et omne convivium*, which caused Wright to translate *omne
convivium* as 'his favourite form of entertainment' (better, 'all his
entertainment'); but it is doubtful whether *convivium* can bear
this kind of sense at all, let alone in the context of taking meals.
To read *erat G* for *et*, or to expunge *et* altogether, does not help;
omne convivium would then have to be taken, implausibly, as an
acc. of extent of time. Schäublin further proposed the deletion of
sermo eius, which he saw as an interpolation going back to a
marginal note. This would have the advantage of making the
series of infinitives from *proponere* to *confiteri* historic (cf. 10. 5
with n. on *subvenire . . . fuit*, 10. 7); but *sermo* seems important,
as indicating that Nepotianus' conversation at table was devoted
entirely to Scriptural and theological matters, and the text as
printed, with the infinitives understood as complementary to
sermo eius ('his talk . . . was to bring forward something from
Scripture . . . '), though perhaps awkward, is, I think, far from
being impossible Latin (cf. perhaps *epist.* 49. 20. 2 'ingenua et
verecunda confessio est, quo ipse careas, id in aliis praedicare'). I
do not share Schäublin's concern that Nepotianus' *sermo* will
thus include his willingness to listen (*libenter audire*); though
this offends strict logic, it sits comfortably in the context.

For *eruditionis . . . habebatur* cf. 10. 4 *eoque . . . indignum*.

10. 9. Tertulliani . . . Arnobius: all Christian writers of some distinction, and all except Hilary (of Poitiers) and Victorinus (of Pettau; though see below), Africans. Jerome himself regarded them sufficiently highly to devote to each, except Lactantius, a section of *De viris illustribus* (cc. 53, 58, 67, 74, 79, 100 (PL 23. 661–701)), and Lactantius is at least mentioned in c. 58, on Minucius Felix. At *epist*. 49. 13. 4 he lists together all but Arnobius, and does so again at 49. 19. 4, though this time omitting Minucius as well. A brief but illuminating critique of their literary styles is given at *epist*. 58. 10 (Minucius is omitted here, too); all but Cyprian and Lactantius face the charge of obscurity in some form or other. At *epist*. 70. 5 Jerome quickly reviews some of their works, again with occasional stylistic comment; Juvencus is added here. There are other references to them scattered throughout the corpus. Nepotianus doubtless knew their writings well, and those of other authors whom Jerome does not choose to name.

It is impossible to be sure that the Victorinus here named is that Victorinus who was Bishop of Pettau and a well-known exegete; it could conceivably be C. Marius Victorinus, the fourth-century rhetor and theologian from Africa, who is also featured in *De viris illustribus* (c. 101 (PL 23. 701)). However, the Victorinus of *epist*. 58. 10 and 70. 5 is certainly the bishop, as Jerome makes reference to his martyrdom (cf. *vir. ill*. 74 (PL 23. 683)), and it is a reasonable assumption, in view of the similarity of the group of names in all three passages, that he has the same man in mind here.

me . . . medium: Jerome cannot resist mentioning what was to him an obvious source of pride. At the same time he stresses again his own close connection with Heliodorus.

lectione . . . Christi: *lectione* (*-nem G*) *quoque GKΨ*, which Hilberg follows, makes no sense: Jerome is not making an entirely new point but summing up what he has just said about Nepotianus' knowledge of the Scriptures and other Christian writings. *quoque* will easily have slipped into the text by dittography after *me quoque* just above. The earlier editors printed *lectioneque*, but this is no better: the connecting particle is out of place (and the whole passage heavily asyndetic), and Jerome might well have avoided *-que* after a short *e* (on this tendency of Latin see KS 2. 14). *lectione adsidua B* must be read.

c. 11. Continuing the theme of Nepotianus' reading of the works of the Fathers, including himself, Jerome lays stress on his own friendship with Nepotianus by telling how the young man persistently requested that Jerome should write something specifically

for him, and how the request was eventually, after some initial
resistance, fulfilled. Nepotianus' favourable reaction to the *libellus*
is fulsomely described, and Jerome goes on to praise his love of the
written word, which contrasted strongly with the materialistic
attitude of many *monachi* of the time.

11. 1. Quotiens ille . . . inpetraret: similarly, Paula made an
  insistent request that Jerome should read the Bible with Eustochium and expound it to her; for a time Jerome refused, 'propter
  verecundiam', but finally consented (cf. *epist.* 108. 26. 2).
     With the present case one might compare those instances in
  literary prefaces where the author displays reluctance to undertake a literary task imposed by someone else, for which see on 1.
  1 *Grandes . . . explicare.* The points of contact are clear: a
  request, a refusal for reasons of (affected) modesty, and eventual
  acceptance because personal ties with the maker of the request
  demand compliance. In the letter he actually wrote, Jerome
  again refers to the frequency of Nepotianus' request (*epist.* 52. 1.
  1, quoted below at *deprecatus est . . . scriberem*; though certainty
  is impossible, this letter is surely the one to which Jerome here
  alludes), though without saying that his refusal to undertake the
  task earlier had been due to *pudor* or *verecundia*; he does,
  however, claim to have had no option but to comply (cf. *epist.* 52.
  17. 1 'coegisti me', etc.).
     deprecatus est . . . scriberem: in fact Nepotianus' request
  was more specific; cf. *epist.* 52. 1. 1 'petis, Nepotiane carissime,
  litteris transmarinis [cf. transmarinis epistulis] et crebro petis, ut
  tibi brevi volumine digeram praecepta vivendi et qua ratione is,
  qui saeculi militia derelicta vel monachus coeperit esse vel
  clericus, rectum Christi tramitem teneat, ne ad diversa vitiorum
  diverticula rapiatur'.
     nocturnum . . . viduam: Jerome borrows two parables from
  Luke to illustrate how importunate and persistent requests are
  rewarded. *nocturnum . . . petitorem* refers to the parable of the
  friend who calls with a request in the middle of the night (Luke
  11: 5–8); cf. esp. v. 8 '[some MSS: + et ille si perseveraverit
  pulsans] dico vobis, et si non dabit illi surgens eo quod amicus
  eius sit, propter inprobitatem tamen eius surget et dabit illi
  quotquot habet necessarios'. *interpellatricem . . . viduam* alludes
  to Luke 18: 1–8, the parable of the persistent woman and the
  judge who finally agreed to avenge her on her adversary, saying
  (v. 5) 'quia molesta est mihi haec vidua vindicabo illam, ne in
  novissimo veniens suggillet me'. Like Jerome in the case of
  Nepotianus' request, the judge here 'nolebat per multum tempus' (v. 4).

In the gospel the parables illustrate how one should pray; but they easily lend themselves to the use Jerome makes of them here.

interpellatricem . . . iudicis: *TLL*, 7. 1. 2240, records only five instances of *interpellatrix*. Three of them are by Jerome, the others being *epist*. 79. 1. 4 and *in Is*. 62. 6–7 (CCSL 73A. 716 = PL 24. 607); in both cases the word occurs in the phrase *interpellatricem duri iudicis*, alluding to the same passage in Luke, and the context of the phrase at *epist*. 79. 1. 4 is very similar to that here. These are the earliest examples. The masculine *interpellator* naturally appears more frequently, and as early as *Rhet. Her*. 2. 16.

The fact that Jerome uses the expression *interpellatricem duri iudicis* in referring to this parable on three occasions is especially interesting in that in neither Vulgate nor VL does the account in Luke include *interpellatrix* or any cognate word, and the judge is not described as *durus* (though Jerome is accurate in representing him as such). This freedom from dependence on the language of the Biblical account stands in contrast to other passages in which Jerome clearly reveals his indebtedness to it; cf. e.g. 7. 2, where *ne haberet tristitiam super tristitiam* is almost a direct quotation of Paul's own words in describing the situation to which Jerome there refers (see on 7. 2 *apostolus . . . caritatis*). The repeated use of the phrase also marks it down as another Jeromian cliché (cf. on 10. 5 *nullam . . . fabulam*). For the use of *interpellatrix* in referring to the parable cf., however, Aug. *quaest. evang*. 2. 45 (AD 397–400) 'quid est quod ad semper orandum et non deficiendum de iudice iniquo voluit parabolam ponere, qui cum deum non timeret et hominem non revereretur, viduae tamen assiduis interpellationibus cessit ut eam vindicaret, ne sibi ab illa taedium fieret?'.

suffunderem: 'overspread'. In the context the word also suggests a blush; it is commonly used with *rubor* in this sense (cf. e.g. Virg. *georg*. 1. 430, Liv. 30. 15. 1).

precatorem: 'as an intercessor', 'to ask on his behalf'. The word is not merely 'ante-classical', as Lewis–Short have it; cf. e.g. Stat. *silv*. 5. 3. 152, Fronto p. 192 Naber, Ambr. *in Luc*. 5. 11.

sacerdotii: as Nepotianus himself was a presbyter, this must refer specifically to the episcopate. It perhaps reflects an old usage. According to E. W. Benson, *Cyprian: His Life, his Times, his Work* (London, 1897), 33 n. 3, in Cyprian the term nearly always refers to the episcopate, and is applied to presbyters only by extension; more recently M. Bévenot, ' "Sacerdos" as

Understood by Cyprian', *JThS* 30 (1979), 413–29, at 421–3, has argued that Cyprian uses *sacerdos* of bishops exclusively. Normally both bishops and presbyters are covered by the word (see on 10. 4 *sacerdotio*).

11. 2. brevi libello: *epist.* 52. A few lines further on Jerome refers to his work as *opusculo*, and *scedulas* (11. 3), though it has wider connotations, primarily relates to *epist.* 52 as well (see on 11. 3 *scedulas consectatur*). But it is doubtful whether the use of any of these diminutives represents an affectation of modesty. *libellus* often occurs virtually as a synonym for *liber*, and Arns, 106, points out that the fact that in the fourth century it is found accompanied by adjectives such as *brevis*, *parvus*, and *parvulus*, suggests that it has by then lost its diminutive force. Equally, *opusculum* is frequently employed simply to refer to something written (cf. e.g. *epist.* 65. 6. 2); and Jerome seems to have a clear preference for *scedula* over *scheda* generally. Furthermore, the context lends no weight to the idea that Jerome is modestly playing down *epist.* 52, especially in the case of *libello*, immediately followed as it is by the rather pompous *amicitias . . . consecravi*. Some observations on Jerome's use of diminutives in general are made by Bartelink (1980), 29, 39–40.

amicitias . . . consecravi: at *epist.* 125. 8. 2 Jerome describes *epist.* 52 as 'editus ad Nepotianum liber'. Certainly he conceived of it as something more than a personal letter; it was intended for wider circulation, and, to judge from the present comment, designed still to be read in later times. The outline of the life of the *clericus* it presents was of course applicable not only to Nepotianus. Other ostensibly personal letters too received a wide readership; see Introduction, pp. 13–15.

By *nostras amicitias* Jerome presumably means his friendships with both Nepotianus and Heliodorus, who is mentioned at *epist.* 52. 1. 1 and 52. 4. 4.

Croesi . . . divitias: the wealth of Darius, King of Persia 521–486 BC, and more especially of Croesus, King of Lydia *c.* 560–546 BC, was proverbial among classical writers, and Christian authors continued to use the motif; see the many examples collected by Otto, 98–9, sect. 468, and in the *Nachträge*. Darius' riches are mentioned in a proverbial way as early as Plato (*Lysis* 211E), and in Latin first at Plaut. *Aul.* 85–6. It was Croesus, however, who particularly caught the imagination of the Romans, and in Latin literature there are numerous instances from Catull. 115. 3 on. Sometimes there is reference to the wealth of the Persians generally; cf. e.g. Plaut. *Stich.* 24–5, Stat. *silv.* 1. 3. 105. Jerome is particularly fond of the expression. At times he refers only to Croesus (cf. e.g. *epist.* 53. 11. 3, 125. 10. 1, 127. 4. 2, *vir. ill.* 75 (PL 23. 685), at others he adds Darius: indeed, to judge from Otto, he connects the two more frequently than any other writer (cf. *epist.* 118. 5. 4 'neque enim Darei opes et Croesi explere valent pauperes mundi', *adv. Rufin.* 1. 17 (CCSL 79. 16 = PL 23. 411), 3. 4 (CCSL 79. 76 = PL 23. 459)).

For the notion of a letter from a friend as great wealth cf. [Julian] *epist.* 184 Bidez–Cumont (40 Hertlein) δεξαίμην ἂν ἔγωγε Ἰαμβλίχου μᾶλλον ἐπιστολὴν μίαν ἢ τὸν ἐκ Λυδίας χρυσὸν κεκτῆσθαι, Liban. *epist.* 1525. 3 Εὐανθίου δὲ ἥκοντος καὶ δῶρόν μοι φέροντος παντὸς χρυσίου κάλλιον, γράμματα σά . . ., and other examples collected by Thraede, 89; perhaps also Demet. *de eloc.* 224 ἡ δὲ [sc. ἐπιστολὴ] γράφεται καὶ δῶρον πέμπεται τρόπον τινά.

The image of riches here is picked up at 11. 3; Nepotianus contrasts with those monks who pursue worldly wealth, by regarding the written word (of God and Christians only, one may suspect) as the true thing of value.

laetabatur . . . testimonio: i.e. by showing, or reciting, the letter to his visitor. One might have expected the order *nostro super se testimonio*.

distinctione . . . varietate: in the context of spoken language *distinctio* generally refers to the careful separation of words and phrases from each other, resulting in clarity of diction; cf. e.g. Quint. *inst.* 11. 3. 52 'nec volubilitate nimia confundenda quae dicimus, qua . . . distinctio perit'. *pronuntiatio* may involve all aspects of oratorical delivery, including facial expression and gesture (cf. e.g. *Rhet. Her.* 1. 3), or refer simply to manner of speech, 'pronunciation', 'inflexion', or 'tone', which seems more likely here: *epist.* 52 does not give great scope for gesture in recitation.

in recitando . . . videretur: I cannot extract satisfactory sense from this passage as it stands. The problem lies partly with whether *ipso* or *ipse* (or neither) should be read, partly with *displicere*. The earlier editors printed *ipse DΦB*, which puts the emphasis on Nepotianus: 'in reading it out it was *he* [not Jerome] who each day seemed to please or displease'. Whether *illo* is taken to refer to the whole *opusculum* or only to the weaker parts of it (cf. *quidquid . . . erat* above), this comment has little point. In neither case does it make sense for Jerome to say that Nepotianus sometimes failed to please; and in the latter case, it is absurd to stress Nepotianus in contrast to Jerome, as if Jerome could have given any pleasure by the shortcomings in the letter. Hilberg read *ipso GK*[acm2] *Ψ* without substantially improving the sense. The meaning must then be something of this sort: 'in reading out those very parts [i.e. *quidquid minus in opusculo erat*] he seemed to please or displease, varying from day to day'; i.e. if he was on form in his recitation, he could make the less satisfactory parts of the letter appear good, whereas, if he was not, all the weaknesses would stand out. But it is doubtful whether *cotidie* can bear the required sense, 'according to the day'; and again one would have expected Jerome to say that Nepotianus' delivery always made the poorer passages seem good, without any notion of displeasure. To omit *ipse* or *ipso* altogether, with 𝔄, does not dispose of the problem, and I see no merit in Vallarsi's suggested emendation, *sibi*. The solution may be to delete *vel displicere*, which could easily have been added by an over-zealous copyist after *vel placere*; *vel placere* can stand alone, the particle intensifying the verb (i.e. 'really to please'; cf. Cic. *de orat.* 2. 325). This does not in itself help us with *ipso* and *ipse*, either of which—or their omission—would now do; but Nepotianus' ability to compensate in his delivery for deficiencies in the text is best underlined by *ipso*—'in reading out those very (unsatisfactory) parts he seemed [or, was seen] each day really to please'—and the rhetorical juxtaposition of *illo ipso*, understood in this sense, with *vel placere* lends support to this reading.

11. 3. unde hic . . . dei?: at last Jerome moves on from his absorbing interest in his own work and focuses more clearly on Nepotianus.

unde legis . . . dedit?: in the context of reading, which continues through 11. 3 (cf. *scedulas*), *legis Christi* should refer not just to Christian teaching and principles but specifically to the Scriptures, or at least the NT. Consideration of Nepotianus' reading of his letter has led Jerome to think also of his Biblical reading, his fondness for which has already been suggested at 10. 8–9.

legis . . . indefessa meditatio recalls *epist.* 52. 7. 1, where Jerome urges Nepotianus to read the Scriptures continually. For the phrase cf. *epist.* 100. 3. 3 (tr. from Theophilus) 'medicina praeteritorum ac praesentium futurorumque vitiorum legis indefessa meditatio'; it owes something to Ps. 1: 2 'in lege domini voluntas eius, et in lege eius meditabitur die ac nocte [sc. beatus vir]' (LXX, Hebr.). Marcella too is said to have practised *legis meditatio*, and for her that involved acting on what she had read; cf. *epist.* 127. 4. 1 'meditationem legis non replicando quae scripta sunt . . . sed in opere intellegens'. Nepotianus' social actions (cf. 10. 5) could be seen in the same light.

For praise of enthusiasm for Scripture in others cf. *epist.* 75. 4. 1 (Lucinus), 77. 7 (Fabiola), 108. 26. 1 (Paula).

alii . . . mendicos: Jerome frequently attacks corruption of

Church, clergy, and monks by satire such as this; see the well-documented account of Wiesen, 65–112. Often it is against rich and money-seeking monks and clerics that he inveighs; cf. e.g. *epist.* 40. 2. 2 'volo in nummarios invehi sacerdotes', 52. 6. 4–5 (legacy-hunting), 52. 9. 1 'sunt, qui pauperibus parum tribuunt, ut amplius accipiant, et sub praetextu elemosynae quaerunt divitias: quae magis venatio appellanda est quam elemosyna. sic bestiae, sic aves, sic capiuntur et pisces: modica in hamo esca ponitur, ut matronarum in eo sacculi protrahantur', *in Soph.* 3. 1–7 (CCSL 76A. 696 = PL 25. 1374). The problem was certainly a real one. The worldliness of the Church was notorious (cf. Wiesen, 65–7, who quotes a wide range of sources), and in 370 clergy were legally forbidden by Valentinian I to receive legacies from women to whom 'se privatim sub praetextu religionis adiunxerint' (*Cod. Theod.* 16. 2. 20). To this law Jerome refers at *epist.* 52. 6. 1 (from where it appears that its operation extended to *monachi* as well as to *clerici*), complaining bitterly that its passing was deserved.

marsuppium . . . obsequiis: *marsuppium suffocantes* is a good clausula, requiring that *matronarum* be taken not with *marsuppium* but with *opes*; *marsuppium* must refer to the purses of the monks themselves, which they refuse to open, as they should, to give money to the poor (cf. *epist.* 52. 9. 1, quoted above at *alii . . . mendicos*). *suffocantes* offers a striking image. The verb is sometimes used metaphorically (cf. e.g. Cic. *ad Att.* 9. 7. 4, *Aetna* 320, Just. 4. 1. 15), but I have found no close parallel to the present instance, where the image has a strong physical, and hence quasi-literal, character; the monks 'strangle' their purses, either by their grip or by the tight drawing of the purse-strings.

marsuppium = μαρσίππιον. Common in Plautus, the word is thereafter found on very few occasions until Jerome, who employs it frequently (cf. e.g. *epist.* 84. 3. 5, 127. 3. 4, *in Agg.* 1. 6 (CCSL 76A. 720 = PL 25. 1394)); cf. *TLL*, 8. 415, and see on 4. 2 *melos*.

diabolo: διάβολος fundamentally = 'slanderer', but comes often to represent Satan or the devil; cf. e.g. LXX 1 Chr. 21: 1, Matt. 4: 1. There are numerous instances of the Latin form with this meaning.

suspiret . . . mendicos: the contrast and paradox are made more marked by the emphatic position given to *mendicos* and by its verbal similarity with *mundus*.

scedulas consectatur: Jerome uses the word *scedula* (*schedula, scidula*, etc.), the diminutive of *scida* or *scheda*, 'a sheet of

paper', many times; cf. e.g. *epist.* 59.4. 1, 114. 1. 2, *adv. Rufin.* 3.
5 (CCSL 79. 76–8 = PL 23. 460–1). Here one thinks primarily of
epist. 52, but the contrast with *aurum* strongly suggests that
scedulas should be taken to have a more general reference: 'bits
of paper', i.e. the Scriptures (cf. on *unde legis . . . dedit?* above),
and other written works, of which *epist.* 52 is representative. It is
significant that in place of *scedulas* Γ has *scripturas*.

   consectatur = 'seeks', 'strives to obtain', 'goes after'. The present tense, like those which follow, is vivid, as though Nepotianus
is still alive.

   paupertate . . . ornatum: the contrast between Nepotianus'
attitude to himself and to the Church is brought out clearly by
the combination of the repetitious *ornatior–ornatum*, with both
words emphatically placed, and the oxymoron in *paupertate
ornatior*, with which cf. *epist.* 108. 1. 1 'potens quondam divitiis,
sed nunc Christi paupertate insignior [sc. Paula]'.

c. 12. In matters of lesser importance, too, Nepotianus displayed
the same virtuous spirit. He took great trouble to keep his church
clean, tidy, and beautifully adorned, and was careful not to neglect
any of his priestly duties. Jerome draws parallels from Biblical and
classical history to Nepotianus' artistry in church decoration.

12. 1. Ad conparationem . . . dicturi sumus: cf. Tac. *dial.* 39. 1
'parvum et ridiculum fortasse vide⟨bi⟩tur quod dicturus sum,
dicam tamen'. *ex conparatione* or *in conparatione/-em* would be
more usual than *ad conparationem*, but cf. e.g. [Aug.] *quaest. test.*
1. 1. 6, Pelag. *in II Tim.* 1. 11 'ad comparationem aliorum
possunt dici magistri'.

   ut . . . sollertiam: there are a number of passages in Jerome
such as this, in which the power of God the creator is represented as being clearly manifested in little animals; often there
are close verbal similarities. The extracts are conveniently
collected and discussed by G. J. M. Bartelink, 'Hieronymus
über die Minuta Animalia', *VChr* 32 (1978), 289–300.

   In art Jerome is often depicted in the company of animals. H.
Friedmann, *A Bestiary for Saint Jerome: Animal Symbolism in
European Religious Art* (Washington, DC, 1980), 23–4, suggests
that artists may have been prompted to include specific animals
in their work by this passage and others like it. This will not,
however, have been true in the case of Jerome's most famous
bestial companion, the lion, who owes his frequent appearance
in the Jerome iconography to the familiar legend of how the
saint removed a thorn from a lion's paw and was thereafter
'adopted' by the creature (for which see Kelly, 333).

et ... animalibus: perhaps 'even in tiny animals too'; but *et ... quoque* is more probably straightforward tautology.

formica, culice: the switch to the singular is for reasons of stylistic variation; cf. the list of barbarian tribes at 16. 2, with n. on *Scythiam . . . rapiunt.*

pro otioso ... rationem: cf. Matt. 12: 36 (Jesus speaking to the Pharisees) 'dico autem vobis quoniam omne verbum otiosum quod locuti fuerint homines, reddent rationem de eo in die iudicii'. If one is held liable for so slight a thing as an idle word, argues Jerome, one ought to be careful in all matters, even those which seem quite unimportant. For a curious parallel cf. Cato ap. Cic. *Planc.* 66 'clarorum virorum atque magnorum non minus oti quam negoti rationem exstare oportere'.

12. 2. sollicitus si: *sollicitus sum* generally functions like a verb of fearing, introducing the subordinate clause by *ne* or *ne non/ut*; so here one might have expected *sollicitus ne non niteret altare*, i.e. 'anxious that the altar should shine'. The construction we have may be that of an indirect question, where *si* is equivalent to *num*. For indirect questions after *sollicitus* see *OLD* s.v., sect. 2c; for the use of *si* in indirect questions see LHS 2. 543–4, Löfstedt (1911), 327–8. Alternatively, though less certainly, the *si*-clauses may be explained by postulating a transition of thought from an idea of mental state (*sollicitus*) to one of action, which might have been expressed by a verb of attempting, such as *conari* or *experiri*: these are often followed by a *si*-clause (cf. KS 2. 425, LHS 2. 666). One might then translate: 'anxiously made efforts to ensure that . . . '.

niteret . . . lucentia: Bingham, bk. 8, gives a full account of the construction and furnishings of early churches. For the sanctuary (*sacrarium*) and altar see his c. 6, sects. 1–3. Veils and hangings (*vela*) are discussed at c. 6, sect. 8; they were used to cover doors, as here, and for other purposes, such as to divide the chancel from the rest of the church. *vasa* are probably utensils of the altar, used for administering the eucharist; for these see c. 6, sect. 21.

altare: until Petronius this word is found only in the plural, *altaria*, which represents one altar or many. Petronius is the first to give an instance of the singular *altare* (135. 3), and subsequently the forms *altaris*, *altarium*, and *altar* also occur; *altarius* is uncertain. See *TLL* 1. 1725.

disposita: 'accorded', 'devoted'; the sense of ordering or arrangement seems untranslatable.

12. 3–4. nobilem . . . testaretur: Jerome's thoughts now pass

from Nepotianus' care in keeping his church clean and tidy to
his attention to its adornment (and perhaps that of others; cf. on
12. 4 *basilicas . . . conciliabula*). *exempla* are introduced to
parallel the artistry he displayed in decorating the church
buildings. The cases of Hiram and Bezalel perform this function adequately, and Fabius Pictor is an apposite choice, as his
renown came from painting a temple (see on 12. 3 *nobilem . . .
invenit*). The inclusion of Hippias of Elis (*philosophus ille*),
whose artistry had nothing to do with the adornment of a
religious building, is less apt, but the *exemplum* follows fairly
easily after the simile *quomodo . . . elegantiam*. For *exempla*
generally see on 5. 2–3 *proponunt . . . explicavit*.

The adornment of Nepotianus' church is unlikely to have
gone beyond the flowers and greenery mentioned at 12. 4, as
Jerome had warned the young priest against such extravagance;
cf. *epist.* 52. 10. 1–2 'multi aedificant parietes et columnas
ecclesiae subtrahunt: marmora nitent, auro splendent lacunaria,
gemmis altare distinguitur et ministrorum Christi nulla electio
est. neque vero mihi aliquis opponat dives in Iudaea templum,
mensam, lucernas, turibula, patellas, scyphos, mortariola et
cetera ex auro fabre facta. tunc haec probabantur a domino,
quando sacerdotes hostias immolabant . . . nunc vero, cum
paupertatem domus suae pauper dominus dedicarit, cogitemus
crucem et divitias lutum putabimus. quid miramur, quod
Christus vocat iniquum mammonam?'. Lack of enthusiasm for
decorating churches with precious metals, jewels, and other
luxury materials is evident too at *epist.* 130. 14. 7. Jerome's
staunch opposition to Christian women over-adorning themselves (see on 10. 2 *excepta . . . reservavit*), which often includes
criticism of the wearing of jewellery (cf. e.g. *epist.* 24. 3. 2, 45. 3.
1, 107. 5. 1, 130. 7. 13), stems principally from his association of
physical adornment with sex, but in this area too one can detect
a distaste for extravagance and a recognition that the world had
other needs; cf. *epist.* 66. 5. 1 'ardentes gemmae, quibus ante
collum et facies ornabatur, egentium ventres saturant', 127. 3. 4
(continuing directly from the quotation at n. on 10. 2) ' . . .
aurum usque ad anuli signaculum repudians et magis in ventri-
bus egenorum quam in marsuppiis recondens'.

12. 3. **nobilem . . . invenit:** Jerome confuses two Fabii and makes
them the same person. The *Romanae scriptor historiae* was Q.
Fabius Pictor, the earliest Roman annalist, whose history of
Rome, written in Greek, appeared around the end of the third
century BC; for details of his life and work see *RE* s.n. Fabius

126. The name Pictor, however, was first acquired by his ancestor C. Fabius (*RE* s.n. Fabius 122), who in 304 BC painted the walls of the temple of Salus on the Quirinal, and added his name (cf. Val. Max. 8. 14. 6, Plin. *nat.* 35. 19); he is mentioned also at Cic. *Tusc.* 1. 4. It is this Fabius who makes the true parallel to the case of Nepotianus. We may suppose that Jerome was familiar with the story, though he need not have got it from Valerius or Pliny (as an aetiology for a famous name it is likely to have been well known): the parallel with Nepotianus clearly works much better if Jerome knew of Fabius as a temple-decorator and not simply as a painter.

At *Tusc.* 1. 4 Fabius is called 'nobilissimo homini', at Val. Max. 8. 14. 6 'nobilissimus civis'. Jerome will, however, naturally have thought of the Fabii, an ancient consular family, as *nobiles*, and there is no reason to suppose that the phrase *nobilem virum* betrays a debt to one or other of these works.

Beselehel . . . fabricati sunt: for Bezalel cf. Exod. 31: 1–11, where God tells Moses that he has called Bezalel and Oholiab to make the tabernacle and the ark and all the furnishings of the tabernacle; cf. esp. v. 3 'implevi eum spiritu dei, sapientia, intellegentia, et scientia in omni opere'. To make the parallel with Nepotianus closer Jerome omits to say that Bezalel made the tabernacle as well as its contents.

For Hiram cf. 1 Kgs. 7, where he makes the bronze furnishings for Solomon's temple; cf. esp. vv. 13–14 'misit quoque rex Salomon et tulit Hiram de Tyro, filium mulieris viduae de tribu Nepthali patre Tyrio, artificem aerarium et plenum sapientia et intellegentia et doctrina'.

quomodo . . . luxuriant: Hilberg suggested that this passage might owe something to Virg. *georg.* 1. 111–12 ' . . . ne gravidis procumbat culmus aristis, / luxuriem segetum tenera depascit in herba'; equally, *laetae segetes* occurs at *georg.* 1. 1 (a parallel Hilberg misses). It is true that Jerome was familiar with the *Georgics* (cf. Hagendahl (1958), with his index), but the reasons for supposing a debt to Virgil in this sentence are slight. The verbal parallels with *georg.* 1. 111–12 are not especially close; *laetae segetes* had the status of a cliché as early as Cicero (cf. *de orat.* 3. 155 'gemmare vitis, luxuriem esse in herbis, laetas segetes etiam rustici dicunt', *orat.* 81), and the adjective, with its sense of burgeoning, is regularly used of crops and other plant growth; likewise *culmus, arista*, and *luxuriare* all belong to the basic language of agriculture. An agricultural simile of this kind would naturally employ such terms.

Similes are an important feature of rhetoric, their function being to help prove a point in argument, to clarify, sometimes simply to add colour, and so on; see the material collected by Lausberg, 1. 232–4, sects. 422–5, and 1. 420–2, sects. 845–7. They are closely related to *exempla*, both being types of comparison, and hence highly appropriate here; cf. e.g. *Rhet. Her.* 4. 62 'id [sc. exemplum] sumitur isdem de causis, quibus similitudo [cf. 4. 59]', Quint. *inst.* 5. 11. 22 'proximas exemplo vires habet similitudo'. One case of *similitudo* given by Quintilian is especially interesting in the present context: 'si animum dicas excolendum, similitudine utaris terrae, quae neglecta sentes ac dumos, culta fructus creat' (*inst.* 5. 11. 24).

redundat: singular after the nearer subject, *mens*.

12. 4. apud Graecos . . . gloriatus est: the philosopher is Hippias of Elis; the story comes from Plato, *Hipp. Min.* 368B: πάντως δὲ πλείστας τέχνας πάντων σοφώτατος εἶ ἀνθρώπων . . . ἔφησθα δὲ ἀφικέσθαι ποτὲ εἰς Ὀλυμπίαν ἃ εἶχες περὶ τὸ σῶμα ἅπαντα σαυτοῦ ἔργα ἔχων· πρῶτον μὲν δακτύλιον . . . ὃν εἶχες σαυτοῦ ἔχειν ἔργον . . . ἔπειτα ὑποδήματα ἃ εἶχες ἔφησθα αὐτὸς σκυτομῆσαι, καὶ τὸ ἱμάτιον ὑφῆναι καὶ τὸν χιτωνίσκον. The reference does not, however, necessarily presuppose direct knowledge of Plato's text; it may be drawn from another writer who had alluded to the passage (possibly from Cic. *de orat.* 3. 127, though Cicero, while mentioning Hippias' boast that he had made his own cloak, ring, and boots, does not say explicitly that the the boast extended to all his attire). In fact, had Jerome read the dialogue at first hand, he could hardly have failed to notice that Socrates' praise of Hippias is ironical (noted by Courcelle (1948), 56 n. 10), making the allusion singularly inappropriate in the present context. For Jerome's knowledge of Plato generally see on 5. 2 *Platonis . . . percucurrimus*.

omne quod uteretur: there is no good reason to read *quo ΦB* for *quod*; for the use of the acc. after *utor*, a feature of pre-Ciceronian and late Latin, but rarely found in between, see LHS 2. 123.

basilicas . . . conciliabula: up to this point the impression has been that Nepotianus was in charge of a single church; but the plurals *basilicas* and *conciliabula* suggest the adornment of several. As it is most improbable that as a presbyter he was responsible for more than one church (cf. Hatch, 196), a possible explanation is that he took it upon himself to decorate other churches of Altinum, which were under the overall jurisdiction of Heliodorus: a good instance of his enthusiasm for the faith. We may be nearer the mark, however, in following a clue offered by Paulinus, who tells, at *epist.* 32. 10 (AD 403), of a

complex of five basilicas on one site at Nola, and, at *carm.* 28.
37 ff. (AD 404), of three basilicas on one square; he also informs
us (*epist.* 32. 1, 32. 5) that Sulpicius Severus built a baptistery
between two basilicas. Though the evidence of Paulinus himself
and from the excavations at Nola is too sketchy to give a clear
picture of the situation (cf. R. C. Goldschmidt, *Paulinus'
Churches at Nola* (Amsterdam, 1940), 94–5), it may be that
Nepotianus' church was similarly multiple.

basilica was used of churches from before the time of Constantine (cf. the appendix to Optatus, CSEL 26. 199. 29–200. 1
(citing a letter written shortly after 303), and other evidence
cited by Goldschmidt, 93), many pagan *basilicae* (halls of
exchange and judicature) first being converted to Christian use
(cf. e.g. Auson. *grat. act.* 1. 3), and the name then being applied
to Christian churches generally; this is a much more likely
explanation of the Christian use of the term than that proposed
by Isidore, that in churches worship was offered to God, king
(βασιλεύς) of all (*orig.* 15. 4. 11). The word could, interestingly,
be applied to a very small edifice indeed; cf. *ILC* 1. 1789, cited
by Goldschmidt, 168 (a child's grave at Puteoli called a *basilica*).

For *conciliabula* = 'churches' cf. e.g. *epist.* 123. 11. 2, *in Zach.*
8. 6 (CCSL 76A. 810 = PL 25. 1467): a natural extension of its
basic meaning of 'meeting-places'. By *martyrum conciliabula*
must be meant those churches built over a martyr's grave or
called by his name to preserve his memory, such as those of
Thomas the Apostle at Edessa and of Peter and Paul at Rome,
and referred to at e.g. *epist.* 107. 9. 2, 127. 4. 2, and *c. Vigil.* 10
(PL 23. 348) as *martyrum basilicae*. For the history of the
development of *martyria*, their architecture and iconography,
see A. Grabar, *Martyrium: recherches sur le culte des reliques et
l'art chrétien antique* (2 vols., Paris, 1943–6), and J. B. Ward-
Perkins, 'Memoria, Martyr's Tomb and Martyr's Church',
JThS 17 (1966), 20–38 (with Grabar's review, 'Martyrium ou
"vingt ans après"', *Cahiers archéologiques* 18 (1968), 239–44);
and for martyr-cults in the early Church, H. Delehaye, *Les
Origines du culte des martyrs* (Brussels, 1933). Jerome's own
attitude to the veneration of martyrs was favourable, and he
defends the practice against Vigilantius, both in the *Contra
Vigilantium* and in *epist.* 109, where see esp. 1. 3 'honoramus
autem reliquias martyrum, ut eum, cuius sunt martyres, adore-
mus, honoramus servos, ut honor servorum redundet ad
dominum'. The word *martyr* (μάρτυς, μάρτυρ) itself, though
fundamentally equivalent to *testis*, is used in Latin almost

exclusively to refer to those Christians who by suffering testified
to the truth of their faith; cf. *TLL* 8. 416–19.

   diversis . . . adumbraret: for the practice of adorning
churches with flowers and foliage cf. Aug. *civ.* 22. 8 'aliquid de
altari florum, quod occurrit, tulit', and perhaps Paul. Nol. *carm.*
14. 108–10.

   visu: appearance *per se*, as opposed to arrangement (*dispositione*).

c. 13. Having described Nepotianus' virtues, Jerome turns to his
death, and recounts in vivid language how, suffering from fever, he
came to the end of his life with calmness and confidence. The
happiness he showed was in stark contrast to the grief of those
around him, clearly indicating his deep faith (another instance of
virtue), and to the end he was mindful of others.

   As Jerome was not present when Nepotianus died this account
must be a reconstruction, involving a greater or lesser degree of
imagination, based—like many of the details in cc. 9–12—on what
he had heard from other sources, and above all, one may suspect,
from Heliodorus himself. This may seem curious, but it did not
matter. Jerone's concern was not to provide Heliodorus with
information about his nephew, but to eulogize the young man
using whatever facts he possessed.

   Similar passages, describing the subject's last days and the
deathbed scene, are found in other consolations by Jerome.
Marcella too died smiling, while Principia wept (*epist.* 127. 14).
Blesilla died of fever, pale and weak, surrounded by her *propin-
qui*, and humbly asking them to pray to Jesus to pardon her
(*epist.* 39. 1. 3–4). The best parallel, however, is the account of
the death of Paula (*epist.* 108. 27–8), to which more space is
devoted even than to the death of Nepotianus here. She fell ill,
and was tended lovingly by Eustochium, until at last she died
peacefully, in the presence of countless virgins, monks, and
clergy. In all cases the consoland is encouraged by being
reminded with what fortitude and confidence the subject faced
death.

   The passage is in certain respects reminiscent of Quint. *inst.* 6
pref., where the author recalls the early deaths of his wife and his
two sons. In particular one should observe the representation of
the author's own grief, and the fortitude displayed by the elder
son, who is the prime object of attention, during his terminal
illness; for the latter feature see esp. 6 pref. 11, and below on 13. 2
avunculum consolabatur and 13. 3 *studiorum*.

13. 1. Macte virtute!: for other instances where Jerome uses this common stereotyped phrase cf. *epist.* 58. 8. 2, 86. 1. 2, 141. 1. 2.

o miserabilis . . . vivimus!: cf. *epist.* 22. 15. 2 (on the early death of Blesilla) 'o infelix humana condicio et futuri nescia', 108. 27. 3 (on the death of Paula) 'o mortalium fragilis et caduca natura et, nisi Christi fides nos extollat ad caelum et aeternitas animae promittatur, cum bestiis ac iumentis corporum una condicio!'.

Hilberg suggested that there is here a reminiscence of Ps. 38: 6 'ecce mensurabiles posuisti dies meos, et substantia mea tamquam nihilum ante te. verumtamen universa vanitas, omnis homo vivens' (LXX), 'ecce breves posuisti dies meos, et vita mea quasi non sit in conspectu meo; omnia enim vanitas, omnis homo stans' (Hebr.). But the thought seems natural, and it is stretching credibility to see a direct connection.

vanum . . . vivimus: not 'the fact that we live is utterly meaningless [without Christ]', where *totum* would be more in place than *omne*, but 'our whole life is meaningless', *vivimus* being treated as a transitive verb; cf. *epist.* 21. 5. 1, 140. 13. 2 'quicquid igitur vivimus et in quo delectabilis est vita mortalium, septuaginta annorum spatio comprehenditur', 140. 14. 2 'et cum pertransierit, inquit, omne quod vivimus, subita morte dissolvimur', *in Is. lib.* 14 pref. (CCSL 73A. 552 = PL 24. 477). This transitive usage is very rare; the verb is sometimes found in the passive (most often impersonally) (cf. e.g. Cic. *Tusc.* 3. 49, Hor. *carm.* 2. 16. 13, Ov. *met.* 12. 188), and there are a few instances of the phrase *vivere vitam* (cf. e.g. Plaut. *Mil.* 628, *Persa* 494, Apul. *Plat.* 2. 16). Beyond this the only sure case of *vivere* + acc. object known to me is Boeth. *cons.* 4 pros. 3 'pavidus ac fugax non metuenda formidat? cervis similis habeatur. segnis ac stupidus torpit? asinum vivit', i.e. 'he lives an ass's life'.

quid te . . . faeni: with the address to *oratio* cf. those to *mors* (2. 2) and to Jerome's own *anima* (5. 1), both of which, however, are understandably represented in more vividly concrete terms, and belong to specific individual traditions of personification (see on 2. 2 *o mors . . . dissocias!* and 5. 1 *Quid agimus, anima?*).

For the notion of hesitation in coming to describe the death of the subject of the *consolatio* cf. *epist.* 79. 6. 1 'quid ultra differimus? omnis caro fenum et omnis gloria eius quasi flos feni. reversa est terra in terram suam: dormivit in domino', 108. 27. 1 'quid agimus, anima? cur ad mortem eius venire formidas? iam dudum prolixior liber cuditur, dum timemus ad ultima pervenire, quasi tacentibus nobis et in laudibus illius occupatis

differri possit occubitus'. *tergiversaris* lends a very Ciceronian
touch; cf. esp. *Tusc.* 3. 41, *Planc.* 48.

    omnis . . . faeni comes from 1 Pet. 1: 24 'omnis caro ut faenum,
et omnis gloria eius tamquam flos faeni; exaruit faenum et flos
decidit', and Isa. 40: 6, from where Peter himself took the
image: 'vox dicentis: clama. et dixi: quid clamabo? omnis caro
faenum, et omnis gloria eius quasi flos agri'; cf. Ps. 102: 15,
Ecclus. 14: 18. By representing the inevitability of mortal death
in these terms, Jerome calls to mind the other aspect of the
situation too: both Isaiah and Peter are contrasting the corrupti-
bility of the flesh with the eternal nature of God, and Heliodorus will naturally have thought that although Nepotianus
could not avoid death it would not be the end.

13. 2. marcescebat . . . migrabat: for the image of the dying
person as a flower cf. e.g. Hom. *Il.* 8. 306–8, Virg. *Aen.* 9. 433–7
'volvitur Euryalus leto, pulchrosque per artus / it cruor inque
umeros cervix conlapsa recumbit: / purpureus veluti cum flos
succisus aratro / languescit moriens, lassove papavera collo /
demisere caput pluvia cum forte gravantur', 11. 67–70 'hic
iuvenem agresti sublimem stramine ponunt: / qualem virgineo
demessum pollice florem / seu mollis violae seu languentis
hyacinthi, / cui neque fulgor adhuc nec dum sua forma recessit'.
In these instances, however, the flower is cut down rather than
simply dried up; and in the third, the object of the comparison is
already dead. Jerome could no doubt have produced a flower-
image of this kind by suggesting that Nepotianus was cut off
before his prime, as he does with Paulina (cf. *epist.* 66. 1. 2 'quis
parturientem rosam et papillatum corymbum, antequam in
calathum fundatur orbis et tota rubentium foliorum pandatur
ambitio, inmature demessum aequis oculis marcescere videat?'),
but instead he represents him, with some accuracy, as gradually
fading away.

    The image has been prepared for by *flos faeni* above. It is,
however, made more striking by the postponement of *lilium* to
the last word in the clause, which effects chiastic balance
between *marcescebat . . . lilium* and *purpura . . . migrabat*: to this
point, even through *flante austro*, it has been natural to think of
Nepotianus himself as subject of *marcescebat*. The colour-
contrast in *purpura* and *pallorem* is especially appropriate to one
who turns from health to sickness, *pallor* regularly being used of
a person's complexion. *migrare*, which seems very grand, is
quite appropriate to a colour-change; cf. Lucr. 2. 774–5 'caerula
quae sint / numquam in marmoreum possunt migrare colorem'.
Altogether the image is very successful.

For the image of flowers perishing in the wind in quite different contexts cf. *epist.* 79. 8. 1 'tenera res in feminis fama pudicitiae est et quasi flos pulcherrimus cito ad levem marcescit auram levique flatu corrumpitur, maxime ubi et aetas consentit ad vitium et maritalis deest auctoritas', 107. 9. 1.

pro dolor: the interjection *pro* is often followed by the acc. of exclamation, generally in the expression *pro fidem*, but at other times it takes a vocative, acting like *o*; cf. KS 1. 273–4. For *pro dolor* cf. e.g. Stat. *Theb.* 1. 77, *Paneg.* 4. 12. 2, Jer. *epist.* 15. 3. 1.

flante austro: *auster* is the south wind (Greek νότος; cf. e.g. Sen. *nat.* 5. 16. 6, Gell. 2. 22. 14). Often it is regarded as the bringer of rain; cf. e.g. Virg. *georg.* 1. 462 'umidus auster', and many other examples (see *TLL* 2. 1553–4). Here, however, Jerome seems to consider it a drying, withering wind, as at *in Ezech.* 27. 26 (CCSL 75. 379 = PL 25. 261) 'ventus auster contrivit te in corde maris. omnes divitiae Tyri austro flante dispereunt, qui significantius hebraice cadim, graece καύσων interpretatur, quem nos in ventum urentem transferre possumus . . . hoc vento Iacob exustus erat et tamen non contritus, dum loquitur: fui per diem exustus aestu et gelu noctis [cf. VL Gen. 31. 40]'. The truth appears to be that at different seasons the wind had a different character (cf. Plin. *nat.* 2. 127 'noxius auster et magis siccus, fortassis quia umidus frigidior est'); in either case it could be destructive to flowers (cf. — in contrast to the present instance — Isid. *nat.* 37 'tertius ventorum auster plagae meridianae cardinalis, qui et notus, ex humili flans tumidus calidus atque fulmineus, generans largas nubes et pluvias latissimas, solvens etiam flores'). Virgil too noted this damaging effect; cf. *ecl.* 2. 58–9.

aestuaret . . . anhelitu: *aestuare/aestus* and *febris* go together readily; cf. e.g. Cic. *Catil.* 1. 31 'aestu febrique iactantur', Oros. *hist.* 6. 12. 2 'post illas ardentissimas febres internosque aestus' (metaphorically, in reference to Gaul), Jer. *epist.* 38. 2. 1 'Blesillam nostram vidimus ardore febrium . . . aestuasse', 99. 1. 2 'febre aestuans'. *aestuare, anhelitus,* and *lassus* are also easily associated; cf. e.g. [Sen.] *Herc. O.* 1339 'reclinis ecce corde anhelante aestuat', Sen. *nat.* 6. 14. 2 'suspiria atque anhelitus laborantis ac fessi signa sunt', *epist.* 11. 2, Colum. 6. 13. 3 'aestuantes anhelantesque', 6. 38. 4 'lassae et aestuanti mulae'.

venarum . . . calor: i.e. the heat was causing him to lose colour (cf. *pallorem* above); *fontes hauriret* also suggests dehydration.

avunculum consolabatur: a clever touch, to recall to Heliodorus how Nepotianus himself tried to console him. Statius employs the same technique at *silv.* 5. 1. 176–93. For other cases where a dying person consoles or encourages loved ones cf. Quint. *inst.* 6 pref. 11, Plin. *epist.* 5. 16. 4.

universis . . . ridebat: the contrast with those around him weeping — emphasized by *universis* and *solus* — sets Nepotianus' faith in a very good light. It is not, however, a criticism of the faith of the others, of whom some expression of grief was demanded by *pietas* (cf. on 7. 2 *flebant . . . caritatis*), but Jerome naturally ignores this aspect here.

proicere . . . venientes: Nepotianus, close to death, has a vision of life on the other side, so to speak. For the historic infinitives cf. on 10. 5 *subvenire . . . fuit*.

in occursum: this phrase (often + gen. or dat.) appears almost exclusively in Christian Latin; *ad occursum* too is much more common in Christian writers than in pagan. See *TLL* 9. 2. 406–7.

intellegeres: cf. on 10. 6.

non emori sed migrare: *migrare*, and similar words, such as *proficisci*, *excedere*, and *praecedere*, are sometimes used by pagan authors to express, or in expressing, the notion of dying; cf. e.g. Cic. *Tusc.* 1. 97 'necesse est enim sit alterum de duobus, ut aut sensus omnino omnes mors auferat aut in alium quendam locum ex his locis morte migretur', Varro, *rust.* 1. 1. 1 'annus enim octogesimus admonet me ut sarcinas conligam antequam proficiscar e vita', Vell. 1. 11. 7 'hoc est nimirum magis feliciter de vita migrare quam mori', Sen. *epist.* 99. 7 'quem putas perisse praemissus est', *dial.* 6. 25. 1 'integer ille nihilque in terris relinquens sui fugit et totus excessit', 11. 9. 9 'non reliquit ille nos sed antecessit', [Sen.] *Herc. O.* 772–3 'ad fata et umbras atque peiorem polum / praecedere illum dicis?'. Christian writers, with their firm belief in an afterlife, found it natural to adopt such expressions, and there are numerous instances. Favez (1937), 156, collects examples in Christian consolation, where it was an obvious τόπος (to them can be added Aug. *epist.* 92. 1, *serm.* 172. 1); in Jerome cf. e.g. *epist.* 39. 3. 3 'de tenebris migravit ad lucem', 39. 3. 6, 79. 1. 3 'mortem iuvenis mariti . . . sic tulit, ut eum profectum crederet, non amissum', 118. 4. 1, and below, 14. 1 *praecessit* with n. In Greek, words such as οἴχεσθαι, ἀπέρχεσθαι, and προπέμπειν are used similarly; cf. e.g. Plato, *Phaedo* 115D, Diog. Laert. 3. 6, Plot. 4. 7. 15, John Chrys. *epist.* 197.

Closely connected is the idea that the dead are abroad, or merely absent; cf. e.g. (in consolation) [Plut.] *ad Apoll.* 12 (107C) Ὁ δὲ Σωκράτης παραπλήσιον ἔλεγεν εἶναι τὸν θάνατον . . .

ἀποδημίᾳ μακρᾷ, John Chrys. *epist.* 197 πράως οἴσεις τοῦ μακαρίου ἀδελφοῦ τῆς μεγαλοπρεπείας τῆς σῆς τὴν ἀποδημίαν· οὐ γὰρ ἂν αὐτὴν καλέσαιμι θάνατον, Jer. *epist.* 75. 1. 3 (quoted at 5. 1 *Anaxagorae . . . mortalem*), 77. 1. 1 (*peregrinatio*), and 14. 6 below. For the euphemism of death as a sleep see on 2. 1 *iungam . . . suscitatus est.*

13. 3. volvuntur . . . patior: cf. *epist.* 108. 27. 2 'quis enim possit siccis oculis Paulam narrare morientem?'. For Jerome's inability to restrain his grief cf. 2. 2 *invito et repugnanti per genas lacrimae fluunt*; and for the exaggeration cf. 1. 2 *cui iam . . . in funere sum* and *inplentur oculi* with nn.

offirmare, which occurs regularly in Plautus (cf. e.g. *Amph.* 646, *Bacch.* 1199, *Persa* 222), appears only sporadically thereafter (and, after Terence, never more than once in any author) until Apuleius (*met.* 7. 28, 10. 10) and later; cf. *TLL* 9. 2. 527–8. In Jerome cf. e.g. *vita Pauli* 9 (PL 23. 25), *in Ezech.* 38. 1–23 (CCSL 75. 525 = PL 25. 356). By contrast *firmare*, rare in early Latin, is found consistently from the time of Cicero and never loses currency; cf. *TLL* 6. 1. 809–12. For the decline and resurgence of *offirmare* cf. on 4. 2 *melos*; the general tendency of Silver Latin to prefer simple verbs will not have encouraged an earlier revival. Both *offirmare* and *firmare* occur with *animus* and similar words as object; cf. e.g. (*offirmare*) Plaut. *Amph.* 646, Plin. *epist.* 7. 27. 8, Oros. *hist.* 5. 5. 15 (*animus*), Sen. *epist.* 98. 7 (*mens*); (*firmare*) Cic. *Tusc.* 2. 28, Ov. *Pont.* 1. 3. 27 (*animus*), Sen. *Tro.* 951 (*spiritus*).

in tali illum tempore: the odd placing of *illum* arises from the fact that it acts here as an enclitic, reverting to second position in the clause (the tendency known as 'Wackernagel's Law'); cf. KS 2. 592–4, E. Fraenkel, 'Kolon and Satz: Beobachtungen zur Gliederung des antiken Satzes: 2', *NGG* 1933, 319–54 (= Fraenkel, *Kleine Beiträge zur klassischen Philologie* (2 vols., Rome, 1964), 1. 93–130). The positioning of *nobis* at 14. 3 and again at 19. 2 is to be explained similarly.

luctante anima: for *luctari* used of the soul of someone on the point of death cf. Virg. *Aen.* 4. 693–5 'Iuno . . . Irim demisit . . . quae luctantem animam nexosque resolveret artus', Sen. *Phoen.* 141–3 'hoc animo sedet / effundere hanc cum morte luctantem diu / animam', Ov. *Ib.* 125–6 'luctatus . . . diu cruciatos spiritus artus / deserat', *TLL* 7. 2. 1731–2. The poetic colour of the phrase is not at all out of place in a passage as stylistically elevated as the present.

studiorum: a reference to academic interests may seem odd in the context, and it is possible that Jerome was thinking simply of the affectionate personal ties between Nepotianus and himself; for *studium* in this kind of sense cf. e.g. Cic. *ad Att.* 2. 19. 4, Lucan 2. 377 'studiis odiisque carenti'. Labourt translates, 'l'amitié'. But Nepotianus may have associated his friendship with Jerome with theological study (cf. 10. 9); and cf. Quint. *inst.* 6 pref. 11 'quam etiam deficiens iamque non noster ipsum illum alienatae mentis errorem circa scholas, litteras habuit'.

hanc . . . defecit: so too Jerome records the last words of Blesilla; cf. *epist.* 39. 1. 4 'haec in extrema verba mandabat: orate dominum Iesum, ut mihi agnoscat, quia inplere non potui quid volebam'. Whether Jerome was present at Blesilla's deathbed and heard these words for himself is not clear. In the present case it is not impossible that he is quoting to Heliodorus words which Heliodorus himself had transmitted to him in the first place; but they are too polished to have an altogether genuine ring. In using the imperfects *debebatur* and *diligebas* Nepotianus speaks as if he is dead already and addressing his uncle from heaven, and that presumably is the point; we would have expected the present, and I have so rendered in my translation.

Last instructions seem to have been expected from persons on their deathbed; cf. Tac. *Agr.* 45. 4. For poems where such instructions are given see Nisbet–Hubbard (1978), 336.

ministerio Christi: 'the service of Christ', as a presbyter. *ministerium* was capable of being applied to all orders of the clergy (for which see on 10. 3 *fit . . . ordinatur*). For the use of the word, and its Greek equivalent, λειτουργία, in the early Church, see *Dict. spir.*, 10. 1255–60, s.v. 'Ministères'.

aetate . . . collegio: cf. *epist.* 52. 4. 3 (Jerome to Nepotianus) 'audi fratrem collegio, patrem senio'; also *epist.* 105. 5. 2 'vale, mi amice carissime, aetate fili, dignitate parens', Aug. *epist.* 166. 2 (= Jer. *epist.* 131. 2. 1) 'venit ad me religiosus iuvenis catholica pace frater, aetate filius, honore conpresbyter noster Orosius'. By *collegio* is presumably meant the priesthood.

in talia verba defecit: one might have expected an expression with the ablative, as at Suet. *Aug.* 99. 1 'in hac voce defecit'; but the accusative is perfectly acceptable (cf. e.g. Apul. *met.* 1. 26 'me . . . sensit . . . in verba media somnolentum desinere'). Jer. *epist.* 39. 1. 4 (quoted above at *hanc . . . defecit*) is similar. The construction is closely akin to that where *in* + acc. expresses a point in time (cf. e.g. Liv. 29. 23. 3 'ex Hispania forte in idem tempus Scipio atque Hasdrubal convenerunt').

avunculum . . . contrectans: a good case of zeugma, *contrectans* being used in two senses at once. Literally *contrectare* = 'to touch, handle', but often = 'to contemplate, consider' (cf. e.g. Cic. *Tusc.* 3. 33 'incitat ad conspiciendas totaque mente contrectandas varias voluptates'). On zeugma of this semantically complex kind see Lausberg, i. 351–3, sects. 705–8.

c. 14. Nepotianus' death occasioned much sorrow. His loss was mourned by Altinum and the whole of Italy, and in him the Church lost a priest who had the potential to succeed Heliodorus as bishop (14. 1).

The rest of the chapter is difficult. At the end (14. 5–6) Jerome urges Heliodorus to control his grief for his nephew; as a bishop he is in the public eye, and should on no account give the impression that he lacks faith in God. This is not at all unexpected after the *laudes Nepotiani* and the account of his death, by which feelings of grief could easily be aroused. The intervening section (14. 2–4), however, is less easily explained. Jerome moves through a range of ideas which are quite in place in a consolatory context, but which are not presented in a specifically consolatory way, still less related directly to the case of Nepotianus. The overall impression is of a drift in his thought in the course of composing the passage, resulting in a lack of clarity and direction. The flow of thought is scrutinized more closely in the notes which follow.

14. 1. Scio . . . prosperis: it is not completely clear how this sentence is to be understood. If both *probare* and *quaesisse* are held to be dependent on *nolueris*, we have to believe that the negative idea in *nolueris* evaporates after the first clause, and to explain the difference in the tense of the infinitives. The latter difficulty disappears if we suppose, rather, that Jerome changes construction in mid-sentence, switching from a *quod*-clause to an acc. + inf. after *scio* — the tense of *quaesisse* will then balance that of *nolueris* — but this interpretation is open to perhaps weightier objections: there is no good reason for the change in construction (stylistic *variatio* will hardly serve), *te* has to be understood with *affectum . . . in prosperis*, and the sense seems inferior. On the first interpretation it is not, I think, impossible to maintain that the negativity of *nolueris* is lost by the time we get to the second clause, though it is awkward, particularly with *et* rather than *sed* as the connecting particle; and explanations for the tense-variation in *probare* and *quaesisse* can at least be attempted. Might *quaesisse* be taken as equivalent to *quaerere*, the wish looking forward rather than back? The use of the perf. inf. where we should expect the present is not unusual after verbs of wishing and ability (cf. LHS 2. 351–2), and for the combination of the two cf. Virg. *georg.* 3. 435–6 'ne mihi tum mollis sub divo carpere somnos / neu dorso nemoris libeat iacuisse per herbas'. But Virgil's *iacuisse* is explained at least partly by metrical considerations, and, if Jerome intended the wish to look forward, it is bizarre that he should mislead us by using the perfect. It seems possible only to take *quaesisse* as a genuine perfect, i.e. 'you did not wish to prove the love of the citizens for you in this way, you wished rather that you had already gained expression of your country's affection under prosperous circumstances'. But it is difficult to be convinced that this is what Jerome really wrote, and there is a good case for an emendation. *quaesieris* would balance *nolueris*, dispose of all the problems of sense, and give a reasonably good clausula (resolved double cretic) into the bargain.

huiusce . . . gratius: verbally dependent on Ambr. *exc. Sat.* 1. 28 (AD 378) 'habeo sane vobis . . . maximam gratiam, quod non alium meum dolorem quam vestrum putatis . . . non enim misericordiae privatae dolor, sed quoddam publicum officium et munus est gratiae, aut, si qua vos mei tangit misericordia, quod talem fratrem amiserim, habeo fructum uberem, habeo vestri pignus adfectus. mallem fratrem viventem, sed tamen publicum officium in secundis rebus iucundius est, in adversis gratius', as pointed out by Duval (1977), 241 n. 3.

tota hunc . . . Italia: the *civitas* is Altinum. For this exaggerated expression of public grief cf. Ambr. *exc. Sat.* 1. 29 'illam . . . Tabitham viduae, hunc tota civitas flevit' (and see above on *huiusce . . . gratius*); for the same fundamental idea expressed in a more colourful and extreme fashion cf. Bas. *epist.* 5. 1 πάντες δὲ ἄνθρωποι, μεθ' ἡμῶν στένοντες, παρισῶσαι τῷ πάθει τὸν ὀδυρμὸν οὐ δυνήσονται· ἀλλὰ κἂν τὸ τῶν ποταμῶν ῥεῦμα δάκρυον γένηται, ἐκπληρῶσαι τῶν συμβάντων τὸν θρῆνον οὐκ ἐξαρκέσει. Jerome's descriptions of the funerals of Fabiola and Paula are similar, though in the case of Paula at least, a woman whose reputation was undoubtedly widespread, the exaggeration is likely to be less extreme; cf. *epist.* 77. 11. 2–3 (Fabiola) 'et iam fama volans, tanti praenuntia luctus [Virg. *Aen.* 11. 139], totius urbis populos exsequias congregabat . . . tunc suos in unum populos Roma conspexit', 108. 29. 1 (Paula) 'tota ad funus eius Palaestinarum urbium turba convenit'. By such passages the writer increases the stature of the deceased and comforts the bereaved by suggesting, or reminding him, that his grief is shared by many others.

For exaggeration of this kind in different contexts cf. e.g. Cic. *p. red. in sen.* 39 'Italia cuncta paene suis umeris reportarit [sc. me]', *Mil.* 20 'tota civitas confecta senio est' (in irony), Jer. *epist.*

1. 7. 1, 147. 10. 3 'noverat te [sc. Sabinianum diaconum] omnis Italia'. Sometimes the idea is pushed even further; cf. e.g. *epist.* 108. 2. 1, 130. 6. 2–5 (on Demetrias' adoption of the life of virginity) 'per omnes domos fervebat virginitatis professio . . . cunctae per Africam ecclesiae quodam exultavere tripudio . . . omnes inter Africam Italiamque insulae hoc rumore repletae sunt . . . penetravit hic rumor orientis litora et in mediterraneis quoque urbibus Christianae gloriae triumphus auditus est . . . quam sponsam hominis una tantum provincia noverat, virginem Christi totus orbis audivit', and the examples relating to the spread of Christianity at n. on 4. 2 *totius . . . est.*

The careful verbal balance of the sentence is striking. Jerome likes such features; for an extreme example cf. *epist.* 1. 1 'otium quasi quaedam ingenii robigo parvulam licet facultatem pristini siccasset eloquii', where he indulges to the full his taste (which we also see here) for separating a noun from an attributive adjective or a dependent genitive (for which see Appendix 2, p. 241).

corpus . . . tuus: the antithesis in these three short, asyndetic sentences is very marked, particularly in the last (though admittedly this is not antithesis proper, but a kind of word-play with antithesis built into it), which makes pointed the reversal of the natural order of things: for this cf. 1. 3 *rerum . . . senes* with n. Virtually the whole of 14. 1, indeed, is built up by antitheses; there are contrasts in *nolueris . . . prosperis, in bonis . . . gratius, quod tu . . . merebatur,* and *in altero gratulatio . . . teneret.* On rhetorical antithesis generally see the evidence collected by Lausberg, 1. 389–98, sects. 787–807, esp. 1. 389–92, sects. 787–96.

At *part.* 21 Cicero considers antithesis to be a feature of the *suave genus dicendi,* nor is this the only characteristic of this style as described by Cicero, present in 14. 1: one might note particularly the combination of asyndeton and conjunction (cf. Cic. *part.* 21 'constructioque verborum tum coniunctionibus copuletur tum dissolutionibus quasi relaxetur').

praecessit: exactly the sort of word used euphemistically of dying; see on 13. 2 *non emori sed migrare,* and cf. *epist.* 66. 15 'prima de vobis praecessit ad dominum', 77. 10. 1 'praecedit maritum, ut Christo famulum derelinquat', 118. 4. 6. The play with *successor* is thus easy.

quod tu eras: i.e. bishop, as the next sentence makes clear.

pontificatus: episcopate; see on 10. 2 *pontificem.*

raptus sit ne teneret: *raptus sit* should perhaps be regarded as functioning like a verb of preventing; if, alternatively, it is

taken to introduce a purpose clause, the sense of purpose in *ne
teneret* will be very slight: 'he was snatched away [by God, or
fate] that he might not hold the episcopate'. Jerome does not
intend to suggest a grand design to prevent Nepotianus becoming bishop. English calls rather for a temporal clause.

14. 2. Platonis . . . mortis: at this point Jerome begins a new
section, marked by the asyndetic opening; the direction he is
taking is not immediately obvious, but becomes clearer when he
introduces the Pauline quotation just below.

The *sententia* is mentioned by Jerome also at *epist.* 127. 6. 1
(quoted at 14. 3 *debemus . . . non potest*) and *adv. Rufin.* 3. 39–40
(CCSL 79. 109–10 = PL 23. 486) 'audi quid apud Graecos
Pythagoras primus invenerit . . . philosophiam meditationem
esse mortis, cottidie de corporis carcere nitentem animae edu-
cere libertatem; μαθήσεις ἀναμνήσεις, id est discentias remini-
scentias esse; et multa alia quae Plato in libris suis et maxime in
Phaedone Timaeoque prosequitur'. For the attribution of the
sententia to Pythagoras see below; as far as Plato is concerned, it
is derived from passages in the *Phaedo* (cf. 64A οὐδὲν ἄλλο αὐτοὶ
[sc. φιλόσοφοι] ἐπιτηδεύουσιν ἢ ἀποθνήσκειν τε καὶ τεθνάναι, 67D τὸ
μελέτημα αὐτὸ τοῦτό ἐστιν τῶν φιλοσόφων, λύσις καὶ χωρισμὸς ψυχῆς
ἀπὸ σώματος, 67E οἱ ὀρθῶς φιλοσοφοῦντες ἀποθνήσκειν μελετῶσι,
80E–81A). Jerome's *meditatio*, which can denote practice as well
as thought or study, represents Plato's ἐπιτηδεύειν and μελετᾶν. It
is, however, doubtful whether Jerome had got at the *sententia*
directly through the *Phaedo*. As in the case of other works of
Plato (see on 5. 2 *Platonis . . . percucurrimus*), convincing
evidence that he knew the dialogue at first hand is lacking. He
knows about the debate on the immortality of the soul held by
Socrates in prison, which is its subject (cf. 4. 2 with n. on *in
consolationem . . . carcere*), and the doctrine that learning is
recollection, which forms part of the debate (*Phaedo* 72E–78B;
cf. *Meno* 80D–86C, *Phaedr.* 249E–250C) (cf. *adv. Rufin.* 3. 39–40
(quoted above)), but this scarcely presupposes that he was
personally acquainted with the Greek text; nor does his comment (ibid.) that it was in the *Phaedo* and *Timaeus* especially
that Plato followed up Pythagorean ideas. At *in Os.* 1. 2 (CCSL
76. 9 = PL 25. 823), where he again refers to the work by name,
there is no indication that he had actually read it.

As for the *sententia* itself, Jerome never attributes it directly to
the *Phaedo*, and it appears to have been well known: cf. Sen.
dial. 6. 23. 2 'inde est quod Platon clamat: sapientis animum
totum in mortem prominere, hoc velle, hoc meditari', Clem.
Alex. *strom.* 5. 11 (quoted at 14. 3 *debemus . . . non potest*;

Courcelle (1948), 87, shows that at least parts of this work were known to Jerome), Greg. Naz. *epist.* 31. 4, Ambr. *exc. Sat.* 2. 35 (quoted below at *multo . . . ad gloriam*, where see n.), where, however, the author is vague about its origin. If nowhere else, Jerome will have come across it at Cic. *Tusc.* 1. 74 'tota enim philosophorum vita, ut ait idem [sc. Socrates], commentatio mortis est'; there is some verbal similarity, and Jerome knew the work well (cf. Hagendahl (1958), with his index). The weight of evidence is very much in favour of the view that Jerome knew the maxim only at second hand.

The suggestion made at *adv. Rufin.* 3. 39–40 that the *sententia* came originally from Pythagoras is curious, but plausibly explained by Kunst, 139, who regards it as an inference from a passage in Porphyry's *Vita Pythagorae*, on which Jerome was drawing in this part of the *Adversus Rufinum* (cf. Courcelle (1948), 61), made in the light of Cic. *Tusc.* 1. 74–5. A story about Pythagoras is also raised in connection with the idea at Clem. Alex. *strom.* 5. 11.

multo . . . ad gloriam: the quotation comes from 1 Cor. 15: 31 'cotidie morior per vestram gloriam, fratres, quam habeo in Christo Iesu domino nostro'. In its Pauline context 'cotidie morior' seems primarily to mean 'every day I risk death' from external dangers (cf. A. Robertson and A. Plummer, *A Critical and Exegetical Commentary on the First Epistle of St. Paul to the Corinthians* (2nd edn., Edinburgh, 1914), 361). If Jerome did understand the phrase to bear this meaning, however, he is not interested in it here, wishing to take it rather more literally. He is concerned to draw a comparison between the standpoint of the pagan philosopher, who only contemplates or practises dying, and that of Paul, the model for Christians, who actually does 'die'. *aliud est conari, aliud agere* makes the comparison clear. Jerome may have felt that Paul 'died' in the sense that he shared in the death of Jesus, an idea which occurs in 2 Cor. and Col. (cf. e.g. 2 Cor. 4: 9–12, esp. 9–10 'persecutionem patimur, sed non derelinquimur, deicimur, sed non perimus, semper mortificationem Iesu in corpore nostro circumferentes, ut et vita Iesu in corporibus nostris manifestetur', Col. 2: 20 'si mortui estis cum Christo ab elementis mundi, quid adhuc tamquam viventes in mundo decernitis?'), or died to sin (cf. Rom. 6: 10–11). The play on the senses of *mori* continues to the end of the section.

The statement of Paul is connected with the Platonic *sententia* also at Ambr. *exc. Sat.* 2. 35 'cottidie morior, apostolus dicit, melius quam illi, qui meditationem mortis philosophiam esse

Commentary on 14. 3

185

dixerunt; illi enim studium praedicarunt, hic usum ipsum mortis exercuit' — the same comparison is drawn here — and at Jer. *epist.* 127. 6. 1–2, where they are not regarded as being in conflict (see on 14. 3 *debemus . . . non potest*). This may be an indication that Jerome was directly acquainted with the second speech on Satyrus as well as the first (for which see on 14. 1 *huiusce . . . gratius*).

per vestram gloriam = νὴ τὴν ὑμετέραν καύχησιν, understood by Robertson–Plummer as an assurance given by Paul to the Corinthians for the truth of his statement 'cotidie morior'; i.e. 'by the glorying in you which I have in Christ Jesus our Lord (ἣν ἔχω ἐν Χριστῷ Ἰησοῦ τῷ κυρίῳ ἡμῶν)'. In Jerome's context the words have no real value, but he takes advantage of *gloriam* to play on the possibilities of that word just below.

ille . . . iste: i.e. the pagan philosopher . . . the Christian.

14. 3. debemus . . . non potest: in the context this statement is awkward and surprising. In the first place it would, on the face of it, have been more natural for Jerome to comment on how Nepotianus lived than on how 'we' should do so. Secondly, *praemeditari* recalls *meditationem*, and as Jerome has apparently rejected the Platonic maxim as insufficient, it is odd that he should now effectively set it up as a principle for himself, Heliodorus, and whoever else may be included in *et nos* — possibly all Christians — to follow. It is as though he has forgotten that he has criticized the *sententia* at all.

The picture would have been clearer if Jerome had combined the idea of *meditatio mortis* with that of 'dying' in one's life without drawing a distinction between them: the idea of appropriate Christian action (seen in terms of 'dying') could then easily be understood to be implied by *praemeditari*. In itself the Platonic maxim does not necessarily conflict with the Christian position. Clement of Alexandria understands it to fall in easily with the way in which Christians should worship God; cf. *strom.* 5. 11 θυσία δὲ ἡ τῷ θεῷ δεκτὴ σώματός τε καὶ τῶν τούτου παθῶν ἀμετανόητος χωρισμός· ἡ ἀληθὴς τῷ ὄντι θεοσέβεια αὕτη. καὶ μήτι εἰκότως μελέτη θανάτου διὰ τοῦτο εἴρηται τῷ Σωκράτει ἡ φιλοσοφία; At *epist.* 127. 6 Jerome does indeed link, in a complementary way, the maxim with the words of Paul quoted here; the passage is worth setting out in its entirety:

annis igitur plurimis sic suam transegit aetatem [sc. Marcella], ut ante se vetulam cerneret quam adulescentulam fuisse meminisset, laudans illud Platonicum, qui philosophiam meditationem mortis esse dixisset. unde et noster apostolus: cotidie morior per vestram salutem; et dominus iuxta antiqua exemplaria: nisi quis tulerit crucem suam

cotidie et secutus fuerit me, non potest meus esse discipulus [Luke 14:
27]; multoque ante per prophetam spiritus sanctus: propter te mortifi-
camur tota die, aestimati sumus ut oves occisionis [Ps. 43: 22]; et post
multas aetates illa sententia: memento semper diem mortis et numquam peccabis [Ecclus. 7: 40]; disertissimeque praeceptum satirici: vive
memor leti, fugit hora, hoc quod loquor inde est [Pers. 5. 153]. sic
ergo — ut dicere coeperamus — aetatem duxit et vixit, ut semper se
crederet morituram. sic induta est vestibus, ut meminisset sepulchri,
offerens hostiam rationabilem, vivam, placentem deo.

The same point might easily have been made about Nepotianus. It is possible that originally Jerome intended to apply the
sententia directly to his case — he was mindful of death (and
lived accordingly), he 'practised' death (in the sense of Christian
preparation for the next world, which might be seen in terms of
'dying'); this would have set him again in a favourable light, and
been a comfort to Heliodorus — but, carried along by the drift of
his thought, and failing to see the logical shortcomings in what
he was saying, he ended up on a rather different course.

For the idea that one should reflect that one will eventually die
cf. e.g. Sen. *epist.* 63. 15 'itaque adsidue cogitemus tam de
nostra quam omnium quos diligimus mortalitate . . . nunc
cogito omnia et mortalia esse et incerta lege mortalia', 93. 6 'non
enim ad eum diem me aptavi quem ultimum mihi spes avida
promiserat, sed nullum non tamquam ultimum aspexi', [Plut.]
ad Apoll. 6 (103F), Lier (1904), 63–4. The notion can have
consolatory effect when combined with the idea that one's own
death will reunite one with the deceased presently mourned.
Seneca does this at *epist.* 63. 15, and Jerome might have done so
here, though there is no indication that he contemplated it.

For other examples in Jerome cf. *epist.* 23. 4, 54. 18. 3 'cogita
te cottidie esse morituram, et numquam de secundis nuptiis
cogitabis', 140. 16. 2–3 'numerum annorum dierumque nostrorum, quos in hoc saeculo nos vivere decrevisti, ostende nobis,
ut praeparemus nos adventui tuo . . . nihil enim ita decipit
humanum genus, quam, dum ignorant spatia vitae suae, longiorem sibi saeculi huius possessionem repromittunt. unde et
egregie dictum est: nullum tam senem esse et sic decrepitae
senectutis, ut non se adhuc uno plus anno vivere suspicetur. ad
hunc sensum pertinet et illud, quod dicitur: memento mortis
tuae et non peccabis. qui enim se recordatur cotidie esse
moriturum, contemnit praesentia et ad futura festinat', (perhaps) 147. 2. 1.

For *praemeditatio* not of one's own death, but of ills which may befall one in the future, see on 5. 1 *Anaxagorae* . . . *mortalem*.

velimus nolimus: for examples of this very common formula, first attested in Cicero (cf. *ad Q. fr.* 3. 6(8). 4, *nat. deor.* 1. 17), see Otto, 362, sect. 1852, and the *Nachträge*. Number and person are of course variable. The expression is frequent in Jerome; cf. e.g. *epist.* 45. 7 'saluta Paulam et Eustochium — velit nolit mundus, in Christo meae sunt', 112. 15. 2, 130. 19. 1, *adv. Iovin.* 1. 12, 2. 21 (PL 23. 228, 316), *in Zach.* pref. (CCSL 76A. 748 = PL 25. 1418).

nam . . . proficiscitur: Jerome now develops the idea, expressed in the last sentence, that death cannot be far away. Everyone is bound to die, and ultimately it makes no difference whether one's life is long or short, except in so far as (a Christian point) the older a man is, the heavier his burden of sin. The implication is that it is better to die young, an idea with which it is difficult not to associate Nepotianus, even though the point is not explicitly related to him. An early death might also be thought advantageous when death is seen as an escape from the miseries of human life (cf. on 14. 4 *optima . . . mortis* and 15. 1 *ut . . . evaserit*, and introductory n. to cc. 15–16).

The notion of *inrecusabilis mortis necessitas*, though not used here in a consolatory way, is nevertheless an obvious τόπος of consolation, and is connected more directly with the case of Nepotianus at 5. 1, where see n. on *Anaxagorae . . . mortalem*.

For the idea that there is effectively no difference between long life and short cf. e.g. Lucr. 3. 1087–94, Cic. *sen.* 69 'quid est in hominis natura diu? da enim summum tempus, expectemus Tartessiorum regis aetatem . . . mihi ne diuturnum quidem quicquam videtur, in quo est aliquid extremum. cum enim id advenit, tum illud, quod praeteriit, effluxit', *Tusc.* 1. 94, Sen. *dial.* 6. 21. 3 'cum ad omne tempus dimiseris animum, nulla erit illa brevissimi longissimique aevi differentia, si inspecto quanto quis vixerit spatio comparaveris quanto non vixerit', *epist.* 99. 4, 99. 31 'omnes, quantum ad brevitatem aevi, si universo compares, et iuvenes et senes, in aequo sumus', [Plut.] *ad Apoll.* 17 (111C), M. Aur. 4. 50 βλέπε . . . ὀπίσω τὸ ἀχανὲς τοῦ αἰῶνος καὶ τὸ πρόσω ἄλλο ἄπειρον. ἐν δὴ τούτῳ τί διαφέρει ὁ τριήμερος τοῦ τριγερηνίου;, Kunst, 139–40. The majority of these passages occur in conjunction with the consolatory idea that one should not grieve at someone's death on the ground that they died young, because to have lived longer would not have been of any benefit to them. On the relativity of time cf. also Tac. *dial.* 16. 6.

In a wholly different context cf. Jer. *adv. Iovin.* 1. 13 (PL 23. 230) 'etiamsi nongentis viveremus annis, ut antiqui homines, tamen breve putandum esset, quod haberet aliquando finem, et esse cessaret. nunc vero cum brevis sit non tam laetitia, quam tribulatio nuptiarum, quid accipimus uxores, quas cogemur cito amittere?'.

si ... donarentur: for Methuselah cf. Gen. 5: 27 'et facti sunt omnes dies Mathusalae nongenti sexaginta novem anni, et mortuus est'. He was the oldest of a number of patriarchs living before the Flood to whom extraordinary longevity is attributed in the OT; a further five of them (Adam, Seth, Enos, Kenan, Jered) are said to have lived beyond their 900th year, six if we include Noah, who was in his 600th year when the Flood began and survived a further 350 years after it. See Gen. 5: 5–31, (for Noah) 7: 11, 9: 28–9.

excedere is not infrequently used of time; cf. Liv. 9. 34. 15 'ne excedas finitum tempus', Plin. *epist.* 2. 1. 4, *TLL* 5. 2. 1208–9; also 16. 1 below. For the position of *nobis* cf. 13. 3 *in tali illum tempore* with n., 19. 2.

transactum ... tantundem est: there is a slight anacoluthon here. After *inter eum ... et illum ...* we should have expected a phrase such as *nihil interest*; Jerome, however, writes 'everything that has been accomplished is just as much', i.e. it all amounts to the same thing, as if *ab eo ...* and *ab illo ...*, in close conjunction with *transactum omne*, had preceded.

magis ... proficiscitur: cf. Ambr. *bon. mort.* (AD 387–9) 6–7 'quid igitur tantopere vitam istam desideramus, in qua quanto diutius quis fuerit tanto maiore oneratur sarcina? ... nullus enim dies sine nostro peccato praeterit', *exc. Sat.* 2. 34. Similarly, one of the consolations Basil offers his correspondent, whose child has died young, in *epist.* 300 is that οὐχ ὑπέμεινεν ἀνάγκην ἁμαρτημάτων.

peccatorum fasce: in late Latin *fascis* is sometimes used to mean a metaphorical burden; cf. Symm. *epist.* 8.13 'praevenisse me arbitror famam, quae te absolutum non modo honoris verum etiam curarum fasce vulgavit', Ambr. *Iob* 1. 3. 7 'fasce delicti', Prud. *ham.* 551, *TLL* 6. 1. 307–8.

proficiscitur: for the use of words of this kind in describing death see on 13. 2 *non emori sed migrare*.

14. 4. optima ... mortis: Virg. *georg.* 3. 66–8. Having just implied that it is better to die young (*magis ... proficiscitur*), Jerome now does so again; not, however, on the ground that the longer one lives, the more sin one accumulates, but because after youth is past one becomes a prey to disease and the suffering which old age brings. Death, no doubt, is equally *inclemens* when it comes to someone young, but at least the intervening miseries are then avoided. Jerome has no interest in the Virgilian context, where the lines occur in connection with the idea that cattle should be mated while still young.

The passage is also quoted, in part, and with some grammatical tailoring, at *epist.* 58. 11. 2 'praepara tibi divitias, quas cotidie eroges et numquam deficiant, dum viget aetas, dum adhuc canis spargitur caput, antequam subeant morbi tristisque senectus et labor et durae rapiat inclementia mortis'; for other cases of borrowing cf. Sen. *epist.* 108. 24 (all three verses; parts are quoted also at 108. 26 and 29), *dial.* 10. 9. 2, [Acro] *Hor. carm.* 2. 11. 5 (in part), Don. *Ter. Phorm.* 1. 2. 42 (in part). In none of these instances are Virgil's words used, as they are here, to suggest that to die young is a good thing.

Naevius . . . mala: the senarius of Naevius quoted here (Naev. *com.* 106) is not recorded elsewhere, and it is not known from what play it comes. It is most improbable that Jerome was directly acquainted with a text of Naevius; he refers to him elsewhere only in his translation of Eusebius' *Chronicle* (p. 135 Helm = PL 27. 495–6), in connection with the time and place of his death (and calling him 'Naevius comicus', a description which, according to M. Barchiesi, *Nevio epico* (Padua, 1962), 106, determined Naevius' future for centuries; for Petrarch he was still a comic poet, his epic, the *Bellum Poenicum*, long forgotten). It seems quite likely that he found the line — and the Ennian verses quoted below (see n. on *prudenterque . . . non licet*) — in Cicero's *Consolatio*, his source for much of c. 5 (where see nn.); cf. Luebeck, 105–6, 157, Kunst, 142. For the phrase *Naevius poeta* cf. Powell, 145 (on Cic. *sen.* 20); and for the theme of the wretchedness of human life, Powell, 263–4.

unde . . . antiquitas: the connection between the Naevius quotation, which links easily with the lines from the *Georgics*, and the present passage seems to be this: taking hold of the general human truth that every mortal must inevitably experience many ills, people in antiquity gave it a mythological extension, imagining Niobe, a woman who suffered great evils (her children were slain by Apollo and Artemis) and grieved accordingly, undergoing metamorphosis. For the full story see e.g. Hom. *Il.* 24. 602–17, Ov. *met.* 6. 146–312; references to other ancient sources may now conveniently be found in P. M. C. Forbes Irving, *Metamorphosis in Greek Myths* (Oxford, 1990), 294–7. Jerome refers to the myth again, in a different context, at *epist.* 69. 2. 7.

The textual problem is a major one which has been much discussed, most recently by C. Vitelli, 'Nota a Gerolamo, *epist*. 60. 14', *RFIC* 101 (1973), 352–5. Four of the MSS, and the fragment m, read *in lapidem et in diversas bestias com(n* m)*mutatam*; two omit the second *in*, and one has *commutatum*. As there is no record elsewhere of Niobe being changed *in diversas bestias*, and as such a multiple metamorphosis would seem to have no point in the myth, it is natural to suppose that something is amiss with the text.

The most usual approach has been to assume a lacuna. Believing that Jerome might have consolidated his point with further examples, Hilberg, following Buresch (1886), 101, took his cue from Cic. *Tusc*. 3. 63 'et Nioba fingitur lapidea propter aeternum, credo, in luctu silentium. Hecubam autem putant propter animi acerbitatem quandam et rabiem fingi in canem esse conversam'; Hecuba's rage is connected with her bitter grief at the deaths of her children. Hilberg's conjecture, *in lapidem et in diversas bestias ⟨conversas alias ut Hecubam in canem⟩ commutatam*, seems to assume this passage — or a similar one from the closely-related *Consolatio* (for the connection see Introduction, p. 19) — to have been Jerome's direct source here. A similar solution is proposed by Kunst, 141 n. 5, who offers an ingenious explanation of how the lacuna arose; according to his reconstruction of the text, a copyist could easily have omitted a line by parablepsy. Buresch names Alcyone, Cycnus, and Daedalion as the kind of figures whom Jerome will have meant to be included among those metamorphosed *in diversas bestias*.

Hilberg's approach, however, is highly questionable. It is dangerous to suppose that in this case Jerome was following a specific source. The story of Niobe was well known and used by consolers in various ways (see below); and by themselves words such as *finxit* and *commutatam*, which recall Cicero's 'fingitur', 'fingi', and 'conversam', are scarcely enough to clinch a connection. His conjecture seems, additionally, grammatically awkward: the position of *commutatam* makes it hard to take it with *Niobam*, where one feels it should belong, and it is redundant with *Hecubam* after *conversas*. The lacuna was filled in a more general, and grammatically more satisfactory, way by Vallarsi: *in lapidem et ⟨alios⟩ in diversas bestias commutatos*. Following the same basic line, but showing greater subtlety and less simplicity than Vallarsi, Vitelli offered as a reconstruction *Niobam . . . in lapidem et ⟨diversas⟩* [or *-os*] *in diversas bestias commutatas* [or *-os*], his essential point being that the repetition

of *diversus* in polyptoton is frequent in late Latin (he gives two
further instances in Jerome, including c. 5. 2 of this very letter).

The presence of a lacuna at all is, however, far less certain than
has sometimes been supposed ('lacunam manifestam explere
conatus sum', wrote Hilberg). As an alternative to the conjecture cited above, Vallarsi suggested that *et in diversas bestias*
might have been interpolated, drawn in, one may presume,
from a marginal comment in an early MS, where other cases of
metamorphosis had been jotted down or alluded to. This idea is
more attractive than most scholars seem to have found it. It
easily explains the corruption, disposes of the need to assume a
corruption of two stages (Vallarsi (above), Vitelli), and avoids
the awkwardness and endless speculation of the Hilberg-type
approach. Though certainty is impossible, I have therefore
opted for deletion.

For the use of the story of Niobe in consolation cf. Cic. *Tusc.*
3. 63 (quoted above), Sen. *epist.* 63. 2 'duram tibi legem videor
ponere, cum poetarum Graecorum maximus ius flendi dederit
in unam dumtaxat diem, cum dixerit etiam Niobam de cibo
cogitasse?', [Plut.] *ad Apoll.* 28 (116B–C) εἰ γοῦν ἡ Νιόβη κατὰ τοὺς
μύθους πρόχειρον εἶχε τὴν ὑπόληψιν ταύτην ὅτι καὶ ἡ . . . βλάσταις . . .
τέκνων βριθομένα . . . τελευτήσει, οὐκ ἂν οὕτως ἐδυσχέραινεν ὡς καὶ τὸ
ζῆν ἐθέλειν ἐκλιπεῖν διὰ τὸ μέγεθος τῆς συμφορᾶς. It is noteworthy
that the myth is used each time in a different context: Cicero
introduces it in connection with his discussion of people who
exaggerate their grief because they think they ought to show the
deepest possible sorrow at the death of loved ones, Seneca uses
it to fortify his exhortation to Lucilius not to weep too much,
pseudo-Plutarch links it with the idea that it is sensible to
remember that people are mortal, for their deaths then occasion
less grief and resentment. So Jerome here employs the myth in
his own way, giving it as one case in which the ancients put into
mythological terms the general truth that people must suffer
many ills.

†**Hesiodus**† . . . **funere:** a second conclusion is now drawn
from the words of Naevius: as men are subject to *mala*, death
must be a good thing and a matter for rejoicing. This point
squares neatly with the implication of the quotation from the
Georgics above and the sentence which precedes it, that to die
young is to avoid the accumulation of sin and the sufferings of
old age. The passage about Niobe sits a little uncomfortably in
the middle of all this.

For the notion that death should be an occasion for joy, and
birth for sorrow, cf. Herod. 5. 4 Τραῦσοι . . . ποιεῦσι τοιάδε· τὸν

μὲν γενόμενον περιιζόμενοι οἱ προσήκοντες ὀλοφύρονται, ὅσα μιν δεῖ
ἐπείτε ἐγένετο ἀναπλῆσαι κακά, ἀνηγεόμενοι τὰ ἀνθρωπήια πάντα
πάθεα, τὸν δ' ἀπογενόμενον παίζοντές τε καὶ ἡδόμενοι γῇ κρύπτουσι,
ἐπιλέγοντες ὅσων κακῶν ἐξαπαλλαχθείς ἐστι ἐν πάσῃ εὐδαιμονίῃ, Val.
Max. 2. 6. 12 'Thraciae vero illa natio merito sibi sapientiae
laudem vindicaverit, quae natales hominum flebiliter, exequias
cum hilaritate celebrans sine ullis doctorum praeceptis verum
condicionis nostrae habitum pervidit', Quint. *inst.* 5. 11. 38 'an
vero me de incommodis vitae disserentem non adiuvabit earum
persuasio nationum quae fletibus natos, laetitia defunctos prose-
cuntur?', Ambr. *exc. Sat.* 2. 5 'fuisse etiam quidam feruntur
populi, qui ortus hominum lugerent obitusque celebrarent; nec
inprudenter enim eos, qui in hoc vitae salum venissent, maeren-
dos putabant, eos vero, qui ex istius mundi procellis et fluctibus
emersissent, non iniusto gaudio prosequendos arbitrabantur.
nos quoque ipsi natales dies defunctorum obliviscimur et eum,
quo obierunt, diem celebri sollemnitate renovamus', Bas. *de
morte* 7 (PG 32. 1265–8); closely related is the idea that it is best
not to be born, or else to die as soon as possible, for which see
e.g. Theognis 425–7, Soph. *OC* 1224–7, Cic. *cons.* fr. 9 Mueller.
See also on 15. 1 *ut . . . evaserit.*

    All the MSS give the name of Hesiod in one form or another.
Hilberg understood Jerome to be referring to *Op.* 174–8 μηκέτ'
ἔπειτ' ὤφελλον ἐγὼ πέμπτοισι μετεῖναι / ἀνδράσιν, ἀλλ' ἢ πρόσθε
θανεῖν ἢ ἔπειτα γενέσθαι. / νῦν γὰρ δὴ γένος ἐστὶ σιδήρεον· οὐδέ ποτ'
ἦμαρ / παύσονται καμάτου καὶ ὀϊζύος οὐδέ τι νύκτωρ / φθειρόμενοι·
χαλεπὰς δὲ θεοὶ δώσουσι μερίμνας; but it is scarcely possible to see
how these words could be summed up by *natales . . . funere*, and
Hilberg himself was forced to say, 'Hesiodi versum male
intellexit Hieronymus'. No other passage in the extant writings
of Hesiod will fit the bill either. Jerome is most unlikely to have
known Hesiod's work at first hand anyway. He mentions him in
two other passages (*epist.* 52. 3. 5, *in Is.* 2. 3 (CCSL 73. 45 = PL
24. 69)), but neither presupposes direct acquaintance with the
Greek text. In the first Hesiod is merely mentioned in a list of
Greek poets, in the second he is referred to simply as 'Graeci
poetae', and the *sententia* attributed to him there may have
reached Jerome through another such commentary on Isaiah
(cf. Hagendahl (1958), 229) or through Clem. Alex. *paedag.* 3. 8
(cf. Luebeck, 11–12, Courcelle (1948), 50); it is quite possible
that Jerome was not even aware of the identity of the 'Graeci
poetae'. Equally, there appears to be no extant intermediate
source, naming Hesiod, from which Jerome could have drawn
the allusion in the present passage. These difficulties have given

rise to much discussion whether *Hesiodus* should remain in the text, and what could replace it, the fullest treatment being that of Kunst, 143–50.

In brief, two possible corrections for *Hesiodus* have been proposed, on the assumption that the error was due to an early copyist or to Jerome himself in a moment of forgetfulness:

(*a*) *Euripides*: the passage in question being the fragment of Euripides' *Cresphontes* quoted in translation by Cicero at *Tusc.* 1. 115: 'nam nos decebat coetus celebrantis domum / lugere, ubi esset aliquis in lucem editus, / humanae vitae varia reputantis mala; / at qui labores morte finisset gravis, / hunc omni amicos laude et laetitia exsequi'. *natales . . . funere* would represent these lines well, and they will have been familiar to Jerome at least through his reading of the *Tusculans* or Cicero's *Consolatio*, where they are almost certain to have occurred (they were in any case famous, and much quoted; cf. esp. Menand. Rhet. *epid.* 2. 9 (413. 24–31) Russell–Wilson, Kassel, 76); but a scribal error of this magnitude, at least, seems most unlikely;

(*b*) *Herodotus*; in which case a copyist, as long as he was familiar with the name of Hesiod, could more easily have misread the text from which he was working and blundered in the transcription. This emendation, first proposed by Susemihl, has been widely favoured (cf. Luebeck, 20, Kunst, 145–9, Courcelle (1948), 68, Hagendahl (1958), 204), and the allusion generally considered to refer to the story of Cleobis and Biton at Herod. 1. 31, in which διέδεξέ . . . ὁ θεός, ὡς ἄμεινον εἴη ἀνθρώπῳ τεθνάναι μᾶλλον ἢ ζώειν. Jerome will certainly have been familiar with the story, which is mentioned at Cic. *Tusc.* 1. 113, and there declared to be well known, but *natales . . . funere* does not, on the face of it, represent it with great accuracy. Clement of Alexandria, however, says that in this story Herodotus οὐκ ἄλλο τι βούλεται ἀλλ' ἢ ψέγειν μὲν τὴν γένεσιν, τὸν θάνατον δὲ ἐπαινεῖν (*strom.* 3. 3), which prompted Luebeck, followed by Courcelle, to hold that Clement was Jerome's direct source; Courcelle further suggested that Jerome may have read Hesiod's name in place of Herodotus' in his text of Clement. As an alternative possibility, Kunst, 147–9, proposed as the original source Herod. 5. 4 (quoted above), arguing that Jerome got at this passage through Cicero's *Consolatio*.

Both conjectures are plausible; the second may have the edge, as allowing more easily the possibility of a mistake by a scribe, albeit one literate enough to know the name of Hesiod. It is, however, far from inconceivable that Jerome's memory failed him at this point, or that *Hesiodus* simply represents a slip of the tongue or pen. As it is impossible to be sure what he intended to write, I have had recourse to the obelus.

prudenterque . . . non licet: this Ennian fragment is somewhat loosely attached to what has preceded. It does not follow directly from the *sententia* of Naevius; it rather looks forward to the subsequent section, where Jerome turns again to the particular case of Heliodorus.

The trimeters are not found elsewhere. Editors from Columna on assigned them to Ennius' *Iphigenia*, on the strength of their similarity to Eur. *IA* 446–9, but the caution of Jocelyn, 323, that it is dangerous to assign to particular plays fragments which have the character of a *sententia*, is well founded. The fragment appears as no. 215 in Jocelyn's edition. Jerome is likely to have found it in Cicero's *Consolatio*; cf. Luebeck, 109–10, 157, who demonstrates that where Jerome cites Ennius elsewhere he is almost certainly dependent on Cicero.

The text and punctuation I have adopted are Jocelyn's; in reading *regi* mD in the first line he followed I. Vahlen, *Ennianae poesis reliquiae* (2nd edn., Leipzig, 1928), 158 (= *Iphigenia*, fr. 7), but the punctuation is his own. By contrast Hilberg printed *regio*, the reading of the majority of the MSS, and, like Vahlen, placed the colon after *loco*. Certainly, if *regio* is right, it can go only with *loco*; *in hoc* must mean 'in this respect'. Metrically this is acceptable, and the sense is adequate. But with *plebes antestat*, *regi* seems more in place than *regio loco*. *loco* must then be put on the other side of the colon; *in hoc loco* would make no sense here. The natural meaning of *loco* is then 'opportunely', 'at the appropriate moment' (cf. *OLD* s.v. *locus* 21*b*), and it balances *honeste*.

14. 5. ut regi . . . quam episcopo: at last Jerome gets back to the specific case of Heliodorus. In addition to all the other reasons why Heliodorus should not grieve for his nephew, some of which have just been hinted at obliquely — that death is an escape from *mala*, and so on — there is another of some importance: it is not honourable for him, as a bishop, to do so. In the rest of the chapter Jerome elaborates on this point.

With *minus . . . episcopo* the effective governing verb is still *non licet*: grief is less unlawful for a king than for a bishop.

servitute dominatur: the Christian paradox of mastery by service, rooted in the gospels; cf. e.g. John 13: 4–10, where Christ washes the feet of his disciples, Mark 9: 34 'ait [sc. Iesus] illis [sc. discipulis]: si quis vult primus esse, erit omnium novissimus et omnium minister'.

in te . . . putant: Heliodorus' position as bishop marks him out as a man in the public eye; people look to him for an example, and he must be careful not to set a bad one. Cf. in general Pind. *Pyth.* 1. 86–8.

Cicero writes to Brutus in similar vein after the death of the latter's wife Porcia: 'mihi tum, Brute, officio solum erat et naturae, tibi nunc populo et scaenae, ut dicitur, serviendum est; nam cum in te non solum exercitus tui sed omnium civium ac paene gentium coniecti oculi sint, minime decet propter quem fortiores ceteri sumus eum ipsum animo debilitatum videri' (*ad Brut.* 1. 9. 2). Buresch (1886), 103–4, and Kunst, 150–1, argue plausibly that Cicero said something similar about himself in his *Consolatio*, comparing himself also with the king mentioned in the Ennian fragment, and that Jerome took over the idea directly from there. Seneca too makes the same sort of point at *dial.* 11. 6. 1 'potest et illa res a luctu te prohibere nimio, si tibi ipse renuntiaveris nihil horum quae facis posse subduci. magnam tibi personam hominum consensus inposuit: haec tibi tuenda est'.

14. 6. delinquere: transitive, with *quod* as object; 'commit' (with pejorative connotation). Labourt's understanding of the word, = 'y renoncer', is certainly wrong.

ubertim . . . in deum: a τόπος of Christian consolation, albeit not a very common one; cf. *epist.* 39. 6. 1 'grandis in suos pietas inpietas in deum est', Paul. Nol. *carm.* 31. 45–50, Cypr. *mort.* 20 'praedicarem . . . occasionem dandam non esse gentilibus, ut nos merito ac iure reprehendant, quod quos vivere aput deum dicimus ut extinctos et perditos lugeamus et fidem quam sermone ac voce depromimus cordis et pectoris testimonio non probemus'. Such a τόπος must be essentially Christian, but the notion that one should cease grieving in order not to give a handle to those who may draw false conclusions from that grief is found occasionally in pagan consolation; cf. Cic. *ad fam.* 4. 5. 6 (Sulpicius) 'noli committere ut quisquam te putet non tam filiam quam reipublicae tempora et aliorum victoriam lugere', Sen. *dial.* 12. 19. 7 'huic parem virtutem exhibeas oportet et animum a luctu recipias et id agas ne quis te putet partus tui paenitere'.

In different circumstances — when she was leaving Rome for Palestine — Paula made sure that her *pietas* towards her children did not make her *impia* towards God: 'siccos oculos tendebat ad caelum pietatem in filios pietate in deum superans' (*epist.* 108. 6. 3).

On exercising restraint in grief generally see on 7. 3 *obsecro . . . nimis*.

incredulas mentes: for the phrase cf. e.g. [Sen.] *Herc. O.*
1979, (in a specifically Christian sense) Cypr. *eleem.* 12 ('incre-
dula cogitatio'), Arnob. *nat.* 1. 51, [Jer.] *epist.* 148. 23. 1. See
further on 2. 2 *credulam . . . affectus.*

desperatio . . . deum: *desperatio* regularly takes the genitive
of the thing despaired of (cf. *TLL* 5. 1. 737–8), and I have
noticed no other instances where it is followed by *in* + acc.
Jerome presumably wrote *in deum* here to balance *in nepotem, in*
+ acc. being quite regular after *pietas.*

desiderandus . . . videaris: for the notion that the dead are
merely absent, and related ideas and expressions, see on 13. 2
non emori sed migrare.

In saying *desiderandus . . . mortuus* Jerome is of course
encouraging Heliodorus not to weep: Nepotianus is simply
absent, and he will see him again. He forgets, conveniently, that
he has earlier (7. 1) said that it is absence from the deceased
itself which causes grief in the bereaved.

cc. 15–16. Jerome now presents a fairly lengthy account of some of
the disasters which have befallen the Roman world in recent years.
Calamities have struck emperors and leading *privati* alike, and
general havoc has been wrought by barbarian invasions throughout the Empire. How fortunate Nepotianus has been in dying and
escaping from it all!

With this passage it is worth comparing particularly Cic. *de orat.*
3. 8 and Tac. *Agr.* 45, where the deaths of L. Crassus and Agricola
are seen as a happy avoidance of specific ills which subsequently
afflicted the state; Q. Hortensius' death is regarded similarly at
Cic. *Brut.* 329. Ambrose, too, represents his dead brother as
having escaped impending disaster in the nick of time (cf. *exc. Sat.*
1. 30–2 (quoted in part at 2. 1 *laeter . . . illius?*)), and Jerome says of
Olybrius that he was 'felix morte sua, qui non vidit patriam
corruentem' (*epist.* 130. 3. 2). Nepotianus' case is slightly different,
in as much as the evil situation from which he escapes is regarded
as having already long been in existence when he dies; cf. Cypr.
mort. 25 (quoted at 16. 3 *Romanus . . . non flectitur*).

Trillitzsch, 51, sees an 'unmistakable' ('nicht zu verkennen')
parallel between Jerome's list of ill-fated emperors and other
leaders and Sen. *dial.* 6. 26. 2, where Seneca, assuming the person
of Cremutius Cordus, urges Marcia not to grieve for her son's
early death: 'regesne tibi nominem felicissimos futuros si maturius
illos mors instantibus subtraxisset malis? an Romanos duces,
quorum nihil magnitudini deerit si aliquid aetati detraxeris?'. It
may be that Jerome had this passage in mind when he wrote these

chapters, but the parallel is not especially close: Jerome is talking of *reges* and *duces*, but he is not interested in the idea that they would have done better to have died sooner. For him, Constantius and the rest are not so much examples against which Nepotianus' good fortune in dying young is to be measured, as representative cases of the particular catastrophic situation from which he has escaped.

In a letter of consolation to a young widow John Chrysostom mentions that of the nine emperors (τῶν βασιλευσάντων) of his time—he is probably reckoning from Constantine to Valens and including the Caesar Gallus—only two died a natural death (*vid. iun.* 4). In the same chapter he also gives cases of private citizens of recent times who died wretched deaths when they had attained high station. But despite the superficial similarity to the present passage Chrysostom's purpose is different: his concern is not to show from what a dreadful situation Therasius has escaped but rather to suggest that he has done well for himself and his widow to die before reaching a higher position, such is the fate of those who gain it, and indeed of their wives.

For general accounts of the history of the period from the death of Constantine to AD 396 see Gibbon, cc. 22–30, A. Piganiol, *L'Empire chrétien (325–395)* (2nd edn., Paris, 1972), 81–299, E. Stein, *Histoire du bas-empire*, 1. *De l'état romain à l'état byzantin (284–476)*, ed. J.-R. Palanque (Paris, 1959), 156–231.

15. 1. quid . . . sedatum: for the healing qualities of time and reason on *dolor* cf. e.g. Cic. *ad fam.* 4. 5. 6 (Sulpicius) 'nullus dolor est, quem non longinquitas temporis minuat ac molliat. hoc te exspectare tempus tibi turpe est ac non ei rei sapientia tua te occurrere', 5. 16. 6 'neque exspectare temporis medicinam [sc. debemus], quam repraesentare ratione possimus', *Tusc.* 3. 35, Ov. *Pont.* 4. 11. 13–14 'finitumque tuum, si non ratione, dolorem / ipsa iam pridem suspicor esse mora', Sen. *epist.* 63. 12 'finem dolendi etiam qui consilio non fecerat tempore invenit', *dial.* 6. 1. 6, 6. 8. 1 'dolorem dies longa consumit', Bas. *epist.* 269. 1 ἱκανὸς μὲν οὖν καὶ ὁ χρόνος μαλάξαι τὴν καρδίαν καὶ τὴν πάροδον δοῦναι τοῖς λογισμοῖς, Ambr. *exc. Sat.* 2. 8, Jer. *epist.* 39. 5. 2 'quod tempore mitigandum est cur ratione non vincitur?', (in a quite different context) 97. 2. 1; also (on time) C. C. Grollios, *Seneca's Ad Marciam: Tradition and Originality* (Athens, 1956), 22–3. By contrast, the theme of Ov. *trist.* 4. 6 is that the one thing time cannot change is the poet's suffering; cf. esp. 17–18 'cuncta potest igitur tacito pede lapsa vetustas / praeterquam curas attenuare meas'.

In the present passage the suggestion is that Jerome's consolation is of little value, as Heliodorus' grief has already been assuaged; but although Jerome gives the appearance of going on to something quite different (cf. esp. *non potius replico* . . .), it is another τόπος of consolation to which he proceeds in the second half of the sentence. At *epist*. 66. 1. 1 he again feels that he is offering his consolation late, and is afraid that he may even reactivate a wound already healed: 'sanato vulneri et in cicatricem superinductae cuti si medicina colorem reddere voluerit, dum pulchritudinem corporis quaerit, plagam doloris instaurat. ita et ego, serus consolator, qui inportune per biennium tacui, vereor ne nunc inportunius loquar et adtrectans vulnus pectoris tui, quod tempore et ratione curatum est, commemoratione exulcerem'. On ancient views of the right time for offering consolation generally—it was normally held to be not too early, when the consolation might aggravate the fresh wound, nor too late, when the wound had become inveterate—see Johann, 36–40, and Gregg, 136–9.

medens recalls 1. 1 *vulneratos*, where see n. on *desiderii . . . vulneratos*.

ut . . . evaserit: for other cases where death is seen as an escape from specific ills confronting the state see introductory n. to cc. 15–16. Seneca points out how much better off Pompey, Cicero, and Cato would have been if they had died earlier, thus avoiding political troubles which affected them directly (*dial*. 6. 20. 4–6). Equally, by dying one may escape more intimate calamities; cf. Virg. *Aen*. 11. 158–9 'tuque, o sanctissima coniunx, / felix morte tua neque in hunc servata dolorem' (Evander after the death of Pallas; there may be a reminiscence of this passage at *epist*. 130. 3. 2 (quoted in introductory n.)), Ov. *trist*. 4. 10. 81–2 'felices ambo tempestiveque sepulti, / ante diem poenae quod periere meae!'.

Death was often regarded as a release from the *mala* of human life generally (which are much more numerous than the pleasures, according to Teles p. 49. 1–4 Hense, and [Plut.] *ad Apoll*. 28 (115F)); cf. e.g. Herod. 7. 46, [Plato] *Axioch*. 366A–367C, Hyp. *epitaph*. 43 εἰ μέν ἐστι τὸ ἀποθανεῖν ὅμοιον τῷ μὴ γενέσθαι, ἀπηλλαγμένοι εἰσὶ νόσων καὶ λύπης καὶ τῶν ἄλλων τῶν προσπιπτόντων εἰς τὸν ἀνθρώπινον βίον, Caecil. *com*. 175 'diu vivendo multa quae non vult videt' (a *sententia* criticized by the aged Cato at Cic. *sen*. 25), Ov. *trist*. 4. 6. 49–50 'una tamen spes est, quae me soletur in istis, / haec fore morte mea non diuturna mala', Sen. *suas*. 6. 6, Sen. *dial*. 6. 19. 5 'mors dolorum omnium exsolutio est', 11. 9. 4 ff., Stat. *silv*. 2. 1. 220–2 'ast hic quem gemimus, felix hominesque deosque / et dubios casus et caecae lubrica vitae / effugit, immunis fatis', [Plut.] *ad Apoll.* 11 (107C) τοιούτου δὴ τοῦ βίου τῶν ἀνθρώπων ὄντος οἷον οὗτοί φασι, πῶς οὐκ εὐδαιμονίζειν μᾶλλον προσήκει τοὺς ἀπολυθέντας τῆς ἐν αὐτῷ λατρείας ἢ κατοικτείρειν τε καὶ θρηνεῖν, ὅπερ οἱ πολλοὶ δρῶσι δι' ἀμαθίαν;, 34 (119F) ἀλλ' ἄωρος ἐτελεύτησεν. οὐκοῦν εὐποτμότερος διὰ τοῦτο καὶ κακῶν ἀπείρατός ἐστιν, Fronto p. 233 Naber, Cypr. *mort.* 15 'multi ex nostris in hac mortalitate moriuntur, hoc est multi ex nostris de saeculo liberantur', Ambr. *exc. Sat.* 2. 3 'nos saeculi huius absolvat aerumnis [sc. mors]', 2. 21 'si mors carnis et saeculi nos absolvit aerumnis, utique malum non est, quae libertatem restituit, excludit dolorem', Greg. Naz. *orat.* 7. 20 μὴ τοίνυν πενθῶμεν Καισάριον, οἵων ἀπηλλάγη κακῶν εἰδότες, Greg. Nyss. *Pulch.* pp. 465–6 Jaeger, Theodoret, *epist.* 14 (Collectio Sirmondiana; Sources chrétiennes, 98) αὐτῷ μὲν συνησθῶμεν τῆς ἐκδημίας, καὶ τῆς ἐντεῦθεν ἀπαγωγῆς ὅτι τῶν ἀμφιβόλων ἠλευθερώθη πραγμάτων, Boeth. *cons.* 4 pros. 4, Buecheler 436. 1, 1274, Kaibel 650. 6–7, Lier (1903), 592–6. Plutarch similarly sees how to be confined on an island could be viewed as an escape from restless travels and dangers, a positive advantage (cf. *exil.* 11 (603E)); and Jerome regards it as a consolation to the blind that they are freed from at least one temptation (cf. *epist.* 76. 2). By contrast, it is possible to regard death as a deprivation of *suavitas vitae*; cf. Ambr. *exc. Sat.* 2. 14.

Christian writers sometimes present death not, or not merely, as an escape from ills, but as an advance to a better state; cf. e.g. Cypr. *mort.* 22, Ambr. *obit. Valent.* 46 'dolendum est, quod nobis cito raptus sit, consolandum, quod ad meliora transierit', *epist.* 39. 3, Aug. *serm.* 172. 3, John Chrys. *epist.* 192 οὐ γὰρ δὴ θάνατος τοῦτο, ἀλλ' ἀποδημία καὶ μετάστασις ἀπὸ τῶν χειρόνων πρὸς τὰ βελτίω, Jer. *epist.* 39. 3. 6 'si viventem crederet filiam, numquam plangeres ad meliora migrasse', 78. 33. This idea is, of course, virtually identical with the notion that Christians pass to heaven, to the presence of God and Christ, when they die; see on 7. 1 *Scimus . . . dei nostri* for its appearance in consolation. For pagan parallels cf. Cic. *Tusc.* 1. 76 'tantum autem abest ab eo, ut malum mors sit . . . ut verear, ne homini nihil sit non malum aliud, certe sit nihil bonum aliud potius, siquidem vel di ipsi vel cum dis futuri sumus', Sen. *dial.* 6. 24. 5 'imago dumtaxat fili tui perit et effigies non simillima, ipse quidem aeternus meliorisque nunc status est'.

For the simple idea that death is no evil cf. e.g. (among countless instances) Lucr. 3. 866–7, Cic. *ad fam.* 5. 16. 4 'nihil mali esse in morte [sc. legi et audivi], ex qua si resideat sensus,

immortalitas illa potius quam mors ducenda sit, sin sit amissus, nulla videri miseria debeat quae non sentiatur', 6. 3. 3, Sen. *epist.* 123. 16, [Plut.] *ad Apoll.* 19 (111E) ἐν οὐδενὶ κακῷ τυγχάνουσιν ὄντες [sc. οἱ ἀποθανόντες], Epict. 4. 1. 133, M. Aur. 12. 23. Ambrose points out how much better off Christians are, if pagans can be consoled by thoughts such as this; cf. *obit. Valent.* 45 'si gentes, quae spem resurrectionis non habent, hoc uno se consolantur, quo dicant, quod nullus post mortem sensus sit defunctorum ac per hoc nullus remaneat sensus doloris, quanto magis nos consolationem recipere debemus, quia mors metuenda non sit, eo quod finis sit peccatorum, vita autem desperanda non sit, quae resurrectione reparatur?'.

ut: causal, as at 10. 1, where see n. on *ut . . . sit*. Note the similarity of expression, with the use of the gerundive in both cases.

15. 2. Constantius . . . imperium: Flavius Iulius Constantius (*PLRE* 1. 226, *RE* s.n. Constantius 4), b. 317, Augustus 337–61, the third son of Constantine the Great, died of a fever in November 361, at Mopsucrenae (*Mopsi viculo*; cf. Jer. *chron. a Abr.* p. 60B Helm (=PL 27. 263–4) (referring to the time of the Trojan War) 'Mopsus regnavit in Cilicia, a quo Mopsicrenae et Mopsistiae'), near Tarsus, while marching to suppress the rebellion of his cousin Julian (the *inimicus* referred to here). He had been one of the principal supporters of Arianism since his adoption of the doctrine soon after his accession. Julian was subsequently acknowledged as Augustus by the whole Empire.

There is no reason to suppose that Jerome is drawing on any source for the details he gives of Constantius and the rest. He had lived through the period, and the facts he presents are such as would have been widely known or rumoured.

Arrianae . . . hereseos: for details of the Arian *heresis*, which denied the true divinity of Jesus Christ, see *ODCC* s.vv. 'Arianism', 'Arius', and the appended bibliographies.

In the early Church αἵρεσις or *h(a)eresis* (gen. *-eos* or *-is*), which first appears in Latin in reference to Cynic philosophical teaching at Laber. *mim.* 36, was used particularly of non-Catholic doctrines and those groups which held them (cf. e.g. Ign. *Trall.* 6. 1 μόνῃ τῇ χριστιανῇ τροφῇ χρῆσθε, ἀλλοτρίας δὲ βοτάνης ἀπέχεσθε, ἥτις ἐστὶν αἵρεσις, Clem. Alex. *strom.* 1. 19, Jer. *in Tit.* 3. 10–11 (PL 26. 598) 'inter haeresim et schisma hoc esse arbitrantur, quod haeresis perversum dogma habeat, schisma propter episcopalem dissensionem ab ecclesia separetur: quod quidem in principio aliqua ex parte intelligi potest. ceterum nullum schisma non sibi aliquam confingit haeresim, ut recte ab

ecclesia recessisse videatur', Aug. *anim.* 1. 19. 34 'Pelagianam haeresim'); but even as late as the fourth and fifth centuries it was probably not as emotive a term as our 'heresy'. From the third century BC αἵρεσις (fundamentally = 'choice', 'election') was used to denote a set of philosophical principles, a 'persuasion', and thence a 'sect', in the sense of a group of people subscribing to a common set of doctrines or ideology (though not, as has been demonstrated by J. Glucker, *Antiochus and the Late Academy* (Hypomnemata, 56; Göttingen, 1978), 166–92, a philosophical 'school' in an organizational sense). The word, in both its Greek and its Latin form, thus occurs, without a necessarily pejorative connotation, in reference to pagan philosophical doctrines or groups (cf. e.g. Polystr. p. 20 Wilke, Polybius 5. 93. 8, Cic. *parad.* 2, Vitr. 5 pref. 3), Jewish religious sects (cf. e.g. Joseph. *bell. Iud.* 2. 8. 1 (118) (Essenes), Just. mart. *dial.* 80. 4 (Sadducees and others), Acts 15: 5 (Greek NT, Vulg.) (Pharisees)), and indeed the early Christians themselves, when regarded by others as a sect (cf. e.g. Acts 24: 5 (Greek NT; Vulg.: *secta*), Just. mart. *dial.* 108. 2). Jerome and Augustine use it of pagans and Jews no less than of 'heretical' Christians; cf. e.g. Jer. *in Ier. lib.* 4 pref. (CCSL 74. 174 = PL 24. 794), *in Tit.* 3. 10–11 (PL 26. 597) 'philosophi . . . Stoici, Peripatetici, Academici, Epicurei, illius vel illius haereseos appellantur', *epist.* 49. 13. 6, Aug. *c. Cresc.* 1. 12. 15, *civ.* 8. 12, *epist.* 222. 2.

paratur: as Dr Winterbottom suggests to me, the impersonal passive reads somewhat oddly before *fertur*, of which Constantius is the subject, and one might have expected *parat*; *paratur*, the reading of all the MSS, may be corrupt, the ending anticipating that of the following verb.

Iulianus . . . propagatos: Flavius Claudius Iulianus (*PLRE* 1. 477–8, *RE* s.n. Iulianos 26), 'Julian the Apostate', b. 332, Augustus 360–3, son of Iulius Constantius the half-brother of Constantine the Great, was killed in battle in Persia (*Media*) in June 363, while conducting a campaign to recover territory lost by Rome to the Persians and even to subdue Persia itself (hence *Romanos propagare vult fines*). *perdidit propagatos* may conceivably refer to the concession of the five Roman provinces east of the Tigris made by Jovian in July 363, the final outcome of the expedition; but it seems more likely that Jerome means that by his death Julian lost (control over) the territories which had been extended as the Roman Empire had been built up over the course of time, in which Julian himself had played a part by driving the Alamanni and Franks out of Gaul and re-establishing the Rhine frontier (356–9).

perditor animae suae is of course an allusion to Julian's apostasy. He was in Gaul as Caesar from 355 to 360 and remained there as Augustus until well into 361, but his rejection of Christianity was not, as Jerome's words (*quem . . . denegarat*) might suggest, a sudden and clear-cut event which fell in that period. From his youth, well before he went to Gaul, Julian had been attracted to paganism, but he kept his practice of its rites long secret, while outwardly continuing to observe the Christian religion. He does not appear to have performed pagan sacrifices openly until late in 361, when he had left Gaul and was marching through Thrace to Constantinople after Constantius' death, though his true position may have become widely known earlier; Zos. 3. 9 records that, while he was still in Gaul, in response to an angry message from Constantius he declared within public earshot that he would rather entrust himself to the gods than to Constantius' words. Whether this was true or not, Jerome may well have heard it said, or inferred from Julian's later public stance, that he had been practising paganism while in Gaul, and assumed that he had turned from Christianity, in reality though not outwardly, during that time.

Christiani iugulator exercitus probably refers to the anti-Christian measures taken by Julian after becoming sole emperor; it is hard to see how *exercitus* could mean anything other than the whole Christian body here (for the notion of Christians as soldiers in the army of Christ see on 9. 2 *sub alterius . . . militarit*). In fact it seems that at first he tolerated Christianity, later merely discouraged it, and only took a harder line after the burning of the temple of Apollo at Daphne in October 362. *iugulator* (which is extremely rare; cf. *TLL* 7. 2. 634, which gives only four instances, including two in glossaries) is a stronger word than Julian's actions against the Christians may actually have warranted, though he threatened more severe measures once he had returned from the Persian campaign. For Jerome's intense dislike of Julian see Bartelink (1980), 93, and esp. *epist.* 70. 3. 2, where the language is very colourful.

The terms in which Jerome describes Julian's death—*Christum sensit in Media* (cf. *epist.* 70. 3. 2 'Nazareum nostrum . . . statim in proelio senserit [sc. Iulianus]')—indicate that he regarded it as an act of retribution for Julian's apostasy. In the light of this it is a fair inference that he felt similarly about the death of Constantius, *Arrianae fautor hereseos*. Equally, the barbarian incursions into the Empire and the Roman defeats at barbarian hands are viewed as God's vengeance for general Roman sin; see c. 17. 1–2 with nn.

For modern accounts of Julian's life see R. Browning, *The Emperor Julian* (London, 1975), G. W. Bowersock, *Julian the Apostate* (London, 1978).

15. 3. Iovianus ... potentia: Flavius Iovianus (*PLRE* 1. 461, *RE* s.n. Iovianus 1), b. 331, Augustus 363–4, had reigned for less than eight months when suddenly he died. The sources are not unanimous, however, that the cause of his death was asphyxiation; some suggest that he may have died of food poisoning after a meal. It may be that even at the time of his death and among those in the imperial circle there was doubt as to what the true cause was.

Valentinianus ... extinctus est: Flavius Valentinianus (*PLRE* 1. 933–4, *RE* s.n. Valentinianus 1), b. 321, Augustus 364–75 (Valentinian I), was a native of Cibalae in Pannonia (*genitali solo, patriam*). Pannonia was invaded and ravaged in 374 by the Quadi and Sarmatae, angry at Roman interference on the frontier and at the murder of Gabinius, King of the Quadi. The Romans suffered badly. In the following year Valentinian made an expedition of revenge, but in the winter died suddenly, in the course of reviling ambassadors from the Quadi; from the sources it is clear that the cause was an apoplectic stroke (cf. R. S. O. Tomlin, 'The Emperor Valentinian the First', unpublished Oxford D. Phil. thesis 1973, Bodleian MS D. Phil. c. 1154, pp. 236, 246; for *vomitu sanguinis* cf. Jer. *chron. a Abr.* p. 247 Helm (=PL 27. 697–8) 'Valentinianus subita sanguinis eruptione, quod Graece apoplexis vocatur, Brigitione moritur', *epist. ad Praesidium* p. 58. 146–8 Morin 'Valentinianus cum adversus Sarmatos Quadosque ... in consistorio saevus infremeret ... sanguine erumpente discrepuit [?]', [Aur. Vict.] *epit.* 45. 8 'impetu sanguinis voce amissa, sensu integer, exspiravit'). Pannonia was left *inultam* in the sense that Valentinian had not yet completed the destruction of the Quadi, which he had planned to do once the campaigning season had returned.

huius ... sepulchri: Flavius Valens (*PLRE* 1. 930–1, *RE* s.n. Valens 3), b. *c.*328, was proclaimed Augustus by his brother Valentinian in 364, the division of the Empire thus becoming complete, Valentinian ruling the West and Valens the East. The Gothic war here referred to was that occasioned by Roman maltreatment of the Goths after they had implored the protection of Valens against the Huns and been taken across the Danube and into the Empire in 376; heavily oppressed by the leaders of the administration in Thrace, they revolted. Valens' death occurred at the battle of Hadrianople, a calamitous defeat for the Romans, in August 378. The sources present two accounts of the manner of his death: one, that he died in battle, his body never being recovered; the other, that he was taken by some of his own troops to a neighbouring village, or cottage, which was soon, however, surrounded and set on fire by the enemy, Valens dying in the blaze. Jerome gives no indication which of these reports he believes.

Gratianus . . . testantur: Flavius Gratianus (*PLRE* 1. 401, *RE* s.n. Gratianus 3), b. 359, Augustus 367–83, was the son of Valentinian I. In 383 Magnus Maximus was hailed as Augustus by the troops in Britain, and on invading Gaul easily won over the armies there. Gratian, thus betrayed by his troops, fled from Paris towards Lugdunum (Lyons) (Zos. 4. 35 alone says that his flight was to Sigidinum in Moesia), but was caught there by Andragathius, Maximus' cavalry commander, and put to death. One may readily believe that he was denied entry by the towns along the road, where he may have tried to find a refuge or an easier way through Gaul, even though no other authority directly substantiates the point.

Lugdunum is most likely apostrophized for the rhythm: with the vocative, the sentence ends with a cretic-spondee; *Lugduni testantur* would have been much inferior quantitatively. For Jerome's attention to prose-rhythm see Appendix 2.

15. 4. adulescens . . . suspendio: Flavius Valentinianus (*PLRE* 1. 934–5, *RE* s.n. Valentinianus 3), b. 371, Augustus 375–92 (Valentinian II), was the brother of Gratian. In 387 Maximus invaded Italy, driving Valentinian into exile at Thessalonica (cf. *fugam, exilia*). Theodosius, emperor in the East, took up arms on the fugitive's behalf, routed the enemy near Siscia in Pannonia, and trapped Maximus himself in Aquileia, where he was then executed (summer 388). This civil war, of which details are scanty, was indeed bloody (cf. *multo sanguine*), if Pacatus' panegyric on Theodosius can be trusted (cf. *Paneg.* 2. 34 ff.), though it was concluded fairly easily and quickly. The rule of the West was restored to Valentinian, but his power gradually drifted into the hands of the Frankish general Arbogastes. In 392 friction between the two reached a peak, and in May Valentinian died suddenly at Vienne (not far from Lyons; cf. *haut procul . . . conscia*) in shadowy circumstances. The accounts presented by the sources vary considerably; most suspect foul play with Arbogastes at the back of it, but B. Croke, 'Arbogast and the Death of Valentinian II', *Historia*, 25 (1976), 235–44, has demonstrated that the probability of suicide is quite high. Jerome's belief that Valentinian was murdered and his corpse hanged after his death squares with the accounts of Orosius and

Philostorgius, who report—Orosius with a little uncertainty—
that he was strangled and then hanged to give the impression of
suicide (Oros. *hist.* 7. 35. 10, Philostorg. *hist. eccl.* 11. 1), though
whether Jerome believed that the body was hanged as an
attempted cover-up for murder or simply to disgrace Valentinian is not clear. The truth, if Valentinian did indeed commit
suicide, could easily have been thus perverted by those wishing
to bring discredit on Arbogastes.

urbe . . . conscia: the use of *conscius* referring to inanimate
things is common in poetry and well attested in prose; cf. e.g.
Cic. *Verr.* 2. 5. 160 'urbem . . . flagitiorum omnium consciam',
Virg. *Aen.* 4. 519–20, Sen. *epist.* 101. 15, [Quint.] *decl. mai.* 13. 4
p. 269. 10 Håkanson 'conscios natalium parietes', Prud. *cath.* 6.
83–4 'conscium futuri / librum', Jer. *epist.* 22. 7. 3 'cellulam
meam quasi cogitationum consciam'.

quid . . . confossi sunt: for *praeteritio* (*quid loquar . . . ?*) see
on 4. 2 *taceo de . . . .* After his list of bona fide emperors Jerome
now turns to the wretched ends of three usurpers.

Procopius (*PLRE* 1. 742–3, *RE* s.n. Prokopios 2), b. *c.*326,
Augustus 365–6, had some degree of connection with Julian.
After the deaths of Julian and Jovian he found himself a figure of
suspicion to Valentinian I and Valens, and went into hiding.
Eventually he came to Constantinople, and, finding conditions
right for a rebellion, became master of the city and was proclaimed emperor (September 365). At first successful, in the
following year he lost the support he had acquired, and was
finally captured, brought before Valens, and executed.

For the career of Magnus Maximus, Augustus 383–8, see
PLRE 1. 588, *RE* s.n. Maximus 33, and nn. on 15. 3 *Gratianus
. . . testantur* and 15. 4 *adulescens . . . suspendio.*

Flavius Eugenius (*PLRE* 1. 293), Augustus 392–4, was a
grammarian and rhetorician elevated to the throne of the West
by Arbogastes in August 392, three months after the death of
Valentinian II. Theodosius subsequently went to war against
them; in September 394 Eugenius was defeated in battle,
captured, and executed, and Arbogastes committed suicide soon
afterwards. See further *RE* s.n. Arbogastes 1, J. Straub, 'Eugenius', *RAC* 6. 860–77.

Jerome's comment that all three stood captive before their
conquerors receives corroboration from other sources. As for
saying that they were *terrori gentibus*, this may have been true of
Maximus, if unfair (he found himself thrust into the position of
emperor, and could not have maintained himself there, as he had
to do, without use of arms; see the sympathetic judgement of

206 *Commentary on 15. 4*

Sulp. Sev. *dial.* 2. 6. 2), perhaps even of Procopius in the East (he easily subdued Asia and Bithynia), but hardly of Eugenius, if he was indeed a puppet emperor in the hands of Arbogastes, and none of them appears to have had the characteristics of a cruel tyrant. Jerome exaggerates to make a strong contrast with their eventual fate.

dum . . . potirentur: for the use of the subjunctive after *dum* = 'as long as' see KS 2. 374, LHS 2. 612.

16. 1. Dicat aliquis: this kind of formula, involving an imaginary interlocutor, is often used to pose an objection or raise a question, which may then be answered; in Jerome cf. e.g. *epist.* 22. 19. 1, 100. 3. 1 (tr. from Theophilus). Quintilian regards the figure as a sort of prosopopoeia; cf. *inst.* 9. 2. 36. Equally, the raising of the objection or question may be attributed not to a third party but to the addressee, and Jerome does so frequently; cf. e.g. *epist.* 58. 4. 1, 84. 9. 1, 107. 6. 2 ('inquies'); 39. 4. 1, 51. 5. 7 (tr. from Epiphanius) ('dicis'); 31. 2. 2, 120. 1. 11 ('respondebis'). For another approach cf. e.g. *epist.* 123. 12. 1 'at patriarchae non singulas habuerunt uxores', where the objection is expressed by 'at' (on which see KS 2. 85-6). The figure is called *hypophora* or *subiectio*; see Lausberg, 1. 381-2, sects. 771-2.

feriuntque . . . montes: Hor. *carm.* 2. 10. 11-12. Jerome quotes the passage also at *quaest. hebr. in gen.* pref. (CCSL 72. 1 = PL 23. 935) and *epist.* 108. 18. 1, in all three cases using the words as an illustration of the idea that those who stand on a pinnacle in some field or other are especially prone to danger. Paula's great virtue, for instance, makes her highly susceptible to people's envy (*epist.* 108. 18. 1). The passage has a similar function in its original context, where Horace is urging Licinius to keep to the golden mean in life, and not reach too high.

dignitates: in the Later Empire *dignitas*, in its technical sense, covered a wide range of military and civil offices, including at the top of the ranking order those held by Abundantius, Rufinus, and Timasius; cf. Jones, *LRE*, 1. 377 ff. For the metonymy cf. *TLL*, 5. 1. 1139, which collects examples going back to Cic. *orat.* 89.

nec . . . biennium: an apparently curious statement, given that Jerome does not in fact go back more than about six months for his examples; see Appendix 1, p. 232.

consularium: at this time *consularis* appears to have been, strictly, a title borne by provincial governors; cf. Jones, *LRE*, 1. 379. Abundantius and the others ranked higher, but Jerome is not concerned to be precise.

Abundantius . . . exulat: Flavius Abundantius (*PLRE* 1.

3–4, *RE* s.n. Abundantius 1), *magister militum* (East) 392–3, *cos.*
393, fell prey in 396 to the jealousy of Eutropius, the most
influential figure in the East in the early years of the reign of the
young Arcadius after the death of Rufinus, and was banished: to
Pityus on the Black Sea, according to Jerome, with some support
from Aster. *hom.* 4 *prope fin.*; to Sidon, according to Zos. 5. 10. 5.
He was perhaps exiled to the Euxine first, and later allowed to
settle in the Phoenician city. The pun in *Abundantius egens* is
worth noting.

Rufini . . . mendicavit: Flavius Rufinus (*PLRE* 1. 778–81,
RE s.n. Rufinus 23), *praefectus praetorio* in the East 392–5, *cos.*
392, who was effectively in control of the eastern Empire after
the death of Theodosius in January 395, was murdered in
November of that year outside Constantinople, possibly, though
not certainly, at the instigation of Stilicho, his counterpart in the
West (cf. A. Cameron, *Claudian: Poetry and Propaganda at the
Court of Honorius* (Oxford, 1970), 90–2). The details of his head
being impaled on a pike, and his avaricious hand carried around
the city as though begging for alms, are also presented by other
authors; cf. e.g. Philostorg. *hist. eccl.* 11. 3, Zos. 5. 7. 6 (head
merely severed), Claud. *in Rufin.* 2. 433–9. Claudian also
inveighs against his greed generally at *in Rufin.* 1. 183 ff. Picking
up a suggestion of T. Birt, H. L. Levy, 'Claudian's *In Rufinum*
and an Epistle of St. Jerome', *AJPh* 69 (1948), 62–8, argued that
in writing this passage Jerome may have been directly indebted
to the lines of Claudian which deal with the same subject, and
that other passages in this chapter may also betray the influence
of parts of *in Rufin.* 2 (16. 2 *non calamitates . . . statum*, 16. 4 *quid
putas . . . barbari?*, 16. 4–5 *quantae . . . praeterfluunt*; cf. *in Rufin.*
2. 440–1, 187–91, 32–5 respectively). But his argument is far
from conclusive; and in any case the likelihood is that the second
book of *In Rufinum* was not written until summer 397, a year or
so after the date of this letter (see Appendix 1): see the sensible
line taken by Cameron, 76–8.

Jerome seems to take great pleasure in the horrible end of
Rufinus (cf. esp. the tone of *dedecus insatiabilis avaritiae*); this no
doubt has something to do with the fact that Rufinus was almost
certainly instrumental in trying to procure the banishment of
Jerome and his monks from Palestine in 395 (cf. Kelly, 203–4,
E. D. Hunt. 'St. Silvia of Aquitaine: The Role of a Theodosian
Pilgrim in the Society of East and West', *JThS* 23 (1972),
351–73, at 357–8).

ad dedecus insatiabilis avaritiae: this phrase perhaps
bears a sense both of purpose and of result. It should certainly be

taken with *mendicavit* rather than with *abscissa* (so Labourt).

Timasius . . . inglorius: Flavius Timasius (*PLRE* 1. 914–5, *RE* s.n. Timasius 1), *magister equitum* 386, *magister equitum et peditum* 388–*c*.395, *cos.* 389, was an outstanding general of Theodosius. After the latter's death Timasius, like Abundantius, fell victim to Eutropius; he was accused of aiming at the throne, and was convicted and exiled (396).

in Oase, Hilberg's conjecture for the variety of confused readings in the MSS (*osasae, ovasae, ovasse, ovans, asse*), is pretty much right, if not exactly so; it is perhaps possible that we should have the locative. Earlier editors printed *Assae*, which might represent a village in Scythia (cf. *RE* s.n. Assa 2; the only other Assa known to *RE* is a town in Chalcidice so called by Herodotus, and elsewhere otherwise named); but the evidence of Zos. 5. 9. 5 Τιμάσιος δὲ τῇ Ὀάσεως οἰκήσει παραδοθεὶς ἀπηλαύνετο, to which Hilberg draws attention, and Soz. *hist. eccl.* 8. 7. 2 (Timasius banished to τὴν κατ' Αἴγυπτον Ὄασιν), clinches the matter. The place will be the great Oasis in the Libyan desert, about five days' march to the west of Abydus on the Nile; cf. Gibbon, c. 32 n. 14. Timasius' exile there appears to be recorded also by Aster. *hom.* 4 *prope fin.*, though he is not named.

altissimo dignitatis gradu is accurate, Timasius having been *mag. equ. et ped.*; cf. Jones, *LRE*, 1. 378. For the phrase *praecipitatus . . . gradu* cf. Cic. *dom.* 98 'praecipitari ex altissimo dignitatis gradu'; also *p. red. in sen.* 2 'altissimo gradu dignitatis'. Kunst, 160 n. 2, sees a possible pun in *Timasius* (τίμη) and *inglorius*.

16. 2. non calamitates . . . prosequi: Jerome here moves into a wider context, going on to consider the troubles experienced by the Roman world at large in recent years. However, we should not, I think, see a contrast between the *calamitates miserorum*, which Jerome has just finished with, and the general disastrous situation to which he is now coming (so Labourt and Wright); rather, *non calamitates . . . statum* should be taken as stressing that the individual cases are part of that situation. With the rest of the chapter may be compared *epist.* 123. 15–16 (AD 409), a similar account of recent devastation by barbarians, particularly in Gaul. For discussion of the passages in which Jerome refers to the barbarian invasions of this period see J.-R. Palanque, 'St. Jerome and the Barbarians', in Murphy, *Monument*, 171–99, and E. Coleiro, 'The Decay of the Empire and the Fall of Rome in St. Jerome's Letters and *Lives of the Hermits*', *Journal of the Faculty of Arts, the Royal University of Malta*, 1 (1957), 48–57. Rhythmically, one would have expected Jerome to have

preferred the cretic spondee of *condicionis statum narro* to the
molossus cretic of *condicionis narro statum*. But in this case he is
prepared to sacrifice the better rhythm for the sake of another
stylistic feature: the clause *fragilem* . . . *statum* is framed by
adjective and noun in agreement, a verbal arrangement for
which Virgil, in the construction of his hexameter, is rightly
renowned (cf. e.g. E. Norden, *P. Vergilius Maro: Aeneis Buch 6*
(4th edn., Stuttgart, 1957), 391–2). For other cases where
rhythmical considerations yield to a preferred word-order see
Appendix 2, p. 241.

horret . . . **prosequi:** *horrere* is regularly found with *animus*,
and may take a dependent infinitive; for the combination cf.
Virg. *Aen.* 2. 12 'animus meminisse horret', Liv. 28. 29. 4
'horret animus referre quid crediderint homines', *TLL* 6. 3.
2981.

viginti . . . **effunditur:** for the use of *quod* to introduce
temporal clauses see Löfstedt (1911), 56–7. With the present
case, where extent of time is being expressed, cf. (in Jerome)
epist. 133. 12. 1 'multi anni sunt, quod ab adulescentia usque ad
hanc aetatem diversa scripsi opuscula', *pref. in Ezram* 'tertius
annus est quod semper scribitis atque rescribitis, ut Ezrae
librum vobis de Hebraeo transferam'; for a different use, where
quod = ex quo, 'since', cf. *epist.* 77. 1. 1 'plures anni sunt, quod
super dormitione Blesillae Paulam . . . consolatus sum', *adv.
Iovin.* 1. 1 (PL 23. 211) 'pauci admodum dies sunt, quod sancti
ex urbe Roma fratres cuiusdam mihi Ioviniani commentariolos
transmiserunt', *epist. ad Praesidium* p. 56. 57–8 Morin.

Alpes Iulias: the chain of mountains north of Istria, Aquileia
to the south-west, Emona to the east. They were formerly called
the Alpes Venetae; cf. Amm. 31. 16. 7.

Scythiam . . . **rapiunt:** the main barbarian movements of
which Jerome is thinking here are the invasion of Pannonia by
the Quadi and Sarmatae in 374 (see on 15. 3 *Valentinianus* . . .
extinctus est; this was not the first time in recent years that they
had invaded Roman territory (cf. Amm. 16. 10. 20, 17. 12, on
events in 357–8)); the Gothic rebellion of 377–82, in which the
Alani and Huns were implicated (cf. e.g. Amm. 31. 16. 3), and in
the course of which the northern provinces of eastern Europe as
far west as the Julian Alps were overrun (cf. e.g. Amm. 31. 16.
7); and the revolt of the Goths under Alaric in 395–6, when
Macedonia and Thessaly were traversed and the whole of
Greece occupied.

Of the regions of the Empire here mentioned, Scythia and
Thracia were at this time provinces in the diocese of Thracia;

Macedonia was a province of a diocese of the same name which also contained, among others, the provinces of Thessalia, Epirus Nova, and Epirus Vetus; Dacia was a diocese which included, among others, the provinces of Dardania, Dacia Ripensis, and Dacia Mediterranea; Dalmatia was a province of the diocese of Illyricum. *cunctas Pannonias* might include all the remaining provinces of Illyricum, viz. the two Pannonias, Savia, Valeria, Noricum Ripense, and Noricum Mediterraneum (so Labourt); or at least the first four, which were formed by the division of Pannonia Inferior and Pannonia Superior under Diocletian. See generally Jones, *LRE*, 2. 1454–6. However, Jerome is unlikely to have been interested in the precise administrative divisions which the names in the list represent; the picture painted by the sentence is broadly impressionistic, and the list may be taken more or less to represent the whole of south-eastern Europe.

It may be that the list should include Achaea, at this time a province in the diocese of Macedonia (cf. Jones, *LRE*, 2. 1456). The clear implication of Hilberg's apparatus is that it is not found in any of his MSS; but it occurs in a number of MSS I have consulted in London and Oxford (for no better reason than that they were easily accessible), generally between *Thessaliam* (often, erroneously, *Thessalonicam*) and *Epiros* and in place of *Dardaniam, Daciam*. See British Library MSS Harley 3044, Royal 6 C. XI, 6 D. I, 6 D. II, 6 D. III (all twelfth century) and 8 A. XI (early thirteenth century), and Bodleian MSS Laud. Misc. 252 (ninth century) and 423 (twelfth century). *Achaiam* is also printed by the earlier editors, though it does not appear in the *editio princeps*.

The inclusion of the Vandals and Marcomanni in the list of barbarian tribes is odd, for they are not mentioned by other authorities in connection with the incursions of the previous twenty years or so; Ammianus, Orosius, Sozomen, Socrates, Zosimus, and Claudian too, are quite silent. The historians may be guilty of omission, but it seems more likely either that Jerome was misinformed or that he was linking the Vandals and Marcomanni with the recent invasions on the strength of their actions against the Romans at earlier times, e.g. in the Marcomannic wars of the second century AD, when they seem to have been allied with the Quadi and Sarmatae (cf. e.g. Oros. *hist.* 7. 15. 8). (The Vandals, Quadi, and Sarmatae are again mentioned in the same breath, in a quite different context, at *adv. Iovin.* 2. 7 (PL 23. 295).) For the view that the Marcomanni were in fact involved in raids into the Danube provinces in 395 see L. Schmidt, *Geschichte der deutschen Stämme* (2 vols., Berlin,

1910–18), 1. 117. Interestingly, the Vandals caused a lot of trouble ten years later, when they were involved with the Suebi and Alani in overrunning Gaul and Spain; cf. e.g. Oros. *hist.* 7. 38. 3, Soz. *hist. eccl.* 9. 12. 3.

With the list of tribes cf. *epist.* 123. 15. 2 'quicquid inter Alpes et Pyrenaeum est . . . Quadus, Vandalus, Sarmata, Halani, Gypedes, Heruli, Saxones, Burgundiones, Alamanni et—o lugenda res publica!—hostes Pannonii vastaverunt'. In each case Jerome switches from singular to plural in the middle, no doubt for the sake of stylistic *variatio*; cf. the list of animals at 12. 1, where he shifts similarly from plural to singular.

vastant, trahunt, rapiunt: an asyndetic list of verbs like this can have great force; other good cases are *epist.* 24. 2, 107. 2. 2 'specu [*leg.* specum] Mithrae et omnia portentuosa simulacra . . . subvertit, fregit, exussit', and the famous instance at Cic. *Catil.* 2. 1 'abiit, excessit, evasit, erupit' (quoted by Jerome at *epist.* 109. 2. 5). Quintilian says of asyndeton that it is 'apta cum quid instantius dicimus: nam et singula inculcantur et quasi plura fiunt' (*inst.* 9. 3. 50); certainly Jerome is speaking *instantius* here. On the figure generally see Lausberg, 1. 353–5, sects. 709–11.

16. 3. virgines dei: cf. 10. 7 *virgines Christi* with n. on *viduas . . . castitate*.

fuere ludibrio: *fuere* gives a better rhythm than *fuerunt*; but see Appendix 2, p. 242.

diversorum officia clericorum: i.e. *clerici diversorum officiorum*, clerics of various ranks or orders, by a sort of hypallage with a transferred adjective involved. For grades of the clergy see on 10. 3 *fit . . . ordinatur*.

subversae ecclesiae: cf. *epist.* 128. 5. 1 'in cineres ac favillas sacrae quondam ecclesiae conciderunt' (after the sack of Rome in 410).

martyrum . . . reliquiae: for the veneration of martyrs in the early Church, and Jerome's attitude to it, see on 12. 4 *basilicas . . . conciliabula*.

ubique luctus . . . imago: cf. Virg. *Aen.* 2. 368–9 'crudelis ubique / luctus, ubique pavor et plurima mortis imago'. Jerome's *gemitus* in place of Virgil's 'pavor' can hardly be a memory lapse, as it renders the verse unmetrical; he must have wished to strengthen the impression of grief at the expense of the notion of fear. Adaptation and alteration of quoted passages is not uncommon in Jerome; cf. Hagendahl (1958), 306–7.

The present quotation is particularly appropriate here because it comes from that part of the *Aeneid* dealing with the ruin of Troy, and it may be that in the following phrase,

Romanus orbis ruit, there is a reminiscence of *Aen.* 2. 363 'urbs
antiqua ruit multos dominata per annos'. When Rome itself fell,
Virgil's lines made an even better parallel, and at *epist.* 127.
12. 3, while telling of the capture of the city, Jerome quotes
the whole of *Aen.* 2. 361–4 followed by a combination of vv. 365
and 369.
　　Aen. 2. 368–9 ('crudelis . . . imago') is also quoted illustrat-
ively by Lact. *inst.* 5. 11. 5 and Oros. *hist.* 2. 5. 10, though the
contexts are different. For the use of the *Aeneid* to illustrate
contemporary events at this period and later, particularly the
barbarian incursions into the Roman world, see P. Courcelle,
'Les Lecteurs de l'*Énéide* devant les grandes invasions germani-
ques', *RomBarb* 1 (1976), 25–56. In authors who draw on the
Aeneid in this way—above all Claudian, Jerome, and Augustine—Courcelle detects an underlying conviction that the history
of Troy and the history of Rome are identical, and that contemporary events form a part of this long history.
　　Romanus . . . non flectitur: Jerome here hints that the ruin
of the world has something to do with human sin, and that
repentance is necessary; in the next chapter this is made explicit.
See on 17. 1 *olim . . . exercitus.* With the present sentence cf.
epist. 128. 5. 1 'pro nefas, orbis terrarum ruit et in nobis peccata
non corruunt', *in Ezech. lib.* 8 pref. (CCSL 75. 333 = PL 25. 231)
(AD 413) 'cadit mundus et cervix erecta non flectitur; pereunt
divitiae et nequaquam cessat avaritia; congregare festinant, quae
rursum ab aliis occupentur; aruerunt lacrimae, pietas omnis
ablata est; multi qui petant, pauci qui tribuant. nec erubescimus,
paupertatem vili palliolo praeferentes, Croesi opibus incubare,
famemque et interitum plurimorum nostris custodire thesauris'.
　　A century and a half earlier Cyprian too had seen the world in
a state of collapse, and pointed out how advantageous it was to
die and be removed from it; cf. *mort.* 25 'mundus ecce nutat et
labitur et ruinam sui non iam senectute rerum sed fine testatur:
et tu non deo gratias agis, non tibi gratularis quod exitu
maturiore subtractus ruinis et naufragiis et plagis imminentibus
exuaris?'. Jerome has of course already made the point, in
slightly different terms, at 15. 1.
16. 4. quid . . . barbari?: Alaric and the Goths overran Greece in
395. According to Zosimus, our main source for the invasion,
peace terms were struck with Athens and no harm done to her
(5. 6); but Zosimus' account is open to suspicion on several
grounds, and what Jerome says here squares with Claud. *in
Rufin.* 2. 186–91 'si tunc his animis acies collata fuisset, / prodita
non tantas vidisset Graecia caedes, / oppida semoto Pelopeia

Marte vigerent, / starent Arcadiae, starent Lacedaemonis arces; /
non mare fumasset geminum flagrante Corintho / nec fera
Cecropiae traxissent vincula matres' (the possibility that Jerome
was influenced by these lines is very remote; see on 16. 1 *Rufini
. . . mendicavit*). Philostorgius, too, declares that Athens was
taken (*hist. eccl.* 12. 2). Zosimus agrees that Corinth and Sparta
suffered capture.

16. 4–5. **anno . . . captivae:** the invasion of the Huns into the
eastern provinces in 395 is described at greater length by Jerome
at *epist.* 77. 8; he records the rumour that they were making for
Jerusalem, and tells of the precautionary measures taken by
Antioch and Tyre. His description of the carnage wrought and
fear inspired by the invasion (cf. *epist.* 77. 8. 1 ' . . . Hunorum
examina, quae pernicibus equis huc illucque volitantia caedis
pariter ac terroris cuncta conplerent') may not be greatly exaggerated; cf. Claud. *in Rufin.* 2. 28–35 'alii per Caspia claustra /
Armeniasque nives inopino tramite ducti / invadunt orientis
opes. iam pascua fumant / Cappadocum volucrumque parens
Argaeus equorum, / iam rubet altus Halys nec se defendit
iniquo / monte Cilix. Syriae tractus vastantur amoeni / assue-
tumque choris et laeta plebe canorum / proterit imbellem
sonipes hostilis Orontem' (see on 16. 1 *Rufini . . . mendicavit* for
the alleged influence of these lines on Jerome), *in Eutrop.* 2.
569–74 'nuper ab extremo veniens equitatus Araxe / terruit
Antiochi muros ipsumque decorae / paene caput Syriae flammis
hostilibus arsit. / utque gravis spoliis nulloque obstante pro-
funda / laetus caede redit, sequitur mucrone secundo / conti-
nuum vulnus', Philostorg. *hist. eccl.* 11. 8 μέχρι τῆς κοίλης Συρίας
ἤλασαν [sc. οἱ Οὖννοι], καὶ τὴν Κιλικίαν καταδραμόντες φόνον
ἀνθρώπων εἰργάσαντο ἀνιστόρητον. Fear in the East would naturally have been increased by the absence of the Roman army (cf.
epist. 77. 8. 2). The invasion is also mentioned in passing by Soz.
hist. eccl. 8. 1. 2 and Socr. *hist. eccl.* 6. 1. 6–7.

16. 4. **Caucasi rupibus:** the phrase recurs at *epist.* 77. 8. 1.

inmissi: the verb is perhaps carefully chosen to suggest that
the invasion is the design of an outside agency; cf. on 16. 3
Romanus . . . non flectitur, 17. 1 *olim . . . exercitus.*

non Arabiae . . . lupi: *lupi* is natural of attackers; cf. e.g.
Virg. *Aen.* 2. 355, where it is used in a simile in reference to
Aeneas' men on the attack in Troy. However, *Arabiae lupi* calls
to mind specifically a passage in Habakkuk concerning the
Chaldaeans of Babylonia: καὶ ἐξαλοῦνται ὑπὲρ παρδάλεις οἱ ἵπποι
αὐτοῦ [sc. τοῦ τῶν Χαλδαίων ἔθνους] καὶ ὀξύτεροι ὑπὲρ τοὺς λύκους τῆς
Ἀραβίας (Hab. 1: 8, LXX); = 'et exsilient super pardos equi eius,

et velociores erunt lupis Arabiae' (Jerome's translation at *in Hab.* 1. 6–11 (CCSL 76A. 584 = PL 25. 1278)). The Vulgate text reads: 'leviores pardis equi eius et velociores lupis vespertinis'. It would not be an impossible leap from this to represent the Chaldaeans themselves as *lupi*; and they would form a good parallel to the Huns (the *septentrionis lupi*) inasmuch as they were used by God as an instrument of correction for his people (cf. c. 17). The choice of *Arabiae* from the LXX version at a time when Jerome had completed his translation of Habakkuk from the Hebrew (see Introduction, p. 10)—if it is not simply drawn from deep in his memory and used merely for a geographical contrast with *septentrionis*, with no thought of the Biblical context—has no obvious special significance, though it lends the passage a more exotic colour than *vespertini*, and may have made the allusion more easily recognizable to Heliodorus and other potential readers.

   tantas brevi provincias: the juxtaposition of *tantas* and *brevi* is meant to emphasize the speed and force of the invasion.

16. 5. obsessa . . . praeterfluunt: for the dangers faced during the invasion by Antioch, which lay on the Orontes, cf. the passages cited at 16. 4–5 *anno . . . captivae*. It is not clear which other cities on the rivers named were besieged; perhaps such as Ancyra (near the Halys), Tarsus (on the Cydnus), and Circesium (on the Euphrates).

   One might compare *epist.* 123. 15. 3, where Jerome lists, at greater length than here, the cities, provinces, and peoples of Gaul which suffered in the raids of 406–9.

   Arabia . . . captivae: as at 16. 2 *Scythiam . . . Pannonias* Jerome is seeking to give an impression, and he will have had no thought of the particular provinces and dioceses covered by these names. Technically, Arabia, Phoenice, Phoenice Libani, and three provinces of Palaestina (I, II, P. Salutaris) were at this time provinces of the diocese of Oriens, while Aegyptus was the name of both a province and a diocese; cf. Jones, *LRE*, 2. 1458–9. Equally, *oriens* above (16. 4) should naturally mean the East generally, not simply the diocese; the invasion in any case took in the diocese of Pontus (which included the Halys and Cydnus) too.

   For the idea of fear generated in neighbouring areas cf. *epist.* 123. 15. 4 'ipsae Hispaniae iam iamque periturae cotidie contremescunt recordantes inruptionis Cymbricae et, quicquid alii semel passi sunt, illae semper timore patiuntur'. In the present case at least, the statement is not likely to be a gross exaggeration; see on 16. 4–5 *anno . . . captivae*.

non ... possim: Virg. *Aen.* 6. 625–7, with part of the second line omitted, i.e., after *ferrea vox*, 'omnis scelerum comprendere formas'. 'non, mihi . . . vox' occurs also at Virg. *georg.* 2. 43–4. In the *Aeneid* the verses are uttered by the Sibyl and deal with the sufferings of sinners in Tartarus; they are thus very appropriate to the present context, as *poenarum* hints at the retributive character of the barbarian attacks (cf. c. 17)—though it should be observed that the Virgilian context is unimportant when Jerome quotes from the passage elsewhere (see below).

The lines are derived originally from Hom. *Il.* 2. 488–90. After Virgil they gradually became a cliché, and were quoted, adapted, imitated, and echoed by writers deep into the Middle Ages; cf. P. Courcelle, 'Histoire du cliché virgilien des cent bouches', *REL* 33 (1955), 231–40, supplemented by A. Cameron, 'The Vergilian Cliché of the Hundred Mouths in Corippus', *Philologus*, 111 (1967), 308–9; also R. G. Austin, *P. Vergili Maronis Aeneidos liber sextus* (Oxford, 1977), 199–200. Jerome quotes from the passage again at *epist.* 66. 5. 2, 77. 6. 4, and 123. 16. 4: in the first of these cases 'poenarum' refers to the sufferings of the sick and maimed with whom Pammachius associated; in the second it is replaced by 'morborum', which refers to the illnesses of those looked after by Fabiola; in the third, where the context is similar to the present, 'poenarum' is supplanted by 'caesorum', and 'omnes captorum dicere poenas' stands in place of 'omnis scelerum comprendere formas'. For alteration and adaptation by Jerome of quoted passages see on 16. 3 *ubique luctus . . . imago*. Courcelle, 236, notes also the adaptation of the cliché into prose at *epist.* 108. 1. 1 (quoted at 1. 1 *Grandes . . . explicare*).

neque ... miserias: the principal point of *historiam* seems to be to imply a long work, with which *breviter* then contrasts. For Jerome's concern for epistolary brevity generally see on 5. 2 *vel libris vel epistulis*.

enim = 'besides'; for this kind of usage see *TLL* 5. 2. 590–1.

alioquin ... sunt: i.e. even if Jerome had intended to write a history of these events, he could not have succeeded; the task would have been too great even for writers of the stature of Thucydides and Sallust. In this way the seriousness of the troubles is emphasized. For the implicit self-depreciation cf. on 1. 1 *Grandes . . . explicare. alioquin* = 'in any case', 'moreover', 'besides', as often in Jerome; cf. C. Paucker, 'De particularum quarundam in latinitate Hieronymi usu observationes', *RhM* 37 (1882), 556–66, at 556.

In place of *sunt*, we might have expected *essent*; but the MSS, which are followed by Hilberg, are unanimous. Erasmus, Victorius, and Vallarsi (though not Martianay) printed *sint*, an easy correction, and certainly not impossible in a present unreal condition (cf. LHS 2. 332). But *sunt* can be retained if, as Professor Walsh suggests to me, we take *Thucydides et Sallustius* to mean '*a* Thucydides and *a* Sallust'; the pres. indic. is vivid, and the expression has perhaps a colloquial flavour.

For the thought behind the sentence cf. *epist.* 130. 6. 1 'ad explicandam incredibilis gaudii magnitudinem et Tulliani fluvius siccaretur ingenii et contortae Demosthenis vibrataeque sententiae tardius languidiusque ferrentur', Sidon. *epist.* 5. 13. 3 'explicandae bestiae tali nec oratorum princeps Marcus Arpinas nec poetarum Publius Mantuanus sufficere possunt'.

Jerome certainly knew the works of Sallust; cf. Luebeck, 117–21, Hagendahl (1958), with his index. Sallust was highly regarded as a writer by others at this time, too; cf. Symm. *epist.* 5. 68(66). 2, Aug. *civ.* 7. 3 'vir disertissimus Sallustius'. As for Thucydides, Jerome may very well not have known his work at first hand. The only other place where he mentions him by name is *epist.* 58. 5. 2 'historici Thucydiden, Sallustium, Herodotum, Livium [sc. aemulentur]', and the only quotation is a Latin version of a maxim which is attributed merely to the Greeks, and which is also quoted (in Greek) by the younger Pliny, again without being attributed to Thucydides (cf. Jer. *epist.* 73. 10. 1, Plin. *epist.* 4. 7. 3); cf. Courcelle (1948), 67–8. Thucydides and Sallust were linked together also by earlier authors, generally because their styles were thought similar (cf. Vell. 2. 36. 2, Sen. *contr.* 9. 1. 13 'cum sit praecipua in Thucydide virtus brevitas, hac eum Sallustius vicit', *suas.* 6. 21, Quint. *inst.* 10. 1. 101 'nec opponere Thucydidi Sallustium verear'), and Jerome probably thought of them naturally as a pair.

c. 17. Nepotianus' death has happily released him from the troubles besetting the Roman world, and it is those who are left to suffer at the hands of the barbarians that are truly wretched. And yet their case is not hopeless. The ultimate cause of the disasters is sin, which has incurred God's displeasure; repentance would see a complete reversal of fortune.

17. 1. Felix Nepotianus . . . non audit: for the τόπος of death as an escape from ills see on 15. 1 *ut . . . evaserit* and introductory n. to cc. 15–16.

nos . . . perspicimus: cf. *epist.* 75. 2. 1 'nos dolendi magis, qui cotidie stamus in proelio peccatorum, vitiis sordidamur,

accipimus vulnera et de otioso verbo reddituri sumus rationem'
(in contrast to Lucinus, who has died and gone to be with
Christ), Greg. Naz. *orat.* 7. 20.

eosque . . . putamus: not strictly true: no-one would really
believe that those whose death has been a happy escape from
misery ought to be wept over; it is rather that it is impossible not
to weep when a loved one dies (cf. 2. 1–2, 7. 1), and, no doubt,
that the notion of death as an escape is often forgotten. But by
putting it in this way Jerome makes it seem absurd that
Nepotianus should be wept for at all: a good consolatory point.

olim . . . exercitus: Jerome now makes clear what he has
already hinted at at 16. 3 *Romanus . . . non flectitur*: that the
strength of the barbarians and the damage they are inflicting on
the Roman world are the result of Roman sin. God is offended
and angry (cf. 17. 2 *tantum . . . desaeviat*), and uses the
barbarians as a means of punishment. At *epist.* 128. 5. 1, written
after the sack of Rome, Jerome makes a similar connection
between sin and the disastrous state of the world (see on 16. 3
Romanus . . . non flectitur); and at *in Is.* 7. 21–5 (CCSL 73.
109–10 = PL 24. 113) (AD 408–10) barbarian tribes are again
seen as the instrument of God's wrath: 'at nunc magna pars
Romani orbis quondam Iudaeae similis est [i.e. in a state of
devastation], quod absque ira dei factum non putamus, qui
nequaquam contemptui sui per Assyrios ulciscitur et Chal-
daeos, sed per feras gentes et quondam nobis incognitas, quarum
et vultus et sermo terribilis est et ⟨quae⟩ femineas incisasque
facies praeferentes, virorum (et bene barbatorum!) fugientia
terga confodiunt'. The theme of disaster as a divine punishment
for wrongdoing or sin is of course pervasive in ancient pagan
literature, and finds plenty of Christian parallels in the work of
authors such as Orosius and Salvian. To give only two brief
examples (one pagan, one Christian) from late Antiquity, cf.
Liban. *orat.* 24. 5 δοκεῖ μοι θεῶν τις ἡμῖν ὀργιζόμενος ἐκείνοις
συμπολεμεῖν, Max. Taur. *hom.* 94 'omnipotens dominus iram
flendae desolationis huic ecclesiae intulit' (after the capture and
destruction of Milan by Attila in 452). Such beliefs are tena-
cious; one has only to recall (for instance) some of the utterances
made after the damage done by lightning to York Minster
following the consecration there of Bishop Jenkins of Durham in
1984.

bella civilia: e.g. the revolts of Procopius and Maximus (see
on 15. 3 *Gratianus . . . testantur*, 15. 4 *adulescens . . . suspendio*,
quid . . . confossi sunt). Jerome does not make it clear whether he
saw Roman sin and the wrath of God at the back of these events

too. The question had probably not formulated itself in his mind; from 16. 2 to the end of c. 17 his attention is focused almost entirely on the barbarian troubles, which are the immediate problem, and this comment about the civil wars reads very much like an afterthought to the previous statement.

17. 2. miseri ... scribitur: cf. *in Ier.* 27. 6–7 (CCSL 74. 263 = PL 24. 850) (not before AD 414) 'cuius infelicitatis est Israhel, quando conparatione eius Nabuchodonosor servus dei appellatur!', a comment on the text 'et nunc itaque ego [sc. deus] dedi omnes terras istas in manu Nabuchodonosor regis Babylonis servi mei ... et servient ei omnes gentes' (Jeremiah 27: 6–7); also relevant is Jeremiah 25: 8–9 (God addressing the people of Judah) 'pro eo quod non audistis verba mea, ecce ego mittam et adsumam universas cognationes aquilonis, ait dominus, et Nabuchodonosor regem Babylonis servum meum, et adducam eos super terram istam et super habitatores eius'. God favours Nebuchadnezzar against his own people because of their offence. The parallel with the present situation is obvious. Jerome regards the Babylonian king in much the same light as the barbarians, as an instrument of punishment and correction; cf. *in Ier.* 25. 8–9 (CCSL 74. 239 = PL 24. 835) 'quodque vocat servum suum Nabuchodonosor, non sic servus vocatur ut prophetae et omnes sancti, qui vere serviunt domino, sed quo in eversione Hierusalem domini serviat voluntati, secundum quod et apostolus loquitur: quos tradidi satanae, ut discant non blasphemare [1 Tim. 1: 20]'.

Nebuchadnezzar is also referred to as God's *servus* at Jeremiah 43: 10.

tantum ... desaeviat: see on 17. 1 *olim ... exercitus*. For *ira desaeviat* cf. e.g. Num. 16: 22, Josh. 22: 18, Jer. *in Is.* 26. 20–1 (CCSL 73. 342 = PL 24. 304) 'in peccatores et impios ira dei desaeviat'; (with *desaevire* in a different sense, = 'cease to rage') Lucan 5. 303–4 'nec dum desaeviat ira / expectat'.

Ezechias ... pugnavit: by means of these three cases from the OT Jerome seeks to show that, by repentance and prayer, the barbarians may be overcome.

Ezechias ... deleta sunt: for the destruction of the Assyrian army of Sennacherib cf. 2 Kgs. 19: 35 'factum est igitur in nocte illa: venit angelus domini et percussit castra Assyriorum centum octoginta quinque milia', Isa. 37: 36 'egressus est autem angelus domini et percussit in castris Assyriorum centum octoginta quinque milia', 2 Chr. 32: 21 (where the figure is not given). The incident occurred in answer to Hezekiah's prayer to God to deliver Judah from the invading Assyrians. Although the Bibli-

cal accounts do not explicitly say that this was an act involving
paenitentia, or that Hezekiah's troubles had come upon him as
the consequence of sin (a situation which repentance would
rectify), the Deuteronomic historian, especially for Samuel and
Kings, regularly represents invasion as a punishment for sin,
and 2 Kgs. 19 (to which Isa. 37 is parallel) should certainly be
read as describing an act of penitence. Jerome's comment at *in
Is.* 37. 1–7 (CCSL 73. 435 = PL 24. 383) clearly indicates how he
understood the passage: 'scindit et ipse rex [sc. Ezechias] vestimenta sua, quia peccatorum suorum et populi esse credebat,
quod Rabsaces [the chief officer of the Assyrian army] usque ad
portam Hierusalem venerit, et contra dominum talia sit locutus'
(on Isa. 37: 1; Hezekiah's prayer follows not long after).
  Iosaphat . . . superabat: cf. 2 Chr. 20: 21–3 'statuit [sc.
Iosaphat] cantores domini ut laudarent eum in turmis suis et
antecederent exercitum ac voce consona dicerent, confitemini
domino quoniam in aeternum misericordia eius. cumque coepis-
sent laudes canere vertit dominus insidias eorum in semet ipsos,
filiorum scilicet Ammon et Moab et montis Seir qui egressi
fuerant ut pugnarent contra Iudam, et percussi sunt; namque
filii Ammon et Moab consurrexerunt adversum habitatores
montis Seir ut interficerent et delerent eos, cumque hoc opere
perpetrassent etiam in semet ipsos versi mutuis concidere vul-
neribus'. Jehoshaphat had already, prior to this, prayed for
Judah's deliverance and heard through Jahaziel that God would
grant his prayer (cf. vv. 5–17). In this case too the invasion of
Judah, by the Moabites and their allies, is presented as an
expression of divine wrath; cf. 2 Chr. 19: 2.
  Moyses . . . pugnavit: cf. Exod. 17: 9–13, where Moses,
holding the *virga dei* and raising his hands aloft (an attitude of
prayer), enables Joshua and the Israelites to defeat Amalek. The
exemplum is the weakest of the three: there is no suggestion in
Exodus that Amalek's attack came as a punishment from God
and that Moses' prayer was an act of penitence (though Jerome
may have believed that it was so, in consequence, perhaps, of the
Israelites' frequent complaints (cf. e.g. Exod. 16: 2, 17: 2–3)).
17. 3. pro pudor et stolida . . . mens!: cf. on 13. 2 *pro dolor*.
  incredulitas is usually found in a religious sense (see on 7. 2
apostolus . . . caritatis), but *stolida . . . incredulitatem* is much
more naturally understood to mean 'stupid to the point of
disbelief', i.e. unbelievably stupid, than 'stupid to the point of
unbelief', i.e. so stupid as not to believe in God, though in the
context there may be a hint of this second meaning too.
  Romanus . . . cedere: Hilberg placed a question-mark after

cedere. As the first part of the sentence (*Romanus* . . . *arbitrantur*) can be taken only as a statement, the question must begin at *non intellegimus*; but while *non intellegimus* . . . *persequente* is acceptable as a question in the context (the great Roman army is overcome by barbarians who are poor foot-soldiers; do we fail to grasp the meaning of the words in the prophets which suggest how we might reverse this situation? (see below on *prophetarum* . . . *persequente*)), *nec amputamus* . . . *morbi* makes good sense only if regarded as a statement (as a question it seems entirely to lack point). The earlier editors saw this, and punctuated with a question-mark not after *cedere* but after *persequente*; but *nec* is connective, and it seems inconceivable that *non intellegimus* . . . *persequente* and *nec amputamus* . . . *morbi* should be the one a question and the other a statement. A question would be in order after the future *amputabimus*, but rather than espouse a reading for which there is no MS support I have chosen to expunge the question-mark altogether. The sentence follows quite easily after what has preceded, clearly showing up the *stoliditas* of the Roman *mens*.

In printing *cernamus*, which is read only by 𝔄, and that doubtfully, I follow the earlier editors against Hilberg's *cernimus*, the reading of the other MSS: it accords much better with the flow of the sentence that *statimque* . . . *cedere*, like *morbus* . . . *auferatur*, should be a clause of purpose dependent on *amputamus* . . . *ut*.

In their translations Labourt and Wright agree with this interpretation on both counts; but of the two only Wright reads *cernamus*, and both unthinkingly retain the question-mark in their Latin text.

ab his . . . arbitrantur: *qui ingredi* . . . *arbitrantur* makes it almost certain that Jerome is thinking particularly of the Huns, for him at Bethlehem the most immediate of the barbarian invaders (cf. 16. 4–5 with nn.); cf. Amm. 31. 2. 6 'eorumque [sc. Hunorum] calcei formulis nullis aptati vetant incedere gressibus liberis, qua causa ad pedestres parum adcommodati sunt pugnas, verum equis prope adfixi, duris quidem sed deformibus [cf. *caballos* below]', Zos. 4. 20. 4 ἐπήεσαν [sc. οἱ Οὖννοι] Σκύθαις, μάχην μὲν σταδίαν οὔτε δυνάμενοι τὸ παράπαν οὔτε εἰδότες ἐπαγαγεῖν (πῶς γὰρ οἱ μηδὲ εἰς γῆν πῆξαι τοὺς πόδας οἷοί τε ὄντες ἑδραίως, ἀλλ' ἐπὶ τῶν ἵππων καὶ διαιτώμενοι καὶ καθεύδοντες), and the *Suda* s.v. ἀκροσφαλεῖς, which describes them as ἄποδες and ἀκροσφαλεῖς, and says also ἄνευ γὰρ ἵππων οὐ ῥᾳδίως ἂν Οὖννος τὴν γῆν πατήσειεν. For the Huns' terrifying appearance (cf. *horum terretur aspectu*) cf. Amm. 31. 2. 2 'prodigiose deformes [*al.* prodigiosae formae]

et pandi [pavendi *Gardthausen*], ut bipedes existimes bestias',
Claud. *in Rufin.* 1. 325–6 'turpes habitus obscaenaque visu /
corpora', Jord. *Get.* 127 'quos bello forsitan minime superabant,
vultus sui terrore nimium pavorem ingerentes, terribilitate fuga-
bant'. It is possible that in writing this description of the Huns
Jerome was directly influenced by Ammianus. Though we
cannot date Ammianus' history precisely, and though it has
generally been held that Books 26–31 appeared later than the
rest, there is good reason to suppose that the work was published
as a unity in 390 or 391; cf. J. Matthews, *The Roman Empire of
Ammianus* (London, 1989), 22–7 with nn. 34–5. O. J. Maen-
chen-Helfen, 'The Date of Ammianus Marcellinus' Last
Books', *AJPh* 76 (1955), 384–99, who detects Ammianus'
influence on later passages in Jerome which deal with the Huns,
attempts to use this passage to set a *terminus ante quem* for the
publication of the last part of Ammianus' history.

prophetarum . . . persequente: Jerome has in mind Isa. 30:
17, though *fugient . . . persequente* does not represent at all closely
either the text of the Vulgate (Isaiah completed by this time; see
Introduction, p. 10) or that of LXX; it looks like a memory
lapse, or an unconcerned paraphrase. Reference to the full
Biblical context is important for understanding the meaning of
these words here: 'haec dicit dominus deus sanctus Israel: si
revertamini et quiescatis, salvi eritis; in silentio et in spe erit
fortitudo vestra. et noluistis, [16] et dixistis: nequaquam, sed ad
equos fugiemus. ideo fugietis. et: super veloces ascendemus.
ideo veloces erunt qui persequentur vos. [17] mille homines a
facie terroris unius, et a facie terroris quinque fugietis' (Isa. 30:
15–17, Vulg.); 'haec dicit dominus deus sanctus Israel: cum
reversus ingemueris, tunc salvus eris . . . et noluistis audire. sed
dixistis: super equos fugiemus; propterea fugietis; et super
levibus ascensoribus erimus. ideo leves erunt qui persequentur
vos. mille ad vocem unius fugient [διὰ φωνὴν ἑνὸς φεύξονται χίλιοι];
et ad vocem quinque fugient multi' (Jerome's translation from
LXX at *in Is.* 30. 15–17 (CCSL 73. 389 = PL 24. 344) (AD
408–10)). Jerome's comments on the passage are helpful: 'deus
. . . loquitur: si agatis paenitentiam, et vel vitia relinquatis vel
errorem pravi consilii, et maneatis in Iudaea, non Babyloniorum
impetum, sed mea praecepta metuentes, salvi eritis . . . qui
contemnentes praecepta vitalia, desperatione dixistis, nequaquam ita erit ut loqueris; sed ad equos confugiemus Aegyptios,
et concito ad eos atque veloci pergemus gradu. quia igitur ista
dixistis, fugietis quidem et pernici cursu intrabitis Aegyptum;
sed velociores erunt Babylonii, qui vos usque ad Aegyptum

222 *Commentary on 17. 3*

persequentur, tantusque terror atque formido obtinebit Aegyptum, ut uni Chaldaeo mille Aegyptii resistere nequeant' (ibid.).
In the present situation the Romans may be viewed as standing
in the same relation to the barbarians as the Israelites to the
Babylonians: they are 'pursued' by the enemy because of their
failure to turn from wickedness. The implication, given what
Jerome has been saying in this chapter, must be that repentance
will see the situation change.

amputamus ... morbi: for the metaphor cf. esp. Ambr. *Noe*
17. 59 'causae aegritudinis debuerunt amputari' (of a sick soul);
also Cic. *Phil.* 8. 15 'sic in rei publicae corpore ... quicquid est
pestiferum amputetur'. The simple notion that a state can suffer
sickness is of course an old one; cf. e.g. Herod. 5. 28, Soph.
Antig. 1015 νοσεῖ πόλις, Dem. *Phil.* 3. 39 ἀπόλωλε καὶ νενοσήκεν ἡ
Ἑλλάς, Cic. *Catil.* 1. 31, *ad Att.* 2. 20. 3 'novo quodam morbo
civitas moritur', Liv. 24. 2. 8 'unus velut morbus invaserat
omnes Italiae civitates'.
For *amputare* used of *causae* in a quite different context cf.
Sidon. *epist.* 2. 14. 2 'amputabuntur causae morarum'.

sagittas: Amm. 31. 2. 9 gives an interesting description of the
long-range weapons of the Huns: 'missilibus telis, acutis ossibus
pro spiculorum acumine arte mira coagmentatis ... confligunt'.

tiaras: cf. Amm. 31. 2. 6 'galeris incurvis capita tegunt [sc.
Huni]'. Jerome will have had in mind the sort of thing he
describes at *epist.* 64. 13, when discussing the priestly vestments
prescribed in Exod. 28: 'quartum genus est vestimenti rotun-
dum pilleolum, quale pictum in Ulixe conspicimus, quasi
sphaera media sit divisa et pars una ponatur in capite; hoc Graeci
et nostri tiaram, nonnulli galerum vocant. non habet acumen in
summo nec totum usque ad comas caput tegit, sed tertiam
partem a fronte inopertam relinquit atque ita in occipitio vittae
constrictus est taenia, ut non facile labatur ex capite. est autem
byssinum et sic fabre opertum linteolo, ut nulla acus vestigia
forinsecus pareant'. For him the word *tiara* does not signify a
type of headgear exclusive to the Persians, and Labourt's note—
'Il ne connaissait les Huns que par ses lectures; sinon comment
leur eût-il attribué comme coiffure la tiare iranienne?'—is based
on a false premise.

caballos equis: the antithesis is striking, and deliberate; but
Jerome is not speaking pejoratively of the Huns' horses simply
for effect. Ammianus characterizes them as *deformes* (see above
on *ab his ... arbitrantur*).

c. 18. Recognizing that he has already gone beyond the ordinary bounds of consolation, Jerome moves on from consideration of the barbarian invasions to take a broader view of the world. His vision, which has a timeless quality, is one of decay and transience; the earth lies in a state of ruin, and life passes inexorably into death, so that no matter what the various conditions of men, everyone who is now alive will soon be dead.

18. 1. Excessimus . . . planximus: the account of recent disasters begun in c. 15 is undertaken primarily to console Heliodorus by showing him how fortunate Nepotianus has been to die at such a time. But not only is most of c. 17 entirely without consolatory purpose or effect; the section as a whole has something of the character of a general lamentation over the state of the world, and to that extent goes well beyond consolation. The irony that in the process of urging Heliodorus not to weep for his nephew he himself has 'mourned the dead of the whole world' is not lost on Jerome.

    Xerxes . . . esset: the story is told at Herod. 7. 44–6; *subvertit montes* should refer to the canal dug through Mt. Athos (cf. Herod. 7. 22–4), *maria constravit* to the bridge of boats built over the Hellespont (cf. Herod. 7. 33–6). Jerome seems to have been directly acquainted with at least parts of Herodotus' history (cf. Courcelle (1948), 68–9), but the present anecdote had long ago been absorbed into the bloodstream of literature dealing with the brevity of life, and was well known (as *dicitur* may suggest); cf. Val. Max. 9. 13 ext. 1, Plin. *epist.* 3. 7. 13, and esp. Sen. *dial.* 10. 17. 2 'cum per magna camporum spatia porrigeret exercitum nec numerum eius sed mensuram comprehenderet Persarum rex insolentissimus, lacrimas profudit quod intra centum annos nemo ex tanta iuventute superfuturus esset', a passage sufficiently similar to the present to suggest the possibility of a direct debt, though even here it is not explicitly stated, as it is by Herodotus and Jerome, that Xerxes reviewed the army from an elevated position. The story may also have occurred in Cicero's *Consolatio* (cf. Buresch (1886), 106–7, Kunst, 155–6), presumably to illustrate the consolatory τόπος that death is inevitable, but even if this was so it is not likely that Jerome was dependent on the *Consolatio* alone. For the appearance of the Athos canal and the Hellespont bridge as rhetorical τόποι in ancient (especially Latin) literature see K. M. Coleman, *Statius: Silvae IV* (Oxford, 1988), 118 (on *silv.* 4. 3. 56–8). Their inclusion here emphasizes that for all a man's technological achievements and power (cf. *potentissimus*) he has no control over death; for this thought cf. the choral ode at Soph. *Antig.* 332 ff., esp. 361–2. The wording of *subvertit montes, maria constravit* appears to depend on Sall. *Catil.* 13. 1 'quid ea memorem, quae nisi iis qui videre nemini credibilia sunt, a privatis compluribus subvorsos montis, maria constrata esse?' (Sallust is thinking particularly of Lucullus, the 'Xerxen togatum' of Vell. 2. 33. 4). For *maria constravit* cf. also e.g. Liv. 35. 49. 5 'consternit maria classibus', Curt. 9. 6. 7, Lact. *inst.* 3. 24. 8, Auson. *Mos.* 289–90 (referring to Xerxes) 'Chalcedonio constratum ab litore pontum, / regis opus magni'.

infinitam . . . exercitum: the positioning of *vidisset* is important; it produces not only a fine clausula (double cretic; better than *exercitum vidisset*) but notable verbal balance. For the latter feature cf. 14. 1 *tota hunc . . . Italia* with n. (the final clausula in that passage, though less pronounced than here, is also good (cretic tribrach)); and see in general Appendix 2.

18. 2. o si . . . defuturos: for the image of the *specula* see Courcelle (1967), 355–62, who cites a wide range of texts where it is used; in some the viewpoint is a moral one (cf. e.g. Plato, *rep.* 445C, Lucian, *Charon* 2, Cypr. *ad Donat.* 9 (where note the similarity to the present passage: 'o si et possis in illa sublimi specula constitutus oculos tuos inserere secretis . . . ')), in others contemplative (cf. e.g. Plot. 4. 4. 5, Greg. Nyss. *beat.* 1 (PG 44. 1193), Ambr. *Abr.* 2. 76), while in the present passage Jerome unites the two viewpoints, observing from the *specula* both human wickedness and the shortness of human life. For contemplation of the whole world (cf. *universam terram, totius mundi*) cf. [Apul.] *mund.* p. 136 Thomas, Greg. M. *dial.* 2. 35.

For the thought of the passage cf. also Sen. *dial.* 6. 26. 5–6 'tot saecula, tot aetatium contextum, seriem, quidquid annorum est, licet visere; licet surrectura, licet ruitura regna prospicere et magnarum urbium lapsus et maris novos cursus. nam si tibi potest solacio esse desideri tui commune fatum, nihil quo stat loco stabit, omnia sternet abducetque secum vetustas. nec hominibus solum . . . sed locis, sed regionibus, sed mundi partibus ludet. totos supprimet montes et alibi rupes in altum novas exprimet; maria sorbebit, flumina avertet . . . hiatibus vastis subducet urbes, tremoribus quatiet . . . inundationibus quidquid habitatur obducet' (the claim of Guttilla (1977–9), 225–7, that Jerome was dependent on this chapter of the *Ad Marciam* rests on insufficient grounds), 11. 1. 1–3 'nihil perpetuum, pauca diuturna sunt; aliud alio modo fragile est, rerum exitus variantur, ceterum quidquid coepit et desinet. mundo quidam minantur interitum et hoc universum quod omnia divina humanaque complectitur, si fas putas credere, dies aliquis dissipabit et in confusionem veterem tenebrasque demerget: eat nunc aliquis et singulas comploret animas, Carthaginis ac Numantiae Corinthique cinerem et si quid aliud altius cecidit lamentetur, cum etiam hoc quod non habet quo cadat sit interiturum ... maximum ... solacium est cogitare id sibi accidisse quod omnes ante se passi sunt omnesque passuri; et ideo mihi videtur rerum natura quod gravissimum fecerat commune fecisse, ut crudelitatem fati consolaretur aequalitas'. In these extracts the notion that all things are subject to decay and that every human life will come to an end is presented for the distinct purpose of consolation. In this respect the present passage is different. There is no hint that Jerome is attempting to comfort Heliodorus. He has shelved the task of offering consolation and is simply confronting the question of the meaning of existence; and the picture, as so far painted, is bleak. For the τόπος of the inevitability of death see also on 5. 1 *Anaxagorae . . . mortalem* and 14. 3 *nam . . . proficiscitur*.

Jerome makes full use of rhetorical effects in this section; anaphora, antithesis, asyndeton in particular are very pronounced. The language is kept taut, the images change rapidly, and an increase in emotional tension seems to result.

vincitur . . . dicimus: an echo of the first sentence of the letter, *Grandes . . . explicare*, where see n. By claiming to be unable to give adequate expression to his theme, Jerome makes the idea that all things will come to an end seem quite dizzying, and the more horrifying.

c. 19. After the broad sweep of the last chapter Jerome now focuses on the detail, and in a less emotionally-charged passage considers the particular case of Heliodorus and himself. Second by second their lives are ticking away. Where, then, is the meaning of life to be found? In Christ, whose love binds them to each other and to Nepotianus despite the great distance between them and the greater gulf which separates them from the younger man. The pessimistic picture of the world presented by c. 18 gives way, and Jerome leaves Heliodorus with the highly comforting thought that in spite of death he and his nephew are still united. The letter ends with encouragement to the bishop to be strong in his bereavement and ever to have Nepotianus in his thoughts and upon his lips.

19. 1. quasi . . . descendentes: the expression follows naturally after 18. 2 *o si . . . speculam*. Jerome comes down from the height from where he has contemplated the world to look at his own situation.

sentisne . . . credimus: *sentisne . . . factus sis?* = 'are you aware of the actual moment when . . .?'. Gradually and almost imperceptibly we age, drifting towards ultimate death; dying is a process that continues throughout one's whole life. The idea is particularly common in Seneca, by whom Jerome may possibly have been influenced here; cf. *epist.* 4. 9, 26. 4, 58. 23, 120. 18, and esp. 24. 20 'cotidie morimur; cotidie enim demitur aliqua pars vitae, et tunc quoque cum crescimus vita decrescit. infantiam amisimus, deinde pueritiam, deinde adulescentiam', *dial.* 6. 21. 7 'in hoc omnes errore versamur, ut non putemus ad mortem nisi senes inclinatosque iam vergere, cum illo infantia statim et iuventa, omnis aetas ferat. agunt opus suum fata: nobis sensum nostrae necis auferunt, quoque facilius obrepat, mors sub ipso vitae nomine latet: infantiam in se pueritia convertit, pueritiam pubertas, iuvenem senex abstulit. incrementa ipsa, si bene computes, damna sunt'.

It is most unlikely that in *cotidie morimur* there is a reminiscence of 1 Cor. 15: 31 'cotidie morior per vestram gloriam', as Hilberg seems to think. Though the Pauline passage is susceptible of different interpretations (see on 14. 2 *multo . . . ad gloriam*), 'cotidie morior' cannot possibly be taken in the simple sense in which *cotidie morimur* is meant here. *cotidie morimur* is in any case a natural way to express the notion of gradual death, as Seneca found (see above).

aeternos . . . credimus has no part in the argument; but it is a point which would readily have come to Jerome's mind in the context. It was important to him that Christians should be aware that death was on its way, and live appropriately; see on 14. 3 *debemus . . . non potest.*

hoc . . . trahitur: cf. *in Gal.* 6. 10 (PL 26. 433) (*c.* AD 387–8) 'hoc ipsum quod loquor, quod dicto, quod scribo [*al.* scribitur], quod emendo, quod relego, de tempore meo mihi aut crescit, aut deperit'. Although the context of this passage is quite different, the similarity of words and thought is so close that one may suppose that Jerome had recently been rereading his *Commentary on Galatians.* Kunst, 157, notes the possible influence on these lines of Pers. 5. 153 'vive memor leti, fugit hora, hoc quod loquor inde est', which Jerome quotes at *epist.* 127. 6. 2.

quod dicto . . . quod emendo suggests that Jerome's method of composition was to dictate to a secretary, read through what he had dictated, and make any corrections he thought necessary. Such a pattern is highly plausible and he may regularly have followed it; it is clear at least that he often used to dictate his compositions, rather than write them with his own hand (cf. A.

Wikenhauser, 'Der heilige Hieronymus und die Kurzschrift',
ThQ 29 (1910), 50–87, Arns, 37–51, Bartelink (1980), 31). In the
text of *in Gal.* 6. 10, 'scribitur' should certainly be the preferred
reading, after 'dicto'; and one may at least question whether
Jerome actually wrote 'emendo' and 'relego' in that order.

puncta notarii: *puncta* is the perfect word in the context, for
it can denote not only marks made by a pen (as also at e.g.
Auson. *not.* 5) but also (with or without a word such as *temporis*)
moments of time (cf. e.g. Cic. *dom.* 115, Apul. *met.* 9. 39).

19. 2. transeunt . . . minuuntur: Jerome likes nautical imagery;
for his frequent metaphorical use of it see L. M. Kaiser,
'Imagery of Sea and Ship in the Letters of St. Jerome', *Folia*, 5
(1951), 56–60, J. W. Smit, *Studies on the Language and Style
of Columba the Younger (Columbanus)* (Amsterdam, 1971),
172–89, Bartelink (1980), 112–13, and for the tradition in
general, Curtius, 136–8.

Christi . . . sociamur: for the idea see below on *ob hanc . . .
manu*; and for the position of *nobis* cf. 13. 3 *in tali illum tempore*
with n., 14. 3.

caritas patiens . . . excidit: Jerome characterizes the love of
Christ which binds together Nepotianus, Heliodorus, and himself by quoting the words of Paul at 1 Cor. 13: 4 and 7–8 (Vulg.:
'[4] caritas patiens est, benigna est; caritas non aemulatur, non
agit perperam, non inflatur . . . [7] omnia suffert, omnia credit,
omnia sperat, omnia sustinet. [8] caritas numquam excidit . . . ').

agit perperam = περπερεύεται, 'vaunt itself', 'act boastfully,
ostentatiously'. The Greek verb occurs in the NT only here; and
there is no other instance of *perperam* in the Vulgate. Oddly,
perperam does not seem to bear this sense elsewhere; it regularly
means 'wrongly', in the moral sense (cf. e.g. Cic. *Quinct.* 31 'seu
recte seu perperam facere coeperunt'), or 'incorrectly' (cf. e.g.
Sen. *epist.* 9. 13 'hoc . . . plerique perperam interpretantur'), and
at *ad Att.* 1. 14. 4, when Cicero wants a word for 'show off' in the
sense of 'make a rhetorical display', he uses the Greek ἐνεπερπερ-
ευσάμην, not a Latinized phrase. A possible explanation is that
agit perperam may have been used in an early Latin version of
the Bible as a literal rendering of the Greek (which may have
been imperfectly understood), and stuck firmly in the text
thereafter; it appears in citations of the passage as early as
Cyprian (cf. *testim.* 3. 3, *unit. eccl.* 14), though not in Tertullian,
who has instead 'protervum sapit' (*pat.* 12).

ob hanc . . . manu: for the notions of 'absent in body,
present in spirit' and 'united in love' (particularly the love of
Christ) in early Christian epistolography see Thraede, 109–46.

A particularly good parallel, in a letter of consolation, is afforded by John Chrys. *vid. iun.* 3 τοιαύτη γὰρ ἡ τῆς ἀγάπης δύναμις· οὐ τοὺς παρόντας μόνον καὶ πλησίον ὄντας ἡμῶν καὶ ὁρωμένους, ἀλλὰ καὶ τοὺς μακρὰν ἀφεστῶτας περιλαμβάνει καὶ συγκολλᾷ καὶ συνδεῖ· καὶ οὔτε χρόνου πλῆθος, οὔτε ὁδῶν διάστημα, καὶ οὔτε ἄλλο τῶν τοιούτων οὐδὲν ψυχῆς φιλίαν διακόψαι δύναιτ᾽ ἂν καὶ διατεμεῖν. For the oxymoron in *absens praesens* cf. Ter. *Eun.* 192, Cic. *amicit.* 23 'absentes adsunt' (of friends).

19. 3. fortitudinem . . . filio: Chromatius, Bishop of Aquileia, 387–407, was a long-standing friend of both Jerome and Heliodorus. He and his brother Eusebius, to whose death Jerome is presumably referring here (nothing more is known about it), appear to have been very close; cf. *epist.* 7. 1. 1, 8. 1. 2. See generally *RE* s.n. Chromatios 2, *DCB* s.nn. Chromatius, Eusebius 4, Kelly, *passim.*

papa is used of bishops generally at this time; it was not until the sixth century that the term began to be reserved exclusively for the Bishop of Rome. See J. P. Krebs and J. H. Schmalz, *Antibarbarus der lateinischen Sprache* (7th edn., 2 vols., Basle, 1905–7), 2. 239, Bartelink (1980), 28.

filio: in various ways Nepotianus is *filius* to both Heliodorus and Jerome; cf. 7. 3, with n. on *in carne . . . pater,* 13. 3.

illum nostra pagella . . . desinamus: cf. Sen. *dial.* 6. 3. 2 'non desiit denique Drusi sui celebrare nomen, ubique illum sibi privatim publiceque repraesentare, libentissime de illo loqui, de illo audire' (an example presented in recommendation of such action), 11. 18. 7–8 'effice ut frequenter fratris tui memoriam tibi velis occurrere, ut illum et sermonibus celebres et adsidua recordatione repraesentes tibi, quod ita demum consequi poteris, si tibi memoriam eius iucundam magis quam flebilem feceris . . . omnia dicta eius ac facta et aliis expone et tibimet ipse commemora', Plin. *epist.* 2. 1. 12 'Verginium cogito, Verginium video, Verginium iam vanis imaginibus, recentibus tamen, audio adloquor teneo', Jer. *epist.* 39. 8. 1–2 'illam mea lingua resonabit, illi mei dedicabuntur labores, illi sudabit ingenium. nulla erit pagina, quae non Blesillam sonet. quocumque sermonis nostri monumenta pervenerint, illa cum meis opusculis peregrinabitur. hanc in meam mentem defixam legent virgines, viduae, monachi, sacerdotes. breve vitae spatium aeterna memoria pensabit'. The anaphora putting the emphasis very much on the deceased in almost all these passages is noteworthy. Plutarch points out that the remembrance of happy times shared with someone whose death one is now mourning can have a therapeutic effect; cf. *ad uxor.* 8 (610E–F).

pagella: the diminutive is rare; cf. *TLL* 10. 1. 84. In Jerome cf. *epist.* 73. 1. 3; also Jeremiah 36: 23.

quem . . . desinamus: two good antitheses with which to end.

APPENDIX 1

The Date of *Letter* 60

We can be sure that Jerome wrote *Letter* 60 in the year 396. The letter postdates the death of Fl. Rufinus,[1] which occurred on 27 November 395;[2] and belongs to the year following the invasion of the eastern provinces of the Empire by the Huns,[3] which took place after the death of the Emperor Theodosius I on 17 January 395[4] and while Rufinus was still alive.[5]

It was long accepted, on the strength of Jerome's comment at *epist.* 77. 1. 1—'quartae aestatis circulus volvitur, ex quo ad Heliodorum episcopum Nepotiani scribens epitaphium, quidquid habere virium potui in illo tunc dolore consumpsi' —that the piece was written in summer. T. D. Barnes,[6] however, argued that spring, which might easily be subsumed under *aestas*, was more likely. In the preface to his *Commentary on Jonah* Jerome indicates that he had written 'ad Nepotianum vel de Nepotiano duos libros'—i.e. *Letters* 52 and 60—and his commentaries on the prophets Micah, Nahum, Habakkuk, Zephaniah, and Haggai, within the previous three years, or thereabouts: 'triennium circiter fluxit, postquam quinque prophetas interpretatus sum . . .'.[7] These commentaries had in fact been composed by the time Jerome wrote *De viris illustribus* in the fourteenth year of Theodosius' reign,[8] which Barnes took to mean the year ending 18 January 393, Theodosius having acceded on 19 January 379.[9] It therefore made sense for Barnes to seek to push the date of the letter as far back towards the beginning of the year as possible: 'triennium circiter' ought at least to be closer to a three-year period than to a four-year one. A date early in the year is, however, not only precluded by the

[1] Cf. 16. 1.
[2] Cf. Socr. *hist. eccl.* 6. 1.
[3] Cf. 16. 4 *anno praeterito*.
[4] For the date see O. Seeck, *Regesten der Kaiser und Päpste für die Jahre 311 bis 475 n. Chr.* (Stuttgart, 1919), 384.
[5] Cf. e.g. Claud. *in Rufin.* 2. 1–35, Socr. loc. cit. (n. 2).
[6] *Tertullian: A Historical and Literary Study* (Oxford, 1971), 235–6.
[7] *In Ion.* pref. (CCSL 76. 377 = PL 25. 1117).
[8] Cf. *vir. ill.* 135 (PL 23. 717–19).
[9] For this date see O. Seeck, *Geschichte des Untergangs der antiken Welt* (3rd edn., 5 vols., Berlin, 1910–13), 5. 125, 479.

reference to *aestas* at *epist.* 77. 1. 1, but also opposed by the need to allow time for the banishments of Abundantius and Timasius, the responsibility for which lay with Eutropius, whose rise to high power came after Rufinus' death,[10] and for Jerome to have heard about them. On this reckoning, spring 396 looks about right.

Barnes's view was put forward in reaction to a seemingly curious theory of P. Nautin[11] that Jerome calculated imperial years not from the date of the emperor's accession but from 1 January of the following year. Nautin thus maintained that for Jerome the fourteenth year of Theodosius' reign meant the calendar year 393, and if this date can be accepted for the composition of *De viris illustribus* the problems involved in reconciling the evidence of *epist.* 77. 1. 1 and the preface to the Jonah commentary fall away. Scholars have, however, been loath to accept Nautin's theory,[12] principally, it appears, because Jerome's statement in the second book of the *Adversus Rufinum*, which belongs to 401 or 402,[13] that he wrote *De viris illustribus* 'ante annos ferme decem'[14] makes it more difficult to accept a later rather than an earlier date for *De viris illustribus*. But just as much leeway must be allowed a comment as vague as 'ante annos ferme decem' as is granted to 'triennium circiter', if not more; and the difficulty thrown in the way of accepting a later date for *De viris illustribus* is, to my mind, no more serious than that entailed by having to suppose both that *Letter* 60 was written as early in 396 as the term *aestas* will allow, and that *De viris illustribus* was written as close to the end of the year 19 January 392–18 January 393 as possible, when all that we know for certain is that it belongs somewhere in the fourteenth year of Theodosius. Indeed, an argument that seems to have been ignored in the debate is that it is not the *De viris illustribus* itself that has, for these purposes, to be fixed in the three years or so mentioned by Jerome in the preface to the Jonah commentary, but the commentaries on the five minor prophets which preceded it; even if *De viris illustribus* was written as late as December 392 or January 393, we have to allow time prior to that for the composition of these commentaries, pushing the clock back still further. Thus Nautin's theory should not be rejected out of hand on this account; and some (though not all) of the further arguments

---

[10] See 16. 1 with nn. on *Abundantius . . . exulat* and *Timasius . . . inglorius.*

[11] First put forward in 'La Date du "De viris inlustribus" de Jérôme, de la mort de Cyrille de Jérusalem et de celle de Grégoire de Nazianze', *RHE* 56 (1961), 33–5.

[12] Cf., in addition to Barnes, Kelly, 174, Booth (1981), 241.

[13] Cf. Booth (1981), 240–1.

[14] *Adv. Rufin.* 2. 23 (CCSL 79. 59 = PL 23. 446).

adduced by him[15] in support of his case following the criticism of Barnes demand that the theory be accorded much more serious consideration than it has hitherto received.

Further consideration of these matters, which are enmeshed with many other problems concerning the chronology of this period, need not detain us, for they have no bearing on the date of *Letter* 60; on any calculation the letter was written around the middle of 396.[16] But a seemingly curious point arises from this dating. At 16. 1, when Jerome proposes to add to his list of ill-fated emperors the names of private individuals who have also experienced personal disaster, he says that he will go back no more than two years to find them: 'ad privatas veniam dignitates, nec de his loquar qui excedunt biennium; atque, ut ceteros praetermittam, sufficit nobis trium nuper consularium diversos exitus scribere'. But the earliest of his three examples is Rufinus, who can have died only six months or so previously. Why then *biennium*? The answer is perhaps quite simple. Jerome has in mind other figures too, but then chooses not to mention them (cf. 'ut ceteros praetermittam'). The *exitus* of some or all of these men will have gone back further than those of Rufinus, Abundantius, and Timasius.

---

[15] See Nautin (1974), 280–4.

[16] Whether right or wrong, Nautin's theory does not of course preclude the possibility that it does belong to the spring, if we accept that *aestas* can stretch that far. Nautin (1974), 279, himself dates the piece to June–July.

APPENDIX 2

Prose-Rhythm as a Feature of Jerome's Style

One of the stylistic features of *Letter* 60 to which attention is drawn in the commentary on a number of occasions[1] is the use of particular rhythmical patterns at pauses within sentences and especially at sentence-endings.[2] From before the time of Cicero until the late Middle Ages prose-rhythm held an important place in Latin prose style. It is, however, not the most fashionable topic in modern classical studies, and there may be readers of this book who are less familiar with the subject than they would like to be; still more probable is it that there will be some who are unacquainted with the rhythmical practices of the period of transition between the quite different systems of the classical and medieval worlds. It may not go amiss, then, to outline the main currents in the use of rhythm in Latin prose from Cicero to the early Middle Ages, focusing principally on the interim period; to illustrate from *Letter* 60 how Jerome exemplifies some of the rhythmical characteristics of the prose writing of that period; and to make a few observations on certain related points of style, without which the picture would be incomplete.

The prose-rhythm of the classical period was metrical, or

---

[1] See on 1. 1 ⟨*nos*⟩ . . . *confecit*, 4. 2 *totius* . . . *est*, 7. 3 *cuius* . . . *laetatus es*, 8. 1 *eorum* . . . *repetantur*, 10. 4 *clamabat indignum*, 11. 3 *marsuppium* . . . *obsequiis*, 15. 3 *Gratianus* . . . *testantur*, 16. 2 *non calamitates* . . . *prosequi*, 16. 3 *fuere ludibrio*, 18. 1 *infinitam* . . . *exercitum*.

[2] Apart from rhythm, and the related matters examined in this appendix, I have confined discussion of points of style to the commentary, where they can be considered with full regard to their context; to attempt a fuller examination of Jerome's style in the brief space afforded by an appendix, and on the basis of a single letter, would certainly lead to generalization, and perhaps to unwarranted conclusions. This area is, however, one that is greatly in need of further investigation. Such work as has been done has concentrated largely on isolating individual features without regard to context; the study of J. N. Hritzu, *The Style of the Letters of St. Jerome* (Catholic University of America Patristic Studies, 60; Washington, DC, 1939), is a classic model of how not to proceed (see the critical but unduly respectful review of J. W. Pirie, 'The Styles of Jerome and Leo the Great', *CR* 54 (1940), 201–2). I have learned something from G. Harendza, *De oratorio genere dicendi, quo Hieronymus in epistulis usus sit* (Bratislava, 1905), and from E. Coleiro, 'St. Jerome's Letters and *Lives of the Hermits* with reference to (1) Art and Style, (2) Social and Historical Significance' (unpublished London Ph.D. thesis 1949); otherwise most of what has been produced on this subject can safely be ignored.

quantitative, in nature.[3] Authors who wrote with attention to rhythm favoured certain combinations of long and short syllables in the clausula, or end of a sentence, and avoided others; often they display the same preferences, usually maintained a little less rigorously, at pauses within sentences, where we can speak of internal clausulae. The most important exponent of quantitative prose-rhythm in Latin was Cicero, whose practice, though opposed by some, became the basic model for later writers. He shows regular preferences[4] for endings formed on a cretic (–∪–) or molossus (–––) base, notably the cretic spondee[5] (–∪–‿≍), double cretic (–∪––∪≍), cretic ditrochee (–∪––∪–≍), molossus cretic (––––∪≍), and molossus ditrochee (––––∪–≍); among his successors the cretic base becomes preferred to the molossus. Also relatively frequent is the famous (or notorious) *esse videatur* clausula (–∪∪∪–≍), a cretic spondee with the second long syllable resolved into two shorts. Among clausulae which Cicero strongly avoids is the hexameter ending, –∪∪–≍.

In the early Middle Ages the use of quantitative rhythms disappeared entirely from Latin prose. The system that replaced it, known as the *cursus*, was based not on syllable-length but on word-stress, or accent.[6] Though the tradition was not completely homogeneous,[7] three fundamental rhythms were dominant throughout the Middle Ages: the *cursus planus* (x́ x x x́ x), where the stresses in the clausula fell on the penultimate syllable and the third syllable before that, the *cursus tardus* (x́ x x x́ x x), where they fell on the antepenultimate and the third before that, and the *cursus velox* (x́ x x x x x́ x), where they fell on the penultimate and the fifth before that.[8] A fourth rhythm, the *cursus trispondaicus*

---

[3] For a brief bibliography see Oberhelman–Hall (1984), 114 n. 3. The most useful starting-points are probably *OCD*, s.v. 'Prose-Rhythm', and Wilkinson, 135–64.

[4] An author's preference for a particular type of ending is demonstrated not by its absolute frequency in his work but by its frequency relative to its occurrences in 'unrhythmical' prose; this crucial principle was established by A. W. de Groot, *A Handbook of Antique Prose-Rhythm*, 1 (The Hague, 1919). The figures for Cicero's favourite clausulae, together with control figures, are conveniently set out by Wilkinson, 156.

[5] Or cretic trochee; in Cicero's practice, and in general, the last syllable of a clausula was regarded as *anceps*.

[6] The *cursus* was of course not employed in all medieval prose texts any more than metrical rhythms feature in all prose of the classical period. The most important modern studies of the medieval *cursus* are those of Lindholm and Janson (1975); the methodology employed by Janson marked a breakthrough in *cursus* scholarship. For earlier pioneering work see Oberhelman–Hall (1985), 214 n. 2.

[7] Janson (1975), for example, demonstrated that in the tenth and eleventh centuries two distinct versions of the *cursus* coexisted, differentiated by region.

[8] The principal form of the *planus* is a paroxytone word followed by a trisyllabic

(x́ x x x x́ x), also played an important part in the system as employed by certain authors and in certain regions. These four *cursus*-forms can be seen to be descended from particular metrical patterns. The *planus*, for example, is the accentual equivalent of the cretic spondee, the *trispondaicus* of the *esse videatur* clausula. The transition from the quantitative to the accentual system took place over a period of about three hundred years, during which attention moved gradually away from quantity towards accent. Recent studies,[9] using modern techniques of statistical analysis, have demonstrated that in this period two rhythmical systems were in use concurrently. One was the *cursus*, which was in use certainly by the later fourth century; the other, the so-called *cursus mixtus*, a term for which there is no ancient authority but which is used by modern scholars to denote a system in which regard is had to both accentual and metrical patterns. The first certain occurrences of the *cursus mixtus* are found in the third century, in the works of Minucius Felix and Cyprian.[10] It appears, further, that two versions of the *cursus mixtus* were employed alongside each other.[11] In the stricter version, clausulae were confined largely to the three principal forms of the *cursus* in conjunction with (in the case of the *planus*) the cretic spondee, (in the case of the *tardus*) the double cretic or cretic tribrach (–∪–∪∪ ≃) (a resolved cretic spondee),[12] and (in the case of the

paroxytone (x́ x / x x́ x); of the *tardus*, a paroxytone followed by a tetrasyllabic proparoxytone (x́ x / x x́ x x) (also frequent is a proparoxytone followed by a trisyllabic proparoxytone (x́ x x / x́ x x)); and of the *velox*, a proparoxytone followed by a tetrasyllabic paroxytone (x́ x x / x x x́ x), where a secondary stress occurs on the first syllable of the final word. But there were variations on these patterns, involving monosyllables and disyllables, so that in addition to the standard form of, say, the *tardus*, as in e.g. *scírě dūlcédʼiněm* (*epist.* 60. 13. 3), we find endings like *disputávʼit īn cárcěrě* (*epist.* 60. 4. 2), where the accent on *in* is too weak to make any difference to the rhythm.

[9] Oberhelman–Hall (1984), (1985), Hall–Oberhelman (1985), Oberhelman (1988a), (1988b); also R. G. Hall and S. M. Oberhelman, 'Internal Clausulae in Late Latin Prose as Evidence for the Displacement of Metre by Word-Stress', *CQ* 36 (1986), 508–26. The principal studies of the interim period prior to Hall and Oberhelman are M. G. Nicolau, *L'Origine du 'cursus' rythmique et les débuts de l'accent d'intensité en latin* (Collection d'études latines, 5; Paris, 1930), and H. Hagendahl, *La Prose métrique d'Arnobe: contributions à la connaissance de la prose littéraire de l'Empire* (Göteborgs högskolas årsskrift, 42. 1; Göteborg, 1937), and *La Correspondence de Ruricius* (Göteborgs högskolas årsskrift, 58. 3; Göteborg, 1952), 32–50.

[10] Cf. Oberhelman–Hall (1985), 224, Oberhelman (1988b), 237.

[11] Cf. Oberhelman (1988b), 236–7.

[12] Although the cretic tribrach was not a preferred clausula in Cicero, it became a desired ending in the prose of the Empire; cf. Oberhelman–Hall (1985), 216 n. 12, Hall–Oberhelman (1985), 201 n. 4.

velox) the ditrochee.[13] The more relaxed version sought a greater variety of accentual rhythms and metrical forms, though those favoured by the stricter version were still predominant. Equally, *cursus*-only works might be written either with close adherence to the three standard forms, or with greater freedom.

Jerome, along with other authors, seems to have followed the *cursus* in some of his works and the *cursus mixtus* in others, and sometimes to have observed no rhythmical practice at all.[14] It has been shown that the letters, taken as a body, follow the *cursus mixtus*,[15] but there is reason to think that further research may reveal differences in the epistolary corpus as a whole. If Jerome's Scriptural commentaries, for example, employ not the *cursus mixtus* but the *cursus*,[16] it seems possible that the more exegetical of his letters may do the same. The reasons for the choice of one system rather than the other are not clear and await investigation, but it seems a reasonable hypothesis that they may have something to do with the nature of the subject-matter.[17] A careful reading of *Letter* 60, however, makes it plain that here Jerome was writing with attention both to accent and to quantity. This could doubtless be demonstrated statistically; but it may give readers a better feel for what this means in practice to look at the rhythmical characteristics of a number of passages in the letter.

[13] Ditrochee endings in Cicero tend to be preceded by a cretic or molossus, but, according to Oberhelman–Hall (1985), 217 n. 15, writers of the *cursus mixtus* were unconcerned with the syllables preceding the ditrochee. My impression is, however, that in *epist.* 60 Jerome likes to introduce a ditrochee with a cretic whenever possible.

[14] Cf. Oberhelman–Hall (1985), 223, 225, modified in the case of *vir. ill.* by Oberhelman (1988*a*), 147 n. 22. The studies of Jerome's rhythm by Knook and by M. C. Herron, *A Study of the Clausulae in the Writings of St. Jerome* (Catholic University of America Patristic Studies, 51; Washington, DC, 1937), are of very limited value. Knook's conclusions were criticized by H. Hagendahl in his review in *Gnomon* 15 (1939), 84–9; the weakness of Herron's book is that it fails to take account of the notion of relative frequency (for which see n. 4 above; it should be added here that in attempting to determine whether a demonstrably accentual text is also written with attention to quantity, allowance has to be made for the fact that accentual texts tend to produce a higher proportion of standard metrical forms compared with completely unrhythmical texts, even though these metrical forms may not have been intended (cf. Oberhelman–Hall (1985), 217)). There is even less to be got from L. Laurand, 'Le *cursus* dans les lettres de saint Jérôme', *RecSR* 9 (1919), 370–2 (= (in slightly shortened form) Laurand, *Pour mieux comprendre l'Antiquité classique* (= *Supplément au manuel des études grecques et latines*) (2 vols., Paris, 1936–9), 1. 180–2).

[15] Cf. Oberhelman–Hall (1985), 223; Oberhelman (1988*b*), 237, includes Jerome among the practitioners of the less rigorous version.

[16] This is demonstrated by Oberhelman–Hall (1985), 223, for *in Is.*, and by Oberhelman (1988*a*), 143, and (1988*b*), 234, for *in Dan.*

[17] This is also the view of Oberhelman (1988*b*), 239–40.

I begin, however, with a passage not from *Letter* 60 but from
Letter 1, a highly rhetorical piece written some twenty years or so
earlier:[18]

igitur Vercellae Ligurum civitas haud procul a radicibus Álpĭūm sĭtă, olim
potens, nunc raro habitatórĕ sēmĭrŭtă. hanc cum ex more consulárĭs
ínvísĕrĕt, oblatam sibi quandam mulierculam una cum adultero—nam id
crimen marítŭs ínpégĕrăt—poenali carceris horrórĕ cīrcúmdĕdĭt. neque
multo post, cum lividas carnes ungula cruéntă pūlsárĕt et sulcatis lateribus
dolor quáerĕrēt vérĭtátĕm, infelicissimus iuvenis volens conpendio mortis
longos vitárĕ crŭcĭátŭs, dum in suum mēntítūr sánguĭnĕm, accusávĭt
álĭénŭm solusque omnium miser merito vísŭs ēst pércŭtĭ, quia non
relíquĭt ínnóxĭáe, ūndĕ póssēt nĕgárĕ. (*epist.* 1. 3. 1–2)

The high metrical quality of this passage, in both the final and the
internal clausulae, is striking. All but two of the clausulae (and
both those internal) show the rhythms most favoured by Cicero
and the Ciceronian school: cretic spondee, once resolved into
–∪–∪∪⌣ and twice into –∪∪∪–⌣, double cretic (no fewer than
six times in thirteen endings), and cretic ditrochee. They also
follow, with only one exception (*mentitur sanguinem*, where the
pause is weak), the preferred accentual forms of the *cursus* (including the *trispondaicus*), in nearly all cases displaying the tendency of
the transitional period to coincidence of accent and ictus.[19]

The density of good metrical forms in this passage is unusual;
but a serious concern for quantity can also be detected in *Letter* 60.
The first chapter will serve as an example:

Grandes materias ingenia párvă nōn súffĕrŭnt, et in ipso conatu ultra vires
áusă sūccúmbŭnt; quantoque maius fúĕrīt quŏd dīcénd(um) ĕst, tanto
magis obruitur qui magnitudinem rerum verbis nōn pŏtēst ēxplĭcárĕ.
Nepotianus meus, tuus, noster, immo Christi et, quia Christi, idcirco plus
noster, ⟨nós⟩ rĕlíquĭt sĕnĕs et desiderii sui iaculo vulneratos intolerabili
dolórĕ cōnfécĭt. (1. 1)

Considered metrically, five of the six clausulae[20] here are excellent;

---

[18] The passage is analysed also by Knook, 74–5. In this and the following
passages I have marked as internal clausulae only what I take to be the most obvious
pauses in the middle of sentences. Normally the ends of clauses containing
a finite verb, provided that the clause is long enough to permit a meaningful
clausula, and that there is a clear sense-pause at the same point. In the interests of
keeping the picture as simple as possible, I have not involved myself in the tricky
problem of using internal rhythms to fix the boundaries of cola and commata.

[19] I do not enter the debate on the question of the real existence of an ictus in
metrical prose, but employ the term, with Oberhelman–Hall (1985), 216 n. 14,
merely to indicate the first syllable of each metrical unit in the clausula.

[20] I include ⟨*nos*⟩ *reliquit senes*, where the rhythm is a point in favour of the
conjecture (see comm. on 1. 1 ⟨*nos*⟩ . . . *confecit*).

238   *Appendix 2*

as regards the sixth, *fuerit quod dicendum est*, we might observe that
if hiatus is permitted, the result is a molossus cretic, which Jerome
is likely to have regarded as at least tolerable.[21] In the next section
the quality becomes more patchy:

quem herēdēm pŭtávĭmŭs, fúnūs tĕnémŭs. cui iam meum sudábĭt
īngĕnĭŭm? cui litterulae placérĕ gÉstĭ̆ent? ubi est ille ἐργοδιώκτης noster et
cycneo canórĕ vóx dúlcĭŏr? stupet animus, manus tremit, caligant oculi,
língŭă bālbútĭt. quidquid dixero, quia íllĕ nōn aúdĭ̆et, mútūm vĭdétŭr.
stilus ipse quasi sentiens et cera subtristior vel rubigine vēl sĭ̆t(u) ōbdúcĭ-
tŭr. quotienscumque nitor in vérbă prōrúmpĕrĕ et super tumulum eius
epitaphii huiūs flórēs spárgĕrĕ̆, totiens inpléntŭr ŏ̆cŭlĭ̆ et renovato dolore
tótŭs īn fúnĕrĕ̆ sŭ́m. (1. 2)

In certain endings (*heredem putavimus, funus tenemus, mutum
videtur*) accent seems more pronounced than quantity.[22] *placere
gestient* (trochee cretic, *cursus medius*[23]) is at best of moderate
quality both metrically and accentually. But most of the remaining
clausulae in this section are good, and in two of them (*canore vox
dulcior, huius flores spargere*) the metrical quality is perhaps
superior to the accentual.[24] The rhythmical shambles of the last
clausula, *totus in funere sum*, can be explained as stylistic reflection
of its content: at the very point where Jerome claims to be so
overwhelmed by Nepotianus' death that his tears prevent utter-
ance, his rhythm too breaks down completely.

   The remainder of the chapter is quantitatively much on a par
with the first section:

moris quondam fuit ut super cadavera defunctorum in contione pro rostris
laudes lĭ̄bĕrĭ̄ dĭ̆cĕrĕ̆nt, et instar lugubrium carminum ad fletus et gemitus
audientium péctŏră cŏncĭtárĕnt; en rerum in nobis órdŏ̆ mūtátŭs ĕ̆st, et in

[21] On the other hand, to elide permits a much better accentual rhythm (*velox*).
The whole question of hiatus and elision in Latin prose is vexed. The view of late-
antique grammarians was that elision in the clausula was forbidden, and hiatus
avoided; cf. Lindholm, 34. The rule formulated by Hall–Oberhelman (1985), 209,
that 'once the specific rhythmical tendencies of a text have been determined, then
either hiatus or elision is allowed so as to obtain the desired clausula', does not help
us in the present case.
[22] Though Oberhelman–Hall (1985), 217, point out that it is not uncommon for a
ditrochee to coincide with a *planus*.
[23] The *medius* is one of the more important minor forms of the *cursus*; it is
extraordinarily frequent in Jer. *vir. ill.* (cf. Oberhelman (1988a), 147 n. 22).
[24] This is true also in the case of *vel situ obducitur*, if the elision I have marked is
permissible. In *canore vox dulcior*, *vox* seems too important a word to be regarded as
having an accent so weak as not to disturb the rhythm. In most examples of such
'proclitic variants' (for the term see Janson (1975), 37) the monosyllable is a fairly
colourless word, such as *in* in the case quoted in n. 8; for other cases in *epist.* 60 cf.
e.g. 8. 1 *meretrĭcĕ̆ sīt nátŭs*, 10. 5 *cétĕrās nòn hăbérĕ̆t*, 13. 1 ómnĕ quōd vívĭmŭs.

calamitatem nostram perdidit sua iūrā nātūrā: quod exhibere senibus
iŭvĕnīs débŭĭt, hoc iuveni ēxhĭbēmūs sĕnĕs. (1. 3)
The dactyl preceding the ditrochee in *pectora concitarent* would
not have troubled an author of the *cursus mixtus*; see n. 13 above.
Though my discussion of c. 1 has concentrated on its metrical
character, it will not have gone unnoticed that standard metrical
and accentual clausular forms often coincide, and that Jerome has
plainly paid attention to both accent and quantity. Considerations
of accent, however, are perhaps more prominent in certain other
parts of the letter. A case in point is c. 10, where the writing is
descriptive and emotionally less charged than in c. 1. I cite in full
only the opening:

Verumtamen velut incunabula quaedam nascentis fĭdēī cōnprŏbēmŭs, ut,
qui sub alienis signis devŏtūs mĭlēs fŭĭt, donandus laurea sit postquam suo
regi cóepĕrīt mĭlĭtárĕ. balteo posito habitūquĕ mūtátŏ quidquid castrensis
peculii fuit in pāupĕrēs ĕrŏgávĭt. legerat enim, 'quī vŭlt pērfēctŭs ēssĕ,
vendat omnia quae habet et det pauperibus ĕt sĕquátūr mĕ', et iterum,
'non potestis duobus dominis servire, dĕ(o) ĕt māmónaĕ'. excepta vili
tunica et operimento pari, quod tecto tantum corpore frĭgŭs ēxclū-
dĕrĕt, nihil sibi āmplĭūs rĕsērvávĭt. cultus ipse provinciae morem sequens
nec munditiis nec sordibus notábĭlĭs ĕrăt. cumque arderet cotidie aut ad
Aegypti monasteria pergere aut Mesopotamiae invisere choros vel certe
insularum Dalmatiae, quae Altino tantūm frētō dīstănt, solitūdĭnēs ŏccŭ-
párĕ, avunculum pontificem desĕrĕrĕ nŏn āudēbăt, tota in illo cernens
exémplă vīrtūtŭm domique habens ŭndĕ dīscĕrĕt. in uno atque eodem et
imitabatur monachum et epíscŏpūm vĕnĕrābátŭr. non, ut in plerisque
accídĕrĕ sŏlĕt, adsiduitas familiaritatem, familiaritas contemptum īllĭŭs
fēcĕrăt, sed ita eum colebāt quăsĭ păréntĕm, ita admirabatur quasi cotidiē
nŏvūm cérnĕrĕt. (10. 1–3)

Many of the clausulae in this extract are of good metrical quality;[25]
but what is most immediately striking is the presence in a short
space of text of so many *velox* endings. This feature, indeed, can be
observed throughout the whole of the chapter, which, by my
count, contains no fewer than sixteen examples of the regular form
of the *velox* (x́ x x / x x x́ x). Now as Latin displays a tendency to
prefer paroxytone words to proparoxytones as penultimates, the
regular form of the *trispondaicus* (x́ x / x x x́ x) should naturally
occur more frequently than the regular form of the *velox*, and
this is generally observed to be so in authors who write with

[25] This is true even of the clausulae in the adapted Scriptural passage *qui . . .
sequatur me*.

no attention to accent.[26] But in c. 10 there are only two such *trispondaicus* endings (10. 6 *fróntĭs tēmpĕrábāt*, 10. 8 *respondérĕ vĕrēcúndĕ*). The overwhelming preponderance of *velox* endings is a certain indicator that in this part of the letter Jerome is being powerfully influenced by accentual considerations.

The least rhythmical parts of the letter are, as we should expect, those most heavily coloured by Scriptural language and phraseology: the Latin Bible, even as revised by Jerome, shows little evidence of careful clausulation on metrical or accentual principles. Consider the following:

quod si Lazarus videtur in sinu Abraham locóquĕ rĕfrīgĕríĭ, quid simile infernus et régnă cāelórŭm? ante Christum Abraham ắpŭd ínfĕrŏs; post Christum lắtr(o) ĭn părădísŏ. et idcirco in resurrectione eius multa dormientium córpŏră sŭrrēxĕrŭnt et visa sunt in cāelést(i) Hĭĕrúsălĕm. tuncque conpletum est íllŭd ēlóquĭŭm, 'surge, qui dormis, et elevare, et inluminábīt tē Chrístŭs.' Iohannes Baptista in herémō pérsŏnắt, 'paeniténtĭ(am) ắgĭtĕ; adpropinquavit enim régnūm cāelórŭm.' a diebus enim Iohannis Baptistae regnum caelórūm vím páss(um) ĕst et violenti dīrĭpŭérūnt íllŭd. flammea illa rumphea, custos paradisi, et praesidentia foribus cherubin Christi restincta et reserátă sūnt sángŭĭnĕ. nec mirum hoc nobis in resurrectiónĕ prōmíttĭ, cum omnes qui in carne non secundūm cárnēm vivĭmŭs municipatum habeámŭs īn cáelŏ, et hic adhuc positis dicátŭr īn térră, 'regnum dei íntrā vós ĕst.' (3. 2–4)

The contrast with the passages cited above is very clear. In the first part of the extract, rhythm is plainly of no great importance.[27] Whether we assume hiatus or elision to be intended in *latro in paradiso, caelesti Hierusalem*, and *caelorum vim passum est* makes no significant difference.[28] However, in the last two sentences, where the influence of particular passages of Scripture is perhaps less dominating, the rhythmical quality is much higher. Disregarding the quotation *regnum . . . est*, all but one of the clausulae are excellent, and in the exception, *secundum carnem vivimus*, where there is only a slight pause, the rhythm is at least fair (molossus cretic, *medius*).

It should be observed that in two of the clausulae in the above

---

[26] For the '*velox* test' see the review of Janson (1975) by M. Winterbottom, *MAev* 45 (1976), 298–300.

[27] Though in the first sentence Jerome may have written *regna caelorum* rather than *regnum caelorum* for the sake of the cretic spondee.

[28] There is an accentual advantage in allowing elision in *caelesti Hierusalem*, but metrically nothing can be done with it. Conversely it seems marginally better, at least metrically, to suppose hiatus in *caelorum vim passum est*. But I cannot believe that Jerome displays any real interest in rhythm here.

passage (*reserata sunt sanguine, dicatur in terra*) the natural word-order seems to have been altered in order to effect an improved ending. Clearly in these cases the clausula was important to Jerome. The same phenomenon may be observed elsewhere in the letter. For example, at 17. 1 Jerome writes: *nos miseri, qui aut patimur aut patientes fratres nostros tántă pĕrspĭcĭmŭs. tanta* should be the object of both *patimur* and *patientes*, and, from the viewpoint of word-order alone, would be better placed before the first *aut*. But Jerome's verbal arrangement is superior metrically, and equivalent accentually, to any other arrangement of the words in the second part of the clause.[29] A particularly common type of case where considerations of word-order appear to yield to those of rhythm is that where the verb is shifted from its usual position at the end of the clause. Consider, for instance, 2. 2 *desiderii frángĭt ăffĕctŭs* (cretic spondee/*planus*, greatly superior to *ăffĕctūs frángĭt*); 3. 1 *tua ăgĭmūs crĕātúră* (cretic spondee/*velox*; nothing can be done with *creatura agimus*); 16. 1 *ad privatas vĕnĭām dĭgnĭtátĕs* (ditrochee/*velox*; the choice of words does not permit any better metrical arrangement, and a *velox* is much preferable to the alternative, a *medius*); 17. 1 *Romanus supĕrátŭr ĕxĕrcĭtŭs* (double cretic/*tardus*, a fine rhythm which also avoids the hexameter ending of *Romanus superatur* or *exercitus superatur*).

Caution is needed, however. Word-groups of this type also occur where rhythm is of no account. At *epist.* 107. 1. 4 Jerome writes 'auratum squálēt Căpĭtólĭŭm', a clausula of no rhythmical merit, where to have left 'squalet' to the end would have given an excellent ending (cretic spondee, *planus*). There is perhaps nothing quite as notable in *Letter* 60; but, to give three examples to underline the point, there is no rhythmical benefit to be got from writing *Latināē mĭcănt hĭstŏrĭăe* in place of *Latinae histŏrĭāe mĭcănt* or the metrically much superior *historiāe Lătĭnae mĭcănt* at 5. 2, from preferring *ĕxcēdĕrēmŭs ánnŏs* to *ánnōs ĕxcēdĕrēmŭs* at 14. 3, or from opting for the very unrhythmical *artium redúndăt ēlĕgántĭăm* at 12. 3. These cases offer a salutary warning against overestimating the importance of rhythm. It seems, indeed, that Jerome has a liking for separating a noun from an attributive adjective or a dependent genitive, whether or not a clausula is being formed.[30]

---

[29] On the cretic tribrach see n. 12 above. The statistics provided by L. D. Stephens, 'Syllable Quantity in Late Latin Clausulae', *Phoenix*, 40 (1986), 72–91, at 78, suggest that Jerome had a strong preference for this ending (or a double cretic) over a molossus tribrach (or molossus cretic).

[30] J. N. Adams, 'A Type of Hyperbaton in Latin Prose', *PCPhS* NS 17 (1971), 1–16, at 11, makes the interesting observation that 'verbal hyperbaton', where a noun is separated from its adjective by a verb, is not uncommon in the Vulgate OT — Jerome's translation from the Hebrew — but rare in VL.

There are many instances; an extreme example occurs at *epist.* 1. 1
(quoted in the commentary at 14. 1 *tota hunc* . . . *Italia*).
One or two further points may be made along the same lines. It
is at first sight natural to suppose that at 16. 3 *fuére lūdíbrĭŏ* Jerome
chooses *fuere* rather than *fuerunt* because he has a preference for a
double cretic over a molossus cretic.[31] But at 16. 4 *fuere* is used
again, this time with no rhythmic point. His choice of *fuere* at 16. 3
may therefore have been determined at least partly by other
considerations. Again, there are times when Jerome eschews an
easily obtainable good rhythm for no readily apparent reason. I can
find no satisfactory explanation, for instance, for his preferring the
pedestrian *cruórě mūtátāe sŭnt* to the powerful *cruórě mūtátăe* at
16. 4. At this stage of our knowledge, all that can be said is that
while rhythm is an important factor in much of Jerome's composition, it does not always exert as much influence as one might
expect.

---

[31] Cf. n. 29 above. Hall–Oberhelman (1985), 210, maintain that the -*ere* form is
used for similar reasons in *Cod. Theod.*

INDEX OF PASSAGES CITED

(a) *Passages from Scripture and classical texts quoted, alluded to, or echoed by*
Jerome in Letter 60

GENESIS
3: 24: 104
5: 5–31: 188
16: 1–12: 137
25: 25: 138
27: 41: 138
37: 33–5: 122
49: 27: 139

EXODUS
17: 9–13: 219
31: 1–11: 170

NUMBERS
11: 16–17: 153

DEUTERONOMY
34: 8: 123

JOSHUA
24: 29–30: 123

JUDGES
11: 1: 138

2 SAMUEL
18: 33: 122

1 KINGS
7: 170

2 KINGS
19: 35: 218

2 CHRONICLES
20: 21–3: 219
32: 21: 218

PSALMS
1: 2: 165
13: 1: 99–100
13: 3: 99–100
29: 6: 122–3
47: 9: 126
75: 2: 106

WISDOM
4: 8–9: 153
4: 11–14: 89

ISAIAH
30: 17: 221
37: 36: 218
40: 6: 174
53: 7: 140

JEREMIAH
12: 7: 94–5
19: 7: 95
21: 7: 95
22: 25: 95
25: 8–9: 218
27: 6–7: 218
34: 20: 95

EZEKIEL
18: 4: 138
18: 19: 138
18: 20: 138

HOSEA
13: 14: 91, 95
13: 15: 91, 92

JONAH
1: 15: 93
2: 1–11: 93
3: 4–5: 93

HABAKKUK
1: 8: 213–14

MATTHEW
3: 1–2: 103
3: 13 ff.: 140
6: 24: 146
9: 25: 89
11: 12: 103
12: 36: 168
12: 39–41: 93
19: 21: 146
27: 50–3: 101

MARK
1: 9: 140
5: 39: 89

LUKE
8: 52: 89
11: 5–8: 161
11: 29–30: 93
16: 13: 146
16: 19–31: 100
17: 21: 105
18: 1–8: 161
23: 38: 109
23: 39–43: 100

JOHN
3: 5: 139
11: 1–44: 89, 128
19: 20: 109
21: 15–17: 140

ACTS
7: 59: 139
8: 3: 139
9: 1ff.: 139
9: 10–19: 139
10: 144

ROMANS
5: 14: 97
5: 19: 144
6: 1–11: 144
8: 12–13: 105
11: 1: 139
12: 15: 155
13: 12: 123

1 CORINTHIANS
13: 4: 227
13: 7–8: 227
15: 31: 184

2 CORINTHIANS
10: 3: 105

EPHESIANS
5: 14: 102

PHILIPPIANS
1: 21: 129
1: 23: 129
2: 27: 129
3: 5: 139
3: 20: 105

1 THESSALONIANS
4: 13–14: 89

1 TIMOTHY
4: 12: 153

HEBREWS
11: 32ff.: 138

1 PETER
1: 24: 175

CICERO
Cael. 12: 135
69: 154

ENNIUS
trag. fr. 215 Jocelyn: 194

HORACE
carm. 2. 10. 11–12: 206

NAEVIUS
com. 106: 189

VIRGIL
Aen. 2. 363: 212
2. 368–9: 211–12
6. 625–7: 215
8. 723: 108
georg. 3. 66–8: 188–9

(b) *Passages from works of consolation and certain related texts*

AMBROSE
bon. mort. 6–7: 188
epist. 15. 1: 80
15. 2: 125
15. 4: 125
39. 3: 199
39. 5: 114, 126–7
39. 8: 130
exc. Sat. 1. 3: 133, 134
1. 4: 115
1. 10: 128

1. 28: 181
1. 29: 181
1. 30–2: 196
1. 30: 90
1. 35: 114
1. 37: 87
1. 70: 88
2. 3: 115, 199
2. 5: 192
2. 8: 197
2. 11: 130

2. 14: 128, 199
2. 21: 199
2. 34: 188
2. 35: 184–5
2. 40–1: 129
obit. Theod. 54: 128
obit. Valent. 3: 83
  16: 158
  17: 155
  26: 80
  32: 157
  45: 200
  46: 127, 129, 199
  48: 114–15
  58 ff.: 133
  58: 130

ANTHOLOGIA PALATINA
7. 261: 87

AUGUSTINE
epist. 92. 1: 177
  259. 1: 29 n.
  263. 3: 128, 130
serm. 172. 1: 177
  172. 3: 199

BASIL
epist. 5. 1: 181
  5. 2: 133
  6. 2: 115
  28. 1: 130
  29: 80–1
  62: 130
  269. 1: 197
  269. 2: 133
  300: 188
  301: 80
  302: 80

BOETHIUS
cons. 4 pros. 4: 199

CICERO
ad Att. 12. 10: 131
ad Brut. 1. 9. 2: 195
ad fam. 5. 16. 1: 81
  5. 16. 2: 114
  5. 16. 4: 199–200
  5. 16. 6: 197
  5. 18. 1: 81
  5. 18. 2: 131
amicit. 9: 120, 121
  14: 127
  15: 87

cons. fr. 9 Mueller: 192
sen. 12: 121
  25: 198
  66–7: 23 n.
  69: 187
  84: 87, 121
Tusc. 1. 73: 83
  1. 74: 184
  1. 76: 199
  1. 93: 133
  1. 94: 187
  1. 97: 177
  1. 113: 193
  1. 115: 193
  3. 28 ff.: 113
  3. 35: 197
  3. 52: 113
  3. 63: 190, 191
  3. 70: 117–18, 120, 121
  3. 76: 20
  3. 81: 16 n.

CONSOLATIO AD LIVIAM
  263–4: 129
  357–60: 114

CYPRIAN
mort. 15: 199
  20: 88, 195
  22: 199
  23: 89
  25: 196, 212

DEMETRIUS
form. epist. 5: 114

EPICTETUS
4. 1. 133: 200

FRONTO
p. 233 Naber: 199

GREGORY OF NAZIANZUS
epist. 31. 4: 184
  165. 2: 130, 131
  165. 3: 80
orat. 7. 20: 199, 217
  18. 5: 137
  18. 23: 147

GREGORY OF NYSSA
Pulch. pp. 465–6 Jaeger: 199

HORACE
carm. 1. 24. 1–2: 131

HYPERIDES
epitaph. 43: 198

INSCRIPTIONS
Buecheler 164–78: 87
436. 1: 199
556. 2–3: 87
1153: 87
1274: 199
1479–85: 87
Engström 31–4: 87
Kaibel 650. 6–7: 199

JOHN CHRYSOSTOM
epist. 192: 199
197: 88, 130, 177, 178
vid. iun. 3: 228
4: 197

JULIAN
epist. 201 Bidez–Cumont: 81

LIBANIUS
epist. 1473. 1: 81
1473. 3: 134

LUCRETIUS
3. 866–7: 199
3. 1087–94: 187

MARCUS AURELIUS
4. 50: 187
12. 23: 200

MENANDER RHETOR
epid. 2. 9 Russell-Wilson: 114,
126, 193

OVID
Pont. 4. 11. 13–14: 197

PAPYRI
P. Oxy. 115: 32n.

PAULINUS OF NOLA
carm. 31. 7–10: 128
31. 45–50: 195
epist. 13. 4: 128
13. 6: 89, 115, 133
13. 10: 130
13. 13: 133

PLATO
apol. 40C: 23n.
Menex. 247C–248C: 131
Phaedo 64A: 183
67D: 183

67E: 183
80E–81A: 183
115D: 177

[PLATO]
Axioch. 366A–367C: 198

PLUTARCH
ad uxor. 2: 131
8: 134, 228
exil. 11: 199

[PLUTARCH]
ad Apoll. 1: 81
3–4: 131
6: 18n., 114, 186
11: 199
12: 89, 177–8
17: 187
19: 127, 200
21: 114
28: 131, 134, 191, 198
33: 113, 117, 119, 120
34: 87, 199

SENECA (younger)
dial. 6. 1. 2: 87
6. 1. 6: 197
6. 3. 2: 228
6. 7. 1: 131
6. 8. 1: 197
6. 10. 5: 114
6. 12. 1: 127
6. 12. 2: 134
6. 13: 117
6. 13. 1–2: 119, 120
6. 13. 3–4: 120
6. 19. 5: 22–3n., 198
6. 20. 4–6: 198
6. 21. 3: 187
6. 21. 7: 226
6. 23. 2: 183
6. 24. 5: 199
6. 25–6: 22–3n.
6. 25. 1: 177
6. 26. 2: 196–7
6. 26. 5–6: 224
11. 1. 1–3: 224–5
11. 1. 4: 114
11. 5. 4: 91
11. 6. 1: 195
11. 9. 1: 127
11. 9. 4ff.: 198
11. 9. 9: 177
11. 10. 1: 134

11. 11. 2: 113
11. 14. 4: 118
11. 16. 3: 118
11. 18. 6: 131
11. 18. 7–8: 228
12. 14. 1: 127
12. 16. 1: 131
12. 19. 7: 195
epist. 63. 1: 81, 131
  63. 2: 191
  63. 7: 133
  63. 12: 197
  63. 15: 114, 186
  93. 6: 186
  93. 12: 114
  99. 3: 133–4
  99. 4: 187
  99. 6: 118
  99. 7: 177
  99. 8: 114

99. 16: 131
99. 18–19: 90
99. 29–30: 22–3 n.
99. 31: 187

STATIUS
silv. 2. 1. 220–2: 198–9
  2. 6. 1–2: 131
  5. 1. 55–6: 132–3
  5. 1. 176–93: 176–7

SULPICIUS RUFUS ap. Cic. *ad fam.*
  4. 5. 1: 81
  4. 5. 4: 114
  4. 5. 6: 195, 197

SULPICIUS SEVERUS
epist. 2. 7: 90

THEODORET
epist. 14 (Coll. Sirm.): 114, 199

(*c*) *Passages from works by Jerome*

adv. Iovin. 1. 1: 85, 209
  1. 3: 85
  1. 12: 187
  1. 13: 188
  1. 22: 124
  1. 41: 154
  2. 4: 124
  2. 7: 138, 210
  2. 10: 158
  2. 12: 157
  2. 21: 187

adv. Rufin. 1. 17: 164
  2. 23: 231
  3. 4: 164
  3. 39–40: 110, 116, 183–4

chron. a Abr. p. 247 Helm: 203

c. Ioh. 23–36: 102

c. Vigil. 10: 172

epist. 1. 1–2: 79
  1. 1: 182, 241
  1. 2. 1: 88
  1. 3. 1–2: 237
  1. 7. 1: 181–2
  1. 9. 2: 137

1. 12. 2: 85
1. 15. 2: 78
3. 3. 2: 89
3. 4: 148
3. 4. 1: 80
3. 5. 1: 129
4. 1. 2: 109
7. 1. 1: 228
8. 1. 2: 228
14. 2. 1: 144
14. 2. 2–3: 141
14. 6. 1: 149
14. 7. 1: 144
14. 8. 1: 150
14. 8. 4–5: 151
15. 3. 1: 176
21. 5. 1: 85, 174
22. 7. 2: 143
22. 7. 3: 205
22. 8. 1–3: 158–9
22. 11. 1: 157
22. 15. 2: 174
22. 17. 1: 129
22. 17. 2: 144, 158
22. 19. 1: 206
22. 27. 3: 147, 205
22. 27. 4: 154
22. 39. 4: 144
22. 40. 3: 103

epist. (cont.)
22. 41. 3: 102
23. 2. 2: 78, 147, 157
23. 4: 186
24. 2: 211
24. 3. 2: 169
24. 5. 1: 147
27. 1. 3: 82
28. 1: 116
29. 7. 2: 79
31. 2. 2: 206
38. 1: 139
38. 2. 1: 176
38. 3. 2: 146
39. 1. 1: 126
39. 1. 2: 80, 157
39. 1. 3–4: 85, 173, 179
39. 2. 1: 128
39. 2. 3–4: 138
39. 3. 1: 89, 114
39. 3. 2: 88
39. 3. 3: 177
39. 3. 6: 177, 199
39. 3. 7: 89
39. 4: 97
39. 4. 1–2: 99, 104, 122, 206
39. 4. 5: 123–4
39. 4. 6: 88, 122
39. 5. 1: 157
39. 5. 2: 130, 197
39. 5. 4: 121
39. 6. 1: 125, 195
39. 6. 4: 130–1
39. 8. 1–2: 82, 228
40. 2. 2: 166
43. 1: 157
43. 3. 3: 85
45. 2. 2: 150
45. 3. 1: 169
45. 6. 1: 85
45. 7: 187
46. 1. 3: 85
46. 4. 1: 85
46. 7. 6: 101
46. 10. 2: 111
49. 13. 4: 160
49. 19. 4: 160
49. 20. 2: 159
49. 21. 3: 151
51. 1. 5–6: 152
51. 2. 1: 151
51. 5. 7: 101, 206
52. 1. 1–2: 85, 142, 161

52. 2. 1: 121
52. 2. 2: 109
52. 3. 5: 83, 192
52. 4. 3: 145, 179
52. 5. 1: 150
52. 5. 3: 156
52. 5. 4–6: 151, 156
52. 6. 1: 166
52. 6. 4–5: 166
52. 7. 1: 165
52. 7. 6: 149
52. 9. 1: 147, 166
52. 10. 1–2: 169
52. 11. 3: 159
52. 11. 4: 157
52. 12. 1: 157, 159
52. 13. 3: 158
52. 15. 1–2: 155
52. 17. 1: 161
53. 5. 2: 107
53. 8. 4: 124
53. 8. 10: 93
53. 11. 3: 164
54. 5. 4: 138
54. 6. 2: 143
54. 7. 1: 146
54. 10. 2: 158
54. 12. 2: 155
54. 18. 3: 186
58. 1. 2: 153
58. 1. 3: 144
58. 2. 2: 147
58. 3. 2: 106
58. 4. 1: 206
58. 5. 1: 149
58. 5. 2: 216
58. 6. 2: 157
58. 8. 2: 174
58. 10: 160
58. 11. 2: 189
64. 21. 2: 158
65. 12. 3: 112
66. 1. 1: 81, 198
66. 1. 2: 175
66. 2. 2: 158
66. 5. 1: 146, 169
66. 5. 2: 215
66. 5. 3: 85
66. 8. 4: 146
66. 13. 1: 155
66. 15: 182
68. 1. 1: 135
69. 2. 7: 189

69. 3. 6: 109
69. 6. 1: 158
69. 6. 7: 139
69. 8. 3: 154
70. 3. 2: 202
70. 5: 160
71. 3. 2–3: 146
71. 5. 3: 116
73. 5. 1: 134
73. 10. 1: 216
75. 1. 1: 80, 126
75. 1. 2–3: 89, 91–2, 96, 114, 178
75. 2. 1: 89, 125, 128, 216
75. 2. 4: 102
75. 4. 1: 146, 165
75. 4. 2: 79
76. 2: 199
77. 1. 1: 178, 209, 230–1
77. 2. 2: 140, 145
77. 2. 3: 136
77. 6: 155
77. 6. 4: 215
77. 7: 165
77. 7. 1: 153
77. 8: 213
77. 9. 1: 127
77. 9. 2: 142
77. 10. 1: 182
77. 11. 2–3: 181
78. 14. 3: 112
78. 33: 199
78. 36. 4: 124
79. 1. 3: 128, 177
79. 1. 4: 162
79. 2. 1: 136
79. 2. 3: 157
79. 2. 4: 89, 142, 144
79. 4. 1: 146
79. 5. 1–2: 154, 155
79. 6. 1: 145, 174
79. 7. 7: 158
79. 8. 1: 176
79. 9. 2: 157
79. 9. 5: 157
79. 10. 2: 81
82. 8. 1: 154
84. 4. 1: 88
84. 5. 1: 102
84. 6. 2: 116
84. 9. 1: 206
85. 3. 2: 79
86. 1. 2: 174
92. 6. 1: 109

97. 2. 1: 197
98. 3. 5: 109
99. 1. 2: 176
99. 2. 2: 84
100. 3. 1: 206
100. 3. 3: 165
100. 9. 1: 109
105. 5. 2: 179
107. 1. 4: 241
107. 2. 2: 144, 211
107. 2. 3: 111
107. 4. 8: 142, 144
107. 5. 1: 169
107. 6. 2–3: 138, 206
107. 7. 2: 81
107. 8. 2: 159
107. 9. 1: 176
107. 9. 2: 172
107. 9. 3: 157
107. 10. 1: 146
107. 10. 2: 158
107. 10. 3: 158
107. 13. 4: 137
108. 1. 1: 78, 137, 167, 215
108. 1. 2: 133
108. 1. 3: 129
108. 2. 1: 182
108. 3. 1: 136
108. 5: 155
108. 5. 1: 146
108. 6. 1: 149
108. 6. 3: 195
108. 9. 3: 104
108. 13. 2: 138
108. 17. 3: 158
108. 18. 1: 206
108. 20. 7: 109
108. 21. 1: 126
108. 21. 4: 90, 132
108. 26. 1: 165
108. 26. 2: 161
108. 27–8: 173
108. 27. 1: 112, 174–5
108. 27. 2: 178
108. 27. 3: 114, 174
108. 28. 3: 153
108. 29. 1: 181
108. 30. 2: 126, 127
108. 32: 83
112. 2. 5: 109
112. 15. 2: 187
114. 3. 1: 82
118. 1. 2–3: 112–13

epist. (cont.)
118. 4. 1: 177
118. 4. 2: 133
118. 4. 6: 182
118. 5. 4: 164
118. 5. 6: 149
119. 7. 3: 126
119. 10. 6: 102
120. 1. 11: 206
120. 8. 8: 102
121. 10. 23: 159
122. 1. 4: 81
123. 1. 1: 124
123. 7. 1: 121–2
123. 12. 1: 206
123. 13. 1: 134
123. 15–16: 208
123. 15. 2: 211
123. 15. 3: 214
123. 15. 4: 85, 214
123. 16. 4: 215
125. 7. 1: 147, 158
125. 8. 2: 163
125. 10. 1: 164
125. 11. 1: 157
125. 15. 1: 151
127. 1. 3: 80, 136–7
127. 3. 4: 146, 169
127. 4. 1: 165
127. 4. 2: 158, 164, 172
127. 6: 185–6
127. 6. 1: 183
127. 6. 2: 226
127. 7. 1: 159
127. 7. 3: 159
127. 12. 3: 212
127. 14: 173
128. 1. 3: 142
128. 5. 1: 211, 212, 217
129. 2. 1: 99
130. 1. 1–2: 79, 88
130. 3. 1: 137
130. 3. 2: 196, 198
130. 4. 1: 137
130. 4. 4: 143
130. 5. 3: 144
130. 6. 1: 216
130. 6. 2–5: 153, 182
130. 7. 11: 137
130. 7. 13: 169
130. 11. 1–2: 132, 157–8
130. 14. 7–8: 155, 169
130. 19. 1: 187

133. 12. 1: 209
140. 13. 2: 174
140. 14. 2: 174
140. 16. 2–3: 186
141. 1. 2: 174
142. 1. 1: 79
143. 1. 2: 96
147. 2. 1: 186
147. 5. 2: 86
147. 8. 1: 143
147. 10. 3: 182
147. 12: 134
153. 1. 3: 135
epist. ad Praesidium p. 55. 51–2
  Morin: 116
p. 56. 57–8 Morin: 209
p. 58. 146–8 Morin: 203

hom. Orig. in cant.
PL 23. 1138: 81

hom. in Luc. 16: 19–31
CCSL 78. 510. 92–6: 100
  78. 515. 269–72: 100
  78. 515. 274ff.: 101

in Abd. 1: 102

in Agg. 2. 2–10: 124

in Eccl. 3. 18–21: 99

in Eph. 5. 14: 102

in Ezech. lib. 3 pref.: 79, 89, 135
  lib. 8 pref.: 212
  27. 26: 176

in Gal. 6. 10: 226–7

in Ier. 1. 17A: 102
  11. 18–20: 94
  12. 7–8: 94
  27. 6–7: 218
  29 (36). 8–9: 102
  31 (38). 25–6: 102

in Ioel pref.: 79, 135

in Ion. pref.: 230–1
  1. 3: 94
  1. 4: 93
  1. 12: 96

1. 15: 94
2. 1: 93
2. 2–3: 93
4. 3: 94

in Is. 2. 3: 192
2. 4: 108
7. 21–5: 217
21. 13–17: 108
26. 20–1: 218
lib. 14 pref.: 174
58. 3–4: 144
62. 6–7: 162
66. 22–3: 134

in Matt. 11. 12: 103, 104
19. 21: 146
27. 53: 102

in Mich. 4. 1–7: 108

in Os. 1. 2: 183
13. 14–15: 92, 95, 99

in Soph. 3. 1–7: 166

in Tit. 1. 5: 151

in Zach. pref.: 79, 187
lib. 3 pref.: 85

pref. in Ezram: 79, 209

pref. in psalm.: 79, 135

quaest. hebr. in gen. pref.: 206

tract. in psalm. 75. 2: 106–7

vir. ill. 75: 164
135: 116

GENERAL INDEX

References to personal names mentioned in the text are given in italic type.

ability and intention, contrasted 78–9, 135
Abraham *44*, *46*, *52*, *98*, 100–1
abstinence 158–9
  see also fasting
Abundantius, Flavius *68*, 206–7
Adam *44*, 97–8, 100, 104
address to the reader 156
adornment 146–7, 169, 173
adsumere 95
adversarius 97
Aeschylus 18
affected modesty 161, 163
  see also self-depreciation
Alani 209, 211
alioquin 215
Altinum 15, 140, 148, 171, 181
Amalek *70*, 219
Ambrose 4n., 16n., 17n., 25, 27n., 33, *134*, 152, 157
  see also Jerome, and Ambrose
Ammianus Marcellinus 221
amputare 222
Ananias *52*, 139–40
anaphora 225, 228
Anaxagoras *48*, 113, 117, 118, 119
ancestry:
  Christian attitude towards 31, 136–7, 138, 140
  as topic of eulogy 31, 135–7
Antigonus Gonatas 117, 119
Antioch 2n., 3, 4, 5n., 13, 140, 214
Antiphon 18
antithesis 182, 225, 229
Apollinarianism 4
Apollinarius 6
Apollonius of Tyana 21
Aquileia 2, 3, 204
Arbogastes 204–6
arere 116–17

Arianism, Arians 4, 16n., 24n., 200
Aristides, Aelius 21n.
Aristotle 20n.
Armenia, Christianity in 111
Arnobius *58*, 160
Asella 156
Aspasia 18n.
asyndeton 182, 183, 211, 225
Athanasius 157
Atlantic 108
Augustine 13n., 24n., 25, 28, 29n., 152
Augustus 108, 152
Aurelius of Carthage 13n.
auriga, in metaphor 158
auster 176
Auxentius of Milan 2n.

baculus 156
balbutire 83–4
baptism 139–40, 144
barbarian invasions 8, 31, 203, 208, 209–11, 212–13, 217
Basil 16n., 24, 28, 33, 157
basilica 172
Benjamin *52*, 139
Bessi 111
Bethlehem 5, 6, 220
Bezalel 32, *60*, 169, 170
Blesilla 28, 31, 128, 157, 173, 179
Boethius 16n.
Bonosus *80*, 149
brevity, epistolary 26, 116
Britain 107

cachinnare, cachinnus 156
Cadiz 107
Caesarea 9
Caesarius 24

Carneades 18n., 31, *48*, 115–16
Cato, M. Porcius (censor) 117, 121
Chalcis 3
character-sketch 155, 156
cherub 105
Christianity, extent of 110–11
Chromatius 10, *74*, 228
Church, corruption of the 165–6
Cicero 16n., 19, 20, 22–3, 26n., 28, *48*, 113, 115, 234, 235n., 237
  Consolatio 13, 19–20, 22n., 25n., 31, 83, 109, 113, 115, 116, 117–18, 119, 120, 131, 135, 189, 190, 193, 194, 195, 223
  see also Jerome and the pagan classics, and Cicero
cilicium 143
cingulum 144
civil service 142–3
Claudian 207
Cleobis and Biton 193
clergy, grades of the 150–1
clericus 150
Clitomachus 31, *48*, 115–16
conciliabulum, = 'church' 172
confovere 115
conscius, of inanimate things 205
Consolatio ad Liviam 21
consolation 15–33 and *passim*
  Christian 23–5, 27–33, 80–1, 88, 89–90, 114–15, 125, 126–7, 128, 130–1, 133, 145, 177, 195, 199
  letters of 16, 20, 21, 24, 25, 26, 27–33, 132, 145
  on misfortunes other than bereavement 16, 21, 24n., 199
  pagan 17–23, 81, 89, 114, 125–6, 127, 131, 133–4, 195, 199
  right time for 198
  verse 16, 21, 24–5
consolatory decrees 17n.
consolatory topics
  all born mortal/death inevitable 22, 32, 114–15, 187, 191, 223, 224–5

death an advance to a better state 199
death an escape 22, 23, 32, 33, 89–90, 188–9, 196–7, 198–9
death no evil 23, 199–200
deceased abroad or absent 177–8
deceased in heaven 125, 199
do not grieve so much as to put your faith in question 195
do not grieve so much that false conclusions can be drawn 33, 195
do not mourn loved ones but be grateful for having had them 23, 33, 133–4
do not set a bad example by excessive grief 194–5
grief healed by time and reason 22, 197–8
no difference between long life and short 187
praemeditatio futurorum malorum 32, 113–14, 118, 191
put a limit to your grief ('nothing too much') 33, 130–1, 191
we grieve for ourselves, not for the deceased 22, 126–7
see also death, a matter for rejoicing; *memento mori*
Constantine 143
Constantinople 4
Constantius (II) *66*, 200, 202
consularis 206
continentia 155
Cornelius, centurion *54*, 144
Cornelius of Rome 151, 152
Crantor 18–19, 20, 21, 31, *48*, 115, 116, 118, 119, 120, 131
Crassus, L. Licinius 83, 196
creatura 97
credulus 90–1
Croesus *58*, 163–4
Cyprian 24, *58*, 160, 162–3, 235
Cyrenaics 113

Damasus 4, 5, 9, 14
Darius *58*, 163–4
David *50*, 122

deacons 151, 153
death:
  destroyed by Christ 30, 88, 91–6
  a matter for rejoicing 191–2
  personification of 91
  a sleep 88–9, 101–2
  see also consolatory topics
deathbed scene 173, 179
Demetrius, writer on rhetoric (confused with Demetrius of Phalerum) 26
Democritus 18, 46, 109–10
demorari, intransitive 111–12, 123
[Demosthenes] 18 n.
desertum 96
desolare 96
devil, the see Satan
'diatribe' 17
Didymus of Alexandria 6
dignitas 206
diminutives 79, 163, 229
Dio Chrysostom 21 n.
dioceses see provinces and dioceses
Diocletian 143
Diogenes Laertius 19, 115, 119–20
Diogenes of Sinope 18, 31, 48, 115–16
Dion of Syracuse 117, 119
disaster, seen as divine punishment for sin 31, 202, 212, 215, 216, 217–18, 219, 221–2
dissolutio 110
Donatus, Aelius 2, 11
dress 146–7
dying, a continuous process 226

Eden, Garden of 101, 104
Egypt:
  Christianity in 110–11
  monasticism in 148
ἔκφρασις 86
eloquium 102
enim 103–4
Ennius 32, 64, 113, 194
Epaphroditus 50, 127, 128, 129
Ephraim, figure in Hosea 92
epicedion 17, 21 n., 131
Epicureans 18, 22

Epiphanius of Salamis 4, 6, 101, 152
episcopus 129, 151
epitaphioi 18 n.
ἐπιτάφιος λόγος 26, 30, 77
epitaphium 77
ἐργοδιώκτης 82
Esau 52, 138
eschatology 98–9, 100–1, 103
Ethiopia, Ethiopians 107
Eugenius, Flavius 68, 205–6
eulogy 26, 27–8, 29, 30–1, 78, 112, 132–3, 135–7, 145, 146, 155, 157, 158, 165
Euripides 193
Eusebius (brother of Chromatius) 228
Eusebius (father of Jerome) 1
Eusebius of Caesarea 4, 108
Eustochium, Julia 5, 7 n., 12, 13 n., 27, 101, 156, 158, 173
Eutropius 207, 208
Evagrius of Antioch 3, 78
exaggeration 82, 84, 85, 90, 106, 112, 116, 178, 181–2, 206
exempla 31, 32, 33, 112, 117–19, 121, 122, 169, 171, 218–19
fortitude in bereavement 32, 112, 117–18, 122
exile 16 n., 21
external advantages, as topic of eulogy 31, 132–3, 135–6, 137

Fabiola 27–8, 142, 155, 165, 181
Fabius Maximus Cunctator, Q. 117, 121
Fabius Pictor, C. 32, 169, 170
Fabius Pictor, Q. 60, 169–70
fascis 188
fasting 143, 157–8
  see also abstinence
fauces 96
Flacilla 24
flower-imagery 85, 175–6
flowers, scattered over tomb 85
fons 117
fortitude in bereavement see exempla

Fronto 21, 28
funeral speeches 16–17, 18 n., 21, 24, 25, 26–7, 28–30, 132, 145
Furia 155

Galus, C. Sulpicius 117, 121
Ganges 107
gates of heaven/hell 104
General Resurrection 98
Geruchia 13, 124
Gorgonia 24 n.
Goths 8, 111, 203, 209, 212–13
   see also Visigoths
Gratian 4, *66*, 204
Gregory of Nazianzus 4, 16 n., 24, 33, 137
Gregory of Nyssa 4, 24, 33
grey hairs 154
grief:
   appropriateness and legitimacy of 22, 30, 87–8, 122, 123, 125, 127–9
   Christian problem of 30, 87, 126–7
   to be moderated (μετριοπά-θεια) 22, 130–1
   to be suppressed (ἀπάθεια) 22, 131
   see also consolatory topics
Gryllus 119–20

Hades 98
   see also hell, harrowing of
Hebrew, misunderstanding of by Jerome 95
Hecuba 190
hell, harrowing of 98–9
Heliodorus 10, 15, 28, 29, *42*, 80, 124, 129, 140–1, 142, 143, 150, 171, 173, 179, 194–5, 228, and *passim*
Helvidius 7
Hercules, Pillars of 107
heremus 103
heresis 200–1
Herodotus 193, 223
Hesiod 32 n., *64*, 191–4
Hexapla *see* Origen

Hezekiah *70*, 218–19
Hilary of Poitiers *58*, 160
Himerius 21 n.
Hippias of Elis 32, 169, 171
Hiram 32, *60*, 169, 170
honos/onus 154
Horace 17, 31, 206
Hosea *44*
Huns 8, 111, 203, 209, 213, 214, 220–1, 230
   conversion of 111
Hyperides 18 n.
hypophora 206

iaculum 81
incredulitas 129, 219
India, Indians 107
   Christianity in 110–11
inferi 101
infernus 96, 98–9, 100, 101, 102, 122
infinitives, historic 155, 159
instar 86–7
interiora 97
interpellatrix 162
intra 105–6
Isaac *44*, *52*, 98
Ishmael *52*, 137–8
Isis 144
iugulare 96

Jacob *44*, *50*, 98, 122
Jairus' daughter 88
Jehoshaphat *70*, 219
Jephthah *52*, 138
Jeremiah 94–5, 96
Jerome:
   life and works 1–8
   and Ambrose 25 n., 134, 181, 185
   and animals, in art 167
   and the canon of Scripture 8, 10
   and celibacy 7, 8
   consolatory writing 15, 25, 26, 27–33, and *passim*
   correspondence 13–15, 141–2, 163, 236

Jerome (*cont.*)
and the desert 3, 7n., 15n., 140, 141
his dream 12
and the Latin Bible 4–5, 8–11, 102, 105, 116, 129, 139, 214, 240, 241n.
method of composition 226–7
and Origen 4, 6–7, 94, 99, 110, 138
and rhetoric 2, 7, 12, 30, 31, 225
satire 5, 146–7, 165–6
Jerome and the pagan classics 11–13, 31–3
and Cicero 12, 13, 19, 20, 31, 83, 109–10, 113, 115–16, 117–18, 120, 127, 131, 135, 154, 175, 184, 189, 190, 193, 194, 195, 211, 223, 237
and Seneca the younger 6n., 20–1n., 110, 117–18, 120, 196–7, 223, 224, 226
and Virgil 12, 31, 78, 108, 170, 211–12, 215
see also Ammianus Marcellinus; Claudian; Herodotus; Hesiod; Horace; Plato; Sallust; Thucydides
Jerome's writings:
Adversus Helvidium 7
Adversus Iovinianum 7
Adversus Pelagium 8
Adversus Rufinum 7, 231
Chronicle 4
Commentary on Daniel 236n.
Commentary on Galatians 12, 226
Commentary on Isaiah 236n.
Commentary on Matthew 10–11
Contra Ioannem Hierosolymitanum 7
Contra Vigilantium 8, 172
De viris illustribus 6, 230–1, 238n.
Letter 1: 2n.
Letter 14: 141–2
Letters 15–17: 3n.
Letter 22: 5, 12, 14–15

Letter 23: 14, 15n., 27, 29
Letter 39: 15n., 27, 28, 31, 122, 124
Letter 46: 13n.
Letter 52: 14, 15, 163
Letter 54: 14–15
Letter 60: 28–33 and *passim*
Letter 66: 25, 27, 28
Letter 70: 12
Letter 75: 27
Letter 77: 27–8
Letter 79: 14–15, 27
Letter 80: 13n.
Letter 108: 27, 28
Letter 109: 172
Letter 118: 27, 28, 29
Letter 123: 13
Letter 127: 27
Letter 146: 151
Letters 148–50: 13n.
Letter to Aurelius 13n.
Letter to Praesidius 13n.
Vita Hilarionis 6n.
Vita Malchi 6n.
Vita Pauli 6n., 147
Jerusalem 2, 5, 6, 15n., 101–2
Jesus, weeps for Lazarus 30, 128
John the Baptist *46*, 103–4
John Chrysostom 24, 152, 197
John of Jerusalem 6–7, 152
Jonah *44*, 92–6
Jordan 140
Josephus 6n.
Joshua *50*, 123–4
Jovian *66*, 201, 203
Julian (addressee of Jerome, *Letter* 118) 28, 112, 149
Julian (emperor) 21, *66*, 200, 201–3
Julius Victor 26

Lactantius *58*, 160
lactare, = 'beguile', 'deceive' 112, 141
lament, lamentation 26, 30, 86, 131, 223
Last Judgement 99
last words 179

laudatio funebris 86
laughter 156
Lazarus 30, *42, 44, 50,* 88, 89, 127, 128
   and the rich man 100
Lea 157
Libanius 21, 28
[Libanius] 26
libellus 163
litterula 82
longevity in OT 188
Lucinus 146, 165
luctari 178
[Lysias] 18n.

mamona 146
maps 134
Marcella 5, 13n., 14, 27, 80, 137, 146, 158, 159, 165, 173
Marcomanni 210–11
marsuppium 112, 166
martyr, martyrs 172–3
martyria 172
Maximus, Magnus *68,* 152, 204, 205–6
Meletius 24
melos 111–12
memento mori 185–6
Menander Rhetor 26–7, 30, 33, 77
Mesopotamia, monasticism in 148
Methuselah *64,* 188
migrare, of dying 177
military metaphors, Christian 144, 145, 202
military service, Christian attitudes to 142, 145
ministerium 179
Minucius Felix *58,* 160, 235
Mithras 144
monachus 149–50
monasterium 148
monasticism 2, 147–8, 149–50
μονῳδία 26
morderi 154–5
Moses *44, 50, 56, 70,* 97–8, 123–4, 153, 219
municipatus 105
mutus 84

Naevius 32, *64,* 189
Nebridius 142, 145, 146, 155, 157
Nebuchadnezzar *70,* 218
nepos, = nephew 142
Nepotianus 15, *42, 50, 52, 60, 70, 72,* 80, 83, 89, 117, 125, 129, 139, 140–1, 142, 144, 145, 146, 151, 153, 171–2, and *passim*
Nineveh 93
Niobe *64,* 189–91
nobilitas, Christian 137
'nothing too much' 131–2
   see also consolatory topics
noun, separated from attributive adjective or dependent genitive 182, 241

offirmare 112, 178
Old Latin Bible (VL) 9, 11, 227, 241 n.
   see also Jerome, and the Latin Bible
opusculum 163
orare, oratio 157
ordinare 151
ordination, resistance to 151–2
Origen 4, 6–7, 13 n., 94, 99, 138
   Hexapla 9
   see also Jerome, and Origen
ostentation, to be avoided 147, 154
outliving elders, natural and proper 87
Ovid 21

Pacatula 156
Pacuvius 113
pagella 229
Pammachius 7n., 25, 155, 158
papa 228
paradise, *paradisus* 99, 100, 101, 104
παραμυθητικὸς λόγος 26, 30
passio 109
Paul, St *52,* 79, 88, 97–8, 123, 125, 127, 128–9, 138, 139–40, 184, 185

Paula (elder) 5, 10, 13n., 27, 28, 31, *50*, 78, 83, 84, 101, 137, 146, 155, 158, 161, 165, 173, 181
Paula (younger) 156
Paulina 25, 158
Paulinian 1, 5, 151, 152
Paulinus of Antioch 4
Paulinus of Nola 24–5, 137, 152, 171–2
Paulus, L. Aemilius *48*, 117, 120–1
pax Romana 108
Pelagius 8, 13n.
Pericles 18n., *48*, 117, 119, 120
perperam 227
Persia, Christianity in 111
Pharisees 105–6
Philo 6n.
Pindar 17
Plato 18, 31, 32n., *48*, *64*, 110, 115, 171, 183–4
[Plato], *Axiochus* 18, 115
Platonism 22–3n.
Pliny (elder) 20
Plutarch 16n., 21
[Plutarch], *Consolatio ad Apollonium* 21
pontifex, = bishop 149
poor, helping the 146, 155
Porphyrius of Gaza 152
Porphyry 110
portare, with parts of the body 143–4
Posidonius 18n., 31, *48*, 115–16
praecedere, of dying 182
praemeditatio futurorum malorum see consolatory topics
Praesidius 13n.
praeteritio 109, 120, 121, 140, 142, 205
praevaricatio 98
prayer, prayerfulness 133, 157
precator 162
prefaces, literary 78–9, 161
Procopius *68*, 205–6
Propertius 17
prose-rhythm 80, 133, 136, 153,

166, 181, 204, 208–9, 211, 224, 233–42
accentual system (*cursus*) 234–6
cursus mixtus 235–6
hiatus and elision 238n.
internal clausulae 234, 237n.
metrical system 233–4
proclitic variants 238n.
velox test 239–40
and word-order 133, 136, 208–9, 240–2
Protagoras 119
provinces and dioceses 209–10, 214
Psalter 8n., 9–10, 11, 99–100, 106, 122, 126
Pulcheria 24
Pulvillus, M. Horatius *48*, 117, 120
purgatory 99
Pythagoras *46*, 109–10, 183–4

Quadi 203, 209, 210
quod, temporal 209
quotations, altered and adapted by Jerome 211–12, 215

recusatio 78–9, 161
refrigerium 100
'refusal' of Principate 152
resurrection:
of Christ 97, 98–9, 100–1, 102, 103, 106, 109, 122, 123
of the dead 88, 97, 98–9, 101–2, 114, 122
see also General Resurrection
reversal of natural order of things 82, 87, 182
rhetorical precept and theory 31, 77–8, 116, 125, 132, 135–6
on consolation 25–7, 30, 81
ritus 108–9
Rome, Jerome at 2, 4–5, 7, 80
Rufinus, Flavius *68*, 207, 230
Rufinus of Aquileia 6–7, 13n.
rumphea 104–5
rust 84

sacerdos, sacerdotium 153, 162–3
Salamis (Cyprus) 5 n.
Sallust 32 n., *70*, 215–16, 224
salvator 97
Sarmatae 203, 209, 210
Satan 97
Satyrus 25
scedula 166–7
Scripture, reading of 157
sea-imagery 227
self-depreciation 77–9, 82, 135, 215, 225
Seneca (younger) 6 n., 16 n., 20–1, 22–3 n., 25–6, 28, 81, 115, 116, 118, 226
  see also Jerome and the pagan classics, and Seneca the younger
Septuagint (LXX) 9–10
sepulchral epigrams 17, 87
shock 83
simile 170–1
Simonides 17
Socrates 18 n., *46*, 109, 117
solamen 156
sophists 17, 18
soul, address to one's 112
Spain 107
specula 224
Statius 21
Stoics, Stoicism 22, 22–3 n., 24 n., 90, 113
Strabo 108
Stridon 1
stylistic variation 168, 211
subiectio see hypophora
substance of persons in heaven 102
subtristis 84–5
sudare 82
suffocare 166
Sulpicius Rufus, Servius 20
Sulpicius Severus 25, 172
swan, dying 82–3
Symmachus 118, 141
sympathy, expression of 26, 80–1

tears, in prayer 157
Telamon *48*, 113

Terence 12
Tertullian 23, *58*, 160
Themistius 21 n.
Theodoret of Cyrus 24, 28, 97
Theodosius 25, 204, 205, 230
Theophilus of Alexandria 13 n., 84
Thucydides 32 n., *70*, 216
tiara 222
Timasius, Flavius *68*, 208
Timothy *56*, 153
totus, qualifying verb 86
Trajan 152
Trier 2
Trinity, doctrine of the 3
Tullia 19, 20, 115
Turasius, letter to 128
typology 93–6, 123–4

uniform, military 142, 143

Valens *66*, 203–4, 205
Valentinian I: 2, *66*, 166, 203, 205
Valentinian II: 25, *66*, 130, 155, 157, 158, 204–5
Valerius Maximus 117, 118, 120
Vandals 8, 210–11
verbal balance 182, 224
verbal hyperbaton 241 n.
Vetus Latina (VL) *see* Old Latin Bible
Victorinus, C. Marius 160
Victorinus, Q. Fabius Laurentius 26 n.
Victorinus of Pettau *58*, 160
Vigilantius 8, 172
Virgil 31, 108, 209, 211–12, 215
  see also Jerome and the pagan classics, and Virgil
virgines Christi 156–7
viscera 129–30
Visigoths, conversion of 111
vivere, transitive 174
Vulgate 4–5, 8–11, 241 n.
  see also Jerome, and the Latin Bible

Wackernagel's Law 178

wine, to be avoided 158–9

wisdom, possessed by young man 153–4

word-order and considerations of rhythm *see* prose-rhythm

world, extent of 107–8

wound-image 81, 132

wretchedness of human life 189, 191–2

Xenophon *48*, 117, 119–20

Xerxes *72*, 223–4

zeugma 179–80

zones, climatic 107–8